THE GRADUAL CONVERGENCE

The Gradual Convergence

Foreign Ideas, Foreign Influences,

and English Law

on the Eve of the 21st Century

Edited by
B. S. MARKESINIS

CLARENDON PRESS · OXFORD

Oxford University Press, Walton Street, Oxford OX2 6DP

Oxford New York

Athens Auckland Bangkok Bombay
Calcutta Cape Town Dar es Salaam Delhi
Florence Hong Kong Istanbul Karachi
Kuala Lumpur Madras Madrid Melbourne
Mexico City Nairobi Paris Singapore
Taipei Tokyo Toronto
and associated companies in
Berlin Ibadan

Oxford is a trade mark of Oxford University Press

Published in the United States
by Oxford University Press Inc., New York

© *Oxford University Press, unless otherwise stated 1994*

First published 1994

British Library Cataloguing in Publication Data
Data available

Library of Congress Cataloging in Publication Data
The Gradual Convergence : foreign ideas, foreign influences and
English law on the eve of the 21st century / [edited by] B. S.
Markesinis
p. cm.
1. Law—Greta Britain—European influences.   I. Markesinis, B. S.
KD540.G73   1993
349.41—dc20   [344.1]   93–2565
ISBN 0–19–825828–3

3 5 7 9 10 8 6 4 2

Printed and bound in Great Britain
on acid-free paper by
Antony Rowe Ltd, Chippenham

03361720

This volume is dedicated by the staff of the
Centre for Commercial Law Studies

to

The Rt. Hon. Sir Thomas Bingham,
Master of the Rolls

Fellow of Queen Mary and Westfield College
formerly
Charirman of the Advisory Council of the
Centre for Commerical Law Studies;

Honorary Fellow and Visitor of Balliol College, Oxford;

Presentation Fellow
of King's College, London.

in admiration and in deep gratitude for the time he finds
to guide and assist educational institutions.

Preface and Acknowledgements

THIS book embodies many of the ideas and beliefs with which the Centre for Commercial Law Studies has been associated in the minds of many lawyers. For first of all, the text is based on a series of seminars which were designed to bring together judges, practitioners, and academics in order to discuss topics of common theoretical and practical concern. The need for such co-operation has always been championed by Professor Roy Goode, the founder and first director of the Centre, and still forms one of the Centre's main tenets. A more immediate cause was a series of seminars organized in 1990 by Professor Ross Cranston, the Centre's second director, which aimed to demonstrate the growing influence that judges and jurists from other common-law systems were having on the parent system. Almost inevitably, the sequel series had to consider more closely the legal relations with our European partners and the shaping of the final idea owes much to the imagination and the untiring support of Sir Thomas Bingham, Chairman of the Centre's Advisory Committee, Professor Cranston, and Professor Brian Napier, its current director. The five sessions that were held at Queen Mary and Westfield College in the Autumn of 1991 lasted in all nearly twenty hours, attracted close to a total of five hundred lawyers, and generated so much favourable interest in what took place at our meetings that we have been persuaded to publish a substantial part of our proceedings. Thanks to the interest and energies of Mr Richard Hart, the link with the Oxford University Press was forged and the seminar series was well on the way to being transformed into a book.

How the book took shape and the kind of editorial dilemmas that came to haunt me over the past eighteen months or so are explained in the second subsection of the first chapter. But if the shortcomings that have resulted from wrong editorial decisions can be blamed entirely on me, the praise for the venture which was, overall, an undisputed success, must be shared by many.

Three firms of solicitors (in alphabetical order)—Allen & Overy, Norton Rose, and Simmons & Simmons—generously provided essential financial support and, equally importantly, many of their partners and associates as participants to our meetings, and for both we are happy to express our deepest gratitude. We at the Centre were among the very first in the country to advocate close links between teachers and practitioners and we thus feel proud to see so many other Law Faculties now following our example.

Funds can always be found for worthy ventures. And our seminars, intellectually exciting without doubt, acquired additional prestige when it became clear that so many of Her Majesty's judges were willing to attend the meetings. Five of them went even further and agreed, despite their heavy work loads, to chair the five sessions as well as contribute in writing their own thoughts on the papers presented during their sessions. This factor alone makes this volume almost unique; and, once again, we hope it will again set the pattern for further comparative ventures of this kind. I am, therefore, delighted to express the Centre's (and my own) deep appreciation for the invaluable help so selflessly given to us by (in alphabetical order) Sir Robin Auld, Sir Thomas Bingham, Lord Browne-Wilkinson, Lord Goff of Chieveley, and Sir Leonard Hoffmann.* Sincere thanks are also due to Judge David Edward for kindly contributing, at very short notice, an epilogue to the papers here reproduced.

A similar debt of gratitude is due to all our foreign and British colleagues who took part in the series as keynote speakers, promptly presented me with written versions of their papers when asked for and, in a characteristically generous way, allowed me to exercise—sometimes boldly—editorial privileges that I arrogated to myself.

I could not conclude these acknowledgements without recalling what my mentor and dear friend, the late Professor C. J. Hamson, told me when back in 1968 he consented to act as my doctoral supervisor. 'Basil' he said, coughing in a way that I later came to realize indicated the coming of a mischievous statement, 'I accept on condition that you do all the work and I get all the credit'. The statement was, of course, uttered in jest, for no one was more solicitous of his pupils' interests than 'CJH'. Yet it is human, consciously or unconsciously, to seek the credit for the work of others, and in my case I feel duty-bound to avoid such a temptation and to stress the crucial role that Mrs Pamela Celentano, my Personal Assistant, played in ensuring that the seminars series was superbly run and that numerous drafts of texts were finally turned into an attractive book. It is a sad reflection that nowadays academic institutions do not publicly recognize the enormous debt they owe to their underpaid and otherwise unrecognized administrative and clerical staff. For my part, I wish to stress that my work at the Centre would have been both infinitely more difficult and less pleasant if it were not for the caring and loyal assistance I and my colleagues have received from our excellent staff.

B. S. Markesinis

Olous, Crete
1 August 1992

---

* Due to many commitments Lord Justice Hoffmann was unable to provide us with a written version of his contribution. We are grateful to Mr Stephen Tromans, partner in Simmons & Simmons and well-known authority on the subject of environmental law, for stepping in at short notice and making available in writing some of his personal reflections on this topic.

Table of Contents

List of Contributors

The Hon. Mr Justice Auld	A Judge of the High Court of Justice, Queen's Bench Division.
Professor Dr Christian von Bar	Professor of Private Law, Private International Law and Comparative Law in the University of Osnabrück; Director of the Institute of Private International and Comparative Law of the University of Osnabrück.
The Rt. Hon. Sir Thomas Bingham	Master of the Rolls.
Professor Dr H. Bocken	Professor of Law in the University of Ghent.
Professor Dr Michael Joachim Bonell	Professor of Comparative Law in the University of Rome I, 'La Sapienza'; Director of the Institute of Comparative Law of the University of Rome.
The Rt. Hon. the Lord Browne-Wilkinson	A Lord of Appeal in Ordinary.
The Rt. Hon. the Lord Goff of Chieveley	A Lord of Appeal in Ordinary.
Judge David A. O. Edward	A Judge in the Court of Justice of the European Communities.
Professor Dr M. Delmas-Marty	Professor at the University of Paris I.
Professor Dr Francesco Francioni	Professor of International Law in the University of Siena. Director of the Centre of International Peace Studies of the University of Siena.
Professor Dr H. C. Werner Lorenz	Professor of Private Law, Private International Law, and Comparative Law

	(Emeritus) in the University of Munich; Director of the Institute of Foreign and International Law of the University of Munich.
Professor Dr B. S. Markesinis	Denning Professor of Comparative Law in the University of London; Professor of Anglo-American Law in the University of Leiden; Bencher of Gray's Inn; Corresponding Member of the Royal Belgian Academy; Member of the American Law Institute.
Professor Dr H. G. Schermers	Professor of the Law of International Organisations at the University of Leiden and former Dean of the Leiden Law Faculty; Chairman of the Leiden Institute of Anglo-American Law; Member of the European Commission of Human Rights.
Mr John Spencer	Reader in Law in the University of Cambridge and Fellow of Selwyn College.
Professor Dr D. Tallon	Professor in the University of Paris II, Director of the Institute of Comparative Law, Paris.
Mr Stephen Tromans	Partner, Simmons & Simmons Solicitors.
Dr Derrick Wyatt	Fellow of St Edmund Hall, Oxford.

Abbreviations

A.2d	Atlantic Reporter, 2nd series (American Law Reports)
AC	Law Reports, Appeal Cases (Decisions of the House of Lords and the Privy Council from 1891)
AGBG	Gesetz über die Allgemeinen Geschäftsbedingungen (German code on general contract terms)
AJIL	American Journal of International Law
AktG	Aktiengesetz (German code on public limited companies)
All ER	All England Law Reports
Am. J. Comp. L.	American Journal of Comparative Law
App. Cas.	Law Reports, Appeal Cases (1875–90)
BAG	Bundesarbeitsgericht (Germany's Federal (Supreme) Court for labour matters)
BB	Der Betriebs-Berater
BGB	Bürgerliches Gesetzbuch (German Civil Code)
BGBl.	Bundesgesetzblatt (Government Gazette)
BGH	Bundesgerichtshof (Germany's Federal (Supreme) Court)
BGHZ	Entscheidungen des Bundesgerichthofes in Zivilsachen (Decisions of the German Federal Supreme Court in civil matters)
Boston College Int. Comp. Law Rev.	Boston College International and Comparative Law Review
BVerfG	Bundesverfassungsgericht (German Constitutional Court)
BVerfGE	Entscheidungen des Bundesverfassungsgerichts (Decisions of the German Constitutional Court)
BYIL	British Yearbook of International Law
C.A.	Court of Appeal
Cal.L.Rev.	California Law Review
Cal.Rptr.	California Reporter
Cass.	Arrêt de la Cour de Cassation de Belgique
Cass.Ass.plén.	Arrêt de la Cour de Cassation, Assemblée Plénière (France)

Cass.Ch. mixte	Arrêt de la Cour de Cassation, Chambre Mixte (France)
Cass.Ch. réunies	Arrêt de la Cour de Cassation, Chambre Réunies (France)
Cass.Civ.	Arrêt de la Cour de Cassation, Chambre Civile (France)
Cass.Com.	Arrêt de la Cour de Cassation, Chambre Commercial (France)
Cass.Crim.	Arrêt de la Cour de Cassation, Chambre Criminelle (France)
Cass.Soc.	Arrêt de la Cour de Cassation, Chambre Social (France)
C.Civ.	Code Civil (French Civil Code)
CE	Conseil d'Etat (French Supreme Court for administration matters)
C.E.R.C.L.A.	Comprehensive Environmental Response, Compensation and Liability Act 1980 (USA)
C.F.R.	Code of Federal Regulations (USA)
Ch.	*Law Reports, Chancery Division (from 1891)*
CISG	United Nations Convention on Contracts for the International Sale of Goods of 11th April 1980
CLJ	*Cambridge Law Journal*
CMLR	*Common Market Law Reports*
C.O.E. draft convention	Council of Europe draft convention on civil liability for damage resulting from activities dangerous to the environment of 22nd July 1991
C.o.J.	Court of Justice
COM	Council of Ministers (EEC)
Conseil const.	Conseil constitutionel (French Constitutional Court)
CPP	Code de Procédure Pénale (French Code on Criminal Procedure)
CrApR	*Criminal Appeal Reports*
C.R.T.D.	Convention on civil liability for damage caused during carriage of dangerous goods by road, rail and inland navigation vessels
D.	*Recueil Dalloz (till 1964, later: Recueil Dalloz Sirey)*
DB	*Der Betrieb*
D.Chron.	*Recueil Dalloz, Chronique*

Denning L.Journ.	*Denning Law Journal*
DStR	*Deutsches Steurrecht*
ECHR	European Court of Human Rights
ECR	*European Court Reports*
EHRR	*European Human Rights Reports*
EL Rev.	*European Law Review*
Env.Pol.& L.	*Environmental Policy and Law*
EuGRZ	*Europäische Grundrechte Zeitschrift*
Exch.	*Law Reports, Exchequer Cases (1865–1875)*
F2d	*Federal Reporter, 2nd series (American Law Reports)*
FamRZ	*Zeitschrift für das gesamte Familienrecht*
G.U.	*Gazzetta Ufficiale (Italian Government Gazette)*
HGB	*Handelsgesetzbuch (German Commercial Code)*
H.L.	House of Lords
ICJ Reports	*International Court of Justice, Reports of judgments, advisory opinions and orders*
ICLQ	*International and Comparative Law Quarterly*
I.L.M.	*International Legal Materials*
IPrax	*Praxis des Internationalen Privat- und Verfahrensrechts*
JA	*Juristische Arbeitsblätter*
J.C.P.	*Juris Classeur Périodique (Semaine Juridique)*
JEL	*Journal of Environmental Law*
JhJb.	*Jherings Jahrbücher für die Dogmatik des bürgerlichen Rechts*
JLMB	Revue de Jurisprudence de Liège, Mons et Bruxelles
JuS	*Juristische Schulung*
JW	*Juristische Wochenschrift*
JZ	*Juristenzeitung*
KTS	*Konkurs-, Treuhand- und Schiedsgerichtswesen*
L.G.D.J.	Librairie Générale de Droit et de Jurisprudence
LM	*Lindemaier/Möhring, Nachschlagewerk des Bundesgerichtshofs*
LQR	*Law Quarterly Review*
MDR	*Monatsschrift für deutsches Recht*
MLR	*Modern Law Review*

N.E.	North Eastern Reporter (American Law Reports)
NJW	*Neue Juristische Wochenschrift*
NJW-RR	*Neue Juristische Wochenschrift Recht-sprechungs Report*
NLJ	New Law Journal
N.Y.	*New York Court of Appeals Reports*
NZLR	*New Zealand Law Reports*
OECD	Organisation for Economic Cooperation and Development or
O.J.	*Official Journal of the European Communities*
OLG	Oberlandesgericht (German Court of Appeal)
Oxf.J. of Leg. Studies	*Oxford Journal of Legal Studies*
PL	*Public Law*
QB	*Law Reports, Queen's Bench (1891–1900; 1952–)*
RabelsZ	*Rabels Zeitschrift für ausländisches und internationales Privatrecht*
RDCB	see RGDC
Rec.	*Recueil de la jurisprudence de la Cour de Justice des Communnautés Européennes*
Rev.crit.dr.intern.privé	*Revue critique de droit international privé*
Rev.int. de droit comparé	*Revue international de droit comparé*
RG	Reichsgericht
RGBl.	*Reichsgesetzblatt (Government gazette)*
RGDC	*Revue Générale de Droit Civil Belge*
RGZ	*Entscheidungen des Reichsgerichts in Zivil-sachen (Decisions of the German Imperial Court in civil matters)*
Riv.dir.intern.priv.proc.	*Rivista di diritto internazionale privato e processuale*
RSC	Rules of the Supreme Court
RW	*Rechtskundig Weekblad*
SC	United Nations Security Council
SEA	Single European Act
Stanford L.J.	*Stanford Law Journal*
TAR	Tijdschrift voor Agrarisch Recht
Tel Aviv Univ. Studies in Law	*Tel Aviv University Studies in Law*
TGI	Tribunal de grande instance (French Court of First Instance)
TMA	Tijdschrift voor Milieu-Aansprakelijkheid

TPR	*Tijdschrift voor Privaatrecht*
Tul.L.Rev.	*Tulane Law Review*
UCC	Uniform Commercial Code
UNEP	United Nations Environmental Program
UN Rep.Intl.Arb. Award	*United Nations Reports of international arbitral awards*
UNTS	*United Nations Treaty Series*
US	*United States Supreme Court Reports*
VersR	*Versicherungsrecht*
VVG	Versicherungsvertragsgesetz (German Code on Contracts of Insurance)
WLR	*Weekly Law Reports*
WM	*Wertpapier-Mitteilungen*
WPg	*Die Wirtschaftsprüfung*
WPNR	*Weekblad voor Privaatrecht, Notariat en Registratie*
WPO	Wirtschaftsprüfer Ordnung (German Accountants Regulations)
Yale L.J.	*Yale Law Journal*
ZIP	*Zeitschrift für Wirtschaftsrecht und Insolvenzpraxis*

Table of Cases

European Court of Justice

FRANCE

GERMANY – FEDERAL CONSTITUTIONAL COURT

GERMANY – IMPERIAL COURT (REICHSGEREIT)

GERMANY – FEDERAL SUPREME COURT
(BUNDESGERICHTSHOF) AND FEDERAL COURT FOR
LABOUR MATTERS (BUNDESARBEITSGERICHT)

GERMANY – COURT OF APPEALS

INTERNATIONAL COURT OF JUSTICE

ITALY

NETHERLANDS

NEW ZEALAND

UNITED KINGDOM

UNITED NATIONS

UNITED STATES

Table of Legislation

GERMANY

UNITED STATES

Table of International Treaties and Conventions

1

Learning from Europe and Learning in Europe

B. S. MARKESINIS

Gott grüss Euch Brüder
Sämtliche Oner und Aner
Ich bin Weltbewohner
*Bin Weimaraner**

1 The Seminar Series and the Book

Learning from Europe was the title of the seminar series which, as stated in the preface, gave birth to this book. Many of our participants were quick to point out that England was, in fact, part of Europe. Too quick, in fact, for, though geographically this observation is correct, it underestimates the differences in legal history and mentality which were (and, probably, still are) far greater than the distance between Dover and Calais could by itself ever possibly suggest. This insular mentality will, one suspects, survive for some time after the Channel Tunnel technically puts an end to our status as islands off the continent of Europe. It was this 'mentality gap' that the title of the series was meant to capture, stress, and attack. For it was further hoped to show—as some comparatists have demonstrated—that attitudes and phobias still constitute the greatest factor that separates this country from the continent of Europe rather than problems, solutions and, even, methodology. Professor Koopmans, the Advocate General of the Dutch Supreme Court (and formerly a judge in the Court of Justice of the European Communities), put this very same thought in a slightly different way when he wrote in his Harry Street Lecture that 'Lawyers in countries like Great Britain and the Netherlands [and the same can be said of other countries on the Continent] still *think* that their legal systems show profound differences, but they are also discovering how

---

* I greet you, brothers | Partisans of various 'isms' and 'slogans', | As for me, I'm a world citizen | As well as Weimarian [Goethe, Zahme Xenien v, in *Sämtliche Werke* Berliner Ausgabe, Bournal, 2: Teil, Poetiische Werke, 687. Trans. by A. Lenhoff]. Erasmus of Rotterdam expressed the internationalist spirit even more strongly when he maintained that 'for those devoted to studies, it is quite unimportant to belong to one country or another.'

much law they have in common.'[1] Unashamedly, therefore, the series and the book, while not ignoring the differences, were aimed at underlying (and underlining) similarities, common problems, and the advantages of searching together for similar or common answers.

It was at this stage, however, that it became obvious to all who took part in the seminars that the English lawyers (and for obvious reasons I am excluding Scots lawyers who have always struck me as being more internationally-minded) were not only experiencing a Europeanization of their law, which was sometimes conscious but was in other instances unnoticed, but were also teaching European lawyers in more ways than one. For example, one only has to read Professor Kötz's admiring references to English judicial styles,[2] or to listen to foreign lawyers and judges who took part in our seminar series extol the virtues and efficacy of common law advocates when they appear before European courts, or, finally, to read Lord Slynn's Hamlyn Lectures and find some areas of the law where English practice would have a beneficial impact on European law,[3] to realize the most obvious of points, namely that we can both teach in and learn from Europe. Whether one learns from Europe or one learns in Europe, the fact is that these worthy aims can only be pursued through increased contacts and an exchange of ideas of the kind we tried to organize. This is the first and best opening move towards weakening if not destroying what I called the 'mentality gap'. Most, if not all, of those who took part in the seminar series told us that we had been successful. The papers (and our discussions) also demonstrated a remarkable move towards the Europeanization of our law—something that can also be said (but is not here considered) about the other European systems. Though gradual, this move cannot be surprising to anyone accustomed to taking a longer view of legal developments. After all, not so long ago lawyers in Europe operated a fairly advanced *ius commune* before the modern sovereign state interrupted legal and academic as well as political co-operation. So why should not lawyers move again in that general direction, as greater economic co-operation and a growing similarity in the social environment make the world they all inhabit both smaller and its various parts more interdependent?

The purpose of this introductory chapter is to help bring these papers closer together by developing a theme which, in the eyes of this author (though, perhaps, not all the readers of this book) could be seen as emerging from our prolonged deliberations.

---

[1] 'European Public Law: Reality and Prospects', *Public Law* (1991), 53. (Emphasis added.)
[2] 'The Role of the Judge in the Court Room: The Common Law and Civil Law Compared', *Journal of South African Law* (1987–91), 35, 41 *et seq.* 'Einführungsvortrag' in *La Sentenza in Europa: Metodo Techica e Stile* (1988), 129 *et seq.*
[3] *Introducing a European Legal Order*, the Hamlyn Lectures, 43rd series (1992), 155.

2   The problems raised by international conferences

As European integration proceeds apace the need for contacts with our Continental colleagues at different levels increases. Organizing such meetings is time-consuming; and turning part or all of them into a book, so that others can get some second-hand knowledge of what took place, can give rise to difficult problems of methodology. We hope that neither of these drawbacks will deter others from following our example. For their benefit, however, and for those who profess a primary interest in comparative law and comparative methodology, this sub-section has been included in the first chapter. The general reader may thus choose to avoid it altogether, though it is not inconceivable that he too, will derive some ideas and benefits from its inclusion.

The following are some of the problems that arose; and though I explain how and why we arrived at particular solutions, I suspect that they will not meet with everyone's approval. Other choices are clearly available.

1.1   *The Co-ordination of the Contributions*

It can be argued that the best, closely-knit, truly comparative work on a particular topic remains the classic study in parallel of tort and delict by Catala and Weir.[4] Though nearly thirty years old, and despite the increase in the volume of comparative literature, no one to my knowledge has repeated their remarkable feat. One can advance a number of reasons for this.

First, the partnership was self-created or, at any rate, encouraged by the late Professor Ferd Stone who had invited the two co-authors to Tulane.[5] They were colleagues of approximately the same age, with similarly penetrating legal minds, an obsession with an attractive legal writing style, and a caustic sense of humour who combined to produce a piece which, I take it, was substantially written while both authors were in the same location. An organizer of a seminar series (and, subsequently, the editor of the book that emerges from it) can hardly create such partnerships whatever his 'casting' powers. If the partnership is 'enforced' from above, it can rarely achieve the kind of full co-operation we find in Catala and Weir. Harris and Tallon recently produced an excellent book on the English and

---

[4] 'Delict and Torts: A Study in Parallel', *Tul L Rev* 37 (1963), 573; *Tul L Rev* 38 (1964), 221, 663; *Tul L Rev* 39 (1965) 701.

[5] There is a hint of this in Tony Weir's elegant piece 'Friendships in the Law: Essays in Honor of the Life, Legend and Legacy of Ferdinand Fairfax Stone', *Civil Law Forum* 6/7 1991–2, 61–94. Another example, which Professor Kötz reminded me of when he kindly read the manuscript of this chapter, is Professor Schlesinger's great project entitled *Formation of Contracts: A Study of the Common Core of Legal Systems*, 2 vols. (1968) which Max Rheinstein described as 'the most intensive comparison of legal institutions that has ever been undertaken'. (*V. Ch. L. Rev.* 36 (1969), 448.)

French law of contract.[6] Reviewers, including the present writer, expressed some doubts and misgivings about it.[7] Overall, however, the book provided a well-organized, informative, and often stimulating insight into the two systems and, one hopes, others like it will follow soon. One suspects much thought went into setting up the teams of contributors who, in essence, came from Oxford and Paris. There again, one notices that the *collaboration* though no doubt *cordiale* was not always *étroite*; and the 'paired contributions' were in some instances particularly 'independent' whenever one of the partners wrote an overtly comparative piece, while the other merely described and reflected on his or her own legal system.

We could not ignore these lessons from the past—especially since our team was more international, our authors had no chance to get together before or after the seminars, and the time factor was, for different reasons, always working against all of us.[8] If computer-matching of the teams was thus not possible—and sometimes a neglect of the smallest details can impair the combined presentation[9]—the only thing one could do was to assign to pairs of colleagues a common general theme and let them decide between them how best to present it. Inevitably, the two halves reproduced in this book are not as closely connected as one would have liked. But we hoped that the discussions that followed the presentations (and which, in our case, lasted in each session for about two and a half hours) would achieve the desirable unity at the second phase of the proceedings. Thanks to the ability of our chairmen and the warm rapport that our speakers, without exception, established with the audience, we achieved this aim beyond our wildest expectations. This last point, inevitably, leads to the second difficulty that confronted us in this series.

1.2   *The Discussions: to Publish or Not to Publish?*

The previous paragraph makes the point that the unity of presentation was really achieved at the discussion phase of the seminars. It was then that differences started melting away and the search for workable solutions to common problems began in earnest. Often English practitioners would put to our foreign speakers questions that were currently concerning them and one could not help but admire how, when facing a common problem, experienced lawyers were able to by-pass totally obstacles created by

---

[6] *Contract Law Today: Anglo–French Comparisons* (1989).

[7] 49 [1990] *CLJ*, 152–5; Collins 'Methods and Aims of Comparative Contract Law' in *Oxf J of Leg Studies* (1991) 396–406.

[8] Nine months elapsed between the invitation to participate at the conference and the actual seminars themselves.

[9] I have, for example, noticed at international conferences the 'pairing' of a very senior (in age) with a very junior colleague with the result that the former almost eclipsed the latter in the ensuing discussion. The courtesy, common sense, and great international experience of our keynote speakers ensured that this did not happen in our case.

concepts, awkwardly-drafted statutes, or highly specific case law. We had foreign lawyers in the audience and the same feeling of mutual understanding was obvious when they engaged in a dialogue with their English colleagues.

To deprive the reader of these materials was not an easy decision to take. Yet, on balance, it could not have been otherwise. The increase in size and, consequently, cost was not one the publishers were willing to sanction, and one sympathizes with such an attitude. Harris and Tallon found a partial way round this problem by abridging the discussions and reproducing them in the third person. Some reviewers of their book found the compromise an unsatisfactory one. The vivacity of the oral discussion was lost and the abridgement in places made the text (and arguments) difficult to follow. The amount of extra time needed to prepare these summaries would have delayed further the appearance of this book. Additionally, and most significantly, our sessions were well-attended by many judges who, by speaking candidly, gave us immensely valuable insights into many of these problems. They (and others), however, had informed me in advance that the taping of the proceedings would have an inhibiting effect. Taping was omitted; and the preparation of summaries was made correspondingly more difficult. At the end of the day the discussions had to be omitted from this book.

We have tried to make up for this omission in two ways. The first—and this adds to the unusual features of this book—was by asking the judges who presided over the five sessions to give us in writing some of their personal reactions to the papers presented at their sessions. They have selflessly obliged; and their pieces, especially when combined with the keynote presentations, provide a rich, extra dimension to the comparative discussions contained in this volume.

The second way of replicating the discussions is through this introductory chapter. Though the ideas contained in it are largely mine—and in no way can they be attributed to any of our speakers, chairmen, or participants—the theme of unity and convergence was one that dominated the sessions and I have chosen to make it the leitmotiv of the book. This brings me to our third dilemma.

1.3 A Joint or Individual 'Synthesis' of the Proceedings?

The Harris and Tallon model was, again, one that had to be considered. Some reviewers felt that the inevitable process of compromise had deprived their collaborative conclusions of 'punch'.[10] In retrospect, one can argue that for the kind of book that Harris and Tallon were writing this may not have been a fatal flaw; indeed, the repeated meetings held by the

---

[10] See n. 6, above.

participants meant that this step towards formulating 'common reflections' (if not conclusions) could be undertaken with some ease. We, however, did not have the luxury of many meetings; and (mainly for financial reasons) the whole team never met at the same time and place. These special factors gave me, as organizer and general editor, the opportunity to attempt my own synthesis which, inevitably, has been influenced by the aims and goals that I have pursued in my twenty-five years as a teacher of comparative law. These aims are not necessarily shared by the other participants of the seminar series, though some of the points contained here were discussed with a number of colleagues. If my colleagues do not share in the blemishes that this introduction may have, they do, however, share in such credit as may be due since the synthesis, in fair measure, is based on their papers and what was said at the meetings. In any event, it represents one possible interpretation of the large volume of material which was considered during our five sessions. If readers can draw additional or different conclusions, so much the better. Disagreements with the views expressed can only help to further the dialogue we wish to promote. The 'correctness' of our views is very much of secondary importance. After all, there is no claim here of papal infallibility; just a persistent desire for more dialogue and enhanced mutual understanding. On this we all agreed without any reservations.

1.4 *How Broadly should the Comparative Law Net be Cast?*

It would have undoubtedly been closer to the Centre's interests if all five of the seminar series had focused on the law of obligations. The recent Law Commission Report on the Privity of Contract shows how the willingness of English lawyers to look abroad is growing, and can be developed further.[11] One need not cite other instances to show how fruitful the interchange of ideas can be in the areas of contract, tort, and restitution. So why cast the net wider to include, for example, criminal law, environmental law, and the effect that international conventions (or treaties) can have on municipal law? Our reasons for casting the net widely were mainly two (apart, that is, from the intrinsic interest that these subjects present): one practical, the other theoretical.

The practical aim was to show how international instruments are gradually helping to develop a more Europeanized English law. More is said about this in the penultimate section of this chapter. In the case of criminal law we also wished to expose English lawyers to some foreign views about non-English criminal law. The aim was again practical: to stimulate further debate in this country and make lawyers and, perhaps, laymen appreciate

---

[11] 'Privity of Contract: Contracts for the Benefit of Third Parties', Consultation Paper No. 121 (1991).

that 'the other man's grass is not *always* greener'. To put it differently, many comparatists will have been appalled over the last years to read and hear how our media have simplified foreign (mainly French) criminal law, repeatedly indicating that some of our recent infamous miscarriages of justice would not have occurred if we had a system of criminal procedure similar to the French. There can be little doubt that French or, more generally, foreign ideas, could help us rethink our own legal solutions (and, incidentally, stop us seeing our police through rose-tinted spectacles). The idea of whole-hearted transplantation is utopic at best, ludicrous at worst. We needed comparative criminal lawyers to make these points and to respond, with appropriate authority, to the specialists of the English Bar who attended that particular session.

Practical considerations have always been paramount in our minds. Yet, at the end of the day I am among those who have expressed grave doubts about the orientation that comparative law seems to have taken from the 1960s onward. Like Dante in the first tercet of the *Inferno* I felt that in its middle-age comparative law was losing its sense of direction. These doubts were advanced forcefully in the 1989 Shimizu Lecture at the London School of Economics; [12] and ever since the lecture was delivered I had hoped for the chance to organize a conference on comparative law in England which would, in a sense, provide an English answer to the French conferences organized by the *Institut de Droit Comparé de Paris*.[13] Over the years a number of aims have been defined for comparative law for the turn of the century.[14] They are discussed briefly in the next sub-section, but among them was the need to make municipal lawyers more comparatively-minded rather than leave comparative law as the exclusive domain of the small coterie of comparatists. Criminal law seemed an obvious and topical candidate; and John Spencer, whose essay complements perfectly Professor Marty's contribution, has recognized this fact and has responded by setting up a course on comparative criminal procedure at Cambridge University after spending a year as a Visiting Professor in Paris. A great service

---

[12] 'Comparative Law: A Subject in Search of an Audience', *MLR* 53 (1990), 1. In that article I complained of the platitudinous generalities that some comparatists use in presenting their subject. Alas, they show no sign of abatement so that for example a senior colleague in the field was recently telling a *mature audience* that 'The term "civil law" system is a convenient shorthand for those Western legal orders that arose out of the legal culture that began to develop in 1095 with Irnerius' lectures at Bologna on the newly rediscovered *Corpus Iuris Civilis* of Justinian' and that 'The common law emerged in England in the course of the twelfth and thirteenth centuries.' Arthur von Mehren, 'The Comparative Study of Law', Essays in Honor of Ferdinand Fairfax Stone, *Civil Law Forum*, 6/7 (1991–2), 43, 44.

[13] A. Tunc and others, 'L'Enseignement de Droit Comparé', (1988) *Rev int de droit comparé* 4 (1988), 703 *et seq*.

[14] In addition to the article mentioned in n. 11, above, see my inaugural address at the Royal Belgian Academy, 'The Destructive and Constructive Role of the Comparative Lawyer' to be published in the summer 1993 issue of the *Rabels Zeitschrift*.

will have been rendered to comparative law if other national lawyers were to follow John Spencer's example. This book offers yet another incentive that direction.

1.5   *The Language as a Barrier to Greater Co-operation*

Any organizer of an international conference has to face the dilemma of either (*a*) inviting the speakers to talk in their mother language, (*b*) making one or two languages the official languages of the sessions, or (*c*) asking everyone to use the language of the forum. Each approach has advantages and drawbacks, but our opting for English as the language of the seminar series was largely prompted by practical considerations—not linguistic chauvinism.

By presenting their papers in English and continuing in the same language during the tiring question and answer sessions, our foreign visitors made their linguistic talents obvious and enviable! In the course of listening to them and subsequently editing their texts—in some cases constantly comparing the English version to the original—one had cause to reflect on a number of issues, two of which might provide the themes of future joint seminars.

It can be argued that English lawyers labour under a considerable disadvantage by not having access to foreign legal literature. The phenomenal success that the central European *emigrés* had in this country and in the USA in the 1940s, 1950s, and 1960s was in large part due to their linguistic abilities which enabled them to combine European (especially germanic) doctrinal analysis with common law pragmatism in a way that was not seen before in the New World and (alas) may never be seen again in the future.[15] The measure of their success is that they made comparative law and the comparative method a recognized, even admired, topic at a time when there was really little practical need for it. It is a measure of the failure of this generation of comparatists (and the one immediately preceding it) that they have allowed the subject to flounder at a time when a shrinking world needs it more than ever. The immigration from Europe has stopped; the Rabels, the Rheinsteins, the Kesslers, the Ehrenzweigs, the

---

[15] For a collection of interesting essays on the central European *emigrés* see: *Second Chance: Two Centuries of German-speaking Jews in the United Kingdom*, ed. Mosse (1990). The immigration of the German intellectuals is discussed in different contexts by, among others, Göppinger, *Juristen jüdischer Abstammung im 'Dritten Reich': Entrechtung und Verfolgung*, 2nd edn. (1990); Freyermuth, *Reisen in die Verlorenrergangenheit: Auf den Spuren deutscher Emigranten* (1990); Stiefel, 'Die deutsche juristische Emigration in den USA' *JZ* (1988), 421. American accounts include Kent, *The Refugee Intellectual: The Americanization of the Immigrants of 1933–1941* (1953) and, more recently, Grossfeld and Winship, 'The Law Professor Refugee' *Syracuse Journal of International Law and Commerce* 18 (1992), 3. The multiple difficulties these scholars encountered makes their achievements even more remarkable.

Kahn-Freunds have died; the Dawsons and the Lawsons, their indigenous counterparts, have proved difficult to replace.

Yet if we are lacking in the knowledge of foreign languages, how rich is our own; and to what effective use it has been put by the great judicial masters of the common law. Along with others, I have on timeless occasions introduced foreign audiences to the economy and confidence of Blackburn and Willis; and time and again I have recited Denning texts or declaimed those of Cardozo. Astonishingly, they may have their critics in their own countries;[16] but they have never failed to impress, even move, civilian lawyers. How much we ceded to the French, even without a legal battle, when through our absence from Europe in the 1950s we allowed them to shape the procedure and even the style of the European courts. Yet the ground is not totally lost, since the common lawyer's training and ability to refine and constantly redefine evolving case law may prove of great use to the modern civilian lawyers, who find their law developing and adapting through cases rather than through an apparently deductive reasoning from codal article to disputed case. The study of the ways we analyse and reconcile cases, as well as the style of our judgments, could, I think, have some beneficial effects on the way foreign lawyers handle their decisional law. A jurist arguing the 'English case' in Europe, should make this a key point in his presentation.

Yet, as always, the learning process is a two-way road; and it would appear that our stylistic superiority in the area of judge-made law is seriously eroded in the domain of legislature drafting, be it because of our lack of a solid legal tradition,[17] or because of our determination to be mathematically precise and exhaustive.[18] Our legislative drafting techniques could learn a thing or two from the continent of Europe. This statement could be seen as an attempt to be even-handed in one's praise and criticism of the various legal systems. It was Sir William Dale who, after a remarkable study of comparative drafting techniques, argued in favour of a style of draftmanship that would come closer to the Continental style by defining first the appropriate *general principle* and then following it up with only

---

[16] For a recent sympathetic and well-written appraisal see Posner, *Cardozo: A Study in Reputation* (1990).

[17] Professor Honoré's view expressed in *The Quest for Security: Employees, Tenants, Wives,* the Hamlyn Lectures, 34th series (1982), 119.

[18] 'English statutes', claimed Sir Charles David, Legal Adviser to the House of Commons Select Committee on European Secondary Legislation, are 'customarily drafted with almost mathematical precision, the object (not always attained) being in effect to provide a complete answer to virtually every question that can arise'. Evidence submitted to the Renton Committee, Cmnd 6053, para. 52. The draftsmen of the gargantuan (and unsuccessful) Prussian Land Code of 1794 would have heartily endorsed such a statement. Sir Michael Kerr, 'Law Reform in Changing Times' *LQR* 96 (1980), 515, 527–8 thought this was 'a basic and apparently ineradicable feature of our constitutional philosophy'.

so much detail as order and clarity required.[19] This is no place to go into this topic, beyond repeating the claim that it would, on its own, justify a comparative conference and warrant an open mind on behalf of English lawyers who tend to assume that immutability is not only a feature but also an advantage of English law.

But let us return briefly to the impact our language can have on foreign lawyers. Take three German student text books on the law of tort written by Professors Kötz,[20] Deutsch[21] and Medicus.[22] Each of these authors is highly respected in his country for his learning, and rightly so. Yet look at the books, and if you are an English (or indeed a non-German) lawyer you will probably rank them in terms of *readability* in the order in which they were named (and German students—when asked—have always agreed). Has the obvious comparative training of the first of these jurists and his frequent exposure to common law audiences had an obvious effect? I venture the thought—and no conclusive proof can, in the absence of a 'confession', be advanced—that it has. And, more immediately, look how important this attribute is when one reads Professor Lorenz's contribution on third party beneficiaries or Professor Kötz's recent lecture[23] on (roughly) the same area of the law. The reader should note how these jurists adapt their writing for an English-speaking audience. No long sentences, no endless discussion of theory, but a masterly use of factually-similar cases; those are the characteristics of their written work. They manage to make their law look more similar to ours; and make us ponder about theirs when it appears superior. For does not Professor Kötz's piece add further significance to the judgment of Lord Justice Goff (as he then was) in *The Aliakmon*[24] and make Lord Brandon's hasty rejection of it (arguably) even less convincing?[25] One may not, at the end of the day, be convinced of the superiority of German law as a result of such writings; but one will have at least been persuaded to look at it, thus closing what I called the 'mentality gap'.

Much more comparative work remains to be done in the area of legal styles and legal translations; and, one hopes, the masterly treatise of Zweigert and Kötz, which rightly considers matters of style as forming the most substantial differences between the common law and civil law systems, will devote in its next edition more space to this neglected yet important aspect of comparative law.

---

[19] *Legislative Drafting: A New Approach* (1977), 335.
[20] *Deliktsrecht*, 5th edn. (1991).
[21] *Unerlaubte Handlungen und Schadensersatz: Ein Grundriss* (1987).
[22] *Bürgerliches Recht*, 15th edn. (1990). This last book, however, is not limited to tort law.
[23] 'The Doctrine of Privity of Contract', *Tel Aviv University Studies in Law* 10 (1990), 195.   [24] [1985] QB 350.
[25] *Leigh and Sillavan Ltd. v. Aliakmon Shipping Co. Ltd.* [1986] AC 785, 820.

3 The Role of the Expositor of Foreign Law

3.1 *The Art of Making One Legal System Intelligible to Lawyers of Another*

All of us, at one time or another, will have listened to lawyers explaining a legal point to a layman using legal jargon and causing more confusion than enlightenment. Equally we will have witnessed and admired the reverse ability, possessed by some commentators, to minimize the use of jargon, go to the heart of a legal point, and make it easy for a lay audience to follow a fairly sophisticated legal argument. Some experienced legal journalists have this gift;[26] but it has not been totally denied to all law professors either.[27]

Comparative law and the use of the comparative method raise similar difficulties. It is a question of talent and deep understanding of what is being compared rather than professed expertise that gives some authors the ability to present intelligibly to their own colleagues intricate aspects of foreign law. Professor Gray's *Re-allocation of Property on Divorce*[28] is one of the best (fairly) recent monographs in comparative family law; moreover, not only was this the author's first book; the author had never professed a primary interest in comparative law. By contrast, books or articles written by 'professional' comparatists—and for obvious reasons it is best not to be specific—have fallen between the Scylla of excessive conceptualism and the Charybdis of almost condescending simplification. In comparative law, the absence of an impeccable legal pedigree in one system may not be a disadvantage; the qualities of a mongrel may be highly valued.

Professor Lorenz's piece is, arguably, a model of what the presentation of foreign law should be. His written style uses the shorter sentences that appeal to the English rather than the more complicated, grammatical structure associated with the German language. In this paper, though the code is not ignored, the law is presented through cases; and, wherever appropriate, the English counterparts are given. The essay not only describes German law; by giving us its answers to questions that are still vexing us, it subtly makes the reader think about his own law and its rationality. So successfully is this presentation made, that it lulls the reader, who otherwise may know nothing about German law, into thinking that it is easy, clear, and conceptually totally uncluttered. It takes a quick glance at the major treaties and the interminable discussions in the legal

[26] Berlins and Dyer, *The Law Machine* (3rd edn.) is a book in point. Joshua Rosenberg's television presentations of current legal affairs offer another example. Bagehot's *The British Constitution* may be the best example of a book which attained great fame largely, I believe, because of its very readable style.

[27] Professor Brian Simpson's *Invitation to Law* (1988), Professor Glanville Williams' *Learning the Law*, 11th edn. (1982), and even his quite unusual (in style) *Textbook of Criminal Law*, 2nd edn. (1983), offer good illustrations.   [28] Published in 1977.

literature[29] on how the *Vertrag mit Schutzwirkung für Dritte* differs from the notion of *Drittschadensliquidation* to crash-land him back into reality. But a teacher, or come to that an expert witness, who starts his presentation in such a manner, who emphasizes notions rather than actual case law, who stresses differences in classification rather than proceeding with a functional comparison of the system, will end up putting off his audience from foreign law. He will be feeding what we have called the 'mentality gap', and encouraging the attitude that has kept us apart for so long: 'why should I look at German law which is so obscure and different?' Professor Lorenz (and indeed some of the other contributors) show that foreign law need not be obscure; and, if it is suitably clarified, it comes closer to our own. It takes considerable exposure to international audiences to achieve such clarity.

3.2   The Need to Destroy Myths

In my inaugural address to the Royal Belgian Academy I spoke of the need to destroy myths before the work of comparative reconstruction can begin.[30] The interested reader will find there many examples of this. Here let me provide two particular illustrations, the first of which emerged during the lucid presentations made by Professors Delmas-Marty and Spencer, while the second surfaced during the discussion that followed Professor Tallon's essay.

Professor Delmas-Marty's paper is brief. Even in its English version it retains the lightness of touch that so often characterizes French writing. It is uncluttered by footnotes. Yet from the very outset it explodes a leader in *The Times*[31] and other assertions similarly made in the English media about the undiluted merits of the inquisitorial system in general and the French *juge d'instruction* in particular. The Germans and the Italians had

---

[29] The German law can be found discussed in all the classic treatises as well as in the shorter but respected text books of Larenz, *Lehrbuch des Schuldrechts*, 13th edn. (1982), i: 201, esp. 208 *et seq.*; Essser–Schmidt, *Schuldrecht*, 6th edn. (1984), i: 562 *et seq.*; Fikentscher, *Schuldrecht*, 7th edn. (1985), 179 *et seq.*; Medicus, *Bürgerliches Recht*, 15th edn. (1990), 508 *et seq.* The following articles have also proved useful; von Caemmerer, 'Verträge zugunsten Dritter', in *Festschrift Wieacker* (1978), 311 *et seq.*; Krause, 'Untermieter und Mieter im Schutzbereich eines Vertrages', *JZ* 1982, 16 *et seq.*; Lorenz, 'Note to BGH NJW 1965, 1955', in *JZ* 1966, 143 *et seq.*; Ries, 'Grundprobleme der Drittschadensliquidation und des Vertrags mit Schutzwirkung für Dritte', *JA* 1982, 453 *et seq.*; Schlechtriem, 'Deliktshaftung des Subunternehmers gegenüber dem Bauherrn wegen Minderwerts seines Werks: Eine neue Entscheidung des House of Lords', *Karlsruher Forum* (1983), 64 *et seq.*; Schwerdtner, 'Verträge mit Schutzwirkung für Dritte', *Jura* 1980, 493 *et seq.*; Sonnenschein, 'Der Vertrag mit Schutzwirkung für Dritte: und immer neue Fragen', *JA* 1979, 225 *et seq.*; Ziegler, 'Personale Abgrenzungskriterien beim Vertrag mit Schutzwirkung zugunsten Dritter', *JuS* 1979, 328; Strauch, 'Verträge mit Drittschutzwirkung', *JuS* 1982, 823; Assman, 'Grundfälle zum Vertrag mit Schutzwirkung für Dritte', *JuS* 1986, 885. All of these articles contain extensive references to the rich case law.
[30] See n. 13, above.   [31] *The Times,* 8 Mar. 1991.

such an institution but they have abolished it. The French are having serious doubts about it. A book edited by Professor Delmas-Marty shows how comparative law should be used in such instances.[32] As Sir Robin Auld and John Spencer note, English law can be improved by using foreign ideas to adapt and reshape English institutions (for example the Crown Prosecution Service), but to talk of a wholehearted importation of foreign institutions can be naive. In this instance, for example, who would do the 'instruction'? Sir Thomas Bingham, in a lecture delivered in the Institute of Anglo-American Law of the University of Leiden, talked of the English criminal law—warts and all.[33] This was an impressive public statement by a jurist in a position of authority who courageously admitted that we could learn from others but rightly doubted whether we were setting about this task in the right way.

The discussions initiated by the papers presented by Professor Delmas-Marty and John Spencer suggest that English criminal law may have defects but that it also has its strengths. More importantly, the borrowing of foreign ideas must be done in a subtle way that fits in with the existing environment, and does not cause more upheaval than benefit. We see this in other areas of the law. The nordic institution of ombudsman had to be Anglicized before it was allowed to immigrate successfully. Sir David Calcutt's Report of the Committee on Privacy and Related Matters[34] likewise recommended the introduction of greater privacy protection, but in a way that may have made it more palatable to the English environment.[35] Our press is, of course, still flexing its formidable muscles to oppose such moves; but in the long run its current practices, sanctimoniously defended under the banner of public interest, will have to change. This is another area where foreign law and practice will show the way.

The second myth—perhaps more accurately described as a distorted picture—that foreigners have about our law concerns our techniques of statutory interpretation. Different drafting techniques have, especially in the past, undoubtedly led to a more literal interpretation of statutes by English courts. The purposive or teleological interpretation that one finds so often in the civil law system was, when not frowned upon, attributed to their more open-ended, principle-oriented, legislature drafting. For example, in *Customs and Excise Commissioners* v. *ApS Samex*,[36] Mr Justice

---

[32] *Procé Pénal et Droits de L'Homme* (1992).
[33] *The English Criminal Trial: The Credits and the Debits* (Leiden Institute of Anglo-American Law, 1990). [34] Cmnd. 1102 (1990).
[35] I have elaborated this point in 'Subtle Ways of Legal Borrowing: Some Comparative Reflections on the Report of the *Calcutt* Committee "on Privacy and Related Matters"', in *Festschrift für W. Lorenz zum siebzigsten Geburtstag* (1991), 717 *et seq.*
[36] [1983] 1 All ER 1042 at 1056. See, also, *Henn and Darby* v. *DPP* [1981] AC 850 at 905 per Lord Diplock.

Bingham (as he then was) said of Community law (but his views apply equally to codal provisions of Continental systems):

The interpretation of Community instruments involves very often not the process familiar to common lawyers of laboriously extracting the meaning from words used, but the more creative process of supplying flesh to a spare and loosely-constructed skeleton. The choice between alternative submissions may turn not on purely legal considerations but on a broader view of what the orderly development of the Community requires.

Though this statement presents clearly the orthodox position, it must not be allowed to conceal three important and interrelated developments. First, let us not forget the widely-phrased discretions that English statutes are increasingly vesting in judges. There may, of course, be nothing strange in 'restor[ing] to the judges . . . the task of interpreting law according to statements of principle, rather than by painfully hacking their way through the jungles of detailed and intricate legislation'.[37] But this may not only be happening more frequently; it may be done so broadly as to invite the application of the broader principles of interpretation which Lord Justice Bingham thought appropriate to a broad and loosely-constructed codal enactment. At any rate, common-law lawyers might be interested to read Professor Kötz's views on the discretion given by section 33 of the Limitation Act 1980 to English judges allowing them to 'disapply' time-limits for actions involving personal injury or death. Having 'spared' the audience of his Chorley Lecture 'the many words used by the parliamentary draftsmen in section 33(3) to tell the judge what factors he ought to consider in determining whether or not it is "equitable" to disapply these time limits', Professor Kötz concluded that the discretion was so widely phrased 'that a similar rule would, in this particular field of law, be unacceptable to German lawyers and, I believe, to lawyers from other Continental countries as well.'[38]

Such drafting clearly makes the literal rule of interpretation redundant. But even where the legislator has spoken and spoken clearly, courts seem to be increasingly moving towards purposive interpretation. One cannot think easily of a more dry or more narrowly-conceived statute (enacted to rectify a gap in the common law) than the Employers' Liability (Defective Equipment) Act 1969, yet look what the courts did to the literary rule in *Coltman* v. *Bibby Tankers Ltd*.[39] which involved the sinking of a vessel with much of its crew. The plaintiff (the widow of a seaman), sued the defendants under the Employers' Liability (Defective Equipment) Act 1969

[37] Lord Wilberforce speaking on the Law Commissions Bill in the House of Lords, H. L. Debates 264: 1175–6 (1 April 1965).
[38] 'Taking Civil Codes Less Seriously', *MLR* 50 (1987), 1, 5.
[39] [1988] AC 276.

to be met, *inter alia, by* the argument that a ship could not be considered as 'equipment for the purposes of this Act'. Indeed, section 1(3) of the Act defined equipment as including 'any plant and machinery *vehicle, aircraft* and clothing' (emphasis added). Ships were conspicuously absent from this list; and, in any event, as the Court of Appeal pointed out, 'equipment' was ancillary to something else and could not be taken to refer to the workplace itself. The House of Lords reversed this judgment; and though the omission of ships from the definition of section 1(3) was described as 'certainly curious', the view was taken that Parliament could not have intended to exclude ships from the ambit of the Act. The purposive construction of the Act thus won the day.

Yet these changes in the English scene, brought about by new drafting techniques and likely to increase as our courts have to interpret more European-emanating statutory material, are only one side of the coin. The reverse, and equally misunderstood (by us this time and not by our foreign colleagues) situation is the increasingly technical and detailed language used by German (and other European) enactments that have added to or otherwise affected the Civil Codes. For example, section 11(1) of our Unfair Contract Terms Act 1977 may have a counterpart in the German Standard Terms Act of 1976;[40] but the complexity of the other provisions of the German statute, and their close interrelationship with various paragraphs in the Civil Code is so great, that it would be foolish to deny that the German judge who has to apply them does not have to pay very close attention to the text of the statute.

A variety of drafting techniques may call for a variety of rules of interpretation. Whatever judges may say they do, they must, at the end of the day, strive to reach a common sense solution when interpreting statutory law. In this sense, English and Continental judges are not so very different whatever the books may say to the contrary.

3.3 *The Importance of Using Foreign Material to Further a Greater Understanding of One's Own Law*

From the days of the late Professor Gutteridge, if not before, this has been accepted as a significant aim of comparative law. The way in which Professor von Bar pursues it in his erudite contribution makes his piece worthy of study and not just casual reading.

Case law dominates his presentation on negligent misstatements and economic loss. In one sense this is not surprising, given the relative paucity of codal and other statutory provisions on the subject in German law. Yet what is really surprising—arguably troublesome for the reasons which I shall give below—is the excessive wealth of the German case law. Nearly

---

[40] Translated and discussed in *Am J Comp L* 26 (1978), 551.

120 decisions figure in this heavily annotated text—many more than I believe can be found in English law. These are truly American proportions, incontrovertibly proving a point which some comparatists have laboured to stress when combating the 'René David way of teaching comparative law': one cannot begin to understand a foreign legal system simply by studying its codes, its statutes, its text books; one must tackle and understand its case law before one can start acquiring a clear picture of the law.[41] One of the questions Professor von Bar's paper raises is how can one do this in the absence of a visibly practised system of *stare decisis*?

Falling back on the codal or statutory background is, I think, only a partial answer given the fact that, as we have already noted, the statutory signposts are few and far between. Of course, that is how the European courts start their reasoning process, using previous case law merely for illustration or supporting purposes and, in any event, much more loosely than an English court would have to do.[42] Moreover, the reference to the earlier case law does not seem to be either exhaustive or particularly analytical. My own impression—obviously that of a foreign observer of German law—is that the internal consistency of the cases is neither strong nor obvious. For the teacher who is interested in detail as much as the practitioner who is trying to obtain a focused view of the law, this must be something little short of a nightmare. Yet order may come in a different way; and one which holds out useful comparative insights both to the foreign observer and the German jurist.

The *deus ex machina* must, in part, be the German academic. Like his predecessor in the ancient Greek tragedies, his intervention may be contrived and the solution he provides only partially convincing. Yet an answer of sorts he does provide, thereby and—incidentally—continuing the long-established dialogue between judges and academics which is one of the hallmarks of German law. What comparative lessons can one draw from this thesis, assuming it is at least plausible?

Professor von Bar's paper is as rich in ideas as in its citation of primary material. He offers a number of interrelated explanations that could provide a unifying theme that would work as a guideline for future disputes. But are the German courts likely to take advantage of such guidance? Traditionally, of course, the interaction between German judge and jurist was constant and close; certainly closer than one finds in other systems. The latter's theories on numerous occasions were taken over by the former to provide a manageable synthesis and a solid foundation of the ever-

---

[41] My theory is elaborated in my article in *MLR* 53 (1990), 1, and put into practice in my *The German Law of Torts*, 2nd edn. (1990).

[42] See Kötz, 'Einführungsvortrag' etc., n. 2, above, to which add: 'Scholarship and the Courts: A Comparative Survey', in *Comparative and Private International Law, Essays in Honor of J. H. Merryman on his Seventieth Birthday* (1990), 183, 194.

increasing case law. For example, the BGB was still in its infancy when Staub in his monumental *Positive Vertragsverletzungen*[43] provided the theoretical underpinnings for the most important category of breach of contract (i.e. bad performance) which the Code, misled by nineteenth-century Romanists,[44] had omitted to regulate alongside the other types of breach—impossibility and delay—for which codal provisions were provided.[45] Some twenty years later, Oertmann's theory of 'basic assumption of the parties' (*Geschäftsgrundlage*),[46] reviving the doctrine of 'presupposition' (*Voraussetzung*) of his famous father-in-law Bernhard Windscheid,[47] again provided some semblance of order to a hyperactive *Reichsgericht*[48] which was trying to cope with the consequences of hyperinflation provoked in Germany by the narrow-sightedness of the victors of the First World War. Another thirty years later and Karl Larenz was to find the codal regulation of contracts in favour of third parties (*Vertrag zugunsten Dritter*) lacking and was thus forced to elaborate[49] the notion by creating the variant of contracts with protective effects *vis-à-vis* third parties (*Vertrag mit Schutzwirkung für Dritte*) to which both Professors von Bar and Lorenz allude in their papers. Here then—and in our present context of economic loss the third illustration is the key one—are examples where academics can provide (and have provided) the courts with theories which, if not quite as effective as the doctrine of *stare decisis,* have established a rallying theme, an anchoring point, for the purposes of bringing some sense and order to the massive case law. In practice however, things have not always worked out like that.

To an outside observer, the German courts have, in recent times and especially in the context of economic loss, broken loose from academic

---

[43] *Die positiven Vertragsverletzungen* (1904).

[44] Mommsen, 'Die Unmöglichkeit der Leistung in ihrem Einfluss auf obligatorische Verhältnisse', *Beiträge zum Obligationenrecht* (1853) i. It was not until the 1920s that the wider notion of *Leistungsstörungen* entered the scene, again under the influence of academic writers.

[45] e.g. paras. 275, 279, 280, 323–5 BGB (impossibility); 284–7, 326 BGB (delay).

[46] *Die Geschäftsgrundlage* (1921). The theory has nowadays lost some of its wide appeal; but another academic, K. Larenz, *Geschäftsgrundlage und Vertragserfüllung* (1963) has come up with a usable alternative.

[47] *Pandektenrecht* (1862) para. 97. It is highly likely that the Windscheid–Oertmann theories influenced Llewellyn's drafting of section 2–615 UCC even though the latter makes no express references to the former. For Llewellyn taught in Germany when the Oertmann theory was at its height; and in his *Casebook on the Law of Sales* (1930), 178 Llewellyn talks of 'the contract [being] abrogated by the failure of a *presupposition* upon which it was founded.' (Emphasis added). The unusual (for the common law) term 'presupposition' is an accurate rendering of the German term 'Voraussetzung' and this strengthens the view that Llewellyn was drawing strongly on German ideas. The Germanic influence on Llewellyn is discussed by, among others, Whitman, 'Commercial Law and the American Volk: A Note on Llewellyn's German Sources for the Uniform Commercial Code', *Yale L J* 156 97 (1987).

[48] RGZ 103, 328, 331.

[49] *Schuldrecht,* lst edn. (1953), i: 16 III; *idem* in *NJW* 1956, 1193; *NJW* 1960, 79.

tutelage, ignored its criticisms, and set themselves on a course which has proved them—at least so it seems to me—more literally-minded than their English counterparts. The spreading defect theory (*Weiterfresserschaeden*) offers one example,[50] the expansion of the ambit of the contract with protective effects *vis-à-vis* third parties is another.[51] Both developments hold out lessons for English law. Here, because of lack of space, a few words will be said only about the second as it has a close connection with Professor von Bar's paper.

This expansion of the ambit of the contract has taken place largely as a result of the weakening of the requirement of *Wohl und Wehe*. This has been explained elsewhere;[52] and some references are made to this 'controlling device' by Professor von Bar in his paper. The courts, by ignoring it or watering it down, have struck out on a course of their own, rapidly making the compensation of pure economic loss more widely available than ever before. Whether this is the result of the availability of insurance, the possibility of contractual limitation of liability, or a sense of consumerism (far greater it would seem than is currently found in the House of Lords),[53] one cannot be sure. For present purposes it does not matter, other than to show that it has made the reconciliation of numerous decisions difficult if not impossible.

In this context, the German academic, it seems to me, has a crucial role to play, not so much in criticizing the BGH whenever its solutions offend academic purists, but in finding ways to help make its case law more consistent and more predictable. If Professor von Bar shows that German tort law is almost unpresentable and unintelligible without its case-law component, he also indirectly makes a case for the need for a greater sense of order to be brought into this case law. In his Chorley Lecture Professor Kötz quoted[54] Karl Llewellyn (who, it must not be forgotten, was a great Germanophile) who wrote in 1938:[55]

No one who has never seen a puzzled Continental lawyer turn to his little library and then turn out at least a workable understanding of his problem within half an hour will really grasp what the availability of the working leads packed into a

---

[50] On which see Hager, 'Zum Schutzbereich der Produzentenhaftung', *AcP* 1984, 413; Steffen, 'Die Bedeutung der "Stoffgleichheit" mit dem "Mangelunwert" für die Herstellerhaftung aus Weiterfresserschäden', *VersR* 1988, 977; Kullmann, 'Die Rechtsprechung des BGH zum Produkthaftpflichtrecht in den Jahren 1989/90', *NJW* 1991, 675. The academic literature that opposes these judicial trends is given in Kötz, *Deliktsrecht*, 5th edn., 28 *et seq.*

[51] On which see literature in n. 28, above.

[52] 'The Random Element of their Lordships' Infallible Judgment: An Economic and Comparative Analysis of the Tort of Negligence from *Anns* to *Murphy*' (co-authored with S. Deakin) *MLR* 55 (1992), 621, 640 n. 115.

[53] Discussed and criticized by Jane Stapleton in 'Duty of Care and Economic Loss: A Wider Agenda' *LQR*, 107 (1991), 249–97.   [54] N. 37, above, at 14.

[55] 'The Bar's Troubles, and Poultices—and Cures?' *Law and Contemporary Problems* 5, 104, 118.

systematic Code can do to cheapen the rendering of respectably adequate legal service.

One wonders, with the greatest respect to both these masters (Llewellyn and Kötz) of comparative law, to what extent this statement is still true today. Unless 'workable understanding of [the] problem' is taken at the most simple level, my own feeling is that a German lawyer asked to advise on the potential liability for negligent statements towards third parties, has to do almost as much research as an American lawyer in order to find the relevant case law and to come up with a moderately workable answer. Moreover, whereas the American lawyer will have some sense of how to determine binding and persuasive precedents, his German counterpart will have to take his cue from what he finds in the standard treatises. The richness of the case law may, however, be subject to a different interpretation, justifying different and rich variations. It could thus be argued that an English lawyer—uninhibited by language barriers—could present some very intriguing possibilities to a German court as a result of the training he has received in handling cases. If I am right in this, German judges might stand to learn a great deal from the common lawyer's training in handling cases. This, then, is an area where German law can learn from our law; but the argument has not, apparently, been proved.

If the above offers an area of potential interest to German lawyers, what can we learn from them in this area of the law? Professor von Bar offers a number of ideas; indeed, he suggests that we have already picked up something from them via Lord Haldane's German education. It is, however, the wider questions that again concern me here; and the question which deserves to be considered most is how can our courts, also faced with a growing and rapidly changing case law, benefit by enlisting academics in their cause?

Clearly in the English context the role that the academic lawyer will have to play if he is to help a court of law will be new and different from that played by his German counterpart. The role here will not be one of finding a substitute to *stare decisis*, but one of assisting the judge in his research and—equally important—assisting him in placing the isolated instance of litigation that is before him against a more logical and consistent general background. The idea may be anathema to traditional common lawyers who rejoice in talking of 'experience' not 'logic', stressing pragmatism over theory, emphasizing the *casus* over principle. For reasons that have been explained elsewhere,[56] and which a growing number of jurists seem to acknowledge,[57] I think this combination of different talents may

[56] See n. 11 and n. 13, above.
[57] e.g. Lord Goff in 'Judge, Jurist and Legislature', *Denning L Journ* 2 (1988), 79; 'The Search for Principle' Maccabean Lecture in Jurisprudence, *Proceedings of the British Academy* 69 (1983), 169.

have to take place. I think it will; and the growing Europeanization of English law which is currently afoot and to which the next section is devoted will make this change more rapid.

4 The Europeanization of English Law

4.1 *Some General Comments*

The title of this sub-heading needs some explanation to avoid creating too many misunderstandings. Thus, the reader must first be reminded yet again that these are my own conclusions or interpretations from what went on during nearly twenty meeting hours and that none of my colleagues are in any way bound by anything other that what they included in their respective papers. Second, though I am talking of the Europeanization of English law, since I have taken the vantage point of English law, I have no doubt that some of the factors discussed in this section and elaborated in some of the papers apply equally to French law, German law, and the laws of other European States. They, too, are in other words subject to the same transforming pressures. That development, however, is best left to others to document in another paper and it has thus been omitted from their account. Third, one talks of the Europeanization of English law because, as a result of multiple influences, one can argue that a new corpus of law, a kind of European *jus commune*, is gradually developing and, indeed, it may be developing faster than one is prepared to acknowledge. The Court of the European Communities may be playing a crucial role in this development, but it is not the only one. Nevertheless, the term Europeanization may indicate the particular importance that the Luxembourg Court is having on national law and, in this sense, it seems to me even more appropriate. Having said this, however, one must stress that this was a legal conference which avoided, at least overtly, political and ideological issues or emotive terms such as sovereignty. I stress this because, even though I am not willing to hide my own bias for 'things European', I think the aim that we all had was to discuss developments that were actually taking place whether we (or the majority of our compatriots) liked them or not. It thus seems to me that whereas the first four papers (Delmas-Marty, Spencer, Lorenz, and von Bar) discussed similarities—obvious or not yet discovered—and differences—real or apparent—between our various national systems, the next six speakers (Bonell, Tallon, Schermers, Francioni, Bocken, and Stephen Tromans' additional essay) have focused on wider influences or pressures on English law. Once again my colleagues' eloquent presentations speak for themselves. For my part, however, I feel there is enough material here to support the thesis that English law is progressively being Europeanized. For those who are refusing to

accept it here are some points for further thought; and for those for whom
the result is a sign of potential weakness, the following thought made by
an historian[58] but, in my opinion, equally valuable for law could be considered: '. . . in the conflict of cultures, it is more blessed to receive than
to give; and the real quality of any civilisation is shown less perhaps by
its indigenous products than by the way in which it constantly grafts new
shoots on to its own trunk, to stimulate further growth and to achieve
richer and more differentiated products.'

4.2   *From Where do These Unifying or Harmonizing Pressures Stem?*

To this question I would give a list of five headings. The more I think of
them, the more I feel they deserve a paper of their own so that these views
do not become too deformed through compression. Here I shall merely
give the list, in ascending order of importance, and will only elaborate on
two of them which are arguably particularly significant *at this stage of
evolution of our law.*

1 Academic work in universities
2 Judges and practitioners
3 International conventions
4 EC Directives
5 The case law of the Luxembourg court

4.2.1   *Academic Work in Universities*

Academia could play a very significant role in the process described in this
paper and, more generally, in ensuring a stronger British presence in Europe. In reality, however, its contribution has been modest. For the research/
writing currently taking place in England is, in terms of volume at least,
rather meagre. Teaching offerings in comparative law, though rich in some
universities, have low student attendances. Finally, exchange programmes
of real academic merit are, if one is to be honest, limited to the four-year
Anglo-French Programme, organized by King's College, London and Paris
II for over a decade now. Four-year courses (with a one-year foreign
component) are springing up; but their real impact in raising European
awareness has yet to be properly measured. Other currently operating
Erasmus-inspired exchanges tend to be labour-intensive to organize and of
low immediate returns (since the students' stay abroad is so brief). As a
long-term public relations exercise in European affairs these programmes
may have their merit. But their short-term effect on our curriculum is
limited; and on the development of our law in the European direction it
must be close to nil.

---

[58] Sir Hamilton Gibb, 'The Influence of Islamic Culture on Medieval Europe' in *Change
in Medieval Society: Europe North of the Alps, 1050–1500*, ed. Thrupp (1964).

4.2.2 *Judges and practitioners*

We find under this heading an intriguing development of potentially great practical significance. Given that in England there is not the close co-operation between judges and academics, it is not surprising to note that, on the whole, our judges have shown little interest in foreign legal developments (unless the case before them obliges them, so to speak, to take into account foreign law). Academic speculation about foreign law also leaves them indifferent. It is therefore particularly interesting to note that in recent times some of them have broken from the ranks and manifested an open interest in both academic and foreign law attempting, whenever possible, to make use of both of them in their judgments. In his Child Lecture in Oxford, for example, Lord Goff made the outstanding claim that comparative law was the subject of the future![59] Lord Justice Bingham, in his Francis Mann Lecture, catalogued a host of areas where English law had learned (and could continue learning) from foreign (including Scottish) law.[60] In his 1986 Denning Lecture Lord Slynn forcefully reminded his audience that:[61]

In the early days the impact of Community law tended to be confined to certain specialised areas and outside those areas it was unusual for points of Community law to be taken other than by specialised practitioners. What I have said shows, I think, that Community law now applies to such a variety of different areas of law that a practitioner cannot afford to ignore it. He cannot regard it as a marginal field of law to be left to specialists.

Lord Slynn's statement refers, of course, to Community law; but one must never forget that much comparative work is done both by the court's judges and Advocates General before some of their decisions are finally reached. There used to be (and still is) a symbiotic relationship between comparative law and the conflict of law; there is now a *ménage à trois,* with Community law having joined the other two. Together they are changing our law in the way described in this sub-section.

Enlightened judges with strong academic credentials are not the only 'practitioners' who can 'internationalize' our law. Practitioners with an international practice before courts such as the International Court of Justice in the Hague, the Court of Human Rights in Strasbourg, or the Court of the European Communities in Luxembourg are accustomed—indeed obliged by the nature of their work—to handling foreign material, in appropriate circumstances combining it with purely English law. These

---

[59] 'Judge, Jurist and Legislature' n. 55, above, at 92.
[60] 'There is a World Elsewhere: The Changing Perspectives of English Law', *ICLQ* 41 (1992), 513.
[61] Quoted by Lord Griffiths in 'Civil Litigation in the Nineties', *Arbitration* , 57: 7 (Aug. 1991), 168, 171. So far as I have been able to ascertain this lecture was never published.

working habits must, inevitably, find their way back into England when more traditional English work is being handled. Their input, however, on the Europeanization of English law comes from their exposure to the procedure and practices of the international courts. Two examples will help bring out my point more clearly.

Civil procedure in European courts is, as everyone knows, more geared towards a written than an oral presentation of the material and pertinent arguments. Cross-examination may be, as Wigmore once wrote, 'the greatest legal engine ever invented for the discovery of the truth',[62] yet the oral proceedings of the common-law trial, of which cross-examination is an integral part, also has its drawbacks. Recently Lord Griffiths claimed extra-judicially that 'whilst there is value in oral argument and cross-examination the presentation of the trial materials and its assimilation by the judge is more quickly and efficiently performed through the written rather than the spoken word'.[63]

It is difficult to imagine statements such as these coming from the lips of senior English judges thirty or even twenty years ago. In my opinion they have become acceptable (and will become commonplace) as time pressures and increased workloads, in conjunction with exposure to European trial techniques, are forcing us to review the efficiency of our methods of civil trial. Likewise our more umpire-oriented way of defining judicial duties may, in the end, give way to 'court-controlled case management techniques' which are so typical of the continental European method of trial.[64]

Another topic which may soon succumb to foreign influences, (and if it does it will, again, be supported by those of our practitioners who have practised before international courts), is that of oral argument. A hallmark of the English trial since its inception may thus, once again, fall under the pressures created by time and experience acquired abroad. Lord Griffiths, again, could not have been clearer when he said that

I have discussed this with those who *practise* [emphasis added] both before our own appellate courts and at Luxembourg where oral argument is restricted and cases rarely last more than one day, no matter how complicated the issues. They tell me that their written submission is more detailed but they find no disadvantage in the shorter term for oral presentation which is a spur to concentration upon the crucial issues in the argument.[65]

These are remarkable changes, not least because they refer to the law of procedure which is so closely linked to the *modus operandi* of practitioners that traditional comparative lawyers regarded them as being beyond the pale of comparative law and the comparative method. It is,

---

[62] *On Evidence* (1940) para. 1367, 28.
[63] 'Civil Litigation in the Nineties', *Arbitration*, 57: 7 (Aug. 1991), 168, 169.
[64] Ibid. at 169.   [65] Ibid. at 169–70.

therefore, all the more significant to read a senior Law Lord express his vision of tomorrow with such confidence:[66]

As we have closer and closer commercial links and possibly monetary and political links as well, we shall be working with ever-increasing frequency with European lawyers. We shall have to familiarise ourselves with their practices and procedure and, of course, when working with them in Luxembourg or Strasbourg we shall all be using the same procedure. Would it not be a great step forward if we could work towards a common procedure for use by all European lawyers? Some countries who try cases through the inquisitorial procedure are now suggesting that they should make a move towards our adversarial procedures. I have suggested that the orality of our adversarial procedure needs modifying, which is perhaps a step towards the inquisitorial procedure. Can we together with our European colleagues find an acceptable middle ground?

4.2.3   *International Conventions*

Professors Bonnel, Tallon, and Schermers provide rich material about various aspects of international conventions and how they can, directly or indirectly, mould municipal law. Their erudite discussions, when combined with the comments supplied by the judges who presided over the respective sessions, should provide much food for thought. Here I should like to continue with the harmonization/convergence theme that I have been pursuing throughout this paper and which has been described as the Europeanization of English law.

The warning was given earlier on that the emphasis in this chapter is on the Europeanization of *English* law (though French, German, Italian, and the other continental systems have been experiencing similar convergence prompted by supra-State factors such as the activities of the two European Courts). The European Convention on Human Rights, as fleshed out by the Commission and the Court, is having just such an effect, especially in the majority of the European countries which treat it as an integral part of their national law.[67] But from the English side, the old doctrine of 'dualism', '*cette doctrine satanique*' as the French have called it, has provided English judges with a brake, or at least a negative excuse, whenever asked to consider its effects in cases that come before them. Once again, however, the legal explanation for the reluctance to make full use of the Convention provides only part of the answer. The English judge's hesitations on the subject can, no doubt, be traced to deeply ingrained fears about the *political* implications such an activity might have on their functions.

---

[66] 'Civil Litigation in the Nineties', 171.

[67] For example, Francioni, 'Italy and the EC: The Legal Protection of Fundamental Rights' in *Italy and EC Membership Evaluated*, ed. F. Francioni (1992), 191 *et seq*. Koopmans, 'Judicial Review of Legislation in the Netherlands' in *Constitutional Adjudication in European Community and National Law, Essays for the Hon. Mr. Justice T.F. O'Higgins*, ed. Cartin and O'Keeffe (1992), 273.

Professor Jacobs, among others, has rationally confronted these fears in his excellent 'The Convention and the English Judge';[68] but the mentality gap remains, albeit weakening by the day.

The true situation is, in fact, much more complex as those who have studied the attitude of the courts towards the Convention have clearly shown.[69] Our courts have thus been in two minds as to what effect they should give to the Convention. The problem has divided judges, with some like Lord Scarman,[70] Lord Reid,[71] Lord Wilberforce,[72] and, most recently, Lord Goff[73] for example, arguing with varying degrees of conviction that it was hardly credible to interpret English legislation in isolation of the Convention, whereas others[74] opted for the more orthodox view that the Convention is not, technically speaking, part of the law of the United Kingdom and could thus be ignored. More dramatically, it has led distinguished judges to take contradictory views on the subject[75] or reach truly

---

[68] *Protecting Human Rights: The European Dimension (Studies in Honour of Gerard J. Wiarda)* (1988), 273.

[69] For example, Duffy, 'English Law and the European Convention on Human Rights' *ICLQ* (1980) 585; McCouch, 'Implementing the European Convention on Human Rights in the United Kingdom', *Stanford LJ* (1982), 147.

[70] For example in *R v. Secretary of State for the Home Department* ex p. *Phansopkar* [1976] QB 606; *A-G v. British Broadcasting Corporation* [1981] AC 303; *Whitehouse v. Lemon* [1976] AC 617.   [71] *R. v. Miah* [1974] 1 WLR 683.

[72] *Blathwayt v. Baron Cawley* [1976] AC 397.

[73] *Attorney-General v. Guardian Newspapers Ltd. (No. 2)* [1990] 1 AC 109, 283–4. This approach is, in turn, having an important impact on national law as *Derbyshire C. C. v. Times Newspapers* [1992] 3 WLR 28 clearly shows. In the latter case Balcombe LJ following *R v. Secretary of State For the Home Department,* ex p. *Brind* [1991] IAC 477, was of the view that [Article 10 of the Convention] 'may be resorted to in order to help resolve some uncertainty or ambiguity in municipal law' (ibid. 43). But he also went beyond established wisdom in arguing that 'even if the common law is certain the courts will still, when appropriate, consider whether the United Kingdom is in breach of article 10.' (Ibid., at 44.) Commenting on this decision Professor Fleming has asked 'Why should it need a quasi-constitutional text of supranational origin to vindicate to democratic values, in [the] teeth of the traditional boast that the common law is a trusted protector of such values in no need of constitutional reinforcement, such as by adoption of the very Convention here invoked?' LQR 109 (1993), 12, 14. Comparative lawyers have often doubted the validity of the boast; and the case in hand demonstrates the practical significance of the international instrument. No wonder increasing numbers of senior national lawyers are advocating the formal incorporation into our law of the European Convention.

[74] *R v. Chief Immigration Officer, Heathrow Airport* ex p. *Salamat Bibi* [1976] 1 WLR 979, 988 (per Lane LJ); *Malone v. Metropolitan Police Commission* [1979] Ch. 344, 378, (per Megarry VC); *Cheall v. Association of Professional, Executive, Clerical and Computer Staff* [1983] QB 126, 146 (per Donaldson LJ). Contrast, however, Lord Denning's views in the same case at 137.

[75] e.g. Lord Denning in *R v. Secretary of State for the Home Department,* ex p. *Bhajan Singh* [1976] QB 188 in favour of taking into account the Convention; *R v. Chief Immigration Officer, Heathrow Airport* ex p. *Salamat Bibi* [1976] 1 WLR 979 (backtracking from the earlier pronouncements); *Cheall v. Association of Professional, Executive, Clerical and Computer Staff* [1983] QB 126, 137 reverting to his earlier, more robust position. Compare, however, Crawford, *BYIL* 50 (1982), 253, 282–5.

paradoxical conclusions. Professor Jacobs, it is submitted rightly, brings into this category Sir Robert Megarry's judgment in the *Malone* case,[76] for in that case the learned judge at the outset of his judgment declared his willingness to 'give the convention due consideration in discussing English law on the point'. Yet when he comes to the point and finds that there is no English law, he considers himself 'unable to apply the Convention.'

Reviewing English law on this topic might lead one to the over-pessimistic conclusion that the Convention has had no effect on English law except to divide its judges as to how it should be handled. Such a conclusion, however, would be misleading for three reasons.

First, it implies that our difficulties with the effects that international conventions can have on municipal law are not shared by other countries. That is not true. Professor Tallon's paper, for example, refers to the contradictory attitudes taken by the two French Supreme Courts on the relationship of conventions and municipal law, a division which once led Judge Pierre Pescatore to remark that we 'must free ourselves from the idea of the French Republic being "une et indivisible", as contradictory positions on an identical problem of vital importance are taken on the left and on the right banks of the Seine.'[77]

Second, excessive emphasis on our 'dualist' approach might lead us to underestimate (*a*) the 'atmospheric' effect the convention has had on our law and (*b*) the indirect but obvious effect the Convention has had on law via the jurisprudence of the *Luxembourg* Court and this despite the fact that there exists no formal link between these two European Courts. More is said about this in the last subsection.

Finally, if the courts have been unable (or unwilling) to give a decisive effect to the Convention, the Convention has, through the combined activity of Parliament and administrators, in the end resulted in significant changes in our law, bringing it ever closer to European law and practice. Quoting Professor Jacobs[78] again, examples include:

In the field of freedom of expression, the enactment of the Contempt of Court Act 1981 in purported compliance with the *Sunday Times* case;[79] in relation to Article 3 of the Convention, the abandonment of certain interrogation techniques for detainees in Northern Ireland, and the non-use (but not the repeal) of the sentence of birching in the Isle of Man. Corporal punishment in state schools has been abolished in Scotland, and proposals made allowing an element of parental choice in England. The legislation prohibiting homosexual behaviour between male consenting adults in Northern Ireland has been amended, as have the rules governing

[76] [1979] Ch 344, critically discussed in 'The Impact of the European Convention on Human Rights on Judicial Decisions in the United Kingdom' in *Perspectives Canadiennes des Droits de la Personne*, ed. Turp and Beaudouin (1986), 80, 86–8.

[77] i.e. by the Conseil d'Etat and the Cour de Cassation. See Pescatore, 'Conclusion' in *The Effect of Treaties in Domestic Law*, ed. Jacobs and Roberts (1987), 273, 281.

[78] 'The Impact of the European Convention'. n. 76, above, 89.

[79] *The Sunday Times* case, judgment of 26 Apr. 1979, Series A, No. 30.

prisoners' rights of access to the courts, rights of correspondence and right to marry. Legislation on the rights of mental health patients has been amended by the Mental Health (Amendment) Act 1982, the Mental Health Act 1983 and the Mental Health Review Tribunal Rule 1983. Provision has been made for compensation for employees dismissed as a result of the closed shop. The immigration rules concerning finances have been amended and further changes are in prospect as a result of cases currently in Strasbourg, as are changes in the rules of telephone tapping in the light of the *Malone* case. The overall effect that fundamental human rights can have in the processes of European integration is one that deserves closer study and proper credit.[80]

4.2.4 EC Directives

The enormous importance of this source of Europeanization of our law is obvious. It can justify many articles but can clearly not be discussed here. It is mentioned merely for the sake of completeness of my list of 'harmonizing factors'. By contrast a few words may be needed to place in its proper perspective the last and, in my opinion, most important of harmonizing elements.

4.2.5 The Jurisprudence of the Court of the European Communities

More than twenty years have gone by since Lord Denning, with his usual vision and power for imagery, described the arrival of European law.[81] In those twenty years the European Court of Justice has been hyperactive in shaping Community law not only in the way it has effected a common market but also in the way it has affected common people by promoting free movement of workers (and their families), by affecting the professions, by strengthening the legal rules of equality between men and women, and much more. Treatises and case books have multiplied over the years, but this invasion is revolutionizing the contents and substance of the common law, just as the other European invasion, over eight hundred years ago, led to its emergence. The impact, in my opinion, has not been adequately studied; and this is no place (nor am I the right person) to undertake such an awesome task. Yet two illustrations might set the reader's mind in the direction I would like it to take.

What the Court has done with Article 119 of the Treaty—which addresses itself to equal pay between men and women[82]—is remarkable not

---

[80] For further discussion see Frowein, Schulhofer, and Shapiro, 'The Protection of Fundamental Human Rights as a Vehicle of Integration' in *Integration through Law*, ed. Cappalletti, Secombe, and Weiler, Series A, i: 3 (1986), 300.

[81] 'the Treaty is like an incoming tide. It flows into the estuaries and up the rivers. It cannot be held back.' *Bullmer Ltd.* v. *Bolinger SA* [1974] 1 Ch. 401, 418.

[82] 'Each Member State shall during the first stage ensure and subsequently maintain the application of the principle that men and women should receive equal pay for equal work.' . . . 'For the purpose of this Article, "pay" means the ordinary basic or minimum wage in salary and any other consideration, whether in cash or in kind, which the worker receives, directly or indirectly, in respect of his employment from his employer . . .'

only through its wide interpretation of 'pay' but also by then declaring it to have direct effect. The combined effect has been not only to extend equal opportunity law in general but also to provide, in Lord Slynn's words, 'an excellent example of the way in which Community law can have an impact on English law'.[83] The same has happened with the Court's broad interpretation of Article 48 of the Treaty, especially the words 'worker' and 'activity as an employed person'.[84] National judges have, in this respect, followed Community law definitions rather than national legal definitions, and the harmonizing effect achieved in this and related areas of the law has been, again, considerable throughout the Community States.

The second way in which the Court's jurisprudence has affected our law was by its taking over the European Convention on Human Rights, making it part of Community law, and in this way openly penetrating countries (like England and Denmark) which have refused to give direct effect to the Convention. *Johnston* v. *Chief Constable of the Royal Ulster Constabulary*[85] offers a good illustration of this.

Mrs Johnston was in full service with the Royal Ulster Constabulary. When the Northern Ireland police were instructed to carry arms, the Chief Constable decided that women should not be allowed to do so lest they become terrorists targets. Mrs Johnstone was thus dismissed. She considered her dismissal as contravening the Northern Ireland equivalent of the British Sex Discrimination Act, but the police relied on its article 53[86] which expressly stated that nothing in the Order could render unlawful anything done for the purposes of national security and public order. For good measure it added that a certificate from the Secretary of State 'shall be conclusive evidence that these conditions are fulfilled'. The Industrial Tribunal which heard Mrs Johnston's case referred the case to the European Court under Article 177 of the Treaty seeking a preliminary ruling

---

[83] *Introducing a European Legal Order*, the Hamlyn Lectures, 43rd series (1992), 127.

[84] But the 'interference' with national law has come in other ways as well as the *Van Duyn* v. *Home Office* case—[1974] ECR 13337—shows. That dispute stemmed from a decision taken by the British Government in 1969 to consider Scientology as socially harmful and, henceforth, to deny to foreign nationals the right to enter the UK and work for that Church. When in 1973 Miss van Duyn was denied entry, she sought a declaration in the High Court that the refusal was contrary to Article 48 of the EC Treaty and article 3 of directive 64/221. On an Article 177 referral, the European Court held, *inter alia*, that 'By providing that measures taken on grounds of public policy shall be based exclusively on the personal conduct of the individual concerned, Article 3(1) of Directive No. 64/221 is intended to limit the discretionary power which national laws generally confer on the authorities responsible for the entry and expulsion of foreign nationals' and, further down, the Court added: 'It should be emphasised that *the concept of public policy* in the context of the Community and where, in particular, it is used as a justification for derogating from the fundamental principles of freedom of movement for workers, *must be interpreted strictly, so that its scope cannot be unilaterally determined by each member State without being subject to control by the institutions of the Community*.' (Emphasis added.)

[85] Case 222/84, [1986] E.C.R. 1663; [1987] QB 129.

[86] Sex Discrimination (Northern Ireland) Order 1976, SI 1976 No. 1042 (N.I. 15).

as to whether the dismissal, though in conformity with the Northern Ireland Order, contravened the 1976 Directive seeking to establish equal treatment for men and women with regard to employment. For the European Court of Justice the crucial question was whether article 53 could effectively bar English judges from ensuring effective compliance with the Directive. The Court took the view that 'Article 6 of the Directive requires Member States to introduce into their internal legal systems such measures as are needed to enable all persons who consider themselves wronged by discrimination to pursue their claims by judicial process.'[87] It followed, in the Court's reasoning, that Member States had to take all measures necessary to ensure 'that the rights thus conferred may be effectively relied upon before the national courts by all persons concerned.' This need for effective *judicial* control reflected nothing other than a general principle of law found in all Member States and, in fact, reflected in Article 6 of the European Convention on Human Rights.[88] The conclusion, bringing these different strands of thought together was, inevitably, that article 53 was contrary to the Directive as it 'allow[ed] the competent authority to deprive an individual of the possibility of asserting by judicial process the rights conferred by the Directive.' Judge Koopmans has summarized this as follows:[89]

The Court's judgment illustrates the force of the combined effect of different lines of legal evolution in Europe. It extrapolates a provision of the European Convention into a Community Directive because it embodies a general principle. The Directive is not only to be implemented by legislative or administrative action: national courts are to respect its provisions when interpreting and applying their national law. European legal developments have a kind of dynamics of their own.

How right Judge Koopmans is when talking about the European 'dynamics'! A glance at the developing law of European environmental protection makes this obvious, for the protection of the environment was conspicuously absent from the original Treaty of Rome. Then, as those halcyon days receded into the background, and the (largely) self-inflicted destruction of the environment became increasingly apparent, the era of EC activity was ushered in under the general principles of the Community or on the basis of 'implied powers'. As Professor Francioni shows in his thoughtful piece, the foundations were thus firmly laid for future, more specific, regulatory measures. And now, on the eve of the Single European Market and, who knows, one day of some form of European Union, this European activity

---

[87] Quotations from [1986] E.C.R. 1680–1, 1682–3.

[88] Traditionally seen as guaranteeing a fair trial but since the *Golder* case—*Golder* v. *UK* [1975] 1 EHRR 524—increasingly having shaped rights of access to courts—an excellent example of judicial creativity which has ultimately affected national laws.

[89] 'European Public Law: Reality and Prospects', *Public Law* 53 (1991), 61.

is seen by many as a necessary component of the Single Market, and with inevitable harmonizing effects on domestic environmental standards.

5   Are the Common-Law and Civil-Law Systems Converging?

The preceding paragraphs should leave the reader in no doubt that convergence is taking place. The convergence is gradual and, indeed, patchy (i.e. more obvious in some areas than in others despite the dynamics of the case law of the European Court which, I believe, has accelerated the convergence process). There is thus a convergence of solutions in the area of private law as the problems faced by courts and legislators acquire a common and international flavour; there is a convergence in the sources of our law since nowadays case law *de facto* if not *de jure* forms a major source of law in both common and civil law countries; there is a slow convergence in procedural matters as the oral and written types of trials borrow from each other and are slowly moving to occupy a middle position; there may be a greater convergence in drafting techniques than has commonly been appreciated and this is bound to lead English law closer to purposive interpretations; there is a growing *rapprochement* in judicial views (the abolition, for example, of the old prerogative writs brought English law much closer to its continental counterparts); and, I think, the apparently amorphous concepts of 'proportionality' and 'just expectations' may be creeping into English law (assuming that on proper analysis they were not there already). Judicial styles may remain more different since common-law judges still seem to talk to everyone who is prepared to listen (or must listen), German judges only talk to intellectual equals, and French judges (at the highest levels) keep their thoughts to themselves!

This assessment is not, I think, shaped by my international background and European-oriented outlook. The points raised in our various papers and in this first chapter will, I think, if further pursued, substantiate the convergence theory even though it is gradual (as indeed it should be) and the title of the book acknowledges. But I think it is also justified by the underlying socio-economic similarities one finds these days in most of Europe (and this despite the current craze of ethnic separation and violence). Increased travel, enhanced communications, greater urbanization, and closer interdependence of national economics, have all combined to make the kind of problems that have to be resolved by the law similar, to weaken or discredit more traditional ways of resolving such disputes, and to raise (at times unreasonably) the expectations that citizens have of the State and the law. All these factors have, in my opinion, favoured growing assimilation—increasingly through court activity.[90]

[90] See, more generally, Koopmans, 'The Future of Legal Systems', The David Hume Institute, Hume Occasional Paper No. 13 (1990).

Take the first point:—similarity of problems. It would be wrong to assume that this was always as strong as it is today. Look, for example, at the French law of contract or, more particularly, the topic we call frustration. At the turn of the twentieth century or during the First World War, though intellectually French law had an uninterrupted link with Roman law and medieval philosophy, thus presenting impeccable intellectual credentials, its case law was simple, agrarian, and at times very quaint in appearance. When contrasted with the English law of the time, predominantly commercial and maritime in flavour, it leaves one in no doubt that the kind of cases that were shaping the developments of the law in these two countries were as often as not very different in their factual content. Yet look at our law of contracts now and you see in all European countries how the kind of problems that face all our courts are very similar, I suspect to a large extent as a result of the appearance in the 1960s, or thereabouts, of the consumer as a litigating party. To be sure, the richness of national case law is such that there is evidence to support any contrary theory. One should, however, be intrigued by the growing similarity of problems that are litigated by national courts and, indeed, have made this a central theme of a new methodological approach to comparative law.

The second factor I mentioned—the weakening of family ties, religion, neighbourhood bonds, and the growing distrust of authority—also contribute to the assimilation process I have stressed. As traditional ways of coping with the vicissitudes of life are weakened,[91] citizens tend to become more willing to seek their remedies in a court of law. This, combined with the third factor—the growing awareness of entitlements—makes modern citizens more anxious to assert their rights in court. Differences of mentality—for example, is litigation the first or last resort in the dispute resolution process—are changing attitudes and, in the process, reducing long–standing differences with other systems such as that of the United States of America.[92] The growth of litigiousness is equally provoked by the State's increased hyperactivity in favour of the citizen. For more administration inevitably brings more maladministration and more rights generate a greater willingness to assert them. Growing distrust in the political and

---

[91] Cf. the observations of the former Chief Justice of the United States Supreme Court Warren E. Burger: 'One reason our courts have become overburdened is that Americans are increasingly turning to the courts for relief from a range of personal distresses and anxieties. Remedies for personal wrongs that once were considered the responsibility of institutions other than the courts are now boldly asserted as "entitlements". The courts have been expected to fill the void created by the decline of church, family and neighborhood unity.' 'Isn't there a Better Way', *American Bar Association Journal* 68 (1982), 274, 275. As I tried to argue in my 'Litigation Mania in England, Germany and the USA: Are we so very different?' 49 [1990] *CLJ* 232 *et seq.*, those trends may be arriving in Europe as well.

[92] On which see my 'Litigation Mania in England, n. 91, above, at 233 *et seq.*

administrative process can only enhance in the minds of many citizens the importance of the courts in the establishment and protection of rights and entitlements. The task the modern courts face is formidable; the responsibility awesome; their opportunity to harmonize legal systems indisputable (even if not always very obvious). The European Courts are, I think, showing how legal assimilation can by-pass political differences and slowly guide Europe towards a new era of a more internationally-based system of law and order. Time only will show if power politics will cause cracks in the edifice of the rule of law as they have done so many times in the past. But until that happens, the harmonization made in Europe seems, to me at least, unstoppable.

A Scottish Postscript

Scottish law has had its own tradition; and, over the centuries, Scotland has enjoyed fruitful academic links with Europe—France and the Netherlands in particular. For practical considerations there was no distinctly Scottish representation at our seminar series. But the omission would have been unjustifiable in the book. We were therefore delighted when Judge David Edward agreed to contribute a Scottish Epilogue to the whole book since he can speak both as an expert of a great national tradition and as one who is helping create a new, supranational one. It is fitting that the last word should be his; and his contribution can best be described in the language of the *jus commune: multum in parvo.*

2

French and English Criminal Procedure

FRENCH AND ENGLISH CRIMINAL PROCEDURE: A BRIEF COMPARISON

J. R. S. SPENCER

1   The French Criminal System

The two things that most Englishmen know about criminal procedure in France are that the French defendant is presumed guilty until he proves that he is innocent, and that the French have something called the Inquisitorial System. The first of these is false, and the second, if half true, is misleading.

The Englishman's unshakeable belief that French criminal procedure reverses the presumption of innocence is puzzling, because the presumption of innocence, though not set out in the Code of Criminal Procedure, has been part of French law ever since it appeared as article 9 of the Declaration of the Rights of Man in 1789—which now forms part of the French Constitution. Part of the explanation may lie in article 537 of the *Code de procédure pénale* (CPP), which provides that in the French equivalent of summary trial, certain written reports by the police are presumed to be correct unless the defendant shows they are inaccurate: perhaps a regular string of British tourists manage to get prosecuted for summary offences, and bring back the impression that article 537 is the general rule. It may also be a side-effect of the prolonged pre-trial phase which, where serious offences are concerned, quietly weeds out most weak cases long before the final public phase of trial. In consequence, few of those accused of really serious offences reach the trial stage unless they are fairly obviously guilty—and the French newspapers, unhampered by a Contempt of Court Act, are inclined to say so. Indeed, the phrase they commonly use to describe a person who is about to stand trial is *le présumé coupable*. To some extent, they are encouraged to do this by a rather unfortunate word the CPP uses to describe the formal act by which the *juge d'instruction* recognizes that the person he is dealing with has progressed from being a suspect to a potential defendant: *inculpation*.[1] When the case comes before the court of trial, however, there is no question of the defendant's guilt being presumed. If the President of the court were to suggest this in the course of the proceedings, any resulting conviction would certainly be quashed.

As to whether it is true that the French have the inquisitorial system, it all depends, of course, on what you mean by 'the inquisitorial system'.

To the French, the 'inquisitorial system' means the oppressive kind of criminal procedure that was in operation before the Revolution of 1789; a procedure that was secret, written, gave the defendant no rights worth having, and where the functions of judging and inquiring were inextricably confused. The first stage in that procedure was that the witnesses were interrogated, in secret, by a judge. The defendant was then interrogated, on the basis of what they had said. This interrogation was also done in private, and the defendant was neither told in advance of the case against him, nor allowed a lawyer to help him to meet it. Where the defendant refused to confess, the judge, if he thought there was a strong prima facie case, could order the defendant to be tortured, to see if this would change his mind. On the written record of the various interrogations the court—of which the investigating judge was a member—decided whether the suspect was innocent or guilty. If they pronounced him guilty, they could again order him to be tortured. This time to get him to reveal his accomplices (if any).[2]

During the eighteenth century, this heavy-handed and authoritarian procedure came under continuous attack. As French political reformers praised the English constitution as superior to the absolute monarchy, so French penal reformers—often the same people—held up English criminal procedure as the model to be copied. Opposition to the inquisitorial procedure continued even after Louis XVI abolished the use of torture just before the Revolution, and an early act of the revolutionary government was to introduce what it perceived to be criminal procedure on the English model.

In many ways, the change was a disaster. A major difficulty was that the new system, complete with grand juries and petty juries, failed to secure the conviction of the gangs of robbers and bandits with which, following the disturbances of the revolutionary years, the country was infested. This—and a general disenchantment with things English after twenty years of bitter war—made Frenchmen more inclined to see the virtues of the system of criminal procedure they had recently abolished. For all its cruelty and

---

[1] At the time of writing, there is a proposal before the French parliament to substitute the phrase *mise en cause*, which is considerably more neutral.

[2] For the history of French criminal procedure, see A. Esmein, *Histoire de al procédure criminelle in France* (Paris 1882); in English, with extra chapters by other authors, as *A History of Continental Criminal Procedure, with Special Reference to France* (Boston, 1913).

heavy-handedness, eighteenth-century French criminal procedure had at least been thorough, in the sense that the evidence in the case was fully investigated, and recorded in a reliable and permanent form. Many Frenchmen, too, now saw advantages in a system under which a person suspected of a serious offence could be held in custody and resolutely interrogated. So in 1808, when Napoleon was Emperor, a new system was designed which reinforced the new procedure with some of what were now thought to have been the better features of the old.

Under the *Code d'instruction criminelle* of 1808, a sanitized version of the old inquisitorial procedure was introduced, for use in serious cases, as a preliminary stage to trial in open court. A new judicial officer, the *judge d'instruction*, interrogated the witnesses in private, interrogated the suspect, and recorded their statements in writing. The product of his research, in the form of a *dossier*, then formed the basis of the case against the defendant at his final trial: which was held in public, before a jury, controlled by a judge who had not taken part in the *instruction*, and in which the key witnesses made a fresh appearance to give their evidence orally, and in the presence of the defendant. Over the succeeding years there were many changes of detail: notably a reduction in the use of juries, and an increase in the rights of the defence. But the *Code de procédure pénale*, which replaced Napoleon's Code in 1958, kept the same general scheme, and this Code, and the scheme it contains, is still in force today. To the French— and to any serious foreign observer—the French system is not inquisitorial, but mixed, with a blend of both inquisitorial and accusatorial ideas.[3] Obviously, the *instruction* is one major difference between French criminal procedure and ours. But there are others, of which the following seem to me the most important.

First, police powers are very different, and so is the machinery that controls their exercise. A powerful weapon that the French police have is something called the *garde à vue*. This is the power to hold a suspect for twenty-four hours. In France, unlike in England, there is no official Code of Practice limiting the amount of psychological pressure that can officially be put on a person detained for police questioning to make him confess, and the *garde à vue* has no right to consult a lawyer, or even to communicate with anybody. The initial period of twenty-four hours can be extended, once only, for a further period of twenty-four hours if the public prosecutor gives permission. But if French law gives the policeman greater powers against the citizen than English law does, in some ways it controls him more closely in exercising them. The power to use the *garde à vue*

---

[3] For a systematic account of modern French criminal procedure in English, see A. V. Sheehan, *Criminal Procedure in Scotland and France* (Edinburgh, 1975). For a simpler account, written with the prospective English defendant in mind, see Richard Vogler, *A Guide to the French Criminal Justice System* (London, Prisoners Abroad Series, 1989).

may only be exercised by an *officer de la police judiciaire*, who is approximately a detective superintendent, and his use of the power is subject to controls outside the ranks of the police; in an ordinary case, the public prosecutor, and if the affair is serious enough to involve one, the *juge d'instruction*. The French criminal courts, unlike the English ones, do not go in for excluding confessions as a means of sanctioning police malpractice in obtaining them: but unlike the English courts, they have, in certain circumstances, the power to punish the offending policeman in a more straightforward manner by ordering his suspension or disqualification.

Second, the courts are differently constituted, with the lay element much reduced. In England, a minority of serious offences are tried in the Crown Court, with a jury of twelve laymen if the defendant pleads not guilty, and the great majority of offences are tried before a bench of laymen in the magistrates' courts. In France, a much smaller minority of serious cases go before a jury consisting of nine laymen sitting together with three professional judges, and all the rest are tried by courts staffed by professional judges—sitting singly for minor offences, but usually as a panel of three.

Third, there is no such thing as a plea of guilty, and unlike English practice the same procedural rules apply whether the defendant admits his guilt or denies it. For the defendant who denies his guilt, this has the disadvantage that no clear distinction is made between evidence that is relevant to guilt and evidence that is only relevant to sentence, both of which come jumbled up together. However, where the defendant admits the offence it has the great advantage that the facts are properly investigated before the sentence is imposed. In England, by contrast, where the defendant admits the offence he pleads guilty: after which there is usually no proper investigation of the facts at all. Following a plea of guilty, the usual procedure is that the prosecutor says the facts were X, the defence lawyer says the facts were Y, and the court decides the sentence without taking any steps to find out which version is correct.[4] This absence of a guilty plea is an important fact that many Englishmen who watch French trials are unaware of, and this ignorance tends to colour their perception of what is going on. They often compare what they see with the trial of a 'not guilty' plea in England, and conclude that a French trial is a hasty and cut-price affair. But if the case—as it often is—is one that would be resolved by a plea of guilty in England, what takes place in the French court is often longer and more thorough than what would happen in England.

Fourth, the French courts do not recognize the primacy of oral evidence. There is no rule against hearsay, as there is in England, and in particular, the court in deciding guilt or innocence can take account of the *procès*

---

[4] Although where there is a major conflict between prosecution and defence versions, the judge will sometimes hold a '*Newton* hearing' (see Newton (1982) 77 CrApR 13).

verbaus—the depositions taken with due formality by the *juge d'instruction* or the police. These are admissible in evidence whether or not those who made them give oral evidence at the trial, and irrespective of what they say if they do. In French trials, a large amount of evidence comes before the court in this form, and this despite the fact that both prosecution and defence have a virtually unfettered right to call witnesses for oral examination. Influenced by a long tradition of a procedure that was written, French judges and lawyers, unlike English ones, do not automatically accept that oral evidence is necessary.

Fifth, the position of the defendant is radically different. In England, he has a choice as to whether or not he gives evidence, and if he elects to give evidence, he says nothing until after the close of the prosecution case. At a French trial, the first thing that happens is that the defendant is questioned by the judge; first about his background, including his criminal record if he has one, and then about the matters that are now alleged against him. Then the witnesses (if there are any) are called, and as the judge examines them he pauses from time to time to ask the defendant if he has any observations to make about what they have said. The defendant has a right of silence, in as much as he can refuse to answer, or to make any comments; but if he does so, there is no pretence, as there is in England, of his silence not officially counting against him.[5]

Sixth, witnesses are usually examined not by the parties, but by the presiding judge. If the prosecution or the defence want to question the witness about a particular matter, they have in principle to put their questions through the judge. The judge has a discretion to allow them to put their questions directly. Some judges exercise this discretion readily, others do not. This obviously cramps the style of the prosecutor or defending *avocat* who would like to put a witness through a rigorous cross-examination, and cannot do so. On the other hand it is much kinder to rape victims, children, old ladies who have been beaten up and robbed, and other vulnerable witnesses.

Seventh, an important part is played in French criminal procedure by official experts. Instead of relying, as we do, on expert witnesses called by the parties, the French system makes great use of a specially-recruited body of experts, who are appointed by the court, and report to it. In France there are expert witnesses as well—but the part they play is much reduced.

Finally, the victim of the offence has a much higher status in French criminal procedure than has the victim in criminal proceedings in England: as is explained later in this chapter.

---

[5] 'Enfin, la personne poursuivie peut toujours se refuser à répondre si elle estime cette attitude plus conforme aux intérêts de sa défense et sous réserve, pour les magistrats et jurés, du droit de tirer de cette attitude toute conséquence utile à la formation de leur conviction.' (Merle and Vitu, *Procédure Pénalle*, 4th edn. (1989), 150).

2   The English Criminal System

There was a time when no Englishman could pronounce the phrase 'English criminal procedure' without adding the words 'which is the envy of the world': but this is no longer true. For years, we have been used to the police telling us that English criminal procedure is inefficient, in the sense that it enables too many guilty people to escape: but more recently, two new and worse defects have become apparent. From those who concern themselves with the victims of crime we hear the complaint that it neglects the victim's interests, or even works against them—especially where they are children, or otherwise particularly vulnerable. And from the seemingly endless series of miscarriages of justice that have recently been exposed[6] we have learnt to doubt its ability to avoid convicting the innocent. This is particularly shocking, because we have traditionally assumed that protecting the innocent from wrongful conviction is something that the English system is particularly good at, however badly it may do everything else. Indeed, the fact that it safeguards the innocent so thoroughly is often said to justify a number of its most evident defects—in particular its harshness towards victims, and the fact that it lets so many guilty people go free.

The Royal Commission on Criminal Justice is now looking at ways of improving English criminal procedure. Are there any lessons it can learn from France? In my view there are three.

The first concerns the position of the victim. In a public prosecution in England the victim has no special status. He will be a witness if the prosecution care to call him—otherwise he is a nobody. He has no right to be informed, let alone consulted, about what charges are brought against the person who has wronged him, or about the prosecutor's decision to drop the charges that are serious in return for the defendant's offer to plead guilty to the ones that are not. If a man is prosecuted for the rape of a girl of 15—a charge that implies she did not consent to intercourse—the prosecution can accept his plea of guilty to unlawful sexual intercourse with a girl under 16—a charge that implies she did consent—and there is nothing she can do about it. Unless the victim is called as a witness, he or she will have no chance to put his or her side of the story before the court: and where the defendant pleads guilty, usually no witnesses are called.[7] So the defendant, having pleaded guilty, can make a speech in mitigation that casts the blame for the incident upon the victim, and there is nothing the victim can do to put the record straight. Indeed, as the victim has no right to be kept informed of the progress of the case, he may only find out what

---

[6] *McIlkenny* (1991) 93 CrApR 287; *Maguire* (1992) 94 CrApR 133; *Ward*, The *Independent*, 12 May 1992; *Kisko*, The *Independent*, 19 Feb. 1992; *McGranaghan* [1992] Criminal Law Review 430.   [7] But see n. 4, above.

has happened when he reads a report of the speech in mitigation in the local paper. Nor does he have, as such, a right to ask the court to award him damages. Since 1972 the criminal courts have had the power to make compensation orders against convicted defendants, and the Criminal Justice Act 1988 now even requires the court to give reasons if it disposes of the case without making such an order. But no one has thought to give the victim *locus standi* to ask for such an order, or to give the court the information it needs in order to do so. This is important, because before the court can make a compensation order it needs to know what losses the victim has suffered: and if—as often—the Crown Prosecution Service has neglected to obtain this information, the order cannot be made.

The victim in France, by contrast, is immeasurably better off. By article 1 of the CPP he has the right to start a prosecution, and if he does so, the public prosecutor has no right—as he has in England—to take it over, and suppress it; the case can only be stopped by the court. More importantly, the victim also has the right to be joined as a *partie civile* where it is the public prosecutor who has started the proceedings. From that point on, he has the same right to be told about the progress of the case as the defendant, and the same right to be informed about the evidence that has been collected. At the trial the *partie civile* can (and often does) have a lawyer to represent his interests, and for the victim who is poor, legal aid for this is sometimes available. The *partie civile* has the right to address the court. He can tell the court his version of events, say what sentence he thinks should be imposed, and make a claim for damages: even in traffic cases, where, in England, the Powers of Criminal Courts Act 1973 expressly prohibits the criminal courts from making compensation orders. And all this is in addition to the possibility of State compensation under the French equivalent of the Criminal Injuries Compensation Scheme. Indeed, the French state compensation scheme is also more generous to victims than the English one, because whereas the English scheme will only pay the victims of crimes of violence, the French scheme also pays out to poor persons who are ruined as a result of theft or fraud.[8]

In 1985, the complaints of English victims were systematically exposed by Shapland, Willmore, and Duff in *Victims in the Criminal Justice System*. A considerable public debate followed, and in 1990 the Government responded by getting the Home Office to issue the *Victims' Charter*. This document is a statement of what it is good practice for the police, the Crown Prosecution Service and courts to do: but there is nothing, needless to say, that gives the victim any legal leg to stand on if good practice is not followed, and his interests are ignored. To some extent, of course, the

---

[8] See CPP arts. 706-3–706-14.

victim can make sure that notice is taken of his grievances by starting a private prosecution. But he gets no legal aid for this, and in any case, it is not an option where a public prosecution is already taking place. In England there are, however, preliminary signs that the victim will be recognized as a person with a legal status different from that of a mere witness, who deserves special protection. In 1976, the Sexual Offences (Amendment) Act broke new ground by prohibiting the media from publishing the identity of the victim of a rape, and in 1992 a new Act with the same name extended the same protection to all victims of all sexual offences.[9]

The second lesson I believe we have to learn from France is about the use of experts. As I have said at greater length elsewhere,[10] there are a number of defects in the present English system of expert witnesses, who are called adversarially for prosecution and defence. Not all of them are present in all cases, thank heavens: but it is not difficult to think of practical examples.

The first defect is incompetence. There is no systematic quality control on those who may be expert witnesses, and some who appear are less than competent. Unfortunately, experience shows that incompetent experts are not always discredited by cross-examination. The second is bias; it is psychologically difficult for even a conscientious expert to avoid being influenced by the fact that he has been invited to give evidence to support one side or the other; not all expert witnesses even try to be dispassionate; and even the ones who are dispassionate risk accusations of bias, which may lower the credibility of their evidence. The third is inequality of arms; the adversarial method can only work fairly where each side has equal resources. But in practice, the defence does not have the same ability to select and pay for experts as the prosecution does; even if the defence were better funded, they would still be in a weaker position where, as often, the tests and examinations are things that can only be done once, and the prosecution expert has already done them. The fourth, and in some ways the most serious defect, is ineptitude; the adversarial approach often masks the areas of agreement between reputable experts, maximizes the areas of disagreement, and, where the experts for prosecution and defence flatly

---

[9] No thanks to the Government! In 1987, when a proposal was made to extend the anonymity of rape victims to other sexual offence victims as an amendment to the current Criminal Justice Bill, the Government blocked it. When the proposal was made again in 1990 as one of the recommendations of the Calcutt Committee (Report of the committee on Privacy and Related Matters, Cmnd. 1002), the Government ignored it. The legislation to achieve this change had to wait for a Private Member's Bill. Clearly, the Government's professed concern for victims is considerably weaker than its fear of the tabloid press.

[10] Spencer and Flin, *The Evidence of Children: the Law and the Psychology* (Blackstone, 1990), ch. 9; [1991] *Criminal Law Review* 106–10; 'Court Experts and Expert Witnesses: Have we a Lesson to Learn from the French?' (1993) *Current Legal Problems*, 213–36.

contradict one another, gives the tribunal of fact no sensible means of deciding which side is scientifically correct.[11]

Logically, a system of neutral, court-appointed experts ought to counter a number of these problems. An expert who is not called in support of either side is less likely to be biased, and the problem of inequality of arms also disappears if the court undertakes the job of finding suitable experts and paying them. A system of court-appointed experts also largely removes the problem of the 'battle of experts', at the end of which the court does not know who to believe. In a difficult case a French court will appoint a panel of experts to advise it, who will produce a joint report. In this the areas of agreement will be clearly set out, as will the points on which they differ.

Of course, a system of court-appointed experts also has its dangers. If the expert is incompetent the risk is greater, because his official standing is higher. In such a system it is therefore particularly important to make sure that experts are of good quality, and that both sides are able to challenge their opinions. The French system of court experts recognizes these problems, and creates what appears to be effective safeguards against them.

In order to make sure that experts who advise the court are competent, the French have a system of official lists, which are under the control of the Court of Appeal in each area. To be admitted to the list of experts is a considerable public honour, entry to the list is difficult, and in the main, only those who are in good standing in their profession are entered. A French psychiatrist writes 'the judges take care that those who act as experts do so in conjunction with normal professional practice, and make sure that no body of professional experts emerges consisting of people who have lost touch with clinical practice'.[12] Article 157 of the CPP requires the court to choose experts from this list, unless there are exceptional circumstances.

As for enabling the expert's opinion to be challenged, the French system provides four separate means by which this can be done. The expert, or panel of experts, are usually appointed by the *juge d'instruction* in the pre-trial phase, and where this happens, article 165 CPP allows the parties to

---

[11] In the words of Bridge J when directing the jury in the Birmingham Six case: 'Members of the jury, the resolution of scientific argument of this sort is difficult, particularly difficult for a jury of lay people . . . The only way that you can resolve these difficulties is by your impression of the witnesses. Use any technical knowledge that you have, but I suspect that in the end you will judge it primarily by your impression of the witnesses, and secondly perhaps by a comparison of their relative experience.' *McIlkenny* (1991) 93 CrApR 287, at 296.

[12] C. Bardet-Giraudon, 'The Place of the Expert in the French Legal System', in *Children's Evidence in Legal Proceedings: An International Perspective* ed. Spencer, Nicholson, Flin, and Bukll (Cambridge Law Faculty, 1990).

ask him to require the expert to consult with particular people who are thought to be able to provide technical information. Where the parties have a particular theory, this enables them to put it before the court experts at the outset. Second, the court expert (or experts) report to the *juge d'instruction*, who passes their report along to the parties, and invites their comments. At this point they have the right to ask the *juge d'instruction* to call for a *contre-expertise* (second opinion), and if he refuses they can appeal. Third, article 168 CPP requires the official expert to appear at trial and justify his report 'where this is necessary'. In practice, he will do so in any case that is serious, and the presiding judge will often allow the parties to question him direct. Lastly, the parties can, if they wish, call their own experts as witnesses at the trial (though in practice this is rarely done).

Could some such a scheme be grafted on to our present arrangements? Taking the criminal process in reverse order, there would be no practical problem about giving the power to appoint an independent expert to the Court of Appeal. Indeed, it formerly had such a power under section 9(e) of the Criminal Appeal Act 1907. When the 1907 Act was replaced by the Criminal Appeal Act 1968 the power was allowed to lapse, not because it worked badly, but simply it was never used. In fact the court simply refused to use it, piously remarking that juries are able to choose between two sets of diametrically opposed scientific evidence.[13]

The appointment of a court expert at the trial stage looks at first sight more difficult to copy in England, because in France it is all part of the *instruction*—a highly-organized pre-trial phase which the court controls, and which is absent from English criminal procedure. It does not follow, however, that there can be no system of court-appointed experts unless the whole French procedure of *instruction* is introduced as well. In the USA, for example, the Federal Rules of Criminal provide for the appointment of court experts at the trial stage,[14] although there is no equivalent of an *instruction*, any more than there is in England. According to the commentators on the Federal Code the provision is little used—but 'the assumption may be made that the availability of the procedure in itself decreases the need for resorting to it. The ever-present possibility that the judge may appoint an expert in a given case must inevitably exert a sobering effect on the expert witness of a party and upon the person utilising his services.'[15]

---

[13] See *Thorne* (1925) CrApR 185.

[14] Rule 706. 'The court may on its own motion or on the motion of any party enter an order to show cause why expert witnesses should not be appointed, and may request the parties to submit nominations. The court may appoint any expert witnesses agreed upon by the parties, and may appoint expert witnesses of its own selection . . .'.

[15] *Federal Criminal Code and Rules* (West Publishing Company, 1991), 257.

Of course, if English criminal procedure were modified to incorporate a properly-organized pre-trial phase, taking place under judicial control, this would make the appointment of court experts easier. And this leads to the third aspect of French criminal procedure from which there may be a lesson to learn: the existence, in serious cases, of a properly-organized pre-trial phase.

In English criminal procedure as it exists today, nothing much of real importance happens between when the police charge the suspect, and when he eventually comes to trial. Decisions will be made about remanding him in custody, of course, and if he is to be tried in the Crown Court, there will be committal proceedings, in the course of which he will be informed of the evidence the prosecution propose to use against him. But there will be nothing more in the way of an official investigation. No one in authority is permitted to put any further questions to the suspect.[16] Nor is anyone in authority likely to put any further questions to the prosecution witnesses. And the job of collecting defence evidence will be left entirely to the defence.

In France the picture is entirely different. If the case is serious enough for a *juge d'instruction* to be involved, a number of important things will happen in the interval between the police investigation and the trial.

In the first place, the defendant will be interrogated again, this time by the *juge d'instruction*. To the English, this looks oppressive: once the police have finished with him, we feel he ought to be left alone. To the French, however, this re-interrogation is seen as a safeguard for the innocent, because it gives the suspect an official opportunity to retract or qualify any confession he has made to the police, and generally to explain himself. What we regard as an essential safeguard for his right of silence, they see as an outrageous deprivation of his right to speak.

Second, it is likely that the main witnesses will be interrogated again, this time by the *juge d'instruction*. As with the defendant's reinterrogation, this acts as a check against the risk that the police put words into people's mouths. More important, the *juge d'instruction* often arranges for the witness and the defendant to have a confrontation. By this means, it is often possible to find out in advance of trial precisely what the points of dispute are, and to obtain further information that bears upon them. It also means that the witnesses' evidence is preserved in an acceptable form in case they should die, go missing, or be otherwise unable to appear at the trial.

Third, the defence has the chance to put their side of the story to a state official, other than the police, one of whose duties is to investigate it.

---

[16] Questioning the suspect after charge was originally forbidden by the Judges' Rules, and the ban is continued in the Code of Practice issued under the Police and Criminal Evidence Act 1984 (Code C. 16.15).

In England, by contrast, the job of grubbing up defence evidence is left entirely to the defence. This means that in the preliminary stage, prosecution and defence are engaged in a fight with seriously unequal arms. In the first place, the defence may not have the funds to do their researches properly, and second, it lacks the necessary legal powers even where it has the money. A defence lawyer is obviously in a much weaker position to get a prospective witness to give a statement than the police are, and he wholly lacks the coercive powers of the police—for example, to conduct a search, or obtain a bodily sample.

Fourth, in the pre-trial phase experts will be appointed by a neutral person, and their reports disclosed, criticized, and discussed—as has already been explained.

Fifth, a state official other than a member of the police assembles all the available evidence—that which points to innocence as well as that which points to guilt—and communicates it to the defence. In English criminal procedure, this has always been a particularly weak point. In theory, the defendant is nowadays supposed to be informed of all the evidence the police have discovered, including any which points in the direction of his innocence,[17] and he can appeal if he is not;[18] but in practice the difficulty is that he has no means of finding out about the bits of evidence the police keep from him. This problem has led to some spectacular miscarriages of justice.[19] One of the arguments for the creation of the Crown Prosecution Service was that it would solve this problem.[20] Sadly, it has not done so. When the Crown Prosecution Service was created the decision was taken to give it no real powers as against the police, and in consequence it has no power to make them hand over their files, or indeed, to make the police do anything. Thus the Crown Prosecution Service—like the defence—only finds out as much about the evidence as the police care to tell it. I firmly believe that if we had had an organized pre-trial phase, a number of our recent miscarriages of justice would have been avoided.

Does it follow from this that, unlike Mme Delmas-Marty,[21] I am a partisan of the *juge d'instruction*? No, not necessarily. What I favour, in serious cases, is a number of important tasks being done by *someone:* which in France happen to be done by the *juge d'instruction*, and which in English criminal procedure are usually done by nobody at all. It is the *phase préliminaire* I like, in other words, and for me it is open to negotiation whether the

[17] See the Attorney-General's Guidelines on Disclosure of Information to the Defence (1982) 74 CrApR 302.   [18] *Parker* (1990) 90 CrApR 107.
[19] As in the *Kisko* case (see n. 6, above) where a man was convicted of the sexual murder of a little girl, although sixteen years later the police were shown to have had scientific evidence that proved conclusively that her attacker must have been someone else.
[20] See the Report of the Royal Commission on Criminal Procedure, 1981 (Cmnd. 8092) 6.24; the Crown Prosecution Service was created by the Prosecution of Offences Act 1985.
[21] See her contribution to this volume.

tasks of which it is composed should fall to an improved prosecutor, to a junior judge, or some to one and some to the other.

In this connection it is worth noticing that when Germany, Italy, and Portugal altered their criminal procedure to remove the *juge d'instruction*,[22] they redistributed his functions, and did not simply abolish them. This, too, is what was proposed for France by the *Commission justice pénale et droits de l'homme*, when it recommended the abolition of the *juge d'instruction* in France. Indeed, as Mme Delmas-Marty says in her contribution to this volume, the Commission wanted to 'preserve the best feature of the system—which it saw as the careful regulation of the preliminary phase.'

[22] In Italy and Germany, the *juge d'instruction* has been eliminated. Under the new Portuguese Code of Criminal Procedure of 1987 the public prosecutor is normally in charge of the investigation, but a *juge d'instruction* can be called in at the request of the defendant, or of the victim where the public prosecutor fails to act. See generally Jean Pradel, *L'Instruction Préparatoire* (Paris, 1991), ch. 1.

THE JUGE D'INSTRUCTION:
DO THE ENGLISH REALLY NEED HIM?

PROFESSOR M. DELMAS-MARTY

1 Introduction

The English press shows increasing admiration for the French system of criminal justice, and in particular, for the *juge d'instruction*. 'The accusatorial system, which ought in theory to protect the innocent, can become the steam-roller which crushes him', wrote the editor of *The Times* on 8 March 1991. 'An inquisitorial system where the court pursues its own inquiry could be better than our present system of criminal justice.' 'Let Lord Runciman and his commission take a look at the French system, whose sole object is to find the truth', wrote Ludovic Kennedy on 4 April 1991, 'a judicial figure oversees police investigations and the role of counsel is essentially low key.'

To the French lawyer, however patriotic he may be, this sudden admiration in England for the *juge d'instruction* looks distinctly odd. Of the various jurisdictions in Europe that borrowed their criminal procedure from France, a number have abolished him. This has happened in Germany, where a law of 1974 transferred his investigative functions to the public prosecutor, and in Italy, where the *juge d'instruction* disappeared when the new Italian code of criminal procedure came into force in 1989. Even in France itself, where the idea originated, lawyers are far from unanimous in thinking that he ought to remain. His abolition, and the transfer of most of his investigative powers to the public prosecutor, has been seriously proposed on two occasions since the Second World War. In 1949 this was proposed by an official Commission, chaired by Mr Donnedieu de Varbres. In 1990, a similar proposal was put forward in the report of the *Commission justice pénale et droits de l'homme*,[1] of which I had the honour to be the chairman.

All this makes me suspect that the English admire the *juge d'instruction* mainly because they have a rather hazy idea about what he is supposed to do in theory, and what he actually does in practice. In this paper I shall attempt to make these matters plain. In the first section, I shall outline what the functions of the *juge d'instruction* are. In the second, I shall summarize what are thought to be the advantages and the disadvantages of the office, and the proposals that were made by the *Commission justice*

---

[1] Commission justice pénale et droits de l'homme, *La Mise en État des Affaires Pénales* (La Documentation Française, 1991).

pénale et droits de l'homme. And in the final section, I shall briefly outline the response of the French Government to our proposals, and the changes that are now taking place.

2 The Procedure Known as '*Instruction*'

In a serious case in France, the criminal process is divided into two distinct phases. There is a preparatory phase, called the *instruction préparatoire*, and a main phase, the *procédure de jugement*.

Whether or not there is an *instruction* depends partly on the offence the defendant committed, and partly on what the public prosecutor and the victim choose to do about it. In descending order of seriousness there are *crimes*, *délits*, and *contraventions*. Article 79 of the *Code de procédure pénale* provides that where the defendant has committed a *crime*, an *instruction* is mandatory. If it is a *délit*, on the other hand, the public prosecutor has the choice as to whether to start one or not. Usually he will not bother, but he will normally do so if there is a need for detention of the suspect, or if the offence is a complicated one, like a commercial fraud—or if there are likely to be difficulties about the evidence—an indecent assault upon a child, for example. An *instruction* is also possible where the offence is only a *contravention*, although here it is quite exceptional. Irrespective of what the public prosecutor has chosen to do, however, an *instruction* will automatically be opened if the victim takes the initiative by constituting himself a *partie civile*. This step is taken by laying the matter directly before the *juge d'instruction*, who is then bound to investigate it— even where the public prosecutor has decided to take no action. At the time of writing, there is an *instruction* in about 8 per cent of all prosecutions. The remaining 92 per cent go straight through to the final judgment phase, much as they do in England.

Where there is an *instruction*, this involves two jurisdictions:

- the *juge d'instruction* (the first level of *instruction*)
- the *chambre d'accusation* (the second level of *instruction*)

The first level of instruction consists of a judge alone, the *juge d'instruction*. He is a judge of the local court of first instance, formally nominated to act as *juge d'instruction* for an unlimited period by the bench of judges.[2] A '*greffier d'instruction*' (clerk of instruction) is allocated to him, drawn from the secretarial staff of the court. In principle there is one *juge d'instruction* per first instance court, but in the bigger courts there are several.

---

[2] Art. 50(1) CPP.

The *juge d'instruction* has three main tasks:

- First, he is charged, with the help of the *police judiciaire*, with putting together the evidence relating to the offence and building up the *dossier* on the case.
- Second, he also has the power formally to accuse (*inculper*) a person against whom there are 'serious and concordant indications of guilt'. *Inculpation* marks the point at which the suspect becomes a defendant. It makes it possible to take various compulsory measures against him, but also ensures him the protection of various 'defendant's rights'.
- Finally, the *juge d'instruction* rules on the accusations that have been made, decides which ones stand up, and if it seems proper, sends the accused for trial before the appropriate court.

The second level of instruction is the *chambre d'accusation*. This is a section of the court of appeal for the district, and it consists of three judges (a president and two advisors). A clerk is also attached to it. From 1844, it did not have a separate existence, because the members did other judicial tasks and only met once a week, or more often if necessary. But having given the president broad powers to control the *juge d'instruction* and to discipline the *police judiciaire*, the 1958 Code of Criminal Procedure lead to the position that he should be available for service in other courts only in exceptional circumstances.[3] The remaining members of the *chambre d'accusation* may, on the other hand, sit in other divisions of the court.[4]

The jurisdiction of the *chambre d'accusation* is extremely wide. In addition to powers over extradition, the rehabilitation of offenders, and discipline over all grades of the *police judiciaire*, the *chambre d'accusation* deals with three large slices of judicial business. First, it acts as a court of appeal against the decisions of the *juge d'instruction* in its area—whether dealing with *crimes*, *délits* or minor offences.[5] Then, at a second level, it has a duty to review all the *instructions* that have taken place relating to offences that count as *crimes*, before it dispatches the accused for trial at the *cour d'assises*.[6] And lastly, it keeps a general eye on all the *instructions* that are being carried on in its area. In this respect, it is said to have 'complete jurisdiction', or that it is 'sovereign'. This third jurisdiction is exercised either by a procedure called *revision*,[7] which enables it to make decisions concerning any accused person whose case is sent to it under article 181, under investigation for any criminal offence of any legal category to which this procedure is applicable—or else by a procedure called *evocation*,[8] which enables it, for any criminal offence to which this procedure applies, to order the formal accusation of those whose cases have not been forwarded to it.

---

[3] Art. 191(2) and (5) CPP.   [4] Art. 191(2) CPP.   [5] Art. 185 *et seq.* CCP.
[6] Art. 181 CCP.   [7] Art. 202 CCP.   [8] Art. 204 CCP.

3   The *Juge d'Instruction*: Advantages And Disadvantages

It is usual to say or write that the *juge d'instruction* established in France by the *Code d'Instruction criminelle* of 1808 is the descendant or heir or the *lieutenant criminel* of the *ancien regime*. With a few less formalities in the paperwork, a *lieutenant criminel* of the *ancien regime* would find things just as he used to do them.[9]

If the paternity is indisputable, the family likeness has been deliberately exaggerated. In fact, the *lieutenant criminel* of 1670 was given powers over not only the preliminary investigation but over the whole process: not only the preliminary acts, but also the final and decisive steps which are taken nowadays at the trial. By contrast the *juge d'instruction* as created in 1808 operates only in the preliminary stages, his principle function being the enquiry.[10] At that time, the legal decisions were made by a *chambre du conseil* composed of three judges, of whom the *juge d'instruction* was one. This trio handled bail, committal for trial, and the decision to drop the case.

The *juge d'instruction* acquired his recognizably judical status by stages, the main ones being as follows: the Law of 1856 that abolished the *chambre de conseil* (because it merely rubber-stamped the decisions of the *juge d'instruction*); the Law of 1897 which allowed the defence lawyer to be present during the preliminary investigation; the Code of 1958 which gives the President of the court, and not the public prosecutor, the right to select the *juge d'instruction* (a selection which, under the Law of 6 July 1989, is now done according to a rota); the Law of 1970 which requires the *juge d'instruction* to give a reasoned decision for refusing bail to a person accused of a *délit*; the Law of 1975, which allows the accused a lawyer when the bail decision is made, and the Law of 1984 which requires the *juge d'instruction* to hear argument from both sides before refusing bail, and takes away the prosecutor's power to prevent the immediate release of the accused on bail by entering an appeal. Other stages in this process include the Laws, now abolished, which between 1985 and 1987, proposed to increase still further the legal guarantees of the defendant during the *instruction* by requiring certain decisions to be made by a panel of judges (*chambre d'instruction* and *chambre de controle d'instruction*); and the Law of 1989, requiring reasoned decisions for all refusals to grant bail, and authorizing the proceedings before the *chambre d'instruction* to be published provided that court consents: again, reforms enacted in the same spirit.

As the *juge d'instruction* has been turned into more and more of a judge,

---

[9] A. Esmein, *History of Criminal Procedure in France* (Paris, 1882), 536.

[10] Indeed he was classed as 'an officer of the *police judiciaire*' by the *Code d'instruction criminelle* of 1808.

so the powers of the police and the public prosecutor have been progressively increased, and these have come to play an ever more important part in setting a prosecution in motion. In particular, there is the fact that two police practices were legalized in 1958: police detention of suspects (alias *garde à vue*), and their subjection to unofficial questioning in the police station before the *juge d'instruction* became involved—a procedure now called the *enquête préliminaire*.

Thus, although the spotlight in France is still firmly focused on the *juge d'instruction*, the system today enshrines an extreme confusion of roles. Depending on whether the proceedings are set in motion by the public prosecutor or the *partie civile*, the same parts are played by the *juge d'instruction*, the *police judiciaire*, or the public prosecutor—and they may be under the control of a judge who is not a *juge d'instruction* but the president of the *tribunal correctionennel*, or the president of the *tribunal de grande instance*.

Confining myself from now on to the *juge d'instruction*, I shall try to weigh up the advantages and disadvantages of the system as it functions in France today. What I have to say will centre around two dominant ideas, which are:

- in terms of advantage, the existence of a careful and minute regulation of the powers of the *juge d'instruction* during the part of the criminal process that leads up to the trial of the accused;
- in terms of disadvantage, the imbalance which is apparent between his *police judiciaire*: too many in respect of the accused, but too few as against the other authorities (the police and the public prosecutor).

3.1　*Advantages: Powers that are Regulated*

Although the European Court of Human Rights has only decided the point recently and incidentally,[11] it is important, in order that the proceedings should be fair at the final stage of judgment, that the preliminary stages should be organized according to rules that are clear: and clear enough to make sure, from the outset, that the process is not merely efficient, but also fair.

In this respect, the *instruction* has the undoubted advantage of being regulated by rules both detailed and precise. Articles 79 to 230—nearly 150 articles—of the Code of Criminal Procedure are devoted to the *instruction préparatoire*.

In detail, the advantages include the following:

- that the points of dispute are identified and clarified well in advance of the final trial;

---

[11] *Lamy* v. *Belgium*, ECHR, 30 Mar. 1989.

- that the case has been properly investigated, and vital points are not ignored or glossed over (this is important for the innocent defendant);
- that in principle, a reliable record is obtained of what vital witnesses were saying before they forgot, or were intimidated, or died, or became otherwise unavailable;
- that it is a sympathetic way of obtaining the evidence from a vulnerable witness (e.g. a child or an elderly person);
- that the innocent defendant can be identified early, and the proceedings against him dropped without the pain of a public trial.

To these can be added a further advantage, frequently pointed out by the *juges d'instruction* themselves, that is, their judicial status. The *juge d'instruction* is independent of the executive, whereas the prosecutors, for their part, are organized in a hierarchy headed by the *Garde des Sceaux*, (Minister of Justice), who can give them orders.

However, this last argument can cut both ways, for two reasons: on the one hand, the fact that the *juges d'instruction* are independent of the executive does not mean that they are necessarily free from other external influences: in particular, the media, and corporatism, to the extent that a liking for the limelight, or membership of a trade union, are not wholly without influence upon the behaviour of certain *juges d'instruction*. On the other hand, his status as a judge can mean that when the *juge d'instruction* makes a ruling—in particular *inculpation*, a ruling that formally accuses the suspect of the offence—this creates a strong impression that the case has already been decided, although the trial has not yet taken place. This shows the difficulty of drawing a clear line between the advantages and drawbacks of having a *juge d'instruction*.

3.2   Drawbacks: Too Much Power, and yet Too Little

There are certain drawbacks which are peculiar to the French version of the system, and these can be disposed of briefly. In particular, there is the fact that our *juges d'instruction* tend to be young and inexperienced, usually coming to the job straight from the *école Nationale de la Magistrature*, and the fact that antiquated and inefficient methods are sometimes used to record the interrogations—often nothing more than the court clerk typing notes at the dictation of the *juge d'instruction*.

But more must be said about certain other drawbacks, which are inherent in the system. In particular there is the fact that it gives the *juge d'instruction* powers that are at once too great and not great enough.

The *juge d'instruction* has, it seems, too much power over the suspect, because he combines three functions: that of policeman (seeking out evidence for the offence, and where necessary, investigating the character of the suspect); that of accuser (because the *inculpation* involves notifying the person that there exist against him 'serious and concordant indications of guilt'); and that of judge (because he makes decisions about bail, and the charges that are justified when the case is sent to trial). Hence in practice there is a risk of conflict, and in particular, conflict between the roles of policeman and judge when as judge he has to make a decision on the question of bail; hence the additional risk of infringing the principle of impartiality, an essential element in a proper judgment.[12] Indeed, it may be thought that the impartial exercise of judicial functions is simply incompatible with the job of policeman or detective, for legal reasons, and equally for practical ones.

At the legal level, the incompatibility stems from the fact that the judge, in his judicial duties, is supposed to play the part of an impartial arbiter, and 'to appear as such to every eye': as the European Court of Human Rights reminds us when necessary (using the term 'impartiality' in its double sense, both objective and subjective impartiality being required). The very logic of the investigation forces him into making hypotheses about the guilt of some people, and the innocence of others.

At the practical level, the *juge d'instruction*'s double task is extremely heavy, and it is noticeable, at the present day, how the *juge d'instruction* is being forced to give up his various duties. His duties of investigation he unloads by making excessive use of the *commission rogatoire*—which means, in practice, that he delegates the job of questioning people to the police. His judicial duties also tend to be skimped. The adversarial hearing that is supposed to take place before a bail decision is often a sham—the lawyers often being insufficiently organized to provide representation. There is an annoying tendency, when making decisions, to give minimal reasons for them. In practice, the double load of duties—ever heavier as more and more safeguards have been built into the process, has resulted in a worrying increase in the average time that an *instruction* lasts. In 1810, the average time taken was one month, in 1980, nine months. Together with this has come an equally worrying increase in the number of people held in prison awaiting trial. In addition to this, and undoubtedly connected with it, there is the fact that the process of *instruction* has been progressively reduced in importance—even marginalized—in favour of investigations made by the police under the direct supervision of the public prosecutor, and which are hardly governed by any regulations at all. In less than 30 years—from 1960–88, the proportion of prosecutions which go through a *juge d'instruction* has been reduced from around 20 per cent to less than 10 per cent.

If the marginalization of the *juge d'instruction* seems to be the indirect

---

[12] See Arts. 5, 6 of the European Convention, and the case-law of the Commission and the Court of Human Rights.

consequence of overloading him with the tasks that have been mentioned, it is also the result of a structural weakness: in particular, the fact that he is directly dependent on the public prosecutor to send him cases to investigate, and on the *police judiciaire* for the means of investigating them efficiently.

Despite the legislator's continual effort to increase the judicial standing of the *juge d'instruction* and to build legal safeguards into the process he operates, the system originally created by the *Code d'instruction criminelle* in 1808 has left a lasting mark: when it comes to his relations with the public prosecutor and with the police, the powers of the *juge d'instruction* are too weak.

In the first place, it is the public prosecutor who keeps the dominant role. As far as offences classed as *délits* are concerned—*crimes*, the more serious classes accounting for only 3 per cent of the cases in which a *juge d'instruction* is involved—it is the public prosecutor who makes the decision as to whether or not an *instruction* shall take place. In this he has a discretion, the negative exercise of which can only be upset if the victim decides to start proceedings as a *partie civile*. Furthermore, his mandate to the *juge d'instruction* limits the scope of his activities, and he may not investigate matters other than those mentioned in it. At any time, the public prosecutor may have access to the *dossier*, may alter the directions of the investigation, and may go to the *chambre d'accusation* with a complaint about some procedural irregularity or some particular ruling, even one in conformity with his instructions. He also retains the power to ask the president of the local court (the *Cour de Cassation*) to take the case away from the *juge*. In the end, it is the prosecutor who is the wheel without which the machinery of the *instruction préliminaire* is unable to go round.

As far as the *police judiciaire* are concerned, they enjoy a large measure of independence as a result of their being attached to the Home Office rather than to the Ministry of Justice. This autonomy is not absolute, it is true, because the Code of Criminal Procedure provides for supervision by the judicial and prosecuting authorities: but this supervision is not entrusted to the *juge d'instruction*. By various sections of the Code of Criminal Procedure, the *police judiciaire* operates 'under the direction of the prosecutor of the Republic'; in each court area it is placed 'under the surveillance of the chief prosecutor', and 'under the control of the *chambre d'accusation*'.[13]

In addition, articles 224–30 of the Code of Criminal Procedure give the *chambre d'accusation*, when dealing with the case in the ordinary course of business, or when seised of the matter by the chief prosecutor or the

---

[13] See Arts. 12, 13 CPP.

president of the *chambre*, power to hold an inquiry into the behaviour of an officer of the *police judiciaire*. Without prejudice to any disciplinary sanctions that may be imposed, it can forbid the officer concerned, either temporarily or permanently, to act as a member of the *police judiciaire* in that particular court area—or even anywhere in the country. (In fact, these provisions are rarely used.)

Finally, it should also be mentioned that by article 45 of the Code of Criminal Procedure, the public prosecutor adds his comments to the official file that is kept on every member of the *police judiciaire*. (But once again, his observations seem to have little effect on the careers of the persons concerned.)

The *juge d'instruction*, on the other hand, has no special powers that he can invoke: and in particular, none against those who disobey articles R.1 and R.2 of the Code of Criminal Procedure, which lay down in broad terms the relationship between the *police judiciaire* and the legal authorities on which they depend.

The *Commission Justice pénale et droits de l'homme* wanted to preserve the best feature of the system—which it saw as the careful regulation of the preliminary phase of the *instruction*. In order to do this and also rid the system of problems that flow from the imbalance of power as explained above, it proposed new structures, to apply to proceedings for every type of offence. The main features of these would be a distinction between powers of investigation and the judicial function, and a clearer distinction between the roles of all the players. These recommendations are built around four closely interwoven propositions.

- The creation of a 'new public prosecutor', who would direct investigations under the control of the judge. His views would be an element in the promotion process within the *police judiciaire*. He would no longer be under the direct control of the Minister of Justice, except as regards the broad lines of penal policy as laid down in general instructions, written and available to the public.
- Greater initiative to the defence by allowing it to request any kind of investigation that it felt useful, and by allowing it voice in the choice of experts; by giving it the right to raise 'nullities'—procedural errors capable of making a procedural step void; and by allowing it to appeal from decisions of the judge on the same terms as the prosecutor may.
- Harmonization of the rules governing the partie civile.
- Strengthening the powers of the judge to control the process by which a prosecution is got under way, and to protect the freedom of the individual. The judge would be renamed the '*juge des libertés*'. He would be freed of his duties of investigation, which would be transferred to the public prosecutor. But he would keep, or be given, a package of powers

relating to individual liberty: prolongation of the *garde à vue* (police detention), bail and bail conditions, telephone tapping, etc. In addition, this judge would control the length and the development of the investigations. He would decide on any conflicts arising between the public prosecutor, the defence, and—if there is one—the *partie civile*. And he would have the power, in the event of a major breakdown—inaction by the public prosecutor, or serious interruptions in the progress of the inquiry—to inform the *chambre d'accusation* and request the public prosecutor to be removed from the case.

In the eyes of the Commission, these conditions are essential to make more certain, during the investigative phase, the 'pre-eminence of the judge'. This is something which is implicit in the constitutional guarantee of legality. And it is also a condition which is vital to ensure that in practice the accused is not tempted as he often is, to confuse his judge and his accuser.

4 Public Reaction to the Proposals: *The Government's Response*

According to the timetable announced by the Minister on behalf of the Department of Justice, a Bill to reform French criminal procedure will be introduced during the spring session of Parliament. The proposals were given in outline to the Council of Ministers on 20 November 1991. It is already clear that the principle of a separation of functions proposed by the *Commission justice pénale et droits de l'homme* will not be adopted. In other words, the *juge d'instruction* will be staying much as he is.

In essence, the centrepiece of the reform is to bring in an element of collegialitys, borrowing from the law enacted in 1985 at the initiative of M. Badinter, but repealed before it came into force following a change of government, the Department of Justice is now proposing to set up in each court of first instance a panel consisting of the *juge d'instruction*, the president of the court or a deputy nominated by him, and another judge, in order to deal with bail applications and remands in custody. In addition, 'teamwork' by *juges d'instruction* will be introduced for cases that are 'complex, difficult or dangerous'. The introduction of this system of teamwork implies extra resources, notably the creation of a certain number of new *juges d'instruction*—but the exact number of new posts is not mentioned in the ministerial statement.

In addition, the scheme involves a number of new measures, of which some were proposed by the *Commission justice pénale et droits de l'homme*.

* Abolition of the '*privilèges de juridiction*'—the clumsy formula used to describe the rule according to which judges, mayors and deputy mayors,

prefects, and officers of the *police judiciaire*, when they are accused of criminal offences, are at present prosecuted and judged by courts designed by the criminal division of the *Cour de cassation*. Henceforth, these various categories will fall under the normal rules of criminal procedure.

- Abolition of '*inculpation*', the term used to indicate that the moment has come at which the charges are formally notified to the suspect, who then becomes the '*inculpé*', and can exercise his rights of defence. The Bill will sever the connection between these two elements, which at present occur together, and create three stages: a '*mise en examen*' which sets in motion the rights of the defence from when the information is laid, a '*mise en cause*' when the accusations are clear and concordant (at which point the person can be remanded in custody), and a '*mise en accusation*' when the instruction is ended. Similarly, the term '*mise hors de cause*' will replace *non-lieu* as the term for when the case is formally discontinued.[14]

- The reinforcement of the rights of the defence, which are at present very limited by comparison with the rights accorded to the public prosecutor, the main litigant in the criminal process. It is proposed to give the defence and the *partie civile* the right to request the *juge d'instruction* to undertake certain investigations (in particular, hearing witnesses and obtaining reports from exports), which they may not require him to do at present, the judge being obliged to give a reason for refusal, which will be subject to appeal.

- The creation of a panel of judges for bail refusals and the extensions of remands in custody. This principal innovation, previously proposed in 1985 as explained above, comes back to the rules laid down when the *juge d'instruction* was created by the *Code d'instruction criminelle* in 1808. The panel will be constituted by the President of the court, and will consist of the President or a judge to whom he delegates the task, the *juge d'instruction* handling the case and another judge of the court. The presence of the *juge d'instruction* on this panel is justified, according to the Ministry, by the fact that he is 'the person best placed' to inform his colleagues about the case in hand. From the decisions of this panel appeal will lie to the *chambre d'accusation*. (Remember, however, that the similar panel system originally created by the *Code d'instruction criminelle* was abolished in 1856, because in practice the *juge d'instruction* had such a dominant role that it made the participation of his two colleagues a useless formality.)

- Team-working by the *juge d'instruction*, on the other hand, represents a new idea, namely giving the responsibility for the whole of the enquiry

---

[14] Of the 73,649 *inculpations* pronounced in 1990, 7762, or 11.12%, eventually led to a *non-lieu*.

to a team of two or three *juges d'instruction*, nominated by the president of the court, with the agreement of the judge seised of the case, in those cases deemed 'complex, difficult or dangerous'.

• The reform of police detention essentially comes down to defining a legal criterion for placement in police detention, and harmonizing, as between the two sets of police powers—*flagrant, délit*, and *enquête préliminaire*—the terms on which detention can be renewed. On the other hand, the idea of allowing the suspect a lawyer in the police station, as is nowadays done in most of the countries of Europe, has not been taken up.

5 Conclusion

In conclusion, two observations can be made. On the one hand, the project contains some proposals which are good in themselves, but which risk missing their mark because they will have to be grafted onto a structure that will find it difficult to adapt to them. The more the legislator has tried to reinforce the guarantees of the *instruction* by imposing new constraints on the judge, the longer cases take in practice. This is the main cause for the excessive amount of pre-trial detention in France, it has become worse— and the worse it becomes the less use is made of the *juge d'instruction*. (We must not forget that the proportion of cases that are handled by a *juge d'instruction*, in relation to the total number of prosecutions, has fallen from 20 per cent in 1960 to under 10 per cent: so in over 90 per cent of criminal cases, the inquiry is in the hands of the police and the pro-secutor, and from thence goes directly to the court for judgment.) This indeed is why the *Commission justice pénale et droits de l'homme* chose a completely different method. Rather than sticking to piecemeal reforms of those technical questions that were most sensitive, we started out by establishing the spirit of the reform with reference to fundamental principles: from which we then, and only then, went on to create the main structures, and the technical details thereafter.

On the other hand, the project does not seem to take sufficient account of the desire that seems to be emerging everywhere in Europe to break out of the stale confrontation between the accusatorial systems of the common-law model and inquisitorial systems as found on the Continent, and to make an effort to conserve what is best in each. The best feature of the inquisitorial system is the recognition of the importance of the preparatory phase, requiring evidence to be properly sought out and properly pre-served. This should be kept. But we also need to admit that the best thing about the accusatorial system is that it promotes the judge to the level of a genuinely neutral arbitrator, by separating the functions of judge and detective—something which makes it possible to establish a balance between prosecution and defence. This, moreover, is the tendency which has been developing in Europe over the last fifteen years. At the time when Europe is being fashioned,[15] it would be a pity to ignore the support of comparative law.

[15] See *Proces Pénal et Droits de L'Homme: Vers une Conscience Europeene* (PUF, 1992).

Defining the Issues and Preparing for Trial

Professor M. Delmas-Marty, in the title of her contribution to this volume, 'The *Juge d'Instruction*: Do the English Really Need Him?', poses a question familiar to sceptics of the English system of criminal justice. The question, in the use of the word, 'really', suggests the answer—unexpected from a French lawyer—'no'. In fact, her response and that of John Spencer, in his contribution, 'French and English Criminal Procedure: A Brief Comparison', is 'yes, maybe, but in a much modified form'. These are authoritative views on a possible reform that is now being studied by the Royal Commission on Criminal Justice.

Mme Delmas-Marty is a professor of law at the University of Paris I and, over the years, has had much working experience of attempts to reform French criminal law and procedure. In 1988 she was appointed President of the *Commission Justice Pénale et Droits de L'Homme*, a body which, in 1990, recommended certain reforms designed to strengthen the judicial role of the *juge* at the preparatory stage, but to divest him of his present investigative role.

John Spencer is a leading exponent of and commentator on the English system of criminal justice, as well known to his judicial pupils at the Judicial Studies Board as to his undergraduates at Cambridge and the many other students and practitioners who read his publications. He is also an authoritative commentator on the French system of criminal justice, having recently been a Visiting Professor at the Universities of Paris I and II. He favours the strengthening of the preliminary stage of criminal proceedings, but leaves open to further consideration how it should be done.

The Royal Commission was appointed in the wake of public concern about a number of miscarriages of justice which have recently been exposed. Its terms of reference include the powers of the courts to direct proceedings and the possibility of their being given an investigative role before and during trial. The Commission has elaborated upon these terms by asking whether we should introduce a pre-trial procedure similar to that conducted by the *juge d'instruction* in France. This enquiry echoes calls made by academic commentators and practitioners in this country over the years that we should consider importing such a combination of judicial and investigative functions into our system of criminal justice. As Mme Delmas-Marty indicates, it is an irony that the British should at last begin to give that call serious consideration when there has long been a significant division of opinion in France about the value of the *juge d'instruction's* investigative role, and some years after Germany and Italy have abolished his counterpart in their jurisdictions.

The quest is for a system that will enable the early and thorough identification by a court, or by some other body, of the case and supporting evidence of each side, so that the issues are properly defined and the evidence going to them thoroughly investigated before trial. As John Spencer observes, it is at that early stage of the criminal process rather than at the appellate stage where miscarriages of justice from false or inadequate evidence can best be prevented. There are advantages in and drawbacks to the introduction of a greater judicial involvement in the investigative and preparatory stages of the criminal process. Mme Delmas-Marty and John Spencer mention the most important of them as exemplified by the experience of the French in the role of the *juge d'instruction* since his first appearance on the scene in 1808. The main advantages lie in the protection that the court can give to both prosecution and defence during the investigative and preparatory stages, by ensuring early definition of the issues, and by a thorough and fair investigation of the evidence and its preservation. In France, where the victim of the alleged offence, the *partie civile*, may intervene in the proceedings, the *juge d'instruction* is there to protect his or her rights at that stage as well. The main disadvantages include a confusion of the judicial, investigative and prosecuting functions, a tendency to long delays before reaching trial, and a reduction in the importance of the trial function because of the greater input given to the preparatory stage.

Both distinguished contributors consider this balance of advantage and disadvantage in the system as it operates in France, and Mme Delmas-Marty summarizes the recommendations of her Commission for its improvement. As I have indicated, its principal recommendation was the retention and strengthening of the judicial and supervisory role of the *juge*, to be renamed the '*juge des libertés*', in the investigative and preparatory stages of criminal proceedings, but the shedding of his investigative functions. As Mme Delmas-Marty describes, the French Government has rejected that recommendation and is in the process of introducing legislation designed to make more effective the present mix of roles.

Any attempt to transplant the *juge d'instruction*, or someone like him, into this country must first take into account the fundamental difference between the English and French systems of criminal law and procedure. This is commonly characterized as the difference between the accusatorial and the inquisitorial systems, though, as John Spencer emphasizes, the French system is a 'blend of both inquisitorial and accusatorial ideas'. However, there is another and equally fundamental reason why the English system of criminal justice is at present unreceptive to the transplantation of such a procedure of early definition of issues and thorough investigation of evidence. That is the deeply ingrained notion in the common law of the defendant's 'right of silence'.

That expression, as Lord Mustill has observed in a recent speech in the House of Lords,[1] 'arouses strong but unfocused feelings'. It denotes, as he pointed out, a number of distinct immunities. But their common origin lay in a concern to protect an innocent person from wrongful conviction obtained by abuse or other unfairness in the treatment of him before or at trial. If a system can be devised which adequately protects an accused person from such abuse or unfairness, what logical justification can there be for continuing to recognize in the context of criminal proceedings a 'right of silence' in any of its procedural forms? Early and full disclosure of the prosecution case is required; the same should apply to the defence case. Both the innocent and guilty man should be obliged to give his account and to disclose his defence, if any, at the earliest possible stage of a criminal investigation and process. It is in the interest of the innocent man to do so, if he is properly protected by the system; it is in the interest of the public and, though he may not agree, of the guilty man, that he also should do so by way of early admission or disclosure of his defence so that it may be adequately investigated while the matter is still fresh.

The 'right of silence' whilst continuing to serve as some protection to the innocent in the present imperfect system of pre-trial investigation and preparation of criminal cases, has also served the guilty and put the public to much inconvenience and expense. Over the last thirty years at least there have been many initiatives, short of legislation, to introduce some form of preparatory hearing or pre-trial review of the general run of criminal cases. The purpose of these has been to *persuade* the parties to give the court and each other information as to the proposed plea and, if the plea is to be not guilty, the issues and the evidence to be canvassed at the trial. I say 'persuade' because such initiatives, usually in the form of practice directions issued by a particular Crown Court[2] contain no effective sanction against non-compliance by the defence. They do not, and cannot, confer on the court a power to compel the defendant to disclose his hand or to inhibit him in his defence if he chooses not to do so. National practice rules for directions hearings are now in draft and the subject of pilot studies at a number of Crown Court centres, but they similarly contain no effective sanction against non-compliance. There are some statutory exceptions, such as the power given to the court to refuse to admit evidence of alibi unless the defendant has previously given notice

---

[1] R. v. *Director of the Serious Fraud Office*, ex p. *Smith* [1992] 3 WLR 66, HL (E) 74.
[2] See e.g. Central Criminal Court Practice Rules, 21 Nov. 1977, set out in *Archbold, Criminal Pleadings and Practice* (1992) i: para. 4–59.

of its particulars,[3] and in the powers given to the trial court when conducting preparatory hearings in serious fraud cases.[4] In contrast, the prosecution are under general obligations of disclosure which, even though their adequacy and the means of policing them are presently under question, may, if breached, result in a conviction being quashed on appeal.

The result is that the 'right of silence' is frequently invoked or unspokenly relied upon by the defendant and his representatives for refusal or failure at the pre-trial review to inform the court or the prosecution as to the proposed plea or the nature of the defence or the evidence, if any, to be called in support of it. 'Tactical' pleas of not guilty are frequently entered for no other reason than to preserve prison privileges or as 'holding' devices until later consideration of the matter by the defendant and his representatives, often on the eve or on the first day of the trial. It is not unknown for the court and the prosecution to embark upon the hearing without having been informed what the defence is or what issues will have to be considered. And it is a frequent occurrence for the defence to keep every one in the dark until the last moment as to whether the defendant will give or call any evidence. The injustice resulting from the defendant's ability to keep his case to himself until the last minute so as to prevent it from being properly tested speaks for itself. In the case of an innocent defendant who does so, for whatever reason, it prevents the prosecution from verifying the defence case and discontinuing the proceedings at an early stage. As to late pleas of guilty or 'cracked trials', they are a notorious cause of waste of public money and court time, and of inconvenience and distress to witnesses and others.

In my view, the time has come to remove the scope for 'defence by ambush' masquerading as the exercise of the 'right of silence' along with the scope for abuse by the police and prosecution presently at the centre of the Royal Commission's inquiry. Such a proposal in procedural terms would probably amount to giving the court power:

- to refuse to admit defence evidence not notified at the preparatory stage, a power that already exists in the case of a defence of alibi; and
- to draw adverse inferences from the refusal or failure of the defendant to disclose his case and supporting evidence at the preparatory stage and/or to give evidence at his trial.

Whether this is practicable depends upon whether an effective pre-trial procedure can be devised to *ensure* early identification of the issues and a fair and thorough investigation of all the available, relevant, evidence on both sides.

John Spencer also mentions another possible reform which, if implemented, would be well served by a system of effective preparatory hearings

---

[3] Criminal Justice Act 1967, s. 11.   [4] Criminal Justice Act 1987, ss. 7–10.

in which the judge could direct the way in which certain evidence is to be presented to the trial jury. That is the introduction of a scheme of court appointed experts, supplemented where required by evidence from experts instructed by the parties. I warmly support that proposal, enabling as it would the early reduction of such evidence to its essentials, and the identification of and concentration on the precise points of dispute, if any.

Mme Delmas-Marty's and John Spencer's interesting and thought provoking analyses of the problems of preparation for criminal trials on both sides of the Channel suggest the way ahead. It is now for the Royal Commission to plot the route in detail.

3

Contracts and Third-Party Rights in German and English Law

CONTRACT BENEFICIARIES IN GERMAN LAW

WERNER LORENZ

1 Introduction: The Scope of this Paper

'Promise of Performance for the Benefit of a Third Party'—this is the heading of the third title in the second book of the German Civil Code (BGB) which came into force on 1 January 1900. Although law reform has brought about many changes in the text of the Code, the provisions relating to third party beneficiaries (paras. 328–35) have remained unaltered. The reason why these provisions have stood the test of time lies in their flexibility, for most of them are mere rules of construction. Before entering into a discussion of their scope of application it will be necessary to become acquainted with their wording.

para. 328 (Contract for the benefit of a third party).
1 'A contract may stipulate performance for the benefit of a third party, so that the third party acquires the right directly to demand performance.
2 In the absence of express stipulation it is to be deduced from the circumstances, especially from the object of the contract, whether the third party shall acquire the right, whether the right of the third party shall arise forthwith or only under certain conditions, and whether any right shall be reserved to the contracting parties to take away or modify the right of the third party without his consent.'

para. 329 (Rules of interpretation in the event of assuming performance).
'If in a contract one party binds himself to satisfy a creditor of the other party without assuming the debt, it is not to be presumed, in case of doubt, that the creditor shall acquire a direct right to demand satisfaction from him.'

para. 330 (Rules of interpretation in case of life insurance or annuity)
'If, in a contract for life insurance or an annuity, payment of the insurance or annuity to a third party is stipulated for, it is to be presumed, in the case of doubt, that the third party acquires the right directly to demand payment. The same rule applies, if in gratuitous transfer of property the duty to perform an act in favour of a third party is imposed upon the recipient, or if a person, on taking over the whole of another person's property or goods, promises an

act of performance in favour of a third party for the purpose of settling the latter's debts.'

para. 331 (Performance after death)

1 'If the performance in favour of the third party is to be made after the death of the person to whom it was promised, in case of doubt the third party acquires the right to the performance upon the death of the promisee.'

2 'If the promisee dies before the birth of the third party, the promise to perform in favour of the third party can be revoked or altered only if the right to do so has been reserved.'

para. 332 (Change by disposition *mortis causa* because of reservation)

'If the promisee has reserved to himself the right of substituting another for the party named in the contract without the consent of the named third party, this may also be done, in case of doubt, by disposition *mortis causa*.'

para. 333 (Rejection of the right by the third party)

'If the third party rejects, by declaration to the promisor, the right acquired under the contract, the right is deemed not to have been acquired.'

para. 334 (Defences of the promisor as against the third party)

'Defences arising from the contract are available to the promisor even as against the third party.'

para. 335 (Right to claim of promisee)

'The promisee may, unless a contrary intention of the contracting parties is to be presumed, demand performance in favour of the third party, even if it is the latter who has the right to the performance.'[1]

Before proceeding any further with this introduction to German law it may be helpful to take a brief comparative look at American law as laid down in the Second Restatement on Contracts.[2]

The doctrinal difficulties that prevented the recognition in English law of a *ius quaesitum tertio* were overcome in the United States of America some time ago. Neither the rule that consideration must move from the plaintiff, nor the requirement of privity of contract between the promisor and the claimant, are considered obstacles standing in the way of an action brought by the third party against the promisor. From a comparative point of view it is interesting to note that there is basic agreement with German law on at least three points of major importance. First, it depends upon the common intention of the promisor *and* the promisee whether and when the beneficiary acquires a right to performance (sections 302, 304).[3] Second,

---

[1] English translations taken from Forrester, Goren, and Ilgen, *The German Civil Code* (1975), 54.

[2] Second Restatement of the Law on Contracts (1981) ss. 302–15.

[3] Para. 302. Intended and Incidental Beneficiaries.

(1) Unless otherwise agreed between promisor and promisee, a beneficiary of a promise is an intended beneficiary if recognition of a right to performance in the beneficiary is appropriate to effectuate the intention of the parties and either

(a) the performance of the promise will satisfy an obligation of the promisee to pay money to the beneficiary; or

no assent by a beneficiary to the contract and no knowledge on his part is necessary to give him a right of action on it, but like an offeree he may reject this right within a reasonable time after learning of its existence (section 306).[4] Third, the beneficiary's right is generally subject to all the defences that arise out of the contract that the promisor may have against the promisee (section 309).[5]

The few provisions of the German Civil Code relating to contracts in favour of third parties are typical of the style and drafting technique of this enactment: while the basic article is couched in rather general terms, important details of this triangular relationship are laid down with utmost precision. As one can see from para. 328 BGB the area of application of this provision is wide. Although the legislator had in mind mainly contracts for the care of third persons (*Versorgungsverträge*),[6] e.g. contracts for life insurance or an annuity (cf. paras. 330, 331 BGB), he was wise enough not to set any limits to the ambit of the rules of contracts in favour of third parties. This has enabled courts as well as the legal profession to discover all sorts of possible contract beneficiaries. In one of the leading commentaries on the Civil Code, more than a dozen contract types—many of them with subdivisions—are listed where the contracting parties may

(*b*) the circumstances indicate that the promisee intends to give the beneficiary the benefit of the promised performance.

(2) An incidental beneficiary is a beneficiary who is not an intended beneficiary.

Para. 304. Creation of Duty to Beneficiary. 'A promise in a contract creates a duty in the promisor to any intended beneficiary to perform the promise, and the intended beneficiary may enforce the duty.' Compare these sections with para. 328 BGB turning also on the intention of the parties.

[4] Para. 306, Disclaimer by a Beneficiary. 'A beneficiary who has not previously assented to the promise for his benefit may in a reasonable time after learning of its existence and terms render any duty to himself inoperative from the beginning by disclaimer.' Compare this section with section with para. 333 BGB which is to the same effect: *Beneficia non obtruduntur*. But see also Farnsworth, *Contracts* (1982), 738 where three possible views as to the vesting of beneficiary's right are mentioned. The author favours the view that this right does not vest until, having learned of the contract, the third party relies on it.

[5] Para. 309. Defences against the Beneficiary.

(1) A promise creates no duty to a beneficiary unless a contract is formed between the promisor and the promisee; and if a contract is voidable or unenforceable at the time of its formation the right of any beneficiary is subject to the infirmity.

(2) If a contract ceases to be binding in whole or in part because of impracticability, public policy, non-occurance of a condition, or present or prospective failure of performance, the right of any beneficiary is to that extent discharged or modified.

(3) ...

(4) ...

Compare this section with para. 334 BGB which states the same in the typically concise style of the German codification.

[6] As to the history of contracts in favour of third parties in European legal systems, see the celebrated monograph of G. Wesenberg, *Verträge zugunsten Dritter* (1949), 138 *et seq.* concerning 'Versorgungsverträge'.

stipulate performance in favour of a third party who thereby acquires the right directly to demand performance.[7]

No complete list will be given here, but some of the more important contracts for the benefit of third persons should at least be mentioned in order to give the reader an idea of their wide range:

- Labour Relations. Pension schemes for retired workers and their widows.
- Medical Treatment. Contracts made by parents for medical treatment of their child.
- Savings or Deposit Accounts. Nominating a third person as account holder.
- Transportation. Travel agency promising a variety of travel services (e.g. contracts made by such an agency with an airline company for transportation of its customers).
- Carriage of goods. Where the consignee is treated as a third-party beneficiary.
- Sale of Goods. A warranty by a manufacturer running with the goods.
- Sale of land. Restrictive covenants in favour of owners of adjoining land.
- Lease. Family members and persons living in the household of the lessee regarded as contract beneficiaries.
- Fiduciary Relations. Certain dealings between a trustee (in bankruptcy) or receiver with the debtor in favour of his creditors.
- Maintenance. Separation agreements stipulating financial support of children living with one of the spouses.
- Insurance. A variety of insurance contracts stipulating performance to a third party nominated by the insured.

In most of the fact-situations indicated above, the third party benefits from the primary obligation of the promisor, which means that he or she has a direct claim to demand performance of the *main* obligation (*primärer Leistungsanspruch*). However, in some of these situations the contracting parties may not intend to confer this right upon the third party. Nevertheless, the third party may profit from certain *secondary* obligations inherent in the contract between promisor and promisee. Such collateral obligations are not confined to the protection of bodily integrity.[8] The more important

---

[7] Münchener Kommentar (-Gottwald), *Bürgerliches Gesetzbuch*, 2nd edn. i (1985), s. 328, nn. 29–55.

[8] The draftsmen of the German Civil Code must have been well aware of the existence of such 'duties of protection' (*Schutzpflichten*). An outstanding example of this awareness can be found in para. 681 BGB which imposes upon an employer the duty to take a number of protective measures in regard to the health and the well-being of his employees. These duties are contractual in nature because para. 618(3) BGB orders the *analogous* application of paras. 842 to 844 BGB, i.e. the provisions of the law of torts concerning the extent of the obligation to make compensation in case of personal injury. This combines the advantages of contractual liability with certain advantages offered by the law of torts.

branch of the modern development concerns the gradual increase of duties aiming at the protection of persons suffering pure economic loss. This development by the courts was prompted by certain shortcomings of the German law of torts which, at least in principle, does not permit the recovery of pure financial loss. This is because under the basic tort rule (para. 823, I BGB) compensation for economic loss may only be claimed if it is the consequence of an unlawfully inflicted personal injury or if it follows from material damage to property. Commercial loss, which is not connected with the invasion of any of these legally protected interests, is recoverable only under exceptional circumstances.[9]

The following case decided by the Federal Supreme Court in 1965 may serve as an illustration for this important development of the German law of damages.[10] An elderly man, who intended to name his daughter as sole heiress and to give a small legacy to a grandchild (a niece of his daughter), decided to make his will in notarial form.[11] For this reason he first consulted his lawyer who had, in the past, also worked for his daughter. In the presence of his daughter he discussed the matter with the lawyer who took notes as to the proposed testamentary dispositions. The lawyer, who at that time had not yet been appointed notary, promised to arrange for a notary to see the testator very soon in order to take down his last will in the proper form. However, in spite of repeated telephone calls from the daughter, the lawyer delayed the matter in a manner which, in the opinion of the courts, amounted to carelessness. Meanwhile, the health of the prospective testator rapidly deteriorated; and he died without having made the intended will. As a result, his estate devolved according to the rules of intestacy which, in the present case, meant that the daughter and her niece formed a 'community of heirs' (*Erbengemeinschaft*), each of them being entitled to one half of the estate. The daughter's action succeeded; she

[9] See para. 823 II BGB: 'A person who infringes a statute intended for the protection of others (*Schutzgesetz*) is bound to make compensation to the party suffering damage. If, according to the provisions of the statute, an infringement of this is possible even without fault, the duty to make compensation arises only in the event of fault.' See also para. 826 BGB: 'A person who wilfully causes damage to another in a manner *contra bonos mores* is bound to compensate the other for the damage.' Furthermore, liability for endangering the credit of another (para. 824 BGB), and liability for breach of official duty (para. 839 BGB in connection with art. 34 Basic Law), may lead to the compensation of pure economic loss. As to the case-law development concerning the recovery of such loss under para. 823 I BGB, see Lorenz, 'Some Thoughts about Contract and Tort', *Essays in Memory of Professor F. H. Lawson* (1986), 87–8. For a general discussion of German law see: Markesinis, *The German Law of Torts*, 2nd edn. (1990), esp. 32–95 and translated cases at 148–239.

[10] Bundesgerichtshof 6 July 1965, NJW 1965, 1955; see also JZ 1966, 141 with an annotation by the present author.

[11] German law also knows the holographic will (para. 2247 BGB), but the notarial form (para. 2232 BGB) is preferred by those testators who wish to avoid the risk of a legally invalid will. In Germany notaries are usually highly-qualified lawyers. In Bavaria, for instance, the office of notary is open only to a small percentage of the top candidates of the Bar Examination.

recovered judgment against the lawyer for the difference between the amount she would have received as a beneficiary under the intended will (had it been drawn up) and the amount actually inherited. On the facts of this case, as found by the courts below, the attorney had promised performance to the deceased. The court also rejected the idea that the plaintiff could have demanded performance as a third-party beneficiary (para. 328 BGB). In the opinion of the Federal Supreme Court it was not necessary to arrive at such a construction of the contract, for another legal device, (developed *praeter legem* and known as 'contract with protective effects *vis-à-vis* third parties' (*Verträge mit Schutzwirkung für Dritte*)), might serve as a basis for the daughter's claim for damages founding in contract.

Originally regarded as a variant of para. 328 *et seq.* of the Civil Code, this type of contract has since gained definite contours of its own and is now recognized as an independent legal institution belonging to the law of liability, broad enough to grant the persons so protected an action for breach of certain secondary duties (e.g. duties of protection—*Schutzpflichten*). The decisive criterion for such a claim is some special relationship with the promisee usually described as 'proximity to the performance' (*Leistungsnähe*). This requirement places bounds to the number of potential claimants. Moreover, the promisor must have been able to foresee that the third-party (claimant) is likely to suffer damage in case of bad performance. In the testamentary case the Federal Supreme Court was fully aware of the fact that formerly the *Vertrag mit Schutzwirkung für Dritte* had never been used as a vehicle for the recovery of pure financial loss. There are two reasons why this step was taken: first because the defendant must have known that timely performance of his obligation was of essence both to the plaintiff and her father and second because the only person likely to suffer damage due to non-performance by the defendant was the plaintiff.

As has already been pointed out, German courts prefer the contractual approach because the law of torts, at least in principle, provides no remedy if pure economic loss is caused negligently. Therefore the *ratio decidendi* of the testamentary case above would also be applicable to a situation with which the Chancery Division had to deal in *Ross* v. *Caunters*[12] where an intended gift to a residuary beneficiary was void due to the negligence of the solicitors who had prepared a will for the testator. It was held in that case that a solicitor is liable to his client in contract, but may also be liable in tort, not only to his client but also to others to whom he owes a duty of care.

'Legal malpractice' in connection with the drafting of wills has also

---

[12] [1980] 1 Ch. 297. A comparative discussion of these cases can also be found in Kötz, 'The Doctrine of Privity of Contract', *Tel Aviv Univ. Studies in Law* 10 (1990), 195 *et seq.* (Ed. note.)

frequently occupied the American courts. A bold step was taken by the Supreme Court of California in the leading case of *Lucas* v. *Hamm*. In that case, the action brought by the intended beneficiary was treated as founding in both tort and contract. In the words of Chief Justice Gibson

since, in a situation like those presented here ... the main purpose of the testator in making his agreement with the attorney is to benefit the persons named in his will and this intent can be effectuated, in the event of a breach by the attorney, only by giving the beneficiaries a right of action, we should recognize, as a matter of policy, that they are entitled to recover as third-party beneficiaries.[13]

For all practical purposes this contractual approach of the California Supreme Court does not differ from the reasoning of the German Federal Supreme Court in the testamentary case.

In this context it should be emphasized that this expansion of the contractual sphere which enables a third party to bring an action for pure financial loss does not open the 'floodgates', since the only person likely to suffer damage due to the attorney's or solicitor's negligence is the intended beneficiary. This resembles those situations which in German law are regarded as cases of *Schadensverlagerung*—a term which, using a concept introduced by Lord Justice Goff (as he then was) in his judgment in *The Aliakmon*, may be rendered in English as 'transferred loss'.[14] These cases differ from those where third parties have suffered economic loss caused by negligent misstatements (e.g. a bank supplies inaccurate information concerning the creditworthiness of one of its customers and the broker, to whom this information was given, passes it on to potential investors;[15] an accountant negligently certifies the correctness of a balance sheet which afterwards is shown to a number of persons who rely on it to their detriment).[16] In the latter type of case where the crucial question is how far one should expand the sphere of contractual protection, German courts have construed contracts whenever it was deemed desirable. It is, therefore, not surprising that they have also resorted to the notion of *Vertrag mit Schutzwirkung für Dritte*. In one of its more recent judgments, the Federal Supreme Court had to deal with the liability for valuing land and buildings of an expert who had supplied the Danish Consul in Munich

---

[13] *Lucas* v. *Hamm*, 15 Cal Rptr 821 (Supreme Court of California) 1961.

[14] *Leigh and Sillivan Ltd.* v. *Aliakmon Shipping Co. Ltd.* [1985] QB 350, 339 (CA).

[15] Bundesgerichtshof, 12 Feb. 1979, NJW 1979, 1595. An English translation of this decision is contained in Lawson and Markesinis, *Tortious Liability for Unintentional Harm in the Common Law and the Civil Law*, (1982), 170.

[16] See *Ultramares Corporation* v. *Touche*, 255 NY 170, 174 NE 275 (New York Court of Appeals, 1922). The point in that case was that an accountant should not be liable in negligence towards the extensive and indeterminable number of investors at large. It is different, however, where an accountant can foresee that a definable circle of persons is likely to rely on his statement for the purpose of making an investment.

with inaccurate information concerning the commercial value of a certain area of land. The Consul passed this information on to a Danish bank which in reliance thereupon invested money in a building project to be carried out on this land. Even though the loan was secured by a land charge the bank suffered considerable damage due to the incorrect expert valuation.[17] In the opinion of the court the bank was in the position of a third-party beneficiary of a contract which had come about between the expert valuer and the Danish Consul. For this purpose it is not necessary to spell out an express or an implied agreement between the promisor (the valuer) and the promisee (the Danish Consul) as to the inclusion of the third party (the bank) in the sphere of protection of this contract, for the expert could have foreseen that his statement would serve as a basis for an investment decision. In the abstract the decisive question may be reduced to the following formula: is the group of persons to be contractually protected capable of description by objective standards?[18] It goes without saying that this criterion is more easily formulated than applied to concrete situations. This can be compared with the difficult question as to the scope and limits of the varied duties of care with which the House of Lords was recently confronted in the *Caparo* case.[19]

Before going on and concentrating on factual situations where the parties intended to confer upon a third party a direct claim to demand performance of the primary obligation, it should be mentioned that the *Vertrag mit Schutzwirkung für Dritte* is also recognized in American law. The Uniform Commercial Code s. 2-318 thus provides for 'third party beneficiaries of warranties express or implied' which includes a provision that 'a seller may not exclude or limit the effect of this section'.

2   The Case Law Relating to Third-Party Beneficiaries

2.1   *Retirement Benefits and Widows' Pensions under Private Law Agreements*

For the sake of comparison it may be helpful to begin with a factual situation which presents the problem that confronted the House of Lords in *Beswick* v. *Beswick*.[20] It will be recalled that in that case a coal merchant had assigned to his nephew the assets of his business, and the nephew undertook first to pay the uncle a certain sum of money per week for the remainder of his life and then to pay the uncle's wife an annuity in the

---

[17] Bundesgerichtshof, 23 Jan. 1985, JZ 1985, 951. See also the previous decision of this court in the same matter dated 28 Aug. 1982, NJW 1982, 2431. English translation in Markesinis, *The German Law of Torts*, 2nd edn. (1990), 218.

[18] In German: '. . . sofern die zu schützende Personengruppe objektiv abgrenzbar ist.'

[19] *Caparo Industries PLC.* v. *Dickman* [1990] 2 AC 605.

[20] *Beswick* v. *Beswick* [1968] AC 58.

event of his death. After the husband's death, which occurred during the following year, the nephew made just one weekly payment to the widow, and then refused to make any further payments. The widow's action succeeded because she had a right, as administratrix of her husband's estate, to require her husband's nephew to perform his obligation under the agreement. As a mere contract beneficiary, however, she would not have been successful since the contract made by her husband with his nephew did not confer on her a direct right of action.[21]

In German law Mrs Beswick could have sued the promisor by relying on para. 328(1) BGB. This has repeatedly been accepted by the Federal Labour Court (*Bundesarbeitsgericht*), the labour courts exercising jurisdiction whenever the claim originates from labour relations. It must be emphasized, however, that this is not limited to labour law only. The decision would not have been different if—in a fact situation like *Beswick* v. *Beswick*—the Federal Supreme Court (*Bundesgerichtshof*) had been the court of last instance because the dispute was not related to labour relations. Since 1966 it has been clearly established that the contract of employment between employer (promisor) and employee (promisee) is to be regarded as a contract in favour of a third party if it contains a stipulation to the effect that a widow's pension will be paid after the employee's death.[22] In another case, decided by the Federal Labour Court concerning retirement payments, the employer had founded a registered association for the sole purpose of paying extra pensions to employees, the amount of which varied according to the period of their employment.[23] Upon his retirement, an employee brought an action against this association claiming a certain amount believed to be due to him under the articles of association. In the opinion of the court this claim was based upon a contract between the employer and the association in favour of retiring employees (para. 328(1) BGB). For the sake of clarity it should be pointed out that these cases have nothing to do with pensions payable under the general social insurance legislation. The money paid in accordance with these private agreements is in addition to social insurance.

[21] After having quoted from the recommendation of the Law Revision Committee (1937-Cmnd. 5449, 31), which would have enabled the widow to enforce the nephew's promise in her own name, Lord Reid (loc. cit. at 72) expressed his disappointment with what he called 'Parliamentary procrastination'. The foreign observer wonders why the House of Lords has not made use of the freedom given to it by the 'Practice Statement' of 1966. (References to further criticisms levelled against the English doctrine of privity as well as proposals for reform can now be found in The Law Commission's Consultation Paper No. 121 on 'Privity of Contract: Contracts for the Benefit of Third Parties', HMSO 1991. Interestingly enough the Commission's Paper makes extensive use of foreign (including German) material.)

[22] Bundesarbeitsgericht 21 Oct. 1966, NJW 1967, 173; see also Bundesarbeitsgericht 5 Sept. 1972, NJW 1973, 963.

[23] Bundesarbeitsgericht 17 May 1973, NJW 1973, 1946. This association (*Unterstütz-ungskasse*) was a legal entity under para. 55 *et seq.* BGB.

2.2   *Parents Contracting with Physicians for the Treatment of Their Child*

In one of the more recent decisions of the Federal Supreme Court concerning medical malpractice a four-months-old girl had been in urgent need of a kidney operation.[24] Her parents consulted a university hospital. Leaving aside details of the somewhat complicated legal relations that exist in some cases of admission to State-owned hospitals, it is important to realize that directors and chief surgeons of such public institutions are allowed, within certain limits, to make contracts for the private treatment of patients. In the instant case the parents of the child had made such a contract with the director of the urological clinic. The operation was successful, but due to a negligent omission in the phase of post-operative care, the child suffered serious and lasting injuries. The case is complicated, not least by the fact that two different departments of the hospital were involved: the urological clinic and the paediatric clinic. Here, suffice it to say that the urologist, who had carried out the operation, was also held responsible for the proper post-operative care.

The child's action succeeded because the contract for medical treatment concluded by the parents in their own name with the director of the urological clinic was regarded as a contract in favour of the child. In German law it is well established that a minor whose parents arrange for his medical treatment is a contract beneficiary within the meaning of para. 328(1) BGB.[25] However, the present case deserves special attention in so far as the parents had joined in this action personal claims for their own costs of looking after the disabled child. This action, too, was successful. This solution is not as obvious as might seem at first sight. Whether a contract in favour of a third party includes the protection of the promisee's interests as well is, ultimately, a question of construction to be determined by the facts of each case. Since this question is beyond the scope of this paper, however, it will not be discussed here.

2.3   *Savings Accounts: Third Person as Account Holder*

Legal problems arising in connection with savings banks books and third parties are no peculiarity of German law. In *Birch* v. *Treasury Solicitor*[26] the Court of Appeal was confronted with a situation which is typical of the kind of problems with which German courts have to deal from time to time. What makes these cases so difficult is the interaction of the law

---

[24] Bundesgerichtshof 10 Jan. 1984, BGHZ 89, 263.

[25] See Münchener Kommentar (- Gottwald), *Bürgerliches Gesetzbuch*, 2nd edn. (1985) para. ii: 328, n. 30.   [26] [1951] 1 Ch. 298 (CA).

of obligations with the law of succession. The *donatio mortis causa* raises its formidable head. In the English case an elderly lady who had been injured in a road accident was staying in hospital. Her husband had already died and she was without relatives. When the nephew of her husband and his wife visited her in hospital she told them to go to her flat in order to get a black bag containing several savings bank books. She allowed them to take these books home and to keep them, saying 'If anything happens to me I want you and Frank to have the money in the banks'. These were the decisive words on which the judgment proceeded. Lord Evershed, MR, delivering the opinion of the court, raised three questions. (At least two of which would have been relevant if the case had to be decided by a German court). First, whether there was a sufficient 'delivery' to the two plaintiffs of the savings bank books to constitute a gift. Second, whether there was the requisite *animus donandi*. Third, whether it was sufficient to hand over the indicia of title, choses in action being incapable themselves of delivery.[27] All of these questions having been answered in the affirmative, the plaintiff's action succeeded against the Treasury Solicitor acting as administrator *ad colligenda bona* of the deceased's estate.

Turning now to German law it is necessary to distinguish between *donatio mortis causa* (para. 2301 BGB) and performance in favour of a third party to be made upon the death of the promisee (para. 331 BGB). Under para. 2301(1) BGB the promise of a gift which is made subject to the condition that the donee shall survive the donor is valid only if it satisfies the formal requirements of the law of succession upon death. What is needed, therefore, is a contract of inheritance (*Erbvertrag*) which must be authenticated by a notary (para. 2276 BGB). However, para. 2301(2) BGB makes an important exception to this rule: 'If the donor executes the gift by delivery of the object given, the provisions relating to gifts *inter vivos* apply.' This is a reference to para. 518 BGB concerning the form of a promise of a gift. Such promises, in order to be legally valid, are also subject to notarial authentication. But any defect of form is cured by the performance of the promise. Therefore delivery of the subject-matter of the gift, if made *animo donandi*, would be a valid gift *inter vivos*. However, in the present case the subject-matter of the gift is a chose in action not being capable of 'delivery' and therefore the decisive question is whether there had been

---

[27] But see also *Sen* v. *Headley*, [1990] 1 Ch 728. The deceased, who formerly had lived with the plaintiff for ten years, had tried to make an informal gift of land: 'The house is yours, Margaret, You have the keys. They are in your bag. The deeds are in the steel box.' It was held by Mummery, J that mere delivery of title deeds to land could not establish a legal or equitable title in the donee, because the donor had failed to part with dominion over the subject-matter of the gift. An informal gift of land does not comply with the Law of Property Act 1925 or the Wills Act 1837. It is different where a savings bank book is handed over *donandi causa*. This amounts to a transfer so that the possessor is entitled to the money.

an assignment.[28] Since the savings bank book is a mere document of debt within the meaning of para. 952 BGB, ownership of the book belongs to the creditor, i.e. the assignee. In other words, delivery of the savings bank book is merely of evidentiary significance because it serves as an indication of an assignment. The position of both English and German law may, perhaps, be stated thus: *donatio mortis causa* of personal property, tangible as well as intangible, is not subject to the formalities of the law of wills if it is executed by delivery (in case of movables) or by assignment (in case of a chose in action).

In German law, however, difficult questions have arisen in cases where savings accounts had been opened by somebody nominating a third person as beneficiary. In 1966 the Federal Supreme Court had to deal with such a case.[29] A grandmother had paid a substantial amount into two savings bank accounts nominating her grandchild as account holder. The savings bank books were still in her possession when she died. Moreover, she had not told her grandchild of the savings intended for her benefit. Did the money belong to the grandchild or was it still part of the estate of her grandmother? In the latter case it would have been the common property of three daughters of the deceased in their capacity as statutory co-heirs. When the defendant, one of the daughters, took possession of the savings bank books, the grandchild brought an action against her demanding their delivery. This action would have been successful if the plaintiff had been the account holder (paras. 985, 952 BGB).[30]

The case raises the difficult question whether this was a *donatio mortis causa* (para. 2301 BGB) or a contract in favour of a third party, stipulating performance upon the death of the promisee (para. 331 BGB). If para. 2301 BGB were to be applied to a case of this type, the grandchild would not be entitled to the money in the bank because neither the provisions relating to the form of dispositions *mortis causa* were satisfied nor had the gift been executed *inter vivos* by assignment evidenced by delivery of the savings bank books. But the grandchild might be in a more favourable

---

[28] See paras. 398 *et seq.* BGB. A chose in action may, by contract with another person, be assigned by the creditor to him. On the conclusion of the contract the assignee takes the place of the assignor. The debtor need not be notified of the assignment, but if he did not know of the assignment he is entitled to assume that the creditor has not changed (paras. 407, 408 BGB). For this reason an assignee is well advised to notify the debtor forthwith. However, in the case of a savings account, possession of the savings account book is both necessary and sufficient for withdrawing money from the account (para. 808 BGB).

[29] Bundesgerichtshof 9 Nov. 1966, BGHZ 46, 198.

[30] Para. 985 BGB replicates the Roman *rei vindicatio*: (The owner can demand from the possessor the delivery of the thing.) This presupposes, of course, that the possessor cannot raise any objections within the meaning of para. 986 BGB. But in the present case there is no reason for a right to the possession of the savings bank book which could be opposed to the owner. Para. 952 BGB, already mentioned in the text above, states that ownership of a written acknowledgement of debt drawn up for a claim belongs to the creditor.

legal position if para. 331 BGB would apply because the courts are inclined to give priority to this provision in case of conflict with para. 2301
BGB. This case-law development began in 1923 when the former
Reichsgericht held that the regular forms of wills need not be observed if
there was an agreement between the customer and the savings bank with
the effect that upon the death of the payor the money he had paid into his
account should become the property of a third party.[31] This means that the
beneficiary acquires the right to the performance upon the death of the
promisee. The law of succession upon death is thereby ousted. The Federal
Supreme Court has continued along these lines. But in the case of the
grandchild the court was confronted with a difficult question of construction because the savings bank books had always been in the possession of
the deceased. Moreover, she had not told the beneficiary of the money she
had deposited for her. Therefore the case had to be sent back to the court
below for further fact-finding, the decisive question being whether the
deceased had the intention to stipulate performance for the benefit of her
grandchild within the meaning of para. 331 BGB when she made the
contract with the savings bank.

It is not surprising that this tendency to give priority to para. 331 BGB
and to neglect para. 2301 BGB has met with severe criticism in German
legal literature. Although this discussion cannot be repeated here in detail,
at least two points which have emerged in this controversy should be
mentioned briefly. First, the formal requirements of the law of wills are by-
passed at the expense of certainty in the law. The case of the savings bank
books, nominating the grandchild as account holder, shows the evidentiary
difficulties inherent in para. 331 BGB, since the person on whose intention
the case turns is no longer alive. Second, serious problems will arise with
regard to the distribution of assets if creditors of the estate must be satisfied. This leads to the strange consequence that the third-party beneficiary may be in a better position than close relatives who are, by law,
entitled to compulsory portions (*Pflichtteilsberechtigte*).[32] Other creditors
of the estate are in an even worse position; for they must try to contest the
disposition in favour of the third party by special proceedings aiming at
the attachment of the gift of money (*nemo liberalis nisi liberatus*).[33]

[31] Reichsgericht 8 Feb. 1923, RGZ 106, 1. The deceased had reserved the right to with-
draw the money at any time and without the consent of the named beneficiary. But it is
important to note that the deceased had handed over the savings bank book to the beneficiary
before she died.

[32] In a case like this, the compulsory portion may be supplemented by demanding from the
recipient the surrender of the gift. This claim is based upon a theory of unjust enrichment
(cf. paras. 2325, 2329 BGB).

[33] Such proceedings may be initiated if the debtor has acted to the disadvantage of his
creditors, especially where he has made gifts to third persons. The *Anfechtungsgesetz* as well
as the *Konkursordnung* have laid down exact time-limits within which creditors may contest
such dispositions of the debtor.

2.4 *Carriage of Persons in Connection with the Services of Travel Agencies*

It happens very often that travel agents, who are obliged by the travel con-tract (*Reisevertrag*) to provide a number of travel services for the traveller (para. 651a(1) BGB), have made a contract with an airline for carriage of their customers. In a contract such as this the airline company places a fixed number of seats for a certain flight at the disposal of the travel agent (charterer). The charterer, who issues air tickets to the travellers, does not necessarily act as an agent of the airline. Nevertheless, the traveller acquires a right to demand performance from the airline. This follows from a construction of the contract between the airline and the travel agency. In view of the object of the contract, the airline, which has promised the charterer to transport the travellers to their destination, is *deemed* to have stipulated that they acquire the direct right to demand performance, i.e. they are regarded as contract beneficiaries within the meaning of para. 328 BGB.[34]

In 1985 the Federal Supreme Court had to deal with a case which deserves special attention partly because it provides an example of what we are considering here, but also because it offers an illustration of the extent to which the defences that the promisor has against the promisee are also available against the third party.[35] In view of the clear wording of para. 334 BGB this last point seems to be obvious. Since the beneficiary's right is based upon the contract between the promisor and the promisee, it is generally subject to all defences arising out of that contract that the promisor may have against the promisee. For present purposes the some-what complicated situation may be conveniently simplified without fear of distortion. A travel agency had chartered a number of seats for a flight from Frankfurt am Main to Santa Lucia in the Caribbean. When two travellers, who had made a contract with this travel agency, checked in for their flight back to Germany, employees of the airline refused to accept them as passengers because in the meantime the travel agency had become insolvent and was unable to pay for the tickets which had already been paid for by the travellers. The travellers were thus obliged to buy tickets from another airline for their return journey to Frankfurt. They were reimbursed by an insurance company which, in turn, brought an action against the airline based upon *cessio legis*. The action succeeded.

The travellers were regarded as third-party beneficiaries of the contract made between the airline and the travel agency. In this way it did not matter whether or not the tickets were issued by the travel bureau as

---

[34] For this proposition see Bundesgerichtshof 24 June 1969, BGHZ 52, 194 (201–2) where this construction seems to have been applied for the first time.

[35] Bundesgerichtshof 17 Jan. 1985, BGHZ 93, 271.

agents for the airline. Since the contract between the airline and the travel agency is made in the interest of the travellers, the parties must be presumed to have conferred upon them the right to demand direct performance (para. 328(2) BGB). In construing this contract the court took a bold step further by holding that the provision of para. 334 BGB (which is not mandatory) did not apply in this case. As a result of this the promisor could not plead failure of performance on the part of the promisee. Again, this is based upon a construction of the particular contract. An airline contracting with a travel agency must be aware of the fact that travellers usually have to pay in advance. They are not required to understand the somewhat complicated legal relations existing between the parties. Therefore they are entitled to expect that the airline will not plead failure of performance because it did not receive payment from the travel agency. 'It is within its sphere of risk to see to it that payments made by travellers for their flight are received in time', is the sentence concluding the reasoning of the court.[36]

2.5 Sale of Goods: Manufacturer's Warranty of Quality for the Benefit of Third Parties

There exist some cases in which a contract for the benefit of a third party has been deemed to have been made by a manufacturer who sold his goods to a dealer before they reached the ultimate buyer. These cases, however, form the exception and not the rule. Normally the seller of goods warrants to the buyer that, at the time when the risk passes to the buyer, the goods are free from defects which diminish or destroy their value or fitness for their ordinary use, or the use provided for in the contract (para. 459(1) BGB). The ultimate buyer who buys from a retailer cannot sue the manufacturer if his goods do not meet with this standard of quality. He must seek relief from the retailer who, in turn, may recover from the manufacturer.[37] However, it may be different if a manufacturer expressly warrants that the goods he sells possess certain qualities. Such warranties are open to the construction that the manufacturer has made a binding offer of a special contract of guarantee (*Garantievertrag*) to the ultimate buyer who accepted this offer by acting upon it (para. 151 BGB).[38] Thus, a motor car manufacturer who issued certificates of guarantee addressed to the ultimate buyer ('to whom it may concern'), that defects reported within one year after the purchase of the car will be repaired, and defective

---

[36] See n. 35, above, 276.

[37] Bundesgerichtshof 18 June 1968, NJW 1968, 1929: the ultimate buyer is not normally a third-party beneficiary of the contract between the first seller and the intermediate buyer.

[38] Para. 151 BGB regards a contract as having been concluded by the acceptance of the offer, without the necessity that the offeror be notified of the acceptance, if such notification is not to be expected according to common usage, or if the offeror has waived it.

parts will be replaced free of charge, is under a contractual obligation *vis-à-vis* the buyer even though the car was bought from a dealer.[39]

It would thus appear that in cases of this type the desired result can be reached without having recourse to contracts for the benefit of third persons. However, in 1979 the Federal Supreme Court had to deal with a factual situation which did not permit this construction of a direct contract of guarantee concluded simultaneously with the sale of the goods. The reason for this was that the manufacturer's representations as to the qualities of certain special sheets of glass produced by him were contained in a pamphlet headed '*Garantie*' which came to the attention of the ultimate buyer five years after he had purchased the goods from an intermediate seller.[40] In this context one should be reminded that under German law it is possible to become a third-party beneficiary without being aware of it. This is implicit in para. 333 BGB which states that the third party may reject, by declaration to the promisor, the right acquired under the contract. If he rejects it, the right is deemed not to have been acquired. In this case, therefore, the ultimate buyer's ignorance of the '*Garantie*' did not, as a matter of principle, preclude him from taking advantage of it. But a decisive question still had to be answered namely, could the manufacturer and the middleman be taken to have intended to conclude a collateral contract of guarantee for the benefit of a third party? In a case such as this, the idea is not as far-fetched as it might seem at first sight, for it must have been in the interest of the middleman (promisee) to make such a contract because a guarantee of quality in favour of the last buyer would mean direct liability of the manufacturer (promisor) if the glass was defective. For all practical purposes, therefore, (though not as a matter of law), the middleman will be exonerated in such cases and the liability will fall on the party whose promise of guarantee was meant to promote sales of his product to ultimate users. It must, however, be admitted that such contracts for the benefit of a third party represent an 'emergency construction' for those cases in which a direct contractual relationship between the manufacturer and the ultimate buyer cannot be spelled out.

2.6 Sale of Land: Restrictive Covenants for the Benefit of Neighbours

Restrictive covenants always impose purely negative duties on the owner of land, e.g. not to use land for a certain purpose, such as building a

---

[39] Bundesgerichtshof 12 Nov. 1980, BGHZ 78, 369.

[40] Bundesgerichtshof 28 June 1979, BGHZ 75, 75 (reproduced in translated form in Markesinis, *The German Law of Torts*, 2nd edn. (1990), 379–82). In this '*Garantie*' the manufacturer promised that under normal conditions of use these sheets of glass ('ISOLAR-Glas') would remain fully transparent and no dust would penetrate the space left between these sheets. This guarantee was operative for a period of five years which began to run from the moment of the first delivery. The manufacturer promised to replace defective units of 'ISOLAR-Glas' free of charge.

factory or carrying on any trade which would be undesirable in a residential area. The safest way of binding a landowner to such a duty is, of course, a real servitude (*Grunddienstbarkeit*) which the owner of the dominant land can enforce against the owner of the servient land (para. 1018 BGB). Such real servitudes are subject to registration in the Land Register (para. 873(1) BGB). In this way, a right *in rem* is conferred upon the owner of the dominant land.

The present essay is not concerned with problems pertaining to the law of real property. Rather, we are concerned with the question whether restrictive covenants may also take the form of mere contracts between vendors and purchasers of land. In 1974 the Federal Supreme Court had to deal with an action brought by the owner of land against the owner of adjoining land. The complaint was that the neighbour had erected a building which was one metre higher than permitted under the local development plan.[41] Cases of this kind will generally give rise to actions in administrative law. The citizen burdened by an administrative action will contest the validity of this action before the administrative court. The instant case, however, concerned a civil action in which the local development plan was important only insofar as the contract of sale made with the purchaser of the land on which the building had been erected contained an express reference to the provision of this plan in regard to the permissible height of buildings. The court left open the question whether the defendant was liable to the plaintiff in damages. A possible basis for such a claim might have been para. 823, II BGB.[42] But the court hesitated to regard as a *Schutzgesetz* the provision in the local development plan prescribing a maximum height for buildings in a certain residential area, even though the purpose of the relevant provision was to prevent landowners from obstructing the view of their neighbours.

In the opinion of the Federal Supreme Court the judgment of the court of appeal dismissing the action had misapplied para. 328 *et seq*. BGB. The obligation undertaken by the purchaser of the land to refrain from erecting a building which was higher than six metres might very well have been stipulated for the benefit of a third party. Although this would not be the main obligation of a purchaser of a plot of land, it could nevertheless be part of his primary obligation to perform which must be distinguished from secondary obligations giving rise to a 'contract with protective effects *vis-à-vis* third parties' (see above). Therefore it did not matter that in the opinion of the court below the obligation to refrain from acting in a certain way could not be characterized as a 'duty of protection' (*Schutzpflicht*).

[41] Bundesgerichtshof 29 Nov. 1974, NJW 1975, 344.
[42] In Germany a local development plan (*Bebauungsplan*) worked out by a District Council (*Gemeinderat/Stadtrat*) is a municipal bye-law (*Ortssatzung*). (The text of para. 823 II BGB is given in n. 9, above.)

For this reason the case had to be sent back to the court of appeal for further fact-finding: what did the parties intend when they incorporated in their contract of sale the provision of the development plan concerning the maximum height of buildings? This question had to be decided in applying the rule of construction laid down in para. 328(2) BGB.

2.7   *Trustees and Third-Party Beneficiaries*

For the sake of clarity it is necessary to start with a warning. In English law the doctrine of privity militates against the proposition that a stranger to a contract may found an action upon it. However, attempts have been made to avoid this rigid rule, so it seems that in certain instances the rule can be modified by the equitable doctrine of the constructive trust. In a case where A has promised B to pay money to C, the promisee would then have to be regarded as trustee for the third party of the benefit of the contract with the promisor. It is true that the subject-matter of a trust is normally some tangible property or a definite sum of money, but it is doubtful whether one can speak of the 'trust of a promise'.[43] The present writer does not wish to express an opinion as to the state of English case law in this matter. The problem is mentioned only in order to avoid a misunderstanding. For in German law, where contracts for the benefit of third parties are recognized, the function of a trustee in connection with third-party beneficiaries is different in at least one important respect. In the relevant cases the trustee (*Treuhänder*) has always been in the position of a *promisor* against whom a third-party beneficiary within the meaning of para. 328 BGB could bring an action. The problem usually surfaces in situations where a debtor has become insolvent. The cases which have come before the court are mostly concerned with complicated situations which cannot and need not be discussed here. Accepting the risk, of over-simplification they will be presented in an abstract manner.

The first case in which a trustee was regarded as a promisor in the context of a contract for the benefit of a third party arose in 1927. A company had received a large sum of money from a bank as a loan which was secured by several land charges (*Grundschulden*). The company had constituted these encumbrances for the benefit of a trustee who had to hold them in trust for the creditors of the company. For all practical purposes the effect of this settlement was that the creditors were in a position that could be compared with mortgagees. In case of non-payment of the debt these creditors could have demanded satisfaction out of the pieces of land to which the land charges extended. In the opinion of the Supreme Court the creditors were third-party beneficiaries within the

---

[43] See the discussion of this problem in Cheshire, Fifoot, and Furmston's *Law of Contract*, 12th edn. (1991), 456 *et seq.*

meaning of para. 328 BGB, the trustee having been in the position of a promisor.[44]

In 1966 this idea was taken up by the Federal Supreme Court in a case concerning the winding up of a business. The owner of a restaurant, who was also dealing in several commodities, had run into financial difficulties. He had transferred parts of his estate to his principal creditors in order to achieve an accord and satisfaction. For this purpose he had commissioned his tax consultant to act as trustee in the winding-up proceedings. In the opinion of the court the fiduciary relationship between the debtor and the trustee had resulted in a contract for the benefit of the creditors. In this context the court speaks of a 'two-sided trusteeship' (*doppelseitige Treuhand*) because the trustee is deemed to have fiduciary relations with the creditors as well.[45] There are at least two more reported decisions of the Federal Supreme Court concerning winding-up proceedings for the purpose of reaching an accord and satisfaction (*Liquidationsvergleich*) where the fiduciary relationship between the debtor and the trustee was regarded as a contract for the benefit of the creditors who thereby acquire the right directly to demand performance from the trustee.[46] But it should be remembered that creditors need not accept this arrangement made by the debtor. They may reject it (para. 333 BGB).

2.8 *Maintenance Agreements for the Benefit of Children*

The problem to be considered here arises mainly in connection with divorce. If after the divorce, one of the spouses is unable to provide for his or her own maintenance, he or she is entitled to claim maintenance from the other spouse (para. 1569 BGB). Details of the rather complicated provisions implementing this principle can be omitted here, but reference must be made to para. 1570 BGB: a divorced spouse may demand maintenance from the other as long as (and to the extent that) he or she cannot be expected to pursue gainful employment by reason of having to care for or to educate a common child. The child has, of course, a claim of its own under the general rule governing the duty of maintenance according to which relatives in direct line are obliged to furnish maintenance to each other (para. 1601 BGB). A minor unmarried child, even if he owns property, is entitled

---

[44] Reichsgericht 25 May 1927, RGZ 117, 143, 149. It should be added that the original creditor (i.e. the bank) was entitled to assign the claim either wholly or in part. As a result of several such assignments (*Teilabtretungen*) the identity of the creditors could not be determined in advance. The appointment of a trustee must be seen against this background.

[45] Bundesgerichtshof 14 Mar. 1966, NJW 1966, 1116.

[46] Bundesgerichtshof 29 Nov. 1973, BGHZ 62, 1, 3; Bundesgerichtshof 12 Oct. 1989, BGHZ 109, 47, 52. See also Bundesgerichtshof 10 Feb. 1971, BGHZ 55, 307, 309 where the same was held in connection with bankruptcy proceedings. However, in a situation like this, the trustee in bankruptcy (*Konkursverwalter*) may contest the dispositions of property made by the trustee whom the debtor had previously appointed.

to demand maintenance from his parents to the extent that the income from his property and earnings from his work are insufficient for his maintenance (para. 1602(2) BGB). Leaving aside certain modifications, this applies to the maintenance claim of illegitimate children as well (para. 1615(a) BGB). In actual legal practice agreements as to the maintenance obligations for the period after divorce are frequent. The Civil Code permits them (para. 1585(c) BGB). It may happen then that the parties make provisions also for the future maintenance of their children. In such cases the question has arisen whether the child may be regarded as a third-party beneficiary of such agreements. This is important if the maintenance agreement of its parents yields more than would be due to the child *ex lege*. Quite apart from that, it helps to avoid litigation if the maintenance obligation has already been fixed in advance.

In 1952 the Federal Supreme Court had to deal with a written agreement between the father and the mother of a child born out of wedlock. The father had committed himself to make monthly payments for the maintenance of the child. This was regarded as a contract for the benefit of the child which gave the mother a right directly to demand performance. The right of the mother to bring this action in her own name followed from para. 335 BGB: the promisee may, unless a contrary intention of the contracting parties is to be presumed, demand performance in favour of the third party, even if it is the latter who has the right to the performance.[47] A review of more recent cases shows, however, that the Federal Supreme Court hesitates to construe such maintenance agreements as contracts in favour of the children. This is evidenced by at least two reported decisions which concerned maintenance agreements made in the course of divorce proceedings by way of judicial compromise (*Prozessvergleich*).[48] Needless to say, such agreements cannot deprive a child of its claim of maintenance granted by the Civil Code. This being so, the suggestion has already been made in the legal literature that one should not recognize such agreements unless they give a child more than would be payable at law. There is also the fear that such agreements are not necessarily in the best interest of children when it comes to the question whether they may claim larger sums for their maintenance if supervening events have upset the economic basis of the compromise. Moreover, there may be complicated procedural problems in connection with para. 323 Code of Civil Procedure, which grants an action for setting aside judgments and other court orders concerning performances, recurring in the future if there has been a significant change of circumstances since the time when such performances were fixed. In view of the above, it seems unlikely

---

[47] Bundesgerichtshof 3 Apr. 1952, BGHZ 5, 302.
[48] Bundesgerichtshof 16 Jan. 1980, FamRZ 1980, 342; Bundesgerichtshof 17 Mar. 1982, NJW 1983, 684, 685.

that maintenance agreements making provisions for children will readily be regarded as contracts for the benefit of third parties.

2.9 *Insurance Contracts Stipulating Performance to a Third Party*

Even a brief look at para. 328 *et seq.* BGB will suffice to show that insurance contracts in favour of third parties are the paradigm of contracts for the benefit of third parties as conceived by the German legislature. Thus, para. 330 BGB expressly mentions the contract for life insurance (*Lebensversicherungsvertrag*) in which payment of the sum insured is stipulated for the benefit of a third party. In this type of contract it is to be presumed, in case of doubt, that the third party acquires the right directly to demand payment. This rule of construction is supplemented by para. 331(1) BGB: if the performance in favour of the third party is to be made after the death of the person to whom it was promised, the third party in case of doubt acquires the right to the performance upon the death of the promisee.

Shortly after the coming into force of the Civil Code the Supreme Court was given an opportunity to decide a typical case which reveals the social conflict inherent in these provisions. In 1900 a merchant made a contract for life insurance in favour of his wife. After his death, which occurred in 1901, bankruptcy proceedings were instituted against his estate. The trustee in bankruptcy claimed the sum insured for the estate, but the widow insisted that it should be paid to her.[49] It was held that she was entitled to the money. The creditors of the deceased, for whom the trustee in bankruptcy had claimed the sum insured, were left empty-handed. The court arrived at this conclusion by combining para. 330 BGB with para. 331(1) BGB. Such an insurance contract grants the third party a direct right of action (*unmittelbares Klagerecht*). However, the right to the performance is not acquired until the promisee has died. Until that moment, the intended beneficiary has nothing but the hope of getting the sum insured, which is less than a right subject to a condition. What is a mere chance, ripens into a right upon the death of the promisee who had regulated this property in such a way that it did not become part of his estate. The beneficiary thus has no claim against the estate of the deceased. The third party (beneficiary) acquires the right to the performance directly by reason of the contract between the insurance company and the policy holder. This construction of the Code provisions makes good sense and seems to be in keeping with the intention of the legislature. Contracts for life insurance for the benefit of a third party—usually a family member —are 'maintenance contracts' (*Versorgungsverträge*). This being so, it is

---

[49] Reichsgericht 3 June 1902, RGZ 51, 403.

sound legal policy to make the beneficiary's right to such maintenance independent of the distribution of the assets of the deceased, for otherwise, experience suggests, there may be unpleasant disputes or even litigation among heirs. All this is avoided if the beneficiary receives the money directly and without any delay.

The decisions of the Federal Court have not departed from these lines.[50] The rules of construction laid down in paras. 330, 331(1) BGB apply to all types of contracts for life insurance (lump sum or annuity), but if no beneficiary is nominated in the contract, the sum insured becomes part of the estate of the deceased.

It may happen, however, that the promisee has designated his heirs as beneficiaries without mentioning their names. In such circumstances, does the sum insured belong to the estate of the deceased? The question is by no means otiose. Suppose the estate turns out to be insolvent? In such a case the heirs must be careful not to be held liable for the debts incurred by the deceased and other obligations imposed upon the heirs as such. The easiest way to get rid of all liability would be to exercise the right of disclaiming the inheritance (paras. 1942 *et seq.* BGB: *Ausschlagung der Erbschaft*). But what will be the effect upon their claim to the sum insured? The first case in which the promisee had made such a contract for life insurance 'in favour of my heirs' (*zugunsten meiner Erben*) came before the German Supreme Court in 1906. It was held that this was clear enough and equivalent to mentioning the beneficiaries by their names.[51] This result was reached after careful consideration of its merits and demerits. The court took great pains in order to show that a previous decision of another division of the court did not stand in the way of such a conclusion, because it was a judgment which was passed several years before the Civil Code came into force and which had been based upon the Prussian Code of 1794.[52] The decision of 1906 anticipated a rule which a few years later was incorporated in para. 167(2) of the Law relating to Insurance Contracts: the promisee may stipulate payment of the sum insured 'to the heirs' without further explanation. A disclaimer of inheritance does not negate their right to the performance.[53] This law has also introduced a special rule in regard to the nomination of the beneficiary under a lump sum insurance. The promisee may at any time substitute another for the party named in the contract without the consent of the promisor (i.e. the insurance company).[54] It goes almost without saying that no consent of

---

[50] Bundesgerichtshof 8 May 1954, BGHZ 13, 226, 232. Bundesgerichtshof 8 Feb. 1960, BGHZ 32, 44, 47.   [51] Reichsgericht 5 Jan. 1906, RGZ 62, 259.

[52] Reichsgericht 26 Jan. 1894, RGZ 32, 162.

[53] Versicherungsvertragsgesetz (henceforth VVG) first promulgated 30 May 1908, Reichsgesetzblatt I 1908, 263.   [54] Para. 166(1) VVG.

the third party is required for such a change, even though he or she was named in the contract.[55] As long as the promisee is alive the third party has a mere chance, but no right, to receive the sum insured.[56]

The foreign observer of English law notices with some interest that in the area of insurance law the rigour of the common law doctrine has been considerably modified by Acts of Parliament. The Married Women's Property Act 1882 is an outstanding example of this special legislation. The policy taken out by a husband in favour of his wife is regarded as a trust for her benefit. The legal effect of section 11 is comparable to paras. 330, 331(1) BGB; the moneys payable under such policy do not form part of the estate of the insured. Without such statutory intervention there would be no trust, for the insured could have changed the destination of the money at any time.[57]

2.10 *Miscellaneous Types of Contracts for the Benefit of Third Parties*

The preceding survey of some of the more important types of contracts in favour of third parties is not complete. The reason for this is that there is no *numerus clausus* of such contracts. The relevant code provisions are framed in general terms so as to permit the creation of all possible obligations in favour of third parties within the range of freedom of contracting. The subsequent remarks are meant to supplement the above survey by mentioning briefly a few more situations giving rise to a contract in favour of a third party.

1 Contracts for the carriage of goods are normally contracts for work and labour within the meaning of paras. 631 *et seq.* BGB (*Werkvertrag*). But the general provisions of the Civil Code merely form the basis for such contracts which are subject to special rules contained in the Commercial Code (paras. 425 *et seq.* HGB). In the present context para. 435 HGB is the most important provision: the consignee acquires the rights of the consignor against the carrier upon arrival of the goods at their destination if he fulfils the obligations arising from the contract. The right to demand delivery of the consignment note together with the goods is expressly mentioned. This includes the right to claim damages in his own

---

[55] Para. 166(2) VVG. Compare this special rule with the general rule in para. 332 BGB: If the promisee has reserved to himself the right of substituting another person for the party named in the contract without the consent of the named third party, this may also be done, in case of doubt, by disposition *mortis causa*.

[56] See n. 49, above. The German Supreme Court (loc. cit. 404) called it a 'mere hope' (*nur eine Hoffnung*).

[57] See the remarks of Lord Esher in *Cleaver* v. *Mutual Reserve Fund Life Association*, [1892] 1 QB 147, 152.

name if forwarding was unduly delayed or if damage was done to the goods on their way to the consignee.[58]

This right does not depend upon ownership in the goods which, for various reasons, may not yet have passed to the claimant.

The solution to which para. 453 HGB leads is closely related to a legal institution called *Drittschadensliquidation* which has been recognized in German law for a long time. An important group of cases are solved by invoking this rule which concerns the distribution of risk prevailing in sales law. Take the case of a buyer who has requested the seller to dispatch the goods sold to a place other than the place of performance. According to para. 447 BGB, the risk passes to the buyer as soon as the seller has delivered the goods to the forwarder, freighter etc., but the property in the goods is not normally transferred to the buyer until delivery. Thus, the seller still has a claim against the person who damaged the goods during transmission even though he has suffered no loss. The buyer, on the other hand, has suffered a loss, but has no valid claim. In 1906 the first case of this type came before the German Supreme Court. It was held that the seller can recover from the wrongdoer in order to pay the money over to the buyer, or that the seller may assign his claim to the buyer.[59] The seller is even obliged to assign his claim if the buyer so demands. This solution derives some support from para. 281(1) BGB dealing with the consequences of impossibility of performance: if the debtor acquires a substitute or a claim of compensation for the object owed, the creditor may demand delivery of the substitute received or assignment of the claim for compensation. From a comparative point of view it is interesting to see that in English law the problem of 'transferred loss' (see above) presents itself in a similar way. Lord Justice Goff, as he then was, has analysed it with such admirable clarity in his judgment in *The Aliakmon* that it seems impossible to improve on his reasoning. In his opinion the buyer should be entitled, subject to the terms of any contract restricting the wrongdoer's liability to the seller, to bring an action in tort against the wrongdoer.[60]

---

[58] Bundesgerichtshof 9 Nov. 1981, BGHZ 82, 162, 170. See also the following decisions applying Art. 17 CMR (i.e. Convention relative au contrat de transport international de marchandises par route): Bundesgerichtshof 21 Dec. 1973, NJW 1974, 412, 413; Bundesgerichtshof 6 July 1979, BGHZ 75, 92, 94.

[59] Reichsgericht, 29 Jan. 1906, RGZ 62, 331.

[60] *Leigh and Sillivan Ltd.* v. *Aliakmon Shipping Co. Ltd.*, [1985] QB 350, 399 (per Goff, LJ):

Where A owes a duty of care in tort not to cause physical damage to B's property, and commits a breach of that duty in circumstances in which the loss of or physical damage to the property will ordinarily fall on B (as is reasonably foreseeable by A) such loss or damage, by reason of a contractual relationship between B and C, falls upon C, then C will be entitled, subject to the terms of any contract restricting A's liability to B, to bring an action in tort against A in respect of such loss or damage to the extent that it falls on him.

This raises a problem which will be taken up in connection with the defences of the promisor against the promisee and their effect upon the third-party's right (see below).

2 In German law it is well established that a contract of lease (*Mietvertrag*) may have legal effects for the benefit of certain persons who have a special relationship with the lessee. This may be illustrated by a case which was decided in 1980. It should, perhaps, be compared with the decision of the Court of Appeal in *Jackson* v. *Horizon Holidays Ltd.*[61] where the question arose whether Mr Jackson had made a contract for the benefit of his wife and children who had suffered the same mental distress as he himself when the hotel where they wanted to spend their holiday turned out to be a total disappointment. In the case before the Federal Supreme Court the object of the lease was a holiday home (*Ferienhaus*). The plaintiff had rented this house for a definite period of time for a summer holiday with his family. Shortly before his holiday was to start he received a letter from the lessor who wrote to him that he had sold this house. The plaintiff was unable to make new arrangements at such short notice. Therefore the holiday had to be spent at home. It is now recognized in German law that non-material damages may be claimed for the disappointment and frustration caused by the loss of the holiday (*vertane Urlaubszeit*, i.e. spoiled holiday). This enabled the plaintiff to recover damages for himself. His wife had assigned her claim to damages to her husband. The court held that she had a good claim, too. Details as to the amount of damages are not relevant for present purposes. The important point is that she was regarded as a third-party beneficiary of the contract of lease made by her husband with the defendant. The court left it open whether this result followed from a direct application of para. 328 BGB, or whether this was a case of a 'contract with protective effects *vis-à-vis* third parties'.[62]

3 An interesting problem pertaining to third-party beneficiaries has arisen in cases where a person has rented a car with fully comprehensive insurance. Under the usual general conditions of contract such insurance exempts the lessee from liability for damage to the car caused by his negligence. Suppose the lessee did not drive the car himself when the accident happened—the driver was a family member or a friend with whom he went on a trip. Does the exemption from liability extend to the driver? The question does not admit a general answer because it depends upon the construction of the contract with the lessor. If the

---

[61] [1975] 3 All ER 92.
[62] Bundesgerichtshof 12 May 1980, BGHZ 77, 116, 124. For more cases turning on third-party beneficiaries in connection with contracts of lease, see Bundesgerichtshof 22 Jan. 1968, BGHZ 49, 350; Bundesgerichtshof 19 Sept. 1973, BGHZ 61, 227, 233. As to the position of a sub-lessee, see Bundesgerichtshof 15 Feb. 1978, BGHZ 70, 327, 329.

lessee was entitled to have the car driven by such third person, the courts are inclined to let him have the benefit of this exemption from liability. Again, para. 328 BGB makes it possible![63]

3 The Promisor's Defence Against the Promisee: Their Effect upon the Beneficiary's Right.

Since the beneficiary's right is based on the contract between the promisor and the promisee, it is only fair that this right is subject to any defences arising out of that contract that the promisor may have against the promisee. It does not matter that the third party has a good claim against the promisee for the satisfaction of which the promisee had made the contract with the promisor. There can be no doubt that the beneficiary's right under this contract rises no higher than that of the promisee. In German law this follows from para. 334 BGB. The American Restatement Second (Contracts) is to the same effect.[64] It is not necessary to draw up a list of all possible defences a promisor may have. Suffice it to say that this includes anything which renders a contract void, voidable or unenforceable. It should, however, be remembered that the rule contained in para. 334 BGB is not mandatory. Therefore a case could arise where it could be argued that the parties have contracted out of this provision. One such case has already been discussed above.

The clear wording of para. 334 BGB has had the desirable effect that there has not been much litigation about this provision. An interesting problem, however, has arisen in the case of 'contracts with a protective effect *vis-à-vis* third parties' which were developed *praeter legem*. *(see supra I. 2)* Does para. 334 BGB merely apply to the main obligation or may a promisor avail himself of this defence also in regard to the collateral duty of protection extended to persons who are 'in proximity to the performance'? The Federal Supreme Court has dealt with this problem on at least two occasions.

The first case, decided in 1960, concerned a contract for work and labour (*Werkvertrag*).[65] In one of the Siemens factories producing cast steel the ceiling of a workshop was under repair. Due to the negligence of the contractor carrying out this work, several blocks of concrete fell down. Two employees of Siemens were badly hurt. The court did not consider claims arising from tort. Such claims were possibly barred by the Tort

---

[63] Bundesgerichtshof 29 Oct. 1956, BGHZ 22, 109, 120–3; Bundesgerichtshof 16 Dec. 1981, NJW 1982, 987, 988.   [64] Para. 309; for its wording see n. 5, above.
[65] Bundesgerichtshof 7 Nov. 1960, BGHZ 33, 247 (reproduced in translated form in Markesinis, *The German Law of Torts*, 2nd edn. (1990), 585–7.)

Statute of Limitations (para. 852 BGB), but the claimants' position would
have been different if they had been able to bring their actions in contract.
When the case came to trial, the protective ambit of contracts for work
and labour had already been defined. The contractor must have been able
to foresee that persons, for whose safety the employer was responsible,
would suffer damage if the work was carried out negligently. These requirements were fulfilled. The third parties, included under the contractual
umbrella, could be identified in advance (i.e. the Siemens employees working in this building); and their employer owed them special duties of care
under labour law (para. 618 BGB). However, on the facts of this case the
court below had found that negligence on the part of Siemens had contributed to causing the damage. The contractor, therefore, put forward the
defence of contributory negligence (para. 254 BGB) which gives a court
the discretionary power to reduce the amount of damages. Could this
defence be set up against a third party? It was held that the basic idea
inherent in para. 334 BGB was also valid for 'contracts with a protective
effect *vis-à-vis* third parties' which are closely modelled after the original
contract for the benefit of a third party.

This *ratio decidendi* was applied in the second case which also concerned
a contract for work and labour. An employer had put certain scaffolding
at the disposal of a contractor who had undertaken to construct a catwalk
connecting several oil tanks. The work was carried out by a subcontractor.
The employer had agreed to this subcontracting. Although the scaffolding
had been inspected by the contractor and the subcontractor, a hidden
defect caused a serious accident. The scaffolding broke and the subcontractor and several of his workers fell to the ground and were badly
injured. Again, it was not clear whether claims arising from tort were
barred by the limitation period. According to the report in the official
report of Supreme Court decisions, the case turned on the contractual
liability of the employer who had furnished the scaffolding. The action of
the subcontractor failed, the contract between the employer and the (main)
contractor containing an exemption clause: 'The use of our equipment
and tools put at the disposal of a contractor is on his account and at his
risk.' There was, of course, a dispute among the parties as to the meaning
of this exemption clause. The plaintiff maintained that it merely excluded
the liability of the defendant for such defects as a user could have been
expected to notice. Details of this dispute are not relevant for present
purposes. The court was of the opinion that such disclaimers of liability
are common in commercial dealings, and a contractor must take them into
account. The next step in the court's reasoning was obvious: if the employer had validly excluded his liability *vis-à-vis* the contractor, it was
evident that this included any beneficiary under this contract. This followed

from para. 334 BGB: the third party cannot be in a better position than the promisee.[66]

In a legal system which does not recognize contracts in favour of third parties the problems suggested by para. 334 BGB have, of course, no exact parallel. In the absence of a trust or agency a person cannot rely upon a term in a contract to which he is not a party, even if he is the person whom the contract is intended to benefit. Nevertheless, it appears that the question whether an exemption clause may affect a third party has also arisen in English law.[67] An interesting case is, perhaps, that of *Morris v. C. W. Martin & Sons Ltd.*[68] which involved three parties: a bailor (owner of a mink stole), a bailee (a furrier to whom the fur was given for cleaning) and a sub-bailee (a firm which actually did the cleaning), the owner having approved this sub-bailment. The contract with the sub-bailee which the bailee had made as principal, and not as an agent of the owner, contained an exemption clause covering *inter alia* the case of theft. The fur was stolen by a servant and the owner sued the sub-bailee for damages. The exemption clause which referred to 'goods belonging to customers' could not protect the defendant, for the 'customer' of the sub-bailee was the bailee, but not the owner of the fur. However, Lord Denning indicated *obiter* that it might have been different if the owner had expressly or impliedly consented to the bailee making a sub-bailment containing this exemption clause. He was even prepared to assume the implied consent of the owner because such conditions are current in the trade. But in view of its wording the clause was not adequate to meet that assumption.

More recently the present problem was squarely faced by Lord Justice Goff (as he then was) in his judgment in *The Aliakmon* to which reference has already repeatedly been made in this paper. He put the following hypothetical case based upon the facts underlying *Ross v. Caunters*[69] where a third party, C (the disappointed legatee), was held to be entitled to proceed directly against A (the solicitor) for damages flowing from A's

---

[66] Bundesgerichtshof 15 June 1971, BGHZ 56, 269, 274. One may, of course, doubt whether the subcontractor was in the position of a beneficiary of a *Vertrag mit Schutzwirkung für Dritte*. The court had such doubts. The existence of such a relationship was accepted merely for the sake of argument in order to show that the decision would remain the same. For a case where an exemption clause contained in a contract between an industrial enterprise and a private security service was extended to their watchman whose negligence was responsible for damage by fire, see Bundesgerichtshof 7 Dec. 1961, NJW 1962, 388.

[67] See *Elder, Dempster & Co. Ltd. v. Paterson, Zochonis & Co. Ltd.*, [1924] AC 522 (HL) The case stands for the proposition that a non-party can in some circumstances shelter behind an exemption clause contained in a contract between two other parties. Strangely enough, the judges had no problem with the requirement of privity of contract. But see *Midland Silicones Ltd. v. Scruttons Ltd.*, [1962] AC 446 (HL): a clause limiting liability for damage to goods in transit which was contained in a contract between the carriers and the consignees did not protect the stevedores who were not parties to that contract, although damage by the stevedores was expressly referred to in the contract.

[68] [1966] 1 QB 716 (CA).   [69] [1980] Ch. 297.

breach of duty to B (the testator). The testator had asked the solicitor to prepare the will while they spent a holiday together, and the solicitor who had no access to his book of precedents was cautious enough to draft the will without assuming any legal responsibility. The will failed for some defect in point of form. Considering the effect of the disclaimer of liability upon C's right of action in tort against A, Lord Justice Goff was of the opinion that this action must be dismissed because 'C's right against A must be regulated by any provisions which controlled or limited B's rights against A'.[70] The contractual approach to this triangular relationship chosen by the German Federal Supreme Court would lead to the same result because a beneficiary's right is subject to all defences of the promisor against the promisee (para. 334 BGB).

In England the contractual solution is advocated by Professor Markesinis who has recently dealt with the present problem in the light of some building cases[71] where the question arises whether a disclaimer of liability in the contract between the subcontractor and the main contractor would be fatal to an action brought by the building owner against the subcontractor who, for instance, carelessly set fire to the building. In *Norwich City Council* v. *Harvey*[72] the Court of Appeal had to decide such a case, but the facts were different in one respect, for the main contract and the subcontract contained identical exemption clauses. One should have thought that this makes things easier, but solving such cases through tort, as the court did, necessitated the finding that the negligence action of the building owner must fail because there was no sufficiently close and direct relation between them to impose upon the subcontractor any duty of care to the owner of the building. Moreover, the doctrine of privity had to be invoked in support of this reasoning. In the opinion of Lord Justice May, with whom Lord Justices Croom-Johnson and Glidewell concurred, the mere fact that there was no strict privity between the owner and the subcontractor did not make it just and reasonable that a duty of care should be owed. In German law the contractual approach, in a case like this, should start out with the question whether the building owner may be regarded as a third-party beneficiary under the doctrine applied in the testamentary case. If this were deemed possible, it would follow that the building owner's claim against the subcontractor is determined by the latter's contract with

---

[70] *Leigh and Sillivan Ltd.* v. *Aliakmon Shipping Co. Ltd.*, [1985] QB 350, 397 (per Goff, LJ).

[71] Markesinis, 'An Expanding Tort Law: The Price of a Rigid Contract Law,' LQR 103 (1987), 354, 392–5. See, also, the following articles by the same author: 'The Need to Set Acceptable Boundaries Between Contract and Tort: An English Lawyer's Views on some Recent American Trends', *Conflict and Integration: Comparative Law in the World Today. The 40th Anniversary of the Institute of Comparative Law in Japan* (Chuo University, 1988), 313 *et seq.* and 'Doctrinal Clarity in Tort Litigation', *The International Lawyer* 25 (1991), 953.   [72] [1989] 1 WLR 828 (CA).

the main contractor, because a third-party beneficiary derives his legal position mainly from this contractual relationship.[73]

4   The Promisor's Right to Restitution: Unjust Enrichment of the Beneficiary?

The triangular relationship existing between the parties may lead to difficult problems of restitution if the promisor has already performed and thus conferred a benefit on the beneficiary. Suppose the contract between the promisor and the promisee turns out to have been void or voidable. In such a situation, the promisor is not obliged to render performance to the beneficiary, because para. 334 BGB would have given him the right to refuse any performance. As a point of legal logic the answer would certainly be that the promisor has a good restitutionary claim against the beneficiary. This proposition may, perhaps, be tested by the following hypothetical case. A husband makes a contract for life insurance stipulating payment of the sum insured to his wife in case she should survive him. The contract is concluded on the basis of a questionnaire concerning the state of health of the applicant. One of the questions concerns previous illnesses from a heart condition. Although the applicant had already suffered serious heart attacks, he deliberately conceals this vital fact. A few years after the conclusion of the contract, he suddenly dies of cardiac insufficiency. After having made payment to the beneficiary, the insurance company finds out that the insured had not honestly filled in the questionnaire. The insurance company is thereby entitled to rescind the contract on the ground of fraud (para. 143(2) BGB). As a result the contract is deemed to have been rescinded *ex tunc* (para. 142(1) BGB). Although there is no decision of the Federal Supreme Court which is directly to the point, the correct solution of this case would seem to be that the insurance company would have a right to restitution against the beneficiary under the basic rule governing the law of unjust enrichment (para. 812(1) BGB).[74] However, a warning must be added because this does not necessarily mean recovery. For such restitutionary claims are usually subject to the defence that the recipient is no longer enriched (para. 818(3) BGB). If the recipient has already spent the money in good faith, the claim will fail. It is different only if he knew of the absence of a legal ground at the time of the receipt, or if he subsequently learns of it but nevertheless spends the money thus received (para. 819(1) BGB). Money spent in bad faith must be returned.

---

[73] See Lorenz, 'Some Thoughts about Contract and Tort', *Essays in Memory of Professor F. H. Lawson* (1986), 96–7 with a view to the *Junior Books* case; Markesinis, *The International Lawyer* 25 (1991), 953, 959–64.

[74] See Staudinger-Lorenz, *Kommentar zum Bürgerlichen Gesetzbuch*, 12th edn. (1979), para. 812 n. 38.

For this purpose the insurance company would have to convince a court that the beneficiary had known of the fraud committed by the insured.

It should be emphasized that this solution does not commend itself to all types of contracts for the benefit of third parties. The Federal Supreme Court has let it be known in an *obiter dictum* that the promisor's right to restitution against the beneficiary must be confined to cases in which the promisee's legal relationship with the beneficiary was not in the nature of a bargain.[75] In the hypothetical case just discussed the promisee wished to secure the maintenance of his wife if she should survive him. In other words, the rule that the beneficiary must be prepared to make restitution applies to the types of contract dealt with in para. 330 BGB (i.e. 'maintenance contracts', see above 2.9). But where the legal relationship between the promisee and the third party is an exchange contract it is not to be presumed that the promisor and the promisee wished to expose the third party to restitution if the contract with the promisor should prove to be void. Therefore the party liable to make restitution should be the promisee who has been unjustly enriched at the expense of the promisor whose performance has extinguished the promisee's obligation *vis-à-vis* the third party.[76] Against this restitutionary claim the promisee may, of course, set off the money already paid to the promisor.

5 Conclusions

In German law the provisions relating to contracts in favour of third parties have given rise to an ever-increasing body of case law. Originally aimed at securing the maintenance of the intended beneficiaries (*Versorgungsverträge*), these provisions, because of their flexibility, may be applied to a large variety of situations. In all these cases the third party may acquire the right directly to demand performance if the promisor and the promisee have made a contract containing a stipulation to this effect. Thus, a case of the type with which the House of Lords had to deal in *Beswick* v. *Beswick* presents no difficulty, because Mrs Beswick would have been successful as a contract beneficiary. As may be seen from paras. 330, 331 BGB, contracts for life insurance or an annuity are typical examples of contracts in favour of third parties. It is interesting to see that even in English law the doctrine of privity has been considerably modified through Parliamentary intervention in the sphere of insurance. This may, perhaps, have reduced the pressure to change the English rule. However, in German law difficult questions have arisen in situations where savings accounts had been opened in favour of third persons. The English case of *Birch* v. *Treasury Solicitors*

[75] Bundesgerichtshof 24 Feb. 1972, BGHZ 58, 184 (188–9).
[76] To the same effect is the case of *Chrysler* v. *Airtemp Corp.*, 426 A 2d 845 (Supr Ct of Delaware, New Castle County, 1980). See also *Restatement of Restitution* para. 110.

(above 2.3) gives some idea of the kind of problems confronting the courts. The German cases are particularly complicated because such contracts in favour of third parties are in collision with basic rules of the law of succession upon death.

In the cases envisaged by the Civil Code the third party may become creditor of the main obligation of the promisor (*primärer Leistungsanspruch*). However, an important case—law development has brought about a legal institution which is called 'contract with protective effects *vis-à-vis* third parties' (*Vertrag mit Schutzwirkung für Dritte*). The testamentary case of the Federal Supreme Court, which can be compared with *Ross* v. *Caunters*, is a good example of this legal device, which was modelled after the Code provision on contract beneficiaries. In these cases the third party is not seeking performance of the promisor's primary obligation, but he makes him liable for damages for bad performance of this obligation and the resulting economic loss. Originally regarded as a variant of para. 328 *et seq.* of the Civil Code, this type of contract has over the years gained definite contours of its own and is now regarded as an independent legal institution belonging to the law of civil liability, broad enough to grant the persons so protected an action for breach of certain collateral duties called *Schutzpflichten* (i.e. duties of protection). It is, however, necessary to place limits on the number of potential beneficiaries. For this reason some special relationship with the promisee is needed. This requirement is described as 'proximity to the performance' (*Leistungsnähe*). Functionally this is equivalent to the question to whom a duty of care is owed in a tort action for negligence in English law. It must be admitted that it is by no means easy to delimit the scope of these collateral duties *vis-à-vis* third parties. The difficulties are comparable with the task of determining the scope of the duty of care. In German law this limiting function depends upon the proper construction of the contract between the promisor and the promisee and the extent to which third parties may be included within the sphere of protection surrounding this contract. No difficulty is presented by situations which may aptly be described as cases of 'transferred loss' (*Schadensverlagerung*). The testamentary case is a good example for this proposition. It is, however, different in cases where the danger of multiplication of damages exists. The famous Cardozo judgment in *Ultramares Corporation* v. *Touche*, which concerned an action for damages brought by a third party who had relied on an inaccurate balance sheet prepared by an accountant, can be taken as an illustration of this problem. The criteria determining the answer to the question whether a third party relying on such a misstatement should be treated as a contract beneficiary are probably not materially different from the standards by which an English court would judge whether a duty of care was owed to that person. Nevertheless, the contractual approach has at least one great advantage over the tort action, for it can easily explain why a disclaimer of liability contained in the contract between promisor and promisee will be fatal to the claim of a third party. The same problem arises with respect to the period of limitation. In each of these cases the third party merely takes the promisee's place. If this doctrine were applied to the building cases hinted at in this paper, it would follow that the building owner's claim against a subcontractor is determined by the latter's contract with the main contractor. As Professor Markesinis rightly observes, it is important to give the third party a remedy, while not over-exposing the defendant.[77]

[77] Markesinis, 'Doctrinal Clarity in Tort Litigation', *The International Lawyer* 25 (1991), 953.

LIABILITY FOR INFORMATION AND OPINIONS CAUSING PURE ECONOMIC LOSS TO THIRD PARTIES: A COMPARISON OF ENGLISH AND GERMAN CASE LAW

CHRISTIAN VON BAR

Third parties may suffer economic loss as a result of relying on inaccurate and incompetent advice. The precise judicial foundation of the potential liability of those proffering the advice is a problem that plagues many legal systems.[1] This is particularly true in England and Germany where the question is both topical and controversial. Tackling the underlying issues from a comparative perspective may well reveal a great deal about the issues as well as the respective legal systems, though at the end of the day we may reach the conclusion that no clear and convincing answers emerge from either side of the Channel.

1 Information, Opinions, Balance Sheets, Certificates, and References

At the centre of our inquiry are cases with factual situations such as that which formed the basis of the decisions of the Court of Appeal[2] and of the House of Lords[3] in *Caparo Industries PLC* v. *Dickman*. Had *Caparo*, however, occurred in Germany, it would have been decided by the provisions relating to the so-called 'company statutory audit'.[4] In the *Caparo* case, the plaintiff maintained that as a result of relying upon the end-of-year accounts prepared by the defendant, it had purchased a 90 per cent share in the public company in question, and paid too high a price for this share because the accounts contained material inaccuracies attributable solely to the defendant's negligence. The accounting procedure itself was based on section 23 of the Companies Act 1990 (cf. now sections 235 to 246 of the Companies Act 1985). It was thus prescribed by statute. A similar obligatory accounting procedure has existed in German law since

I am grateful to Mr Anthony Webster, BA, Barrister at Law, for helping with the translation of an early version of my manuscript into English.

[1] Monteiro, *Responsibilidade por Conselhos: Recomendaçoes ou Informaçoes* (1989) provides rich references to international literature.

[2] [1989] 1 QB 653.   [3] [1990] 2 AC 605.

[4] The legal basis for the statutory audit derived, incidentally, from English law (Ebke, *Wirtschaftsprüfer und Dritthaftung* (1983), 13), dates back to 1931. Their current version can be found in para. 316(1) of the Commercial Law Code (HGB), the first sentence of which reads as follows: 'The yearly accounts and Annual Report of share companies which are not 'small' within the meaning of para. 267 subsection 1, must be prepared by a qualified accountant.'

1931.[5] In these cases, according to the prevailing view,[6] liability towards third parties is excluded (though one must also note with surprise the absence of any recent case law interpreting this provision).[7] I, personally, incline to this view[8] since para. 323(1), sentence no. 3 of the HGB (as last modified by the '*Bilanzrichtliniengesetz*' of 19 December 1985) makes, in the context of statutory audits, accountants liable for either intentional or negligent breaches of duty only towards the shareholding company itself and towards other companies (legally) associated with it.[9] Liability under this provision is limited to DM 500.000 for each set of accounts (para. 323(2), sentence no. 1 HGB).[10] Others (such as shareholders or creditors of the shareholding company) are not mentioned in the statute. Admittedly,

---

[5] The current text, para. 323 HGB, reads as follows:

The auditor, his assistants and the legal representatives of an auditing firm assisting in the examination are obliged to make conscientious and impartial examination and to maintain confidentiality. They may not exploit without authorisation business secrets learned in their work. Whoever intentionally and negligently violates his duties is obliged to compensate the company for the damage incurred and, if a related enterprise is damaged, that one as well. Several persons are liable as joint and several debtors.

(Translation from Ruester (ed.), *Business Transactions in Germany* (1990)).

[6] See in particular Ebke, op. cit. n. 4, above, at 38–43 and 56–60; Ebke, JZ 1990, 688, 689 (book review); Ebke–Flechtrup, JZ 1986, 1112 (case-note); Lang, 'Zur Dritthaftung der Wirtschaftsprüfer', WPg 1989, 57, 58. Stahl, *Zur Dritthaftung von Rechtsanwälten, Steuerberatern, Wirtschaftsprüfern und öffentlich bestellten und vereidigten Sachverständigen* (1989), 198–9, takes a different view, but, in my opinion, fails to convince.

[7] From the decisions of the BGH BB 1961, 652; OLG Oldenburg VersR 1981, 88; and OLG Karlruhe WM 1985, 940 which interpret para. 826 BGB, one can only conclude that the courts (tacitly) assume that para. 323 HGB (or rather, its identically-worded predecessor) exhausts the accountant's *contractual* liability.

[8] An exception might possibly be found in cases where the accountant induces a special degree of trust in his person, e.g. in reply to a specific question, he expressly reaffirms the accuracy of his work. On such facts, liability in *culpa in contrahendo* or under a separate contract for the supply of information, may exist, alongside para. 323 HGB and quite independently of para. 826 BGB. See: Heymann (-Hermann), *Handelsgesetzbuch*, iii, para. 323, n. 7 and Hopt, 'Die Haftung des Wirtschaftsprüfers: *Rechtsprobleme zu Para 323 HGB* (s. 168 AktG a.F.) und Zur Prospekt—und Auskunftshaftung', in: *Essays in Honour of Pleyer* (1986), 341, 353.

[9] For the special case of mergers para. 340(b)(5) of the Public Stock Corporations (AktG) provides for liability to shareholders of the merging companies.

[10] Schlechtriem, quite rightly, concludes in his article, 'Summenmässige Haftungs-beschränkungen in Allgemeinen Geschäftsbedingungen', BB 1984, 1177, 1183, that an upper limit of DM 500,000 for each set of accounts must be possible outside the applicable scope of para. 323 BGB on the basis of general business conditions. 'The rules relating to statutory audits by virtue of Act of Parliament must also be capable of application to accounts vol-untary undertaken but which are similar in nature (i.e. by simple inclusion in the terms of the contracts)'. Such a limit to liability will also have third-party effect, for it would be quite wrong if third parties were to enjoy more rights under a contract which by definition they are strangers to, than the co-contractor himself: BGH NJW 1987, 1758, 1760. Of no effect, however, is an attempt to limit liability for intentionally caused damage (para. 276(2) BGB; BGH JZ 1986, 1111, 1112); or for damage caused by gross negligence (para. 11 no. 7 of the Law Relating to General Business Conditions—AGBG). This is so, even when the third party in question is also a business person (BGH NJW 1987, 1758, 1760).

taken literally this means no more than that these categories of persons are owed no duty of care under the rules of the Commercial Code. In addition, however, para. 323 HGB does contain the seeds from which a general civil-law principle of liability might be derived. What, however, is meant by that provision becomes clear by casting one's eye back into the history of it, where one finds the idea that para. 323 HGB ought to be regarded as an *exhaustive* norm in respect of any *contractual* liability which might befall an accountant in the preparation of accounts.[11] Only tortious liability thus remains unaffected.[12] At first sight this distinction may appear insignificant to an English lawyer; *Caparo* is after all a tort case. As soon as one realizes, however, that in German law professional liability towards third parties is grounded in the law of contract, and only exceptionally in the law of torts (para. 826 BGB:[13] intentional damage *contra bonos mores*), it then becomes clear just how important is this special provision relating to statutory audits.

In German law, *Caparo* would thus have been decided in precisely the same way as it was by the House of Lords (and unlike the Court of Appeal, which distinguished between existing and potential shareholders). However, this coincidence should not lead us to the mistaken conclusion that our attempts at comparative legal analysis are already at an end, since this common feature, found in statutory audits, might only be coincidental. Moreover, the task of an accountant in Germany (as well as in England) includes a variety of other consultancy, certification, and opinion-related activities, including *contractual* audits,[14] for which he enjoys no express privileges when it comes to questions of liability. It follows that the *Caparo* question is only one of the issues that have to be considered, but not the only one. Thus, one should note that as far as liability towards third parties is concerned, the relevant principles of general liability in both German[15] and in English[16] law do not differ, other than in detail, from those applicable to other experts and service industries. Indeed, it is arguable that the liability of accountants is actually rooted in the rules of liability applicable to other professions. In the following pages, therefore,

---

[11] For a detailed account see Ebke, n. 4, above, at 40 *et seq.*

[12] The applicability of tort law beside para. 323 HGB is settled law. Cf., in addition to the references in n. 7, above, Ebke/Scheel, 'Die Haftung des Wirtschaftsprüfers für fahrlässig verursachte Vermögensschäden Dritter', *WM* 1991, 389 *et seq.*

[13] 'A person who wilfully causes damage to another in a manner *contra bonos mores* is bound to compensate the other for the damage.' Translation from Markesinis, *The German Law of Torts*, 2nd edn. (1990).

[14] Also Lang, op. cit. n. 6, above, 58 and Hopt op. cit. n. 8, above, at 353 *et seq.* Accountants' tasks are set down by law in para. 2, Accountants Regulations (WPO).

[15] Cf. Lang, 'Die Rechtsprechung des Bundesgerichtshofes zur Dritthaftung der Wirtschaftsprüfer und anderer Sachverständiger', *WM* 1988, 1001, 1002.

[16] On this point see, Lord Denning in *Candler* v. *Crane, Christmas & Co.* [1951] 2 KB 164, 179 *et seq.* See also Weir's case-note on the *Caparo* case in 49 [1990] *CLJ* 212.

I shall also deal with tax advisors, publicly employed experts (in whatever field), banks engaged in giving information about the creditworthiness of their clients, lawyers, and others whose professional concern it is to look after the financial interests of their clients. Strictly speaking, information concerning the character of employees also falls within the ambit of this discussion. This issue was, in fact, litigated before the Federal Court in 1979, and its decision provides us with a splendid example for a case-study. Put simply, that case dealt with an employer who in good faith wrote an unusually good reference for his bookkeeper. Armed with this reference, the bookkeeper was able to obtain a highly desirable position elsewhere. However, it subsequently emerged that the bookkeeper had embezzled large sums of money whilst working for his former employer. When asked to return the money, he requested a short time in which to pay. He was granted some time but used this 'period of grace' to embezzle even more money from his new employer using his 'tested' method. The proceeds of this new embezzlement were then used to pay back the debt to his former employer. The Federal Court allowed the second employer's claim against the first employer on the ground that the first employer had, in breach of his duties, failed to revoke the letter of recommendation. This omission was held to be actionable on the grounds that it amounted to a breach of confidence, a concept which was not given a closer definition by the court.[17]

2 Third Parties

The object of this study is the liability of the service professions towards third parties. Precisely what makes these persons 'third parties' is unambiguous in English law: the doctrine of privity of contract clearly states that third parties are those persons not bound by, or enjoying rights under, a valid contract. This criterion, however, is wholly inappropriate in German law since the latter ignores the concept of consideration. Consequently, in Germany it has been possible to base the liability of the service professions towards third parties in contract.[18] If one, therefore, still wished to come up with a common definition of who constitutes a 'third party', one could say that a 'third party' is that person who is neither obliged in law to pay, nor in fact has paid, money in respect of the defective service that caused the damage. This definition includes purchasers of shares in companies, of goods, or of land, whenever they have relied upon the accuracy of professional estimates of the value of these items, but who have not, themselves, paid for such estimates. Above all, however, this definition includes credit

[17] BGHZ JZ 1979, 725 and the accompanying comment by v. Bar and Loewenheim, 'Schadenshaftung unter Arbeitgebern wegen Unrichtiger Arbeitszeugnisse', *JZ* 1980, 469 *et seq.* [18] Compare the previous section.

institutions whose loans have been dishonoured on similar grounds. A potential claimant might thus be a bank who mistakenly believes its client to be creditworthy on the strength of certain essential information provided, for example, by an accountant. The same is true of a supplier or a contractor who postpones immediate payment of sums owed to him by his client on the faith of an incorrect statement by the client's bank, tax adviser, or other trustworthy person.

The above clarification, essential for the sake of describing the relevant case material, can thus serve to elucidate the basic factual problem that confronts us. Third parties who claim damages in these types of cases must know that in a market economy it is only possible to insure against the risk of investments going wrong against remuneration. In other words, courts must be slow to develop principles tending towards 'gratuitous' liability. For the same reasons then it is desirable to proceed carefully on the basis of liability arising out of advice offered and actually relied upon. Otherwise we all too easily confuse the question whether a third party is entitled as of right to rely on the quality of a service commissioned and paid for by another (i.e. under contract).[19] This difficulty is of course not the only one generated by the typical triangular situation in professional liability cases. It is in many cases perfectly possible to adopt a different approach, and to say of those features crucial to establishing liability that the person responsible giving the service ought really to be prevented from being remunerated for shoddy work, without risk to himself and thereby lowering the reputation of his profession in general.[20] Whoever overestimates the value of a company's assets or of a work of art, or whoever proffers over-generous information concerning a debtor's ability to pay, or whoever overestimates an employee's integrity or the progress of construction work (essential for securing credit), almost invariably never inflicts damage upon his client.[21] The latter experiences no disadvantage whatsoever in consequence of an overestimate either of his assets or of his personal qualities; in these situations the potential victim of a second-rate service is and necessarily remains a 'third party'.

3 Types of Fault: Intention and Negligence

The above-mentioned problems commonly arise only in situations in which the defendant has acted negligently and not intentionally. In principle,

---

[19] Cf. also v. Bar, 'Unentgeltliche Investitionsempfehlungen im Wandel der Wirtschaftsverfassungen Deutschlands und Englands', *RabelsZ* 44 (1980), 455, 477 *et seq.*

[20] Cf. Hopt, n. 8, above, 341–4.

[21] With good reason Bingham LJ in *Caparo* v. *Dickman* [1989] 2 WLR 316, 330 says 'The duty contended for would simply extend a right of redress, if the auditor failed to perform his duties with reasonable care and skill, from the company, *which would rarely have a claim*, to shareholders who foreseeably would.' (Emphasis added.)

intentional acts cause fewer problems both in England and in Germany. Thus, those situations which in England are dealt with under the tort of deceit, are in Germany regulated by paras. 823 II[22] and 826 of the Civil Code. We are all entitled not to be deceived wherever we are. The rather blandly worded para. 676 of the German Civil Code, the content of which, incidentally, is crucial to our discussion, expresses this self-evident proposition. It is thus laid down in para. 676 that, 'Whosoever gives to another advice or a recommendation . . . shall not be liable to pay damages resulting from the reliance thereon . . . *irrespective* of any liability which might exist either in contract or by virtue of tort law.' It should be noted that the reference here to the law of torts is confined to *intentional* acts causing the type of loss covered by para. 826 BGB. A specific tort of 'negligence', giving rise to damages for pure economic loss, was a notion wholly alien to the original authors of the German Civil Code. Moreover it remains the prevailing opinion of both the courts and academics that this self-imposed limitation should not be altered.[23]

It is worth noting, however, that there is a clear divide between German and English legal opinion as to what distinguishes negligence-based liability from intention-based liability. A system of tort law such as the English has no need to extend the ambit of intentional torts when it can accommodate damages for pure economic loss caused by negligence through *Hedley Byrne* v. *Heller*[24] type of reasoning. In contrast, a system which, like the German, is restricted by its Code to wilful acts, will go to great lengths in order to expand its 'intentional' torts so as to include elements of negligence. This is precisely what has happened in Germany.

Paragraph 826 of the BGB provides the starting point (apart from para. 823 II BGB, which is not really helpful in this area).[25] According to para.

---

[22] The text of para. 823 BGB reads as follows

(1) A person, who wilfully or negligently injures the life, body, health, freedom, property or other right of another contrary to law is bound to compensate him for any damage arising therefrom. (2) The same obligation attaches to a person who infringes a statutory provision intended for the protection of others. If according to the purview of the statute infringement is possible even without fault, the duty to make compensation arises only if some fault can be imputed to the wrongdoer.

Translation from Markesinis, op. cit., n. 13.

[23] A proposal I favour (cf. v. Bar, *Entwicklungen und Entwicklungstendenzen im Recht der Verkehrs(sicherungs)pflichten, JuS* 1988, 169 *et seq.*), for developing the German law of torts, namely to apply para. 823 II BGB not just to statutes designed to protect persons, but also to established duties developed in case law, i.e. to professional negligence, has been expressly rejected in BGH NJW 1987, 2671. It is interesting to note that the question of whether these cases are better dealt with as a matter of tort or contract also arises in England—albeit under reversed nomenclature! See Markesinis, 'An Expanding Tort Law: the Price of a Rigid Contract Law', *LQR* 103 (1987), 354, 371. [24] [1964] AC 465.

[25] The business laws considered here typically require intention, in which case it is easier to have recourse to para. 826 BGB.

826 liability attaches to whoever 'intentionally and *contra bonos mores* causes damage to another.' Intention here refers to the causing of damage, and not to the immorality. This is only appropriate in the circumstances, for were it otherwise, persons with a greater ethical awareness would be exposed to greater liability than the morally backward. Already in the days of the Reichsgericht the view was taken that the requirement of immorality in para. 826 was satisfied where the defendant was personally aware of the circumstances adjudged 'immoral' in the opinion of the court;[26] and the Federal Court has continued this practice.[27] By 'immoral' however, we understand not only intentional, but also thoughtless and reckless behaviour.[28] Thus, liability within the meaning of para. 826 BGB can arise where a doctor diagnoses a person as being mentally ill for the purposes of an application made by the relatives for the administration of that person's assets, the doctor basing his decision on insufficient information and on an inadequate medical examination.[29] Likewise there is 'immorality' where a bailiff, without careful reflection, advises that an impecunious debtor is good risk as regards a loan.[30] Other illustrations include an expert witness who in court recklessly overestimates the value of real estate;[31] a bank manager who provides false information concerning a client's soundness;[32] and a surveyor who draws up a favourable report without first having tested the entire building for dry rot, thereby leaving the creditor with a mortgage secured against a worthless property.[33] In the finding of careless and thus immoral conduct the German courts, in fact, go even further. For example, it is sufficient that an accountant acting on his client's instructions, sends to that client's bank a statement of the client's assets in which real estate is described as being 'free of charges' when (as could easily have been discovered by looking through the Land Charges Register), it was not so;[34] or that a tax advisor prepares a balance sheet and authenticates it even though the figures presented to him were clearly contradictory;[35] or that counsel attends negotiations on behalf of his client for the purpose of rescheduling a debt, yet does so possessing no knowledge of the state of his client's assets and then maintains during a critical

---

[26] RGZ 79, 17, 23 and RGZ 123, 271, 278.

[27] BGH NJW 1951, 596 (and Coing's note thereto). This has been good law since then.

[28] Good law since RGZ 72, 175, 176 and RGZ 143, 49, 51.

[29] RGZ 72, 175 *et seq.* It is interesting to note that Lord Denning in *Candler* v. *Crane Christmas* [1951] 2 KB 164 at 183 discusses an analogous situation and affirms liability obiter: 'Thus a doctor, who negligently certifies a man to be a lunatic when he is not, is liable to him, although there is no contract in the matter, because the doctor knows that his certificate is required for the very purpose of deciding whether the man should be detained or not.'   [30] RG JW 1917, 540 No. 8.

[31] RG JW 1932, 937 No. 5; cf. also BGH WM 1966, 1150; BGH WM 1962, 935; and BGH WM 1960, 1323.

[32] See RG JW 1911, 584.   [33] BGH WM 1966, 1150.

[34] BGH WM 1986, 711.   [35] OLG Frankfurt WM 1989, 1618.

phase of the negotiations that 'there aren't the slightest grounds' for initiating proceedings against his client: 'If my client says you will have your money by the following days, you can count on it. I know my client and his relations.'[36]

In the light of these decisions I have no doubt that the German courts, in cases such as *Derry v. Peek*,[37] *Angus v. Clifford*,[38] *Le Lievre v. Gould*,[39] *Heilbut Symons & Co. v. Buckleton*,[40] *Nocton v. Lord Ashburton*,[41] *Candler v. Crane, Christmas & Co.*[42] and even *Smith v. Eric S. Bush*[43] would have found reckless and thus immoral conduct. Moreover, in the cases of *Derry v. Peek*, and *Heilbut Symons v. Buckleton* as well as in *Candler v. Crane Christmas* they would also have affirmed an intention to cause damage. For it is settled German law that para. 826 BGB presupposes no actual wish to cause damage (*dolus directus*), but rather the subjective realization by the doer of the act that his conduct might injure or cause loss to another, which the doer accepts even though he may not wish it (*dolus eventualis*).[44] Therefore, he who gives information off-the-cuff must recognize that it could be false; and the very fact that he still goes ahead and gives the information demonstrates that he has reckoned with the possibility of damage to others and that he has accepted it. This at least is the view adopted by the German courts which, as a result, end up by elevating what is essentially careless behaviour to the level of *dolus eventualis* and thereby imposing liability under the terms of para. 826 BGB.[45]

The preceding observations concerning para. 826 provide us with adequate insight into the dogmatic framework of the German legal system; yet for an understanding of just how this provision operates in practice, we need to know a little more. Of importance is the realization that it is entirely irrelevant whether or not the person causing the damage knew of the identity of the third party—at least, this is the German view as far as recklessness is concerned (i.e. a degree of irresponsibility amounting to gross negligence). It is enough—but also essential—that the expert 'foresees and desires both the general direction in which his conduct might develop and the type of damage which might possibly ensue therefrom.'[46] For this reason, it is sufficient to establish liability where a tax advisor realizes that, 'the end-of-year accounts which he prepared might well be

---

[36] BGH WM 1962, 845; NJW 1962, 1500.   [37] [1889] 14 App Cas 337 (HL).
[38] [1891] 2 Ch 449 (CA).   [39] [1893] 1 QB 491 (CA).
[40] [1913] AC 30 (HL).   [41] [1914] AC 932 (HL).   [42] N. 29, above.
[43] [1989] 2 WLR 790; [1989] 2 All ER 514 (HL).
[44] BGH WM 1976, 498, 500; BGH WM 1977, 59, 62; BGH NJW 1986, 180, 182 *et al.* This is accepted law.
[45] For greater detail here, see v. Bar, *Verkehrspflichten* (1980), 216 *et seq.*, as well as Ebke/ Scheel, op. cit. n. 12, above, 390. For the cases, read at least BGH WM 1986, 711, 712 and BGH NJW 1987, 1758, 1759.
[46] BGH LM No. 15 to S. 823 (Be) BGB; BGH WM 1966, 1151, 1152.

used for the purpose of obtaining credit or otherwise in a credit situation and that a potential creditor might thereby be induced unwittingly into concluding a disadvantageous transaction on the strength of those accounts.'[47] But where an architect and publicly employed surveyor of property mistakenly assesses agricultural land as suitable for building purposes and is not aware, given the circumstances of the case, that his estimate could be of relevance in a broader context (especially to banks), then para. 826 BGB will not be applicable.[48]

A further remark concerning para. 826 BGB relates to the issue of third-party insurance protection. Most experts will in these cases have insurance cover; and this may be extended in amount for more important tasks or for individual cases as the need arises. Other professions (such as accountants), are required by statute to take out compulsory insurance.[49] But even the most comprehensive insurance policy is a dead duck, 'when the insured himself has, in breach of the law, intentionally brought about the state of affairs making him responsible to third parties.' In such a situation, 'the insurer is not liable' (see para. 152 VVG).[50] Lack of space makes it impossible to discuss the question whether a finding of liability under para. 826 BGB leads, inevitably, to the loss of insurance cover according to para. 152 VVG; but even without such discussion, it is already evident just what a huge danger para. 826 presents to all concerned.[51] Personally, I am not sure whether the Federal Court has thought through all the various implications in reaching its decisions or not, since these aspects of insurance cover rarely find expressions in claims for damages.[52] Thus, the fact that contractual liability enjoys 'the upper hand', as one Federal judge recently put it,[53] is at least an encouraging sign. For this very reason it is a well-known fact in liability claims that nothing increases the defendant's readiness to settle the dispute more than a hint from the court that it intends to see if para. 826 BGB might be applicable in the case before it.

4   Physical Damage and Pure Economic Loss

A special feature of our discussion is claims for pure economic loss. This phrase probably has the same meaning both in German and English law, namely loss unconnected to physical injury or property, nor arising from

---

[47] BGH NJW 1987, 1758, 1759.

[48] BGH WM 1966, 1148; VersR 1966, 1034, 1035.

[49] Para. 54 of the Accountants' Regulations (WPO).

[50] Law Relating to Insurance Contracts (Versicherungsvertragsgesetz) dated 30 May 1908, RGB l 1908, 263, BGB l III 7632-1.

[51] Schindhelm/Grothe, 'Die Dritthaftung des Steuerberaters nach Vertragsgrundsätzen', *DStR* (1989), 445 *et seq.*

[52] For an exception see BGH JZ 1985, 951, 952; and n. 108, ante.

[53] Lang, *WM* 1988, 1001 (n. 15, above).

other loss or injury to rights having effect against all the world (for this reason called 'absolute' in German legal terminology). That the distinction between 'pure' and 'other' types of economic loss seems also to have taken root in England[54] is, in one sense, quite remarkable, given that the English law of torts thinks in terms of standards of conduct and not, as Germans do, in terms of protected rights and interests. Insofar as a German lawyer can be a judge in these matters, the English aversion to the various categories of pure economic loss seems linked to the fact that the distinction between negligent acts (or omissions) on the one hand and negligent words (or silence) on the other,[55] does not appear a particularly tenable one.[56] The fact that each of our legal systems nowadays provides for a special category of liability known as 'pure economic loss'[57] has a more profound explanation. Two basic tendencies may be distinguished.

4.1 The Market Economy

The first is based upon the observation that damages for 'pure economic loss' can only ever be available in a market economy in exceptional circumstances in any case, since the *raison d'être* of the system depends on maximizing one's own profit and thereby holding one's competitors down, all in the name of competition. Permit competition, and by definition you permit 'pure economic loss' to be inflicted upon people at the same time. Acknowledgement of this long ago led to the basic premise of legal liability, i.e. that whilst you must not deceive others, you are under no further obligation to concern yourself with their economic interests. In this respect, both the German para. 676 BGB[58] and the House of Lords' ruling in *Derry* v. *Peek*[59] were in complete accordance with one another when first pronounced at the turn of this century. Today, some 90 years later, damages for 'pure economic loss' still remain the exception, although the

---

[54] Cf. the contributions of Huxley, 'Economic Loss in Negligence: The 1989 Cases', *MLR* 55 (1990), 369; of Howarth, 'Negligence after Murphy: Time to Re-Think', *CLJ* 58 (1991), 84, 87; and of Cane, 'Economic Loss in Tort: Is the Pendulum out of Control?', *MLR* 52 (1989), 200.

[55] See, for example, the judgment of Bingham LJ in *Caparo* v. *Dickman* [1989] 1 QB 653, 683–4: 'The starting point of the argument was that the peculiar character of words has led to insistence on closer proximity between the parties before a duty of care can arise than is required where physical injury or damage is in issue. That this is so emerges, I think, clearly from the Hedley Byrne case itself . . .'

[56] Since, of course, 'negligent words' or 'negligent silence' can also cause physical injury or damage to property. One only has to think of a surgeon who fails to give a sufficiently detailed explanation to his patient prior to operating, or of inadequate information in the field of product liability. [57] Weir, 49 (1990) CLJ 212, 213.

[58] The BGH on numerous occasions has conceded that the true meaning of this provision militates against the finding of a contract for the supply of information as well as against other contractual mechanisms for extending liability. (See e.g. BGH NJW 1973, 323; BGH WM 1978, 576, 577 and BGH BB 1976, 855.) [59] Note 37, above.

scope of the exceptions in both Germany and in England has, at times, increased noticeably.

Precisely what lies behind this developments is unclear. I assume, however, that various forces are at work.[60] First of all, and in quite a general way, the fact that the wealth of modern man consists more and more of 'pure economic interests' must have played a role in this redirection. Second, it seems to me that in our modern economy there always exists the possibility of re-acquisition, with the result that the distinction between *ownership* (meaning the interest in preserving individual tangible objects) and *money* (representing the *possibility* of acquiring ownership) has lost some of its importance. Third, and closer to our immediate theme of professional liability, a new factor has acquired significance. In this field there is a very strong desire to maintain certain standards of service, otherwise the entire service industry is in danger of collapse. Also relevant these days is the generally higher level of education. The academically trained expert is no longer thought of as exceptional, and the point at which persons are ready to take him to court for malpractice has in general come closer as it has in the field of medical malpractice where this development began. Whether and to what extent the popular opinion that members of the service professions earn too much money has contributed to this effect is very clearly a question which, on account of its speculative and political nature, one dare not even ask.

4.2 *Reliance on Expert Knowledge*

Though I have just said that both our legal systems have developed special rules governing the recovery of damages for pure economic loss, that is not to say that the relevant criteria for determining liability are to be found exclusively in that sphere of the law of torts alone. In reality, amongst all the grounds leading to liability, two factors play a decisive role next to the question of foreseeability—two factors which are also relevant to liability in other contexts. These are reliance on and the increased responsibility of those possessed of expert knowledge which they must, on occasion, place at the disposal of a 'non-paying public', in circumstances where it is blatantly obvious to the former that the latter is likely to harm itself by its own ignorance.

Ten years before *Donoghue* v. *Stevenson*[61] was decided, when German law had already begun the task of consolidating the various 'duty of care' situations, a case came before the Reichsgericht involving a vet who was called upon to deal with a cow stricken by anthrax. The cow had to be put down, but not before the butcher employed to slaughter the animal

---

[60] Cf. Bar, op. cit. (n. 19, above).   [61] [1932] AC 562.

contracted the anthrax virus himself through a wound in his finger. The court upheld the butcher's claim for damages on the grounds that the vet had failed to warn him. Whilst it was true that there existed 'no general duty in law to take up arms on behalf of the health of others', it could be said that persons who practice hazardous professions and who offer their services to the public bear a responsibility 'to ensure that whenever their services are employed, a safe and proper system of work is provided'. The practising of a profession or trade of this nature 'gives rise to general duties of care appropriate to that profession or trade which collectively might be described as duties stemming from dealings with all coming into contact with that profession.'[62] This case marks the birth in German tort law of a concept which has formed ever since an important part of the case law of the courts. This concept has, in a similar way also been accepted in the context of liability for pure economic loss.[63] The first relevant decision in the post-war era was a case of the Federal Court delivered on 29 October 1952[64] in which the defendant professional trustee was asked by a landlord to help him draw up a lease agreement with a person interested in taking the lease. During negotiations, the trustee assured the interested party—who was later to become the plaintiff—that an earlier lessee had terminated his contract with the landlord. This was untrue. The plaintiff obtained no benefit under the lease and brought an action claiming damages for wasted expenditure. The Federal Court allowed the claim on the basis of a breach of a *contract* to give information: 'The status of the defendant, being a doctor in law', was 'a good enough reason on which to establish a relationship of confidence with the plaintiff, lending a special weight to the information actually given.' The Federal Court then went on to say that 'That status is a circumstance on which the plaintiff ought to be able to rely upon as proving the information given was prepared with the requisite care.'[65] Exactly the same idea has been used ever since, albeit using different words. Sometimes our courts talk of lawyers as 'the independent voice of the law, perceived throughout a broad cross-section of society as being trustworthy and held in esteem thereby'.[66] In other cases— for example involving 'publicly employed land surveyors and tax advisors' —the makers of statements are deemed to owe a duty of care towards third parties since they 'possess special expert knowledge recognized by the State.'[67] Put differently, 'lawyers, tax advisors and accountants' owe a greater than normal duty towards investors because 'they occupy a peculiar position of trust having regard to their generally acknowledged and

---

[62] RGZ 102, 372, 375.

[63] It is in fact older, if one thinks of Germany's 'leading case' on liability for information, i.e. RGZ 52, 365 *et seq.* (1902). Cf. here 5.2 above.

[64] BGHZ 7, 371.   [65] BGHZ 7, 371, 375–6.

[66] BGH DB 1972, 676, 677.   [67] BGH NJW 1987, 1758, 1759.

elevated professional or economic status, or on account of their quality as a professional person . . .'[68]

According to the German[69] cases then, it is social status and not financial reward which leads to professional liability.[70] In Germany at least, this has been the case for a long time, not just in the domain of pure economic loss. A few years ago, the Federal Court had to decide a case in which the plaintiff, a school teacher, maintained that he had returned home one evening in severe frost and black ice conditions after the time during which citizens were obliged to scatter grit on their roads. His journey took him past a discotheque: while he did not wish to go inside, the entrance was brightly lit and warm, and so the plaintiff rested there for a few moments. The pavement around the entrance had not been gritted and, during a momentary lapse of attention, the plaintiff fell and injured himself. His claim was upheld. Since the public is entitled to rely on the safety of areas near pubs and shop entrances, a duty of care (consisting in a duty to grit), was owed even towards non-guests.[71]

5 Contractual or Tortious Liability

5.1 *General*

It has already been noted that in German law liability for information and opinions causing pure economic loss is dealt with primarily by means of the law of contract (with the exception of para. 826 BGB), while English law treats this as a tort problem. The essential explanation for this different approach has also been mentioned. Para. 823, I BGB[72] restricts the protection to 'absolute' rights which are listed in that paragraph in an exhaustive manner. In England, on the other hand, the doctrines of consideration and privity of contract have blocked the expansion of contract law. Lord Devlin said as much concerning consideration in *Hedley Byrne*;[73] and Lord Jauncey of Tullichettle extended it to the notion of privity in *Smith* v. *Bush*,[74] whilst Millett J in *Al Saudi Banque* v. *Clark Pixley* stated

---

[68] BGH NJW 1990, 2461, 2462.

[69] This thought of course is not unique to German law. It is also forever appearing in the English cases. See, for example, Lord Bridge in *Caparo* v. *Dickman* [1990] 2 AC 605, 619 ('The question what, if any, duty is owed by the maker of a statement to exercise due care to ensure its accuracy arises typically in relation to statements made by a person in the exercise of his calling or profession.').

[70] The fact that 'an expert receives no reward for the information he provides' does not, according to the German courts, 'exclude the possibility of a finding of a tacit contract for the supply of information.' (BGH DB 1985, 1464; BGH WM 1969, 36; BGH WM 1964, 117; BGH WM 1962, 933).					[71] BGH NJW 1987, 2671.

[72] The text is printed at n. 22, above. For details see Markesinis, *The German Law of Torts* (1990).

[73] [1964] AC 465, 525. Decisions such as *Williams* v. *Roffey Bros. & Nicholls (Contractors) Ltd.* [1990] 2 WLR 1153 lead German lawyers to wonder whether the doctrine of consideration is now becoming dispensable. Lack of space, however, forbids digression into that area.					[74] [1989] 2 WLR 790, 822.

it in the following way, 'in *Hedley Byrne* v. *Heller* there was privity but
no contract because of the absence of consideration, (whereas) in *Smith* v.
Bush . . . there was consideration but no privity.'[75]

It is therefore easy to explain why English law took one direction and
German law another. More difficult (and more interesting) is the subsequent question, namely what actual differences do the two approaches produce in practice? Does classifying these cases as contractual (German law)
or as tortious (English law) make any difference at the end of the day? Or
can one detect behind the technical labels precisely the same factors at
work? I believe that one can prove the latter and, moreover, I believe that
in so doing the respective patterns of argument, hitherto seen (and criticized)
purely in a national context, will suddenly appear in a new light.

5.2 Voluntary Assumption of Liability and the Contract to Give Correct Information

If a German lawyer sees his own case law against the background of
English case law, he is, sooner or later, confronted with a question which
at the outset was impossible for him to imagine in the context of tort law,
namely whether or not the defendant has voluntarily assumed liability
towards the plaintiff. In arriving at just such a conclusion Lord Reid was
the first to make use of this idea by asking the question: was there sufficient proximity in the relationship existing between the plaintiff and the
defendant such as would justify the finding that the defendant did, indeed,
owe a duty to take care *vis-à-vis* the plaintiff? He stated in *Hedley Byrne*
that *Candler* v. *Crane, Christmas & Co.* was wrongly decided; *Candler*
appeared to him to be 'a typical case of agreeing to assume responsibility'.[76] Lord Devlin too, in *Hedley Byrne* spoke of a 'responsibility, that is
voluntarily accepted or undertaken.'[77] The case of *Ministry of Housing and
Local Government* v. *Sharp*[78] helped to answer the question whether and
to what extent the neighbour principle enunciated in *Donoghue* v. *Stevenson*
could be consolidated by means of the voluntary assumption of responsibility test. Bingham LJ described this test in *Caparo* as 'very useful';[79] and
Lord Jauncey of Tullichettle preferred in *Smith* v. *Bush* 'to approach the
matter by asking whether the facts disclose that the appellants . . . must . . . ,
by reason of the proximate relationship between them, be deemed to have
assumed responsibility towards Mrs Smith.'[80] The assumption of liability

---

[75] [1990] 2 WLR 344, 353.   [76] [1964] AC 465, 487.
[77] [1964] AC 465, 529.   [78] [1970] 2 QB 223.   [79] [1989] 2 WLR 316, 326.
[80] [1990] 2 WLR 790, 822. Cf. now *Kuwait Bank* v. *National Nominees Ltd.* (PC) [1991]
1 AC 187, 219 (per Lord Lowry), where one reads the following: 'But although directors are
not liable as such to creditors of the company, a director may by agreement or representation
assume a special duty to a creditor of the company. A director may accept or assume a duty
of care in supplying information to a creditor analogous to the duty described by the House
of Lords in *Hedley Byrne* . . .' One could hardly express the similarity between English tort
law and German contract law any more clearly!

test is, however, anything but uncontroversial. Correcting the law of contract by means of rules borrowed from the law of torts is not acceptable, according to one view;[81] that the test cannot be used in all cases is stressed by others.[82] Even within the House of Lords itself there appears to be a difference of opinion. 'I do not think that voluntary assumption of responsibility is a helpful or realistic test for liability', pronounced Lord Griffiths in *Smith* v. *Bush*,[83] whilst Lord Roskill in *Caparo* expressly declared himself to be in support of Lord Griffiths' view. According to Lord Roskill, it is not a question of voluntary assumption of responsibility; rather that phrase is used to denote the existence of circumstances, 'in which the law will impose a liability.'[84]

Neither these differences in approach nor the matter itself are strange to German lawyers, only in my country the discussion is inverted, for it is asserted that the 'German' doctrine of assumption of liability represents contract law being used to correct a tort law system which is too narrow. The starting point here is an early decision of the Reichsgericht dating back to 1902. A lawyer gave a bank negligent information pertaining to the number of charges registered against his client's land. The result was a loan made to this client which was in effect wholly insecure due to the extent of the charges. The bank's claim for damages could not be supported by the law of torts. The lawyer was personally held liable for, in the view of the Reichsgericht, he had 'entered—tacitly—into a contractual relation'. The court continued: 'Where a person, whose profession it is to give advice of the kind presently under consideration, learns that another person needs reliable information in connection with just such a matter, and proceeds to give that other person written advice on precisely this matter, then he thereby enters into a contractual relation with that other person.'[85] This case represents the beginning of a long series of decisions which have continued up until the present day using the same approach, namely that a so-called contract to supply correct information arises where one person gives another person information which is of considerable importance to the recipient, the latter intending to use the information given to him as the basis for important arrangements having economic, legal, or factual implications.[86] The content of this contract—not supported by 'consideration'—is not a duty to give information, but ultimately an

---

[81] Huxley, *MLR* 53 (1990), 369, 376. On the whole matter see Markesinis, 'An Expanding Tort Law: The Price of a Rigid Contract Law', *LQR* 103 (1987), 354.

[82] See Bingham LJ in *Caparo* v. *Dickman* [1989] 2 WLR 316, 326 and Salmon LJ in *Ministry of Housing and Local Government* v. *Sharp* [1970] 2 QB 223, 279.

[83] [1989] 2 WLR 790, 813.

[84] [1990] 2 AC 605, 628. Also Lord Denning in *Ministry of Housing* (n. 82) at 269.

[85] RGZ 52, 365, 366–7.

[86] See BGHZ 7, 371, 374; BGHZ 74, 103, 106 and BGH JZ 1985, 951; This is accepted law.

'assumption of liability': whoever gives information under such circumstances must ensure that it is correct; he who makes a mistake is liable for it. Para. 676 BGB to which we have already alluded does not apparently contradict this,[87] because it clearly states that this provision does not affect any liability that may arise out of a contract.

It is not my intention here to ask the question whether one can reproach the German courts for playing dogmatic 'tricks' in this area of law. Much more interesting is to find out in which areas they have affirmed the existence of a contract to supply correct information and in which they have rejected it. For in this way one may discover what really lies behind this 'voluntary assumption of responsibility'. The BGH has in principle always affirmed, or rather taken into consideration, the existence of a contract for the supply of correct information in cases of a direct contact between the giver and the recipient of the information. Where the giver of information has himself done something at the behest of his client, such as actually seeking out the third person, the matter is fairly straightforward. This approach goes as far back as 1902 to the aforementioned decision of the Reichsgericht.[88] It formed the basis, too, for the decision, already discussed in the context of para. 826 BGB, concerning the lawyer who acted on behalf of his client in credit negotiations;[89] and for cases involving banks which provided a supplier of goods with details of a client's creditworthiness at the latter's instructions.[90] A contract to supply correct information will also be upheld in circumstances where an accountant compiles credit documents in accordance with his clients' wishes, and then hands them over to a bank,[91] or who permits his client to do so.[92] Nothing here suggests that the identity of the person requesting the information in the first place could be at all decisive. For its part, the BGH has always sought to stress that,

> Whosoever gives information, either in his or her professional capacity or for personal profit, knowing that the information is of considerable importance to the questioner (e.g. that it may form the basis for extensive business decisions) . . . generally acts in the awareness that he is making a binding statement, possibly with legal consequences, and not just an off-the-cuff opinion free of any legal implications whatsoever. At any rate, in the majority of instances, it will be understood thus by the questioner; and it is the latter's understanding which is relevant.[93]

There is then no doubt that *Hedley Byrne* would have been decided in Germany according to the rules relating to the breach of a contract to supply correct information. As the BGH has made clear elsewhere, 'it

---

[87] But cf. n. 58, above.   [88] N. 85, above.   [89] N. 36, above.
[90] BGH WM 1985, 381.   [91] BGH JZ 1986, 1111.   [92] BGH WM 1965, 287.
[93] BGH VersR 1986, 35. Insofar as the published text speaks of non-binding 'statements of *mind*' (Willenserklärung), in my opinion there must be a printing error for it should read 'statements of *knowledge*' (Wissenserklärung).

cannot make any difference in the eyes of the law, whether it was the person seeking the information who went to the bank or vice versa.'[94]

Further examples involving this type of liability may be gleaned from those cases involving advice that led to poor investments. Those who manage investment portfolios, which are subject to preferential tax provisions, are liable in damages towards those persons to whom they send an incorrect market *exposé* accompanied by a 'strong recommendation' that they participate.[95] The same applies to an accountant who works for a limited partnership (*Kommanditgesellschaft*) and who personally advises a partner that he should take a larger stake in the partnership, the accountant providing the necessary bridging finance.[96] On the other hand, no such liability should arise where an employee acting as a 'non-independent tool' sells shares outside the Stock Exchange,[97] or where an accountant, not acting in connection with a statutory audit, is taken to court by a potential shareholder after the company has, on its own initiative (and without the accountant's knowledge), made the results of the accountant's work available to that interested party;[98] or where a lawyer uses merely 'soothing words' to his client's creditor, words which in no way indicate that the lawyer is informed about his client's business relations.[99] If there were no special provisions applicable to statutory audits, then, in my opinion, it would, again, be difficult to find a contract to supply correct information in circumstances like those found in *Caparo*. The BGH has indeed held on numerous occasions that a contract for the supply of information may also arise with more than one person, and that in such situations it is irrelevant that the giver and receiver of the information are not personally known to one another.[100] Conversely however, it is always crucial that the supplier of the information (e.g. a bank or a manager of investment portfolios) has a particular group of people in mind (e.g. lenders), whom he attempts to convince to participate in a given project. Without this aim of wanting to find investors in the open market who are interested in a certain project, liability under a contract for the supply of correct information simply cannot arise.

6   Preliminary conclusions

At this point I think we ought to pause in order to draw some preliminary conclusions. All claims permitted under para. 676 BGB (i.e. for tortious and contractual liability), are exhausted by the dual provisions of para. 826 BGB and of the contract for the supply of correct information. What

---

[94] BGH NJW 1979, 1595, 1596.   [95] BGH WM 1979, 530.
[96] BGH WM 1975, 763.   [97] BGH VersR 1986, 35, 36.
[98] OLG Saarbrücken BB 1978, 1434.   [99] BGH WM 1978, 576.
[100] BGH NJW 1979, 1595; BGH VersR 1986, 35 *et al.*

exists beyond these is entirely a creation of the courts, and therefore it strikes me as appropriate to deal with liability for '*culpa in contrahendo*', together with liability for breach of contracts having effect in favour of third parties at a later point.

Where have our observations led us thus far? Relatively straightforward appear to me those cases in which experts give advice or recommendations, or even an affirmation or off-the-cuff certification, foreseeing in the process a certain course of events and accepting the possibility that within such a course third parties will make use of the information. 'Fraud includes the pretence of knowledge when knowledge there is none', said Mr Justice Cardozo as long ago as 1931 in *Ultramares Corporation* v. *Touche*, adding that 'To creditors and investors to whom the employer exhibited the certificate, the defendants owed a like duty to make it without fraud, since there was notice in the circumstances of its making that the employer did not intend to keep it to himself.'[101] German case law takes exactly the same view, and I, too, consider this to be the correct starting point. German case law has, however, gone a step further and has put the irresponsible mistake on a par with fraud. I must confess that I basically agree with this approach, with the caveat that these cases should be classified as negligence cases so far as insurance law is concerned. Viewed uniquely from the perspective of liability, all these cases may be conveniently grouped together under their own rules. I find unconvincing the traditional English law approach, which recognizes no distinction between categories of carelessness in the tort of negligence. Cardozo's leap from a pretention of knowledge to a 'thoughtless slip or blunder', which cannot be allowed to expose accountants to 'liability for an indeterminate amount for an indeterminate time to an indeterminate class',[102] is, simply, too broad. It may be that the English courts are currently pondering over the same question. *Yianni* v. *Edwin Evans & Sons* provides us with an example here, for Park J expressly stressed in that case that 'the defendant's report and valuation was the result of a grossly incompetent and negligent survey.'[103] Today's service industry is bound by a minimum of professional standards, and the expert must attain this standard in his dealings with all those who he knows will rely on his expertise: *éducation oblige*.

Liability for 'normal' or 'simple' negligence on the other hand comes in for consideration when a particularly close relationship exists between the informer and the informed, which obliges the former to include within his circle of contemplation the financial interests of the informed. Precisely what constitutes this 'particularly close relationship' lies at the heart of our inquiry; and I think few, if any, would be bold enough to try and solve this problem in one single sentence. The best we can do is to divide up the

---

[101] 174 NE 441, 444 (1931).   [102] N. 101, above.   [103] [1982] 1 QB 438, 446.

cases under various headings, and then to list those factors which influence the decision of the court in any given group.

One such factor common to both legal systems is that of 'assumption of liability'. To me it seems self-evident that one cannot do away with this factor simply by saying that on the facts there has been no 'voluntary' assumption of liability. This is so because no one (including a party to a contract) is liable because he wishes to be liable, but rather because he *ought* to be. Contracts for the supply of correct information and the voluntary assumption of liability are designed for situations in which the giver of the information forfeits the protection afforded by the requirement of 'consideration'. Where a service has been provided in circumstances in which remuneration *could* have been demanded but which *in fact* was not so demanded (normally because the supplier of the information accrues a different benefit which he clearly considers as adequate),[104] then that supplier is liable just as a party to a contract would be. In these cases it is only of secondary importance whether this principle is expressed using the language of the law of torts or of the law of contract. In addition, it might well be of importance that the provider of the information enjoys an (actual or perceived) monopoly in a given sphere of information and so owes a higher degree of care. For these reasons, the issues appear clear to me where a giver of information has, himself, a financial interest in the recipient's decision whether or not to go ahead with an investment. This is the case where the informer is seeking investors for a project in which he, himself, has an interest; for this is, essentially, a case of financing via others. Additionally, it is usual in this type of case that the supplier of the information is relied upon as the sole source of information, without the potential investor/recipient making inquiries of his own. *Mutual Life and Citizens' Assurance Co. v. Evatt*[105] would, I think, have been decided by a German court in favour of the plaintiff (although as far as I know there is no exact equivalent in our law). Furthermore, a level of care equivalent to that existing in a contract is expected of persons contacting third parties for the purpose of securing a pecuniary advantage for their own clients and who do so because they feel adequately rewarded under the terms of their relationship with their clients. The giver of information in these circumstances bears a responsibility precisely because, by virtue of his special professional status and his concomitant ability for giving independent advice, he is elevated to a position of trust. As regards a bank's liability for the information it provides, I consider a banker's duty of confidentiality

---

[104] Lang, *WPg* (1989), 57, 62 (n. 6, above) quite rightly states that 'the sharp distinction made in the Civil Code Book between paid transactions (actual and full recompense) and unpaid transactions (understood by the fathers of the Civil Code Book as having an altruistic character), and treated in some respects as less enduring . . . has become questionable today.'

[105] [1971] AC 793 (PC).

a crucial factor, since it means that *a priori* it is forbidden to pass on client information to others. If, then, a bank does supply an outsider with such information, it must realize that, at the very least, it is the main or sole source of that information. Moreover, it must also accept liability because it does not provide this kind of information for altruistic reasons. For a bank, in its own interests as well as those of its clients, has every reason to ensure it is well informed about the local economic situation. Banks seek to be involved, and precisely this motivation generates their particular duty of care. This is not confined just to banks, however, a point well illustrated by an interesting case which went to the BGH twice[106] in the course of the 1980s. This is an interesting case since it also leads us naturally into the law of contracts with protective effects *vis-à-vis* third parties.

In April 1974 the defendant surveyor prepared a report for the owner of land, estimating its value, along with that of the building that was on it, at DM 20 million. Armed with the surveyor's report, the landowner sought further finance. After complex negotiations, a Danish bank became interested. It offered a loan over DM 15 million which, in turn, was secured against the land and other securities to the tune of some DM 18 million. One of the securities was taken over in June of 1975 by the Danish Exportcredit Council, a State-run body. Before concluding this security agreement, however, the Danish Consul in Munich in December 1974, acting on behalf of the Exportcredit Council, contacted the defendant and asked him if he was a publicly employed and commissioned surveyor and whether he still stood by his original report. The defendant replied that the land was likely to have increased in price since the preparation of the report, and confirmed his reply in a letter to the consul. In 1976 a forced sale of the land in question raised a mere DM 1.9 million for the plaintiff, because building regulations made it illegal to build on most of the land. The plaintiff claimed damages from the defendant surveyor. The BGH found that the latter had breached his duties under a contract to supply information. Through the Consul the defendant became aware of the fact that the information requested was to form the basis of an eventual decision concerning the granting of credit worth millions of Deutschmarks. Understandably, the Consul had turned to the defendant because of his expertise. 'The absence of any expectation of financial return does not itself exclude the finding of a tacit contract. Once a contract for the proper supply of information has been found to exist, then the defendant is obliged to give the requested information with the appropriate

---

[106] The case was returned to the appellate court by the BGH in both instances: BGH WM 1982, 762; NJW 1982, 2431 and BGH JZ 1985, 951 (and Honsell, case-note); NJW-RR 1986, 484. Also an informative essay by Damm, 'Entwicklungstendenzen der Expertenhaftung', JZ (1991), 373, 378. Cf. also Hübner, 'Vertrag mit Schutzwirkung für Dritte und Ersatz von Vermögensschäden', VersR 1991, 497 *et seq.*

care and to give it accurately.'[107] Thus, the only question was *with whom* the contract had been concluded. Clearly the Consul, himself, was not a contracting party. It was equally impossible to say that, in his capacity as Consul, he could have acted as the representative of the private bank. The BGH took the view that the Consul had acted for his country and thus on behalf of the Danish Exportcredit Council. A contract had therefore been concluded between the State of Denmark and the surveyor. As a result, the latter's duties were not confined to his immediate co-contractor. It remained open to either party to such a contract to bring third parties within its ambit, and this is precisely what happened with the plaintiff bank. The bank, therefore, had a claim in damages for breach of a contract which had protective effects in its favour. The BGH went on to say that it was not true that this ruling exposed the surveyor to an excessive risk of liability: 'It is possible simply to insure against the risk a surveyor runs for incorrect evaluations. It is also beyond doubt that the defendant is indeed insured against the present liability, and that its extent is sufficient to satisfy the claim.'[108]

7 Judicial Creations: *Culpa in Contrahendo* and Contracts with Protective Effects Towards Third Parties Lying in between Contract and Tort

7.1 *Legal Obligations in the Law of Contract*

Here we are confronted with one of the most peculiar creations of the German courts: contracts having protective effects towards third parties. It is beyond the terms of this essay to describe the precise details of this contract; and this is so not only because the BGH is trying to use this construction in a whole bundle of heterogenous cases. I shall confine myself to the basics.

German tort law as laid down in the BGB has not only failed to provide a satisfactory regime for pure economic loss; equally striking is the absence of rules of strict liability relating to employs' liability for the torts of his employees. Para. 831 BGB[109] states that no liability shall attach to an

---

[107] BGH JZ 1985, 951.

[108] Note 107, above , at p. 952. This reference to the allegedly adequate insurance cover may strike one as a little tongue-in-cheek if it is true that the plaintiff only claimed for DM 500,000 when his total loss amounted to DM 7.5 million at the time of the action complained of (also Ebke/Scheel, WM 1991, 389, 397).

[109] (1) A person who employs another to do any work is bound to compensate for damage which the other unlawfully causes to a third party in the performance of his work. The duty to compensate does not arise if the employer has exercised ordinary care in the choice of the employee and, where he has to supply appliances or implements or to superintend the work, has also exercised ordinary care as regards such supply or superintendence, or if the damage would have arisen, notwithstanding the exercise of such care.
Translation from Markesinis, op. cit., n. 13, above.

employer for the negligent act(s) of his employees if the employer is not himself negligent in connection with those acts. Furthermore, many difficulties have arisen by the limitation period, which for torts is three years,[110] and also the fact that victims of torts must prove the defendant's negligence. All these matters are regulated in a different manner in contract law. This branch of the law makes an employer's liability for his employees independent of fault (para. 278 BGB); the limitation period in contract cases normally runs for 30 years (para. 195 BGB); fault is presumed in cases of breach of contract (para. 282 BGB), and, finally, contract law makes no distinction between 'pure' and 'other' economic loss. One can easily see why the German courts almost always turn their attention to the law of contract and exploit every available opportunity to escape from the strictures of the law of torts. The device of the contract for the supply of information has already given some idea of this.

From the above, one notices that the developments which I wish to trace in the following pages did not begin in the field of pure economic loss but rather in the field of physical damage. The classic cases involve damage suffered by shoppers etc. who slip outside a shop on black ice or who slip inside as a result of stepping on slippery substances such as peeling linoleum floors,[111] banana skins,[112] or vegetable leaves.[113] From a legal point of view, what each of these situations have in common is that they all take place immediately prior to the making of a contract, and for the German courts this is the decisive feature. Relying on an idea developed by *Rudolf v. Jhering*,[114] the Reichsgericht found that legal obligations may arise even before the actual conclusion of the contract. As a result, both parties are obliged to deal with each other with the care reserved for 'co-contractors'.[115] *Culpa in contrahendo* was born. But what was to happen when the victim was not the potential co-contractor, but someone coming into contact with the source of danger, with the 'doer's' blessing, in exactly the same way as the co-contractor? Should children accompanying their mothers doing the shopping be any worse off? This idea, too, was rejected by the courts, which instead 'discovered' the contract with protective effects towards third parties.[116]

German tort law has not stood still since the turn of the century. It has

---

[110] Para. 852 BGB.

[111] RGZ 78, 239; (case no. 65 in Markesinis, op. cit., n. 13, above).

[112] BGH NJW 1962, 31.

[113] BGHZ 66, 51 (case no. 66 in Markesinis, op. cit., n. 13, above).

[114] 'Culpa in Contrahendo oder Schadensersatz bei Nichtigen oder nicht zur Perfektion gelangten Verträgen', *JhJb* 4 (1861), 1 *et seq.*   [115] As n. 111; since settled law.

[116] As n. 113. On contracts with third-party protective effects in the English language see, Markesinis, op. cit. (n. 13, above), 74 and Kötz, 'The Doctrine of Privity of Contract in the Context of Contracts Protecting the Interests of Third Parties', *Tel Aviv Univ Studies in Law* 10 (1991).

conquered a good deal of new territory as far as employers' liability and the burden of proof is concerned.[117] However, it remains intransigent in the field of protection afforded to primary economic interests (quite apart from the question of limitation, which is in the process of reform). It is in the field of primary economic interests, however, that both the doctrine of *culpa in contrahendo* and the contract with third-party protective effects have been applied most vigorously. Indeed, in recent history *culpa in contrahendo* rules have been used to create a special sub-class of liability for the author of a prospectus who circulates it amongst people outside the Stock Exchange (the so-called 'grey' capital market) seeking investment opportunities at advantageous tax rates and who are thus prepared to put money into so-called '*Abschreibungsgesellschaften*' and '*Bauherrenmodelle*'.[118] The extent and basis for this liability was described in a case decided by the BGH in 1980, in the following terms:

'Prospectus liability' . . . is an extension of 'reliance liability' as developed in the cases involving some element of fault in the negotiations stage of making a contract, in an area which Parliament has not seen fit to legislate, yet which is in need of legal regulation . . . It is immaterial when establishing this liability (which protects the investor's reliance on the correctness of information given in a prospectus) . . . , whether the person giving the information is actually mentioned in the prospectus or otherwise known to the recipient of the information; of relevance are that person's participation and responsibility alone.[119]

The *culpa in contrahendo* rule, together with contracts having third-party protective effects and reliance liability (which simultaneously brings both of the above concepts together and extends them)[120] have become familiar features in German law and must, accordingly, be treated as part of customary law. As far as legal classification goes, they obviously oscillate in quite a unique fashion between tort and contract law. One might even be compelled to say that German law has constructed a 'third lane' between tort and contract law. These doctrines fulfil a tortious role insofar as they are aimed at compensating damage to pre-existing interests, and not at compensation for unfulfilled expectations. They furthermore retain an affinity with tort law in that they are the expression of obligations not arising on the basis of mutual declarations which lead to the formation of a contract.[121] This hardly needs mention as far as *culpa in contrahendo* is

---

[117] For more details, v. Bar, *JuS* 1982, 637 *et seq.* and *JuS* 1988, 169 *et seq.*

[118] On this point now BGH NJW 1990, 2461.

[119] BGHZ 79, 337, 339–40 (the text is not a literal translation). It should be noted that it is not necessary to prove that the 'recipient' of the information has in fact read the prospectus.

[120] It should be remembered that the BGH used 'reliance liability' to create liability for the issue of certifications, n. 17, above.

[121] Thus BGHZ 6, 330, 333; BGH DB 1981, 1274 *et al.*

concerned. But as far as contracts with third-party effects go (where the BGH unfortunately employs different reasoning), matters are not so straightforward. In the aforementioned case involving the Danish consul,[122] the BGH attributed liability to the (real or imputed) intentions of the parties, i.e. it argues 'contractually' in a narrow sense. But the BGH does not stop there. Many different approaches are to be found in the case law of our Supreme Court from which just one case dating back to 1977 is chosen here for consideration.

A goods supplier, with his client's authority, was to debit the latter's bank account with all sums payable for goods delivered under the contract (so-called 'reverse transfer'). Even though the client's account became overdrawn, the client's bank failed to notify the supplier's bank of this fact. The bank was, however, under a duty to make such notification by reason of an agreement made between all German banks, the so-called Reverse Transfer Agreement (*Lastschriftabkommen der Banken*). Although this Agreement stated quite *explicitly* that it created no rights for third parties, the BGH nonetheless classified it as a contract having protective effects for third parties, and then surprisingly went on to say that 'The duty to protect rests not on the Agreement, but on the legal relations as outlined in this judgment, on their purpose, and on equitable principles; such duty would moreover be found to exist even if there had been no Reverse Transfer Agreement at all.'[123] It follows that in some cases the will of the parties is decisive, whereas on other occasions the BGH applies an objective test.

7.2 *Those Protected*

I think that these brief remarks are not only sufficient to show how contracts with protective effects for third parties work but also to demonstrate that within their framework German lawyers, like English lawyers, face exactly the same problems of determining the range of protected persons. Both legal systems are preoccupied with the same question, namely who belongs to the group of persons owed a duty of care by the giver of information? Less obvious are the parallels between the two legal systems when it comes to *culpa in contrahendo* and what followed therefrom, i.e. 'reliance liability'. To be sure, oblique connections of a sort do, indeed, exist. For example, Viscount Haldane studied in Göttingen,[124] and this might

---

[122] Note 106, above.

[123] BGHZ 69, 82, 88. (Translated extracts of which can be found in Markesinis, 'An Expanding Tort Law: The Price of a Rigid Contract Law', LQR 103 (1987), 354, 366–8.) For (straightforward) transfers, see OLG Düsseldorf WM 1982, 575, where a contract with third-party protective effects was also upheld in favour of the client requesting the transfer.

[124] Richard Burdon Haldane, *An Autobiography*, 3rd edn. (1921), 21: 'I used at times to hear other great teachers. Ritschl was there, and von Jhering, whose books on Jurisprudence I was to study later.'

explain the similarity between 'fiduciary relationship' as laid down in *Nocton* v. *Lord Ashburton*[125] and the *culpa in contrahendo* doctrine. In addition, I find echoes of German 'reliance liability' in the case of *Dutton* v. *Bognor Regis Urban District Council*[126] and in section 43(1) Companies Act 1948 though the link here is not obvious and this problem has not yet, on the whole, received sufficient attention to provide us with a workable comparative law analysis. For this reason, my following remarks are confined to contracts with protective effects for third parties.

The traditional criteria for ascertaining the persons owed a duty under these contracts (besides actual parties thereto) are given in the question whether or not, '. . . a third person comes into contact with the performance of the contract in a way which is evident to the party owing that performance, and in respect of such third party the person owed the contractual performance in turn owes a duty in that area in which the initial obligation operates.'[127] In answering this question it used to be decisive whether or not the person who owed the obligation under the contract was under any responsibility for the 'well-being' of the third person.[128] Whilst essential for damage caused to persons and to property, originally this formula was not developed for cases of pure economic loss. Nowadays, *this* criterion (responsibility for the 'well-being') has become just one amongst many in this area of law. Nonetheless, it is one which has not wholly disappeared. An illustration of this is provided by a ruling of the BGH in 1965, which may be thought of as the German counterpart to *Ross* v. *Caunters*,[129] and which, like that case, was decided in favour of the plaintiff. The defendant was a lawyer who was asked by the plaintiff to visit her sick father, as he was eager to make a will. This the lawyer did, promising moreover that he would return in due course with a notary. In spite of repeated and pressing telephone calls made by the plaintiff, the defendant failed to keep his word. The father died before the will was drawn up with the result that the plaintiff, instead of being the sole heiress, as she would have been, had the planned will been executed, was forced to share the inheritance with her niece in equal shares. The BGH upheld the plaintiff's claim for damages on the basis that she fell within the scope of the contract made between her father and the lawyer. 'That the plaintiff was to be the sole heiress, was the expression and aim of personal love and care, resting on a close family bond.'[130]

A second criterion with a role to play in these cases is that of concurrence or, as the case may be, of opposition of interests. Inclusion of third parties under the umbrella of contractual protection becomes impossible when their interests are at variance with those of the person enjoying

---

[125] Note 41, above.   [126] [1972] 1 QB 373, 397.   [127] BGHZ 49, 350, 354.
[128] Cf. here BGHZ 51, 91, 96; BGHZ 66, 51, 57 and BGH NJW 1971, 1931.
[129] [1979] 3 WLR 605.   [130] BGH JZ 1966, 141, 142 *et seq*. NJW 1965, 1955.

contractual rights *stricto sensu*. The leading case here was decided by the BGH in 1972:[131] The defendant accountant had for years been responsible for preparing the end-of-year accounts for a sole trader. The defendant certified a number of these accounts in the knowledge that they would be shown to banks with whom the trader had continuing business relations. In total, the trader was working with 17 credit institutions. In 1965 he went bankrupt. The BGH rejected the bank's contention that the end-of-year accounts overestimated the amount of capital invested by the trader himself in the business. The inclusion of the plaintiff bank in the protective sphere of the contract was rejected, 'having regard, inter alia, to the clear conflict of interests in respect of the representation of creditworthiness existing between the contractor (i.e. the trader) on the one hand and the bank on the other.' To uphold contractual liability, 'would bring with it the danger of incalculable, and in view of the interests at stake, unjustifiable, exposure to liability.'[132] The judgment is remarkably restrictive, but distinguishable from the otherwise pro-plaintiff jurisprudence of the BGH, in that the case did not involve a decision whether or not to grant credit for a certain investment, but rather whether or not to put an end to an already-existing loan agreement. Moreover, the number of banks with which the trader had business relations was relatively high and the accountant could not reasonably be expected to bear the risk of such liability. If I understand it correctly, Lord Jauncey's express affirmation in *Caparo*[133] of Millet J's decision in *Al Saudi Banque* v. *Clark Pixley*[134] is sufficient proof that that case before the German BGH would have been decided identically by an English court of law. The conflict of interests factor, however, which to my mind clearly existed and should have played a role in *Caparo*, has hitherto only been considered in English law in cases dealing with lawyers' liability towards third parties.[135] The explanation for this may be that English law seeks to establish a relationship between the *giver* of information and third parties, whereas German law asks itself if there is a sufficient link between the *recipient* of information and the third party.

A relatively recent decision of the BGH, and particularly interesting in the light of current developments in English law, was one decided in 1986,[136] and I shall conclude this essay with that case. The facts were as follows. A film director wished to purchase a limited liability company from its sole owner for approximately DM 500,000. The venture was

---

[131] BGH NJW 1973, 322. Cf. also OLG Saarbrücken BB 1978, 1434; BGH KTS 1988, 314, 316, and OLG Köln VersR 1991, 564, 566.   [132] BGH NJW 1973, 322, 323.

[133] [1990] 2 AC 605, 662.   [134] [1990] Ch 313; [1990] 2 WLR 344.

[135] See Sir Robert Megarry VC in *Ross* v. *Caunters* [1980] Ch 297, 320–3; *Balcombe* LJ in *Clarke* v. *Bruce Lane & Co. (a firm) and others* [1988] 1 All ER 364, 369 and cf. also *Gartside* v. *Sheffield Young & Ellis* [1983] NZLR 37, 43–4.

[136] BGH NJW 1987, 1758; ZIP 1987, 376; DB 1987, 828; WM 1987, 257; VersR 1987, 262.

financed by the film director's bank—the eventual plaintiff. The company had received a set of interim accounts prepared by the defendant tax advisor which, at the very least, amounted to a negligent representation of the company's assets. The bank, which authorized the making of a loan using the company shares as security, was unable to claim the payment of the loan instalments. Having examined para. 826 BGB and the rules relating to contracts for the supply of correct information, the BGH turned its attention to contracts with protective effects for third parties. As already shown in the *Danish Consul* case,[137] the BGH based its decision on a different argument, namely, whether the defendant himself had tacitly assented to the inclusion of the third party in the contract and by this means therefore had established the necessary contact with that third party. Accordingly, it was the parties' intentions which were decisive, the 'assumption of liability' and not the (obviously inadequate) connection between the bank and the company. In the BGH's view, there were on the facts, 'indications that the parties intended to bring third parties within the protective scope of their contract.'[138] The defendant knew that the interim report prepared by himself was by no means intended solely for the purposes of informing the company. Indeed ultimately, the report was irrelevant as far as the company was concerned. True, the defendant knew neither the film director nor his bank, but that was not, according to the BGH, decisive in the instant case. Rather, it was sufficient that the defendant 'recognised that the report was intended either for a purchaser or for persons giving credit (banks).' Of course there are limits to be set on just who falls within this protective scope, for it is, 'necessary that this protective duty be restricted to a clearly defined class of persons.' The BGH decided that this requirement was met on the facts of this case since, 'the scope of protection only [extends to] the purchaser and any would-be supplier of credit to the purchaser.'[139]

This decision has met with strong criticism in academic circles[140]—with good reason, it seems to me, since the BGH has in effect here created the contract with protective effects towards 'fourth' parties by taking into account the bank standing behind the potential purchaser of the company.[141] At the same time the decision fails to explain precisely why banks should deserve protection for financing the original purchase. Should it really make any difference whether a bank puts up money for the takeover of the company itself or whether, the film director having financed the purchase out of his own pocket, the bank then puts up money for another

---

[137] Note 107 and n. 108, above.

[138] BGH NJW 1987, 1758, 1759.   [139] Note 138, above, at 1760.

[140] For greater details see Schindhelm/Grothe, n. 51, above and Ebke/Scheel, n. 12, above.

[141] That only the 'first third party' is protected is a view shared by Hopt, 'Dritthaftung für Testate', *NJW* 1987, 1745 *et seq.*

plan on the basis of that company's balance-sheet?[142] I think that in neither of these situations is a bank particularly well protected; it would only be different had the tax advisor acted with gross negligence and thoughtlessly. The methodology of the BGH in this case is peculiarly reminiscent of Lord Wilberforce's 'two-stage-test' developed in *Anns* v. *Merton London Borough Council*,[143] apparently now[144] confined to legal history since the decision in *Murphy* v. *Brentwood*.[145] For it is not enough to say that prima facie there exists as between the injurer and the injured a sufficient degree of proximity so that the former was able to foresee that an error on his part was likely to injure the latter and then, by way of a balancing act, to ask whether there are good grounds for limiting the class of claimants. For such grounds may always be found, and no one seems to know in advance what they really are. Personally I, therefore, favour the view, first expounded by Lord Denning more than forty years ago, that a duty of care is indeed owed to third parties, when a balance sheet is laid before them for their perusal with a view to persuading them to invest in a company. 'But I do not think', added the learned judge, 'that the duty can be extended still further so as to include strangers of whom they [the accountants] have heard nothing, and to whom their employer, without their knowledge, may choose to show their accounts.'[146]

8   Conclusion

Conscious of just how difficult it is to bring the degree of clarity to the hydra-headed problem of professional liability towards third parties, I venture some conclusions in a very tentative form.

1 For statutory company audits, para. 323 HGB provides a special regime which excludes third-party claims, whenever the accountant was not acting intentionally. Thus *Caparo* would have been decided in just the same way in Germany. The distinction between actual and potential shareholders is thus redundant in this context.

2 In German law, at least for the purpose of establishing liability, a distinction should be made between intention, thoughtless behaviour amounting to gross negligence, and ordinary negligence. The existence of the second type of fault would justify the extension of the class of protected third parties.

---

[142] Cf. *Kötz*, op. cit. (n. 116, above).   [143] [1978] AC 728, 751–2.

[144] Doubts concerning the correctness of the 'two-stages-test' had already been expressed in a number of other cases: e.g. *Governors of Peabody Donation Fund* v. *Sir Lindsay Parkinson & Co. of Hong Kong* [1988] AC 210, 239–41; *Yuen Kun Yeu* v. *Attorney General of Hong Kong* [1988] AC 175, 190–4 and above all by Lord Keith of Kinkel in *Hill* v. *Chief Constable of West Yorkshire* [1989] AC 53, 60.

[145] [1990] 3 WLR 414; [1990] 2 All ER 908.

[146] *Candler* v. *Crane Christmas* [1951] 2 KB 164, 181.

3 Generally, it is of little consequence, whether one decides the individual cases of professional liability towards third parties using the law of torts or the law of contract. Whatever the 'wrapping', the questions inside remain the same. It is conceivable that the traditional tort–contract distinction has in this context lost its justification. Reliance on professional expertise, and the fact that an important economic self-interest often lies at the heart of unpaid information in today's service industry, have altered the landscape of liability.

4 Voluntary assumption of liability exists both in German and English law. This is sensible in cases of direct contact between the giver and receiver of information, where the giver has created such a state of reliance that he shows himself prepared to deal as if he were a co-contractor. This in turn depends on the person acting in his capacity as expert and possessing an economic or other self-interest in being asked questions. To this must come the knowledge (actual or imputed), that the recipient of the information is dependent on the information for making important investment or credit decisions. English law could operate far more convincingly using the concept of voluntary assumption of liability (or voluntary assumption of duty), were it prepared to do without the doctrine of consideration.

5 Where no direct contact exists between the parties, then such contact must be imputed using criteria which to date are incapable of being expressed in one neat, unified formula. Mere foreseeability is insufficient. Inclusion of 'fourth parties behind third parties' ought to be impossible insofar as the supplier of information has not acted thoughtlessly (as defined above).

6 German judges are more interested in proximity between the first recipient of information and third parties, whereas their English brethren in principle examine the connection between the giver of information and third parties. In reality, both approaches are relevant and therefore should be given due consideration in the task of assessing the facts of each case.

7 An easily distinguishable special sub-class of case has developed, at least in Germany, in respect of investment prospectus' circulated outside the stock-market. Moreover, cases involving non-cash payment transactions settled *en masse* have a special place within the context of contracts with protective third-party effects. In this area the courts have made fresh use of general liability, which to date has escaped closer classification, and which is based on the idea of reliance and steps taken as a result of such reliance. The same applies to liability for persons who issue references.

8 Cases falling outside these special categories are dealt with partly by reference to responsibility for an individual's welfare, partly by a finding of concurrent (or conflicting) interests, and partly by inquiring into the

intentions of the immediate co-contractor. The first criterion still plays a considerable role in cases of lawyers' liability,[147] the second insulates accountants against liability *vis-à-vis* banks enjoying a long-standing relationship with the company whose accounts have been audited. By contrast, the third criterion appears less sensible, at least in cases where a tax advisor or accountant has had no direct contact with the investor. The investor himself may be protected, but there exists no reason whatsoever to arm his supplier of credit with the means of claiming against the advisor.

9 Discovering what the German law is requires a constant and careful study of its case law with its codal provisions only providing the starting points of the enquiry. This is a crucial point that both English and comparative lawyers should bear in mind; and it should also make German lawyers keener to study how the common-law lawyers handle their case law.

---

[147] Cf. with BGH JZ 1966, 141 (n. 130, above) and in particular BGH NJW 1977, 2073; OLG Hamm MDR 1986, 1027 and BGH JZ 1988, 656.

On the evening of 4 November 1991 an English audience of practising and academic lawyers spent a happy evening at Queen Mary and Westfield College listening to a presentation by two distinguished German professors, Professor Werner Lorenz of the University of Munich, and Professor Christian von Bar of the University of Osnabrück. Professor Lorenz spoke to us about contract beneficiaries in German law, and Professor von Bar about liability for information and opinions causing pure economic loss to third parties. Each had, with characteristic courtesy and consideration, prepared a paper specially designed for an English audience. Not only were the papers written in the English language; they also deliberately avoided, so far as possible, the high level of abstraction which German lawyers can so easily grasp and by which English lawyers are so easily bemused, and they brought their subjects down to earth with an interesting citation of authority, both German and English, which enabled the English lawyers, tethered as they are to facts, to recognize the problems with which they are familiar, and which revealed a mastery of our case law which is most impressive. Needless to say, the papers were provided with a helpful apparatus of footnotes.

The papers are, of course, available here in this this book; and there is little point in my attempting to summarize their contents. Although at first sight they may appear to relate to distinct subjects, they are both relevant to what appears to many English lawyers to be the no man's land between contract and tort. It is a truism of comparative law that, whereas the English law of contract is unnaturally constricted by the doctrine of consideration with the inevitable result that our law of tort has expanded to deal with problems which, in other jurisdictions, are regarded as contractual, so the German law of negligence is, by virtue of para. 823(1) of the BGB, so drawn as to exclude liability for purely economic loss, with the result that their law of contract (unencumbered by a doctrine of consideration) has expanded to deal with problems which we treat as tortious. This combination of circumstances makes a comparison of the two legal systems in this area a particularly fertile subject of study for both English and German lawyers; but, as these two papers show, it is by no means easy for the English lawyers to grasp the nature of the particular concepts which have been developed by the German courts to do practical justice.

In a sense, the very nature of Professor Lorenz's subject made his paper the easier of the two for us to follow, a task rendered easier still by the deceptively simple clarity of his exposition. It has been my experience, as a commercial lawyer, that very rarely in practice is an English lawyer troubled by the doctrine of consideration, for the simple reason that, in the vast majority of transactions which come to the attention of practising lawyers, consideration is in fact present. This fact has perhaps promoted the survival of a doctrine which experience of other legal systems, including of course the German, demonstrates to be generally of little or no value and occasionally harmful. Perhaps the greatest harm which it has caused is that, through the rule that consideration must move from the promisee, it has prevented the development of rational principles under which contracts may, where appropriate, be enforced by third parties. During our discussion of these papers, Professor von Bar asked us: 'Why don't you get rid of the doctrine of consideration?' It was a fair question; but, so far as third-party beneficiaries are concerned we can at least say that the matter is under consideration by the Law Commission, who have had the benefit of a lucid exposition of the German law on the topic by Professor von Bar himself, which I am sure must have been of great assistance. My only hope is that statutory reform of this subject will not attempt to decide too much, and that the parliamentary draftsman will not be impelled by his inherited discipline to put the judges in a strait-jacket, a point to which I will return at the end of this brief reflection.

It is instructive for us to discover from Professor Lorenz's paper the wide range of circumstances in which the German courts have taken advantage of para. 328 of the BGB. Of particular interest, however, is the development concerned with the imposition of contractual duties designed to provide compensation for third parties who have suffered pure economic losses. These are known as contracts with protective effects *vis-à vis* third parties (*Verträge mit Schutzwirkung für Dritte*). This development was discussed both by Professor Lorenz and Professor von Bar, citing in particular a case (BGH 6 July 1965, 1955) which bears a significant resemblance to the English case of *Ross* v. *Caunters* ([1980] 1 Ch 297) in which liability of a testator's negligent solicitor to a disappointed beneficiary was held to arise in negligence. The jurisprudential basis of this decision perhaps calls for some elucidation, which could well be assisted by study of the parallel German experience. Another related topic, of particular interest to myself, is the legal institution of German law called *Drittschadensliquidation*, which enables the purchaser of goods to recover damages in respect of loss or damage suffered by him at a time when, although he has not yet acquired the property in the goods, they are at his risk. In *The Aliakmon* ([1985] QB 350), I proposed a solution to this problem, which by coincidence bears a marked resemblance to the German institution, a similarity commented upon by Professor Lorenz in his paper. I only discovered the existence of the German institution about a year after I wrote my judgment in that case, when I was reading a book of essays in honour of Professor

Harry Lawson, and found the German principle explained in the essay contributed by Professor Lorenz himself. It was a matter of sadness to me that my proposed solution, which has proved to be so completely acceptable to our German colleagues, did not have the same attraction for my colleagues in the House of Lords who heard the appeal. Fortunately, by subsequently introducing in the House the Bill prepared by the Law Commission now enacted as the Carriage of Goods by Sea Act 1992, I was able to participate in the statutory reversal of that decision which the House made in its judicial capacity. But I cannot help feeling that, in the light of the evident usefulness of the doctrine in German law, the English courts might one day reconsider the possibility of adopting a comparable principle as part of the common law.

Professor von Bar's paper on liability for information and opinions causing pure economic loss is also of great interest to us; though for me it is enlightening, not only as a stimulus to reconsidering the basis upon which we attach liability in such circumstances, but also as demonstrating the variety and sophistication of the concepts which the German courts are able to invoke, basing themselves in their law of contract. There is no doubt to my mind that for a practising lawyer such as myself, it is by no means easy to grasp the true nature of, and interrelationship between, these concepts; and I feel that we all owe a debt of gratitude to Professor von Bar for his admirable account of them. It is of some interest that *Caparo Industries Plc* v. *Dickman* ([1990] 2 AC 605) would have been decided the same way in Germany, because of provisions relating to the company's statutory audit (which, incidentally, limits liability to DM 500,000 for each set of accounts—an application of the principle of limitation of liability to the professions which deserves attention in this country). But, for English lawyers, it is of greater interest to find that para. 826 of the BGB, imposing liability on a person who 'intentionally and *contra bonos mores* causes damage to another', has been gradually expanded by judicial interpretation to embrace cases of thoughtless and reckless behaviour, and even cases of careless conduct, provided that the defendant possesses a subjective realization that his conduct might injure or cause loss to another (*dolus eventualis*). Yet it is plain that the German judges are as sensitive as the English judges about the dangers of allowing liability for pure economic loss to escalate out of control. There is the clear realization that, in a market economy which tolerates, and indeed encourages, competitive activities which, if successful, will inevitably cause economic harm to our rivals, claims for pure economic loss can only be allowed in exceptional circumstances. What we are in fact seeing in both jurisdictions is a carefully controlled development of heads of liability for pure economic loss (I hesitate to call it a carefully controlled opening of the floodgates) in specific circumstances, though in Germany the basis of the development is (for well known reasons) basically contractual rather than tortious. In both countries, there has been reliance upon the notion of 'assumption of liability' or, as we tend to call it, 'assumption of responsibility': though in Germany this is, of course, regarded as a development of contract law to correct the deficiencies of their tort law, and has in the present context developed into a 'contract to supply correct information'. Professor von Bar comments that English law could operate far more convincingly using the concept of voluntary assumption of liability if it were prepared to do so without the doctrine of consideration; yet, as *Hedley Byrne* v. *Heller* ([1964] AC 465) itself shows, English law is in fact prepared to take that step. It is however easier to accommodate the concept if it is regarded, as it is in Germany, as giving rise to a contractual liability, than if the liability is regarded as tortious; though Professor von Bar feels that classification of the principle as contractual or tortious is a matter only of secondary importance.

The judicial developments in German law, outside para. 826 BGB and the contract to supply correct information, include liability for *culpa in contrahendo*, and contracts having protective effects *vis-à-vis* third parties (also discussed by Professor Lorenz). For these two doctrines, I refer the reader to the closing passages of Professor von Bar's essay. They demonstrate, if any demonstration is needed, the ability of German judges to indulge in judicial law-making on a case by case basis, in much the same way as we do in this country. Indeed, developments such as these lead the English observer to wonder whether, in identifying the differences between our judicial methods in the development of the law, the prime difference lies not so much in the influence of codes in providing the framework for the law in a codified legal system such as the German, as in the dead hand of the parliamentary draftsman in a common-law country such as England which inhibits the judicial development of the law within the framework of a statute. That the latter phenomenon has its philosophical origin in the Benthamite determination to imprison judges within an all embracing statute law is, I believe, clear; but the philosophy is now perpetuated by a self-imposed discipline which our parliamentary draftsmen believe, in all good faith, requires them to create statutes so detailed and comprehensive that they are incapable of child-bearing. Perhaps one of the greatest lessons for us from this absorbing seminar lies in the form of para. 328 BGB, praised by Professor Lorenz for its flexibility, which has for that very reason survived unaltered over the years. Is it too much to hope that the Law Commission will bear this in mind as they prepare their proposed reform in relation to contracts for the benefit of third parties?

4

International Conventions and Domestic Law

THE IMPACT OF INTERNATIONAL CONVENTIONS ON MUNICIPAL LAW

DENIS TALLON

The topic I have to address is the impact of international conventions on municipal law. Can a British lawyer 'learn from Europe'? Before trying to answer this question, one must attempt to fix its meaning and limits. By Europe I assume we mean continental Europe and not the Europe of the European Community which, of course, includes the United Kingdom. Moreover, I will confine my comments to the law of my own country since, on this subject, it is doubtful that one finds a monolithic position in Europe.

I also had some difficulties with the wording of the title of this essay. Literally speaking (and a literal rule of interpretation prevails in English law), there is no impact because in French law international conventions form part of municipal law. Once a treaty has been ratified, it is integrated in the purely domestic legal system and becomes *ipso jure* a part of it according to the so-called monist theory. So I shall take the words 'international conventions' as referring to the national rules of supranational origin. Moreover, in this essay I shall look at conventions affecting the rights and obligations of individuals only.

Fifty years ago, the answer to the question as I defined it would have been easy: the impact of international conventions on municipal law was very limited. The legal system was built essentially by the national law-making authorities and was intended for their own citizens. International conventions were scarce and covered few topics: transports, copyrights, patents, and the like. This nationalistic approach was reflected in private international law. At the time, the 'conflictualist' doctrine prevailed. Situations with a foreign element were to be governed by municipal law designated by the national conflict of laws rules of the forum in the unexpressed hope that it would be the *lex fori*. The 'conflictualists' recognized, of course, the existence of international rules to be found in international conventions; but they were rather contemptuous towards these rules which formed a *lex specialis* to general theory. As a result, these rules were rarely discussed in the academic literature and scarcely ever taught in law schools.

Nowadays, the situation is very different. In all countries jurists have become aware of the interconnection between the national legal systems and the international order. Every lawyer is conscious of the international or supranational dimension of law. Rules of international inspiration occupy an ever-growing place in municipal law, the reason being that municipal law is not always well-adapted to regulate international relations. As René David said bluntly, 'the "conflictualist" method is a "barbarian way" of dealing with international legal relations.'[1] There is, of course, also the controversy—very strong in France—concerning the existence and usefulness of the notion of *lex mercatoria*.

Whatever the reasons, the fact is that there is an obvious increase of the role played by international conventions in municipal law, especially by multilateral treaties such as the European Convention for the Protection of Human Rights and Fundamental Liberties or the UN Convention on International Sale of Goods (CISG). Moreover, we now have rules of EC origin, at least as far as 'secondary legislation' is concerned. These are not directly part of my subject, but are nevertheless associated with it. (They are closely related in the principle of primacy). There are also important international conventions of EC origin: the Brussels Convention on Jurisdiction and Enforcement of Judgments and the Rome Convention on the Law Applicable to Contractual Obligations, which recently came into force thanks to UK ratification.

The point of departure from this nationalistic approach came with the (French) Constitution of 1958 which contains a chapter on treaties (articles 52 to 55). It deals with the rule of direct integration of treaties into municipal law. (This is as a result of the so-called 'monist' theory and the principle of primacy of international law over municipal law: article 55). We must also refer to case law. First, the case law of the *Conseil constitutionnel* (which has adopted a strange position on the question of primacy), and the case law of our two supreme courts, the *Cour de cassation* and the *Conseil d'Etat* which do not always coincide, and which have recently brought about major changes through spectacular reversal of judgments. The situation is neither entirely coherent nor finally settled.[2]

According to the 'monist' theory, international conventions become part of domestic law, but this does not mean that they have exactly the same status. Owing to their international origin, they present some specific

---

[1] This is the main object of his fascinating and controversial book *Le Droit du Commercial International: Réflexions d'un Comparatiste sur le Droit International Privé* (Paris, Economica, 1987).

[2] This should give the English reader some views on the structure of French courts, and the authority of precedents.

problems when compared to purely domestic law. These problems concern first the superiority—or primacy—of international conventions over domestic law and second the way in which they are construed.[3]

1 The Primacy of International Conventions over Municipal Law

According to the monist theory, which is adopted by the Constitution of 1958 (and is in line with a well-established French tradition), there is no need for an Act of Parliament (or an Order in Council) to incorporate a treaty into domestic law. Such a treaty becomes directly enforceable as soon as the procedure of ratification (by the President of the Republic) has been completed. Certainly, for the treaties we are concerned with, there must be an authorization by Parliament to endorse ratification (article 53-1 of the Constitution), but this is different from an implementation by Act of Parliament which is required in English law. Once ratification takes place the treaty, like all ordinary statutes, must be published in the *Journal Officiel* (D.14 March 1953) if it 'affects the rights or obligations of private persons'.

Once ratified and published, international conventions become part of the legal system. According to article 55 of the Constitution they then take precedence over ordinary domestic rules. This principle, foreign to traditional English law[4], bears important consequences.

1.1 *The principle*

Article 55[5] provides that treaties have a 'superior authority' to that of domestic legislation: but also contains an important proviso: the treaty must be applied also by the other party. This is generally known as the rule of reciprocity.

1.1.1 *Superior Authority*

The rule is aimed at solving conflicts between domestic statutes and international conventions. It is strongly expressed but does not indicate how

[3] The subject-matter is examined in various textbooks of which the following deserve a special mention. Thus, for 'civil' law see 'Droit Civil': J. Ghestin (éd.) *Traité de Droit Civil*, Introduction générale par J. Ghestin et G. Goubeaux, 3e edn. Paris, 1990, Nos. 282–302; P. Malaurie, Droit civil: Introduction Générale, Paris, 1991, No. 700, 937–41; for private international law see: B. Audit, *Droit International Privé*, Paris, 1991. Nos 51–60; P. Mayer, *Droit International privé*, 4e éd. Paris, 1991, 30–5. Finally, for an EC perspective see: J. Boulouis, *Droit Institutionnel des Communautés Européenes*, 3e éd. (Paris, 1991), 229–34.

[4] Of course, the primacy principle appears with regard to EC law: the *Factortame* case is very instructive, as compared with the *Jacques Vabre* case of the *Cour de cassation*. (Cass. ch. mixte 24 May 1975, D.1975, 497.)

[5] 'Les traités ou accords régulièrement ratifiés ou approuvés ont, dès leur publication, une autorité supérieure à celle des lois, sous réserve, pour chaque accord ou traité, de son application par l'autre partie.'

one should make it effective. Indeed, there has been a difference between the solutions adopted by our superior courts (*Cour de cassation, Conseil d'Etat* and *Conseil constitutionnel*). There is no great difficulty when the treaty is the more recent text. The *lex posterior* rule applies just as it would between successive ordinary statutes. There is a tacit abrogation of the earlier statute insofar as it runs counter to the convention.[6]

But what if a later municipal rule is incompatible or inconsistent with an earlier treaty? Of course, the courts always try to avoid the conflict by construing the later statute as if it had impliedly reserved the application of the earlier convention. There is even—as in English law—a presumption that the State must respect its international obligations,[7] but it may not be possible to presume this if the domestic rule is obviously inconsistent with the treaty. How then can its 'superior authority' manifest itself? There is a minimal interpretation according to which the principle binds the State but does not affect private legal relations. If the subsequent legislation is a statutory instrument, it may be quashed under the normal procedure of judicial review (plea or exception of illegality). The treaty being a superior rule in the hierarchy of sources, a statutory instrument which is contrary to it is illegal. But if the subsequent rule is contained in a statute then, under this interpretation, it cannot be set aside by courts. The reason for this is simple: ordinary French courts have no constitutional control over statutes and are absolutely bound by them. This was for a long time the position taken by the *Conseil d'Etat,* especially with respect to EC treaties and regulations.[8]

On the other hand, the *Cour de cassation* has shown itself more daring. In the famous *Société Cafés Jacques Vabre* case of 1975,[9] it decided that a legislative disposition of the Code of Customs was to be set aside by the judge as it was contrary to Article 95 of the EC Treaty. To do this the court relied on two kinds of arguments. The first was based on the primacy of community law as expressed by the Court of Justice of the European Communities (*Costa* v. *ENEL*[10] and *Simmenthal*[11] cases) as well as the specific nature of the European Communities and the limitation of sovereignty it entailed. The other ground was article 55 of the Constitution

---

[6] Even if the courts sometimes use the primacy principle in this situation: Cass.Soc. 16 February 1987, BV, No. 77: conflict between art. 14 Civil Code and the Franco-Swiss Convention on Jurisdiction and Enforcement of Judgments of 1869.

[7] The so-called 'jurisprudence Matter': Cass.civ. 22 Dec. 1931, DP 1932, 1.113, note Trasbot.

[8] The *Conseil d'Etat* has been rather hostile towards the European Communities and has had a tendency to restrict its impact on municipal law. Its attitude has changed over time.

[9] Cass.ch. mixte 24 May 1975, D.1975, 497, concl. Av. gen. Touffait; only the most important cases in the *Cour de cassation* are quoted by the name of the parties (as it is the rule for the Conseil d'Etat).   [10] *Costa* v. *ENEL,* 15 July 1964, Rec. 1964, 1141.

[11] *Simmenthal,* 9 Mar. 1978, Rec. 1978, 609.

and the 'superior authority' of treaties, so that the primacy principle was not to be confined to EC treaties and regulations. This reasoning was confirmed by other cases involving non-community matters.[12] The opposition between our two superior courts was thus flagrant and rather disconcerting. Happily, it disappeared when, in 1989, the *Conseil d'Etat* overruled its previous position and, in the *Nicolo* case, affirmed that it should interpret an Act of Parliament in conformity with prior international conventions—even though, in that case, it decided that there was no opposition between the two texts. The treaty involved was an EC convention, but it is clear that the new ruling applies to all kinds of treaties.[13]

The picture must be completed by examining the case law of the *Conseil constitutionnel*. One might have thought that the principle of primacy was of a constitutional nature, meaning that the *Conseil* could exercise its control over statutes allegedly infringing on international obligations before their promulgation.[14] Though the *Conseil* never denied the above-mentioned principle, it strangely enough, refused to apply it, deciding instead that it has authority only to check the conformity of statutes, not treaties, to the Constitution.[15] This decision, however, has been much criticized and may well be overruled.[16] The present position, however, has at least one advantage: there is no possibility of conflict between the *Conseil constitutionnel* (were it to declare conformity to prior conventions and let the statute pass) and the two supreme courts (which could decide otherwise).

Litigation in this field is in the hands of the *Cour de cassation* and the *Conseil d'Etat* which nowadays have the same position: if a statute contravenes the rules laid down by an earlier treaty, these courts will refuse to apply the statute; they cannot, however, repeal it. They just ignore it as if it were abrogated.

This position is of major importance. The sovereignty of Parliament (relative in French law) finds its limits in the international obligations of the State. In the words of Philippe Malaurie:[17] 'La jurisprudence *Cafés*

---

[12] For instance, on the application of the European Convention on Human Rights; see nn. 25–9.

[13] CE 20 Oct. 1989, JCP 1989. 11.21371, concl. Commissaire du Gouvt Frydman; conflict between Art. 227(1) EC Treaty and a statute of 1977 organizing the elections for the European Parliament.

[14] The control is an *a priori* one, after the vote and before the promulgation by the President of the Republic, at the request only of the President of the Republic, the Prime Minister, the President of both Houses of Parliament and (since 1974) sixty members of Parliament.

[15] *Conseil const.* 15 Jan. 1975, D.1975, 529, note L. Hamon, *Rev crit dr internat privé* (1975), 1214, note P. Lagarde: the question was about the conformity of the Voluntary Interruption of Pregnancy Act to the European Declaration of Human Rights.

[16] An encouraging sign may be inferred from a decision of 21 Oct. 1988—the *Bischoff* case—(D.1989. 285 note F. Luchaire) where the *Conseil* agreed to review the conformity of an electoral law with the lst Protocol of the European Convention on Human Rights. It should be noted, however, that in this case the *Conseil* was acting not as constitutional court but as the court of elections.   [17] Op. cit. in the bibliography, No. 712.

Jacques Vabre et *Nicolo* a changé le visage de la France'. This is true, at least in theory, as we shall see later. Article 55 of the Constitution has thus been given operative force. But it contains a qualification: the reservation regarding reciprocity.

1.1.2 *The Reservation regarding Reciprocity*

The reservation regarding reciprocity may be compared to the concept of withholding performance (*exception d'inexécution*) in contract law.[18] The primacy of the treaty over domestic rules must be denied if the other party to the treaty fails to fulfil its obligations.[19] But who is to decide if this is the case? The court itself or the executive? The *Cour de cassation* and the *Conseil d'Etat have* both held that they can not decide themselves whether or not the condition of reciprocity has been met. They can only ask the Ministry of Foreign Affairs to give a ruling—a ruling which is binding only for the case before them since circumstances may change . . .'[20]

One may wonder if this would still be the position of the *Conseil d'Etat* after the *GISTI* case[21] in which it decided that the court was totally free to construe international conventions notwithstanding any official interpretation. This could be taken to imply that from now on the *Conseil d'Etat* would also be free to decide by itself if there is reciprocity of international obligations or not.[22] The possibility of consulting the executive could then be maintained, though, one assumes, as a mere option and with no binding authority. As a matter of fact, the reservation regarding reciprocity is seldom used. The principle of primacy is now well established and increasingly decided by the courts and not the Government.

1.2 *Consequences*

The growing importance of the law of supranational origin has many consequences for municipal law. One of these is of a political nature, namely, a reaction of mistrust towards this law which comes from elsewhere. Indeed, a bill was introduced after the Jacques Vabre case, by a private member of Parliament, attempting to prohibit the courts from setting aside a statute for being inconsistent with international or European rules. Though it was not adopted, it underscores a certain nationalistic tendency in France.

The same can be said of the movement towards unification or harmonization of laws. Those engaged in this movement often think that it has the

---

[18] The clause works for bilateral as well as multilateral treaties.

[19] This exception does not apply to the European Communities Treaties, where a specific procedure exists in case of 'infringement'. This was decided in the *Jacques Vabre* case.

[20] P. Lagarde, 'La Condition de Réciprocité dans l'Application des Traité Internationaux: Son Appréciation par le Juge Interne', *Rev critique dr internat privé* (1975), 25, who is in favour of giving to the executive only the initiative and the right to decide on reciprocity.

[21] Below.   [22] This was hinted by the Commissaire du Gouvernement.

unanimous support of the community of French lawyers. Far from it: there are many who see it as a perversion or adulteration of the national legal system. Savigny's brood is not extinct.

The most acute criticisms are of course directed against the European Community's rules, considered as a manifestation of 'Eurocracy', a word coined to describe European bureaucracy.[23] This does not affect international conventions directly.

Moreover, it is difficult not to take into account the growing importance of international conventions, such as the CISG or the Brussels or Rome Conventions. And yet, this is not always fully appreciated. For instance, many lawyers, out of habit, still consider the enforcement of foreign judgments in terms of '*exequatur*' which is the traditional procedure. Yet this has become the exception, the normal rules being those of the Brussels Convention. Nowadays, far more judgments are enforced under the EC rules than under the so-called 'general procedure'.

The main effect of the primacy principle is, of course, the setting-aside[24] of contrary domestic legislation by the courts, now admitted without reservation by the two supreme courts.[25] In practice this has been rarely used, since judges always try to avoid declaring an open conflict and resort to an appropriate construction of the encroaching statute; but it has nevertheless had a strong dissuasive effect on the law-makers.

There are also indirect effects which bring about some rather usual situations. The first is the application of international conventions to situations, where they ought not to be applied as such, yet the rules they contain are considered to be applicable by extension. Thus, in domestic sales, the idea of conformity, introduced by the Uniform Law on International Sales of 1964 (not ratified by France) and taken over by the CISG, has been used by the *Cour de cassation* in order to duplicate the rather stringent rules of *garantie des vices cachés* (warranty of hidden defects). Sometimes, also, a convention is applied by anticipation,[26] before it has come in force, as being the expression of a general principle: this has been the case with the Rome Convention on the Law Applicable to Contractual Obligations.[27]

International conventions, or at least some of them, also play a growing role in orienting rules and practices of domestic law. I refer here particularly to the European Convention on Human Rights.[28] This Convention is

---

[23] B. Oppetit, 'L'Eurocratie ou le Mythe du Législateur Suprême', D.1990, *Chron* 73.

[24] Or the nullification of statutory instruments, by the plea of illegality or the exception of illegality.　　　　　　　　　　　　　　　　　　　[25] P. Malaurie, op. cit., 712.

[26] Or to situations excluded by the convention, by way of analogy.

[27] For instance: Paris 27 Nov. 1986, *Rev crit droit internat privé* 1988, 314, note A. Lyon-Caen.

[28] Independently, of course, of the direct procedures before the European Commission and Court of Human Rights.

referred to more and more in various cases, either criminal or civil, as an argument to construe domestic rules (notably when these rules are rather loose or formulated as standard) in a specific direction.

In a recent example the *Cour de cassation* had to decide if it was possible to modify the description of the sex of an individual on that person's birth certificate in cases of transsexualism (*demande de rectification d'état civil*). One of the arguments that was advanced in favour of this, but which was rejected, was that it was contrary to Article 8(1) (respect for private and family rights . . .) of the European Convention on Human Rights to impose on a person a sex which was not really his or hers.[29]

Another case concerned telephone tapping in criminal proceedings and the rights of the *Juge d'instruction* in view of Article 8(2) of the Convention (Limitations on the right to privacy).[30]

The case law is extensive and one might even suggest that the reference to the Convention tends to become (sometimes abusively) a standard issue . . .[31]

In a more indirect way still, but nearly as important, the preliminary rulings of the Court of Justice of the European Communities may affect domestic case law, as is shown by two recent decisions. In the first, the Court was asked if the French interpretation of article 1643 Civil Code ('*garantie des vices cachés de la chose vendue*'), according to which there is an irrefutable presumption that the manufacturer or professional seller is aware of the defects of the goods he sells unless the buyer is a professional in the same business or trade (with the consequence that exemption clauses are void), was a rule which violated Article 34 (quantitative restrictions) or Article 85(1)(1) (restrictive practices) of the EC Treaty. The answer was in the negative.[32] Yet there is a sting in the tail of this decision: in an international contract, where the parties may choose the applicable law, they need only adopt a different law in order to avoid the bias of the French rule against the professional seller. This may be an incentive for the *Cour de cassation* to moderate this bias and strengthen the doctrinal trend against the present rule.

---

[29] Cass.civ. 1, 21 May 1990, 4 arrêts, rapport Massip, concl. Av.gen.Flipo, JCP (1990), 11.21588.

[30] Cass.crim. 15 May 1990, JCP (1990), 11.21541 note W. Jeandidier.

[31] It was also raised in the *GISTI* case before the *Conseil d'Etat* (below) as well as before the *Conseil constitutionnel* in the abortion statute case (above); see also, among other recent cases: Cass.civ. 1, 19 Mar. 1991, D.1992, IR 110, about the right of the creditor to obtain the address of his debtor from his employer (held as not contrary to art. 9 Civil Code and Art. 8(1) of the European Convention on Human Rights; TGI Montpellier 15 Dec. 1989, JCP 1990, 11.21556 note Gridel in an action against a hospital which had failed to detect congenital malformation in a foetus; the mother held that, had she known of it she would have had an abortion; one of the defence's (unsuccessful) arguments was that abortion was against Article 2(4) of the European declaration.

[32] Court of Justice at the EC, 24 Jan. 1991, D.1991, 237, note J. Berr.

The second example is taken from the interpretation of Article 5(1) of the Brussels Convention of 17 September 1968, involving a case of successive contracts (sale and resale). According to French case law, the remedy of the ultimate buyer against the first seller (generally the manufacturer) is 'necessarily contractual', which means, in French law, that he cannot use a remedy in tort. Should this rule apply to the special jurisdiction for contractual remedies in Article 5(1)? This was the question which was recently put by the *Cour de cassation* to the European Court of Justice.[33] If the answer (which we still do not know), turns out to be negative, there will be a messy discrepancy between the European and French regimes of contractual liability. And this again will be a major argument in the controversy which presently rages in this area.[34]

From cases such as these one must conclude that even in what appear to be purely domestic matters it is nowadays impossible to disregard the European or international context. In a general way, rules of international origin are not to be separated from rules of purely domestic origin, though this statement is subject to some qualification, because of the primacy principle and its direct and indirect consequences. (Similarly, there are some differences as regards interpretation but this point is best discussed under a separate heading.)

2   The Peculiarities of Interpretation

Even though integrated in the national system, international conventions cannot be construed in exactly the same way as purely domestic rules.

One of the peculiarities of interpretation of international treaties raises a question of principle: what is the relative place of the courts and of the Government in the interpretative process? A recent decision of the *Conseil d'Etat* seems to tip the scale in favour of judicial interpretation. On the other hand, it is quite clear that a judge cannot use exactly the same interpretation techniques in cases of international and municipal rules.

2.1   *The principle of judicial interpretation*

There may, of course, be an official joint interpretation by the contracting parties to an international treaty, for instance by an exchange of letters published in the Official Gazette. This interpretation has the same strength as the treaty itself. There is also, as regards EC law, the preliminary ruling of the Court of Justice of the EC, pursuant to Article 177 of the Treaty of

---

[33] Cass.civ. 1, 8 Jan. 1991, *Rev crit dr internat privé* 1991, 411, note Y.L.
[34] Cass.Ass.plén. 12 July 1991, JCP 1991, II.21743, note G. Viney (arrêt Besse); C. Larroumet, 'L'Effet Relatif des Contrats et La Négation de l'Existence d'une Action en Responsabilité Nécessairement Contractuelle dans les Ensembles Contractuels, *JCP* 1991 i: 3531.

Rome, which is binding on national courts; in addition, we know that this procedure has been or will be extended to some conventions (such as the Brussels Convention on Jurisdiction).

However, in the absence of such procedure in a monist system such as the French one, how should one interpret international conventions? We find there are two conflicting ideas. The first is that the judge has the natural power to construe the rule of law which he has to apply. Article 4 of the French Civil Code reminds him that he cannot refuse to adjudicate by using the pretext of silence, obscurity, or inadequacy of the law, but on the other hand, a wrong interpretation involves the international liability of the State. Thus the interpretation of conventions may well be considered as a duty of the executive: since the Government has negotiated the treaty it should bear the duty of providing its own 'official' interpretation. Arguably, the Government is better equipped to do so because it knows of the *travaux préparatoires* and is aware of the intentions of the contracting parties. Moreover, an official interpretation has the advantage of being unique, whereas interpretations by the courts (in the absence of a rule of precedent) may be contradictory.

Such is the debate—a debate which led, up to very recently, to difference of opinion between our two supreme courts. The change of attitude of the *Conseil d'Etat* may induce the *Cour de cassation* to follow suit.

The traditional position of the *Cour de cassation* (at least of its civil divisions) has been, since 1839, that it has the right to construe international conventions[35] unless the interpretation raises questions affecting international public order (as opposed to questions of private interest). In this case, the courts must conform to the interpretation given by the Government (in general, a circular of the Ministry of Foreign Affairs published in the *Journal Officiel*); if there is none, they must ask for it. In matters of private interest, the courts may ask for an official interpretation and if one is given (and published) the courts have to adopt it. In all other cases, the court has a complete freedom of interpretation (subject to what shall be said later under 2.2).

It must be noted that the criterion is somewhat vague: what are the issues affecting international public order (or public law)? It seems to include all cases where the interpretation may lead to diplomatic difficulties. And the courts are, as a rule, very prudent: in case of doubt, they ask for an official interpretation.[36] Conflicts may arise if in one case governmental

---

[35] Cass.Ch.Réunies 27 Apr. 1950, *Sirey* (1950) 1.165 note Metzger; JCP 1950.II.5650 note Lerebourg-Pigeonniere.

[36] For instance: Cass.Com. 7 Mar. 1984, D.1983, 284, where an official ruling was asked for the interpretation of Art. 22 of the Warsaw Convention of 1929, on the method of assessing damages for loss of luggage, because monetary public policy was involved; also Cass.Civ. 1, 19 Mar. 1963, D.1963, 529 note P. Malaurie.

interpretation is not asked for and if in another it is and is answered differently from what has been decided by the judge in the previous case. There is some doubt also about the value of a previous interpretation of the same legislation, but in a different context. On the whole, however, the system is working well.

Up until recently, the position of the *Conseil d'Etat* (and of the criminal division of the *Cour de cassation*) was totally different. These courts decided as early as 1823 that in every matter, an interpretation was to be asked from the executive. The Court had no power whatsoever to provide one itself. There was, however, a reservation: an interpretation must first of all be deemed to be necessary, that is there had to be an ambiguity. In case of an *acte clair*, there was no need for an interpretation, hence no need to consult the Ministry of Foreign Affairs.[37] This attitude was widely criticized for various reasons. The strongest criticism was that in administrative litigation the State is generally the defendant and thus, when asked for an official interpretation, acted both as judge and party. This argument was strengthened by the European Convention on Human Rights and was used when the *Conseil d'Etat* reversed its position in the *GISTI*[38] case in June 1990.[39] This was a highly political affair concerning a Franco-Algerian Convention of 1985 on the entry into and residence in France of Algerian workers, which had been interpreted by a ministerial circular, to which the Ministry of Foreign Affairs had referred the Court. The *Conseil d'Etat* decided that it was not bound by the official interpretation and that it was free to construe all kinds of treaties—going thus further than the *Cour de cassation*. The *Conseil* may ask for the official interpretation but, if given, is not bound by it: it is just an opinion which it may or may not follow. As a matter of fact, in the *GISTI* case, the *Conseil d'Etat* approved the official interpretation. We are thus faced with a curious situation: an official interpretation, regularly published, binds the *Cour de cassation* but not the *Conseil d'Etat*. The general opinion is that the *Cour de cassation* should fall into line with the *Conseil d'Etat*.[40]

It is the second time we have noted a major change in the case law of the *Conseil d'Etat*, and such changes are not without reciprocal effects. Under the *Nicolo* rule, the *Conseil d'Etat* will now have to solve the conflict between domestic law and international conventions and this will open more opportunities to interpret international conventions pursuant to the

[37] The theory of *acte clair* was also used extensively by the *Conseil d'Etat* to escape the preliminary ruling of the EC Court of Justice.

[38] Initials of an association for the support of immigrant workers.

[39] CE 29 June 1990, *GISTI*, *Revue crit dr internat privé* 1990, 61 avec les conclusions du *Commissaire du Gouvernement* Abraham et la note de P. Lagarde: this case has been reported and commented in many other legal publications.

[40] We have seen that this change will probably modify the position of the *Conseil d'Etat* on the condition of reciprocity.

GISTI precedent. And, of course, it will not be necessary to resort to the '*acte clair*' doctrine any more in order to avoid an external interpretation.

We are therefore heading towards a situation where all Courts will be entitled to interpret international conventions without any restrictions. Does this mean that they should resort to the same techniques as are used for domestic rules?

2.2   *The techniques of interpretation*

The problem is different in French law and in English law. In England, the Courts have to deviate from their traditional method of interpretation—the literal rule[41]—when they have to construe a treaty. In France, the basic principles are the same, they just have to be adapted. Interpretation must be done according to the spirit and not the letter of the text. The spirit must prevail over the letter when the letter leads to a result which is not compatible with the aim of the text (statute or convention). This is what is called the 'teleological' or purposive method.[42] In an international convention there is always a common general purpose, for example as described in Article 7 of the Vienna Convention on the UN CISG: 'The need to promote uniformity in its application' and to have 'regard to its international character'. French courts have not waited for the Vienna Convention to adopt this position.

Thus the court will have to look at the *travaux préparatoires* (now frequently published, or to be requested from the Ministry of Foreign Affairs). Again, this process is not a novelty for French judges who are accustomed to do so for domestic rules in order to ascertain the purpose of legislation. They may compare the different linguistic versions of the text and refer to the foreign cases dealing with same text.[43] This is not foreign to the French judge who is accustomed to rely on such external aids. In short, some techniques developed for the interpretation of domestic law are used, but are adapted in order to have regard to the international character of the text.

3   Conclusion

When one comes to reflect on the above I do not know if there is much that an English lawyer stands to learn from (continental) Europe. In many

---

[41] Even though, if I am rightly informed, this rule tends to lose ground, in favour of a purposive approach.

[42] In the *GISTI* case, the *Commissaire du Gouvernement* notes that a literal interpretation would have been clearly against the objectives pursued by the negotiations of the international agreement.

[43] This is less foreign to English law: *Fothergills* v. *Monarch Airlines* [1980] 2 All ER 696 (HL).

respects the impact of international conventions on domestic law appears to be different in French and English law, but some differences are more apparent than real. For instance, the opposition between the so-called monist and dualist theory of international conventions may not be as fundamental as it appears at first sight. In both there is the intervention of Parliament, though with different powers,[44] it must be admitted. As regards the technique of interpretation, the starting points of both systems are in theory far apart, though in recent years one feels there has been a marked convergence. The primacy principle (of constitutional value in France) is a major difference; but something like it also seems to be appearing in English law as well, as far as European Community legislation is concerned. The English courts would thus seem to be confronted with the same problems as the French *Cour de cassation* and *Conseil d'Etat*. Moreover the original structure of the courts in the French system leads to a strange situation: the ordinary courts cannot control the constitutionality of statutes—this control being reserved to the *Cour constitutionnel*, in a limited way (a priori control);[45] but they must check the statutes' international conformity—which the *Conseil constitutionnel* refuses to do. Despite all this, however, this power of the judicial and administrative courts has not brought a major upheaval in the legal system. The primacy principle has thus not proved a threat to the domestic legal order.

Does it then matter that no specific lessons can be drawn from the topic I have been examining? I think not. In my experience, the most important thing in these kind of discussions is to acquire a better understanding of each other, for I have discovered over the years that it is very easy to talk at cross-purposes. An enlightened appreciation of another's legal system is a necessary preliminary step to a useful exchange of ideas; and in appropriate circumstances, lessons may also be learned.

---

[44] The French Parliament can only give or refuse its authorization; it cannot amend the Treaty.

[45] No such control is possible once the statute has been promulgated by the President of the Republic.

THE 1968 BRUSSELS CIVIL JURISDICTION AND JUDGMENTS CONVENTION AND THE 1980 ROME CONVENTION ON APPLICABLE LAW

MICHAEL JOACHIM BONELL

1 Introduction

It is an open secret that States often use their conflict of laws rules, as well as their rules on jurisdiction, to serve specific national interests. Take, for instance, the tendency of United States courts to extend their personal jurisdiction as much as possible in cases brought by US citizens against foreigners[1] and to deny their competence and to refer the parties to a foreign court if it is the foreign party who is the plaintiff.[2] This is no co-incidence, but rather reflects a deliberate choice of policy aiming at favour-ing national industry to the detriment of foreign competitors. Indeed, in this way, among other things, the notoriously strict rules in force in the United States in the field of product liability are imposed on foreign companies merely because their products are sold in the United States, whereas American companies which export their products abroad succeed in avoiding them, thus obtaining an obvious advantage both in terms of image and extra costs.[3]

Similarly, note how Italian courts, notwithstanding the principle *jura novit curia*, in practice make the application of foreign law (even when applica-ble under the conflict of laws rules) dependent on the demonstration by the party invoking it that, in relation to the matter in dispute, it contains rules different from those of Italian law.[4] This must, in part at least, be due to the desire to favour those among lawyers and judges who wish to see Italian law prevail so as to avoid having to deal with a foreign law with

---

[1] To the point that even the courts in the US speak of a 'long-arm jurisdiction', based on 'minimum contacts' between the single controversy and the territory of the State in question: *International Shoe Co. v. Washington*, 326 US, 310.

[2] Thus invoking the doctrine of *forum non conveniens*, on which see Stewart, 'Forum Non Conveniens: A Doctrine in Search of a Role', *Cal L Rev*, 74(1986), 125 *et seq.*

[3] For an impressive list of cases of European or Japanese companies which, due to an action brought against them by an American consumer for defects in their products, have found themselves subjected to the jurisdiction of United States courts, with the consequent risk of being condemned to pay astronomical sums, apart from the inconveniences of the so-called pre-trial discovery, see Junker, 'Der Lange Arm Amerikanischer Gerichte: Gerichtsgewalt, Zustellung und Jurisdictional Discovery', *IPrax* 1986, 197 *et seq.*

[4] See most recently *Corte di Cassazione*, 19 Jan. 1985 No. 149, in *Riv dir intern priv proc* (1986), 344.—It may incidentally be recalled that a quite similar approach is adopted also by English judges: the rule is that 'Foreign law must in general be proved by expert evidence. [I]t cannot be proved merely by putting the text of a foreign enactment before the court nor merely by citing foreign decisions or books of authority' (Dicey and Morris, *On the Conflict of Laws*, 11th edn, (1987), i: 220.

which they are not familiar and which they would obviously find much more difficult to apply.

The United Kingdom is in this respect, no exception. What distinguishes English judges from their colleagues in other countries is that they normally do not hesitate to admit openly their partisan attitude and to justify it by the alleged superiority of English law and of the way it is administered by English courts. A foreign observer cannot but admire the confidence with which it is submitted that even in the absence of any other link with the English legal system, foreign parties 'may reasonably desire that the familiar principles of English commercial law should apply'.[5] Equally, one is surprised by the nonchalance with which the commercial court in London is presented as '. . . far more than a national or domestic court . . .', namely as a *'curia franca* of international commerce, in so far as commerce is based upon the rules and concepts of English law . . .'.[6] On the other hand it is a well-known fact that for London, or more precisely for the legal profession that is based there, the application of English law and its administration by English courts is not only a question of prestige, but also represents a real business opportunity or, as has been said, an actual 'industry',[7] to be jealously cultivated and guarded for obvious economic reasons.[8]

The last few years have, however, seen developments which should bring about important changes in this respect, at least for the member States of the European Communities. I am referring to the adoption and entry into force of the 1968 Brussels Convention on Jurisdiction and the Enforcement of Judgments in Civil and Commercial Matters,[9] and of the 1980 Rome Convention on the Law Applicable to Contractual Obligations.[10]

The peculiarity of these two conventions is that their impact on the

[5] Lord Wright in *Vita Food Products Inc.* v. *Unus Shipping Co. Ltd.*, [1939] AC, 277, 290.

[6] Sir John Donaldson MR in *Amin Rasheed Corp.* v. *Kuwait Insurance*, [1983] 1 WLR, 228, 240.

[7] Paulson, Introduction to the first issue of the *International Arbitration Review* (1985), 2.

[8] It is not easy to furnish precise statistical data on the volume of business involved. However, it has been estimated that the contribution made by the legal profession of the City of London to the UK balance of payments amounts to not less than £200 million per year, cf. Liston–Reeves, *The Invisible Economy: A Profile of Britain's Invisible Exports* (1988), 237.

[9] The Convention, signed at Brussels on behalf of the six original member States of the Communities on 27 Sept. 1968, entered into force on 1 Feb. 1973 following the completion of the process of ratification by all six signatories. The United Kingdom, along with Denmark and Ireland, signed the 1978 Accession Convention which was brought into force by the Civil Jurisdiction and Judgment Act 1982.

[10] The Convention, signed in Rome on 19 June 1980 by the then nine member States, came into force on 1 Apr. 1991 following the deposit of the seventh instrument of ratification, i.e. that of the United Kingdom, which implemented the Convention by the Contracts (Applicable Law) Act of 1990.

municipal laws of the contracting States is not limited to the subject-matters specifically dealt by them. Indeed, not only do they provide uniform rules on jurisdiction and enforcement of judgments in civil and commercial matters and on conflict of laws in the field of contractual obligations, but the way in which they do so may well reduce, if not eliminate, the 'legal imperialism' exercised by national courts when imposing their jurisdiction over foreigners and/or following a marked 'homeward trend' in the determination of the proper law of the contract.

2   The Impact of the 1968 Brussels Civil Jurisdiction and Judgments Convention on the Exercise of Jurisdiction by the Courts of the Contracting States

2.1   *Strict and Uniform Jurisdictional Rules to the Exclusion of National Exorbitant Jurisdiction*

The Brussels Convention is based on Article 220 of the EC Treaty but, notwithstanding the fact that this provision merely invites member States to provide for '[the] simplification of formalities governing the reciprocal recognition and enforcement of judgments', it goes much further than this. Indeed, it also aims at establishing a uniform system of rules for the determination of the jurisdiction of the courts originally seised. In other words, contrary to the traditional judgment-recognition conventions which contain jurisdictional rules (if any) only for the purpose of the recognition and enforcement of judgments in States different from those in which they were rendered (so-called 'indirect' rules of jurisdiction), the Brussels Convention lays down jurisdictional rules intended to be directly binding on the judgment-rendering courts in replacement of the existing national rules (so-called 'direct' rules of jurisdiction). As a consequence, courts with jurisdiction to hear a given case will be the same for all contracting States, with the result that not only is it no longer necessary to make the recognition and enforcement of foreign judgments subject to any jurisdictional test on the part of the recognizing court, but also the risk of forum shopping should be considerably reduced.

Regarding the allocation of jurisdiction among the different national courts, the general rule is that persons domiciled in a contracting State must be sued in that State, irrespective of their nationality (Article 2). The concept of 'domicile' is not defined by the Convention itself. In order to determine whether a party is domiciled in the contracting state whose courts are seised of the matter, the court shall apply its internal law, whereas if a party is not domiciled in the state whose courts are seised of the matter, the determination of whether the party is domiciled in another contracting State shall be made in accordance with the law of that State

(Article 52(1) and (2)). Corporations and other legal persons are considered to be domiciled where they have their 'seat'. In order to determine that seat, the court shall apply its rules of private international law (Article 53(1)).[11]

In addition to the general jurisdiction of the court of the defendant's domicile, the Convention provides also for cases of special jurisdiction which may be either concurrent with or alternative to the former. Disputes where, in addition to the court of the domicile, a court of another contracting State may equally exercise jurisdiction are, among others, those relating to contracts, maintenance, torts, trusts, salvage, and, in general, those arising out of any kind of operations of a branch, agency or other establishment of a particular company or a firm (Article 5). Exclusive jurisdiction is provided for in disputes relating to immoveable property, companies, public registers, industrial property rights, and enforcement of judgments (Article 16). Finally, special rules are laid down for insurance and consumer contracts, in order to protect policyholders and consumers (Articles 7–15).

With the exception of the cases of exclusive jurisdiction and, to a certain extent, insurance and consumer contracts, jurisdiction may be extended either by contractual agreement between the parties (Article 17) or by submission by the defendant (Article 18).

Where proceedings between the same parties and involving the same cause of action are brought in the courts of different contracting States, any court other than the court first seised shall of its own motion decline jurisdiction in favour of that court (Article 21); if the actions are only related, it may, but must not necessarily, stay its proceedings (Article 22).

In general the Convention is concerned only with the so-called 'international' jurisdiction, i.e. with the allocation of jurisdiction between the contracting States. There are, however, cases where it covers also the so-called 'internal' or 'local' jurisdiction, i.e. it indicates which court within the contracting State concerned will have jurisdiction. Thus, when Article 5(1) states that in matters relating to a contract a person may be sued 'in the courts for the place of performance of the obligation in question', it determines both the State which has jurisdiction and the particular court within that State in which the action must be brought.[12] The importance of this aspect is evident: with respect to matters falling within its scope, the Convention replaces not only existing national rules on international jurisdiction,

---

[11] Such an approach was adopted because, given the differences between the various domestic laws in this field, a jurisdiction convention was not the proper place to attempt to lay down a uniform definition of 'domicile'. (See Report by Jenard on the 1968 Convention (hereafter Jenard Report), [1979] OJ C59/1, esp. 15–16.

[12] Other provisions of this kind can be found in Arts. 6 and 6a, 8(1) (nos. 2, 3), 9, 10, 11(2), 14(3), 17 (if parties so agree), and 18.

but also the rules concerning internal jurisdiction, thus contradicting the traditional view that in the field of procedural law unification at an international level is extremely difficult if not impossible.

Within the sphere of application of the Convention, i.e. if the defendant is domiciled in a contracting State,[13] the uniform jurisdiction rules are intended to replace the existing national rules on jurisdiction in their entirety. Indeed, according to Article 4, the latter continue to apply only against defendants not domiciled in a contracting State.[14]

The Convention expressly lists the most important national rules on jurisdiction which will no longer be applicable. Some of them do refer to well known cases of 'excessive' jurisdiction: suffice it to mention articles 14 and 15 of the French Civil Code which, as applied in practice, grant a French plaintiff the right to sue a foreign defendant in French courts even if the dispute has no connection at all with France. Likewise, these articles allow a French defendant the possibility of insisting on being sued in France, thereby rendering the foreign judgment not enforceable in France.[15] Again, article 23 of the German Code of Civil Procedure, according to which a foreign defendant may be sued before a German court merely because there are assets of his in Germany, whatever their value.[16] Finally, article 2 of the Italian Code of Civil Procedure prohibits the possibility of excluding the jurisdiction of Italian courts in favour of that of a foreign court whenever one of the parties to the agreement is an Italian citizen domiciled in Italy.[17]

The list, however, is not exhaustive. Thus, for instance, as far as the United Kingdom is concerned, express mention is made only of the common-law rules which establish jurisdiction merely by service of summons during the temporary presence within the United Kingdom of the defendant, or the existence or seizure within the United Kingdom of property belonging to the defendant. There is no doubt, however, that, in all cases where the defendant is domiciled in one of the contracting States, other domestic

---

[13] Contracting States to the 1968 Brussels Convention are, in addition to the six original member States of the Communities, the other six member States to which, after their accession to the Communities, the Convention was extended by means of special accession conventions. It should be noted, however, that after the 1988 Lugano Convention on Jurisdiction and the Enforcement of Judgments in Civil and Commercial Matters between the EEC and the EFTA member States comes into force (which should take place in the near future), the uniform regime provided by the Brussels Convention will, in substance, be extended to include Austria, Finland, Iceland, Norway, Sweden, and Switzerland.

[14] The only exception expressly mentioned in Article 4 concerns the cases of exclusive jurisdiction provided for in Article 16, which are governed by the conventional regime even if the defendant is not domiciled within a contracting State.

[15] Cf. Gaudemet-Tallon, 'Nationalisme et Compétence Judiciaire: Déclin ou Renouveau?', *Travaux du Comité français de droit international privé*, (1986–8), 177 *et seq.*

[16] Cf. Kropholler, in *Handbuch des Internationalen Zivilverfahrensrechts*, I (1982), i: 314 *et seq.*   [17] Cf. Ballarino, *Diritto internazionale privato* (1982), 125 *et seq.*

jurisdiction rules are also no longer applicable. This is particularly so for those rules that grant 'discretionary' jurisdiction under Order 11 r. 1(1) of the Rules of the Supreme Court.[18]

For the six founding States of the European Communities there was no doubt that any new member State should be required to accept the substance of the Brussels Convention as originally agreed upon. A special provision to this effect was included in the text of the Convention (Article 63(1)), the only 'adjustments' admitted being those strictly necessary to accommodate the legal systems of the adhering States (Article 63(2)).

The first occasion for a renegotiation of the Convention arose when in 1973 Denmark, Ireland, and the United Kingdom joined the EEC. Subsequently the same situation was to arise after the entry into the Communities of Greece, Portugal, and Spain. The result of all these negotiations was the adoption in 1978 of the Convention on the Accession to the 1968 Convention and the 1971 Protocol of Denmark, the Republic of Ireland, and the United Kingdom,[19] in 1982 of the Accession Convention with Greece[20] and in 1989 of the Accession Convention with Portugal and Spain.[21]

As a whole, the adjustments made in order to accommodate the legal systems of the new contracting States were, however, not as relevant as one might have expected. In other words, the Convention, originally negotiated between the six EC founding States, and therefore clearly reflecting the civil-law approach to jurisdiction and to the recognition and enforcement, fundamentally maintained its character even after the accession of the two common-law States.

On the other hand, however, it should not be overlooked that when negotiating its accession to the Convention the United Kingdom succeeded in introducing a number of amendments aiming at the maintenance of London as the privileged forum for the settlement of disputes arising in the context of international trade relationships. Suffice it to mention Article 17(1) which, admitting in its amended version that extension of jurisdiction may be validly agreed not only in writing (or evidenced in writing) but also in the other general forms used in international trade or commerce, in fact legalizes the widespread practice in the field of maritime transport of inserting a clause in the bill of lading naming London as the competent forum even for disputes arising with third-party endorsees. The same can be said of the changes made to Article 12, which deals with

---

[18] Under these circumstances it is hardly surprising that in the UK the Convention is considered to be 'revolutionary' and the implementing legislation defined as 'perhaps the most important piece of legislation relating to civil procedure enacted in [the] country this century': cf. Collins, *The Civil Jurisdiction and Judgments Act 1982*, (1983), iii and 4.

[19] OJ, L 304, 1 of 30 October 1978.   [20] OJ, L 388, 1 of 31 December 1982.

[21] OJ, L 285, 1 of 3 October 1989.

extension of jurisdiction in the area of insurance. Whereas originally the possibility of derogating from the jurisdictional provisions of the Convention in this field was greatly limited in the interests of the insured (who was deemed to be the weaker party), now, as a result of the 1978 revision the extension of jurisdiction is permitted without any limitation whatsoever in relation to subjects of non-contracting States. As between subjects of contracting States such a possibility exists in the important branch of insurance against risks arising out of transport by sea or air. This is yet again to the advantage of London, which the insurance companies operating there can continue to impose on their foreign clients as the competent forum for determining eventual disputes.

2.2   The Atlantic Emperor: *A Case in Point*

A recent case concerning a dispute between an Italian and a Swiss company and which is still pending before the courts of both Italy and England would appear to be particularly appropriate to illustrate the changes which will follow as a result of the introduction of the Brussels Convention.[22]

Marc Rich & Co. AG, a Swiss company with its head office in Zug, wanted to buy a quantity of Iranian crude oil f.o.b. Valfajr Terminal from an Italian company, Società Italiana Impianti PA, based in Genoa. The contract was concluded in Italy, after the purchaser had communicated to the seller by telex its acceptance of the conditions proposed by the latter. Two days later, the purchaser sent a further telex in which, apart from setting out the terms in greater detail, it inserted a clause indicating English law as the proper law of the contract and referring any possible disputes arising between the parties to an *ad hoc* arbitration to be held in London. The seller did not reply to this further communication; however, it duly consigned the cargo at the port of shipment to the carrier indicated to it by the purchaser. Once loaded, the cargo was found to be seriously contaminated.

On request for damages by the purchaser, the seller denied all liability and, given the insistence of the other party, applied to the Court of Genoa for a decision in its favour. On receipt of the citation to appear before the Italian judge, the purchaser commenced arbitration in London. It nominated its own arbitrator, and since the seller refused to do likewise, it asked the High Court to appoint an arbitrator on the defendants behalf in terms

---

[22] Reference is here made to '*The Atlantic Emperor*', a case with respect to which decisions have already been rendered by Mr Justice Hirst and by the Court of Appeal (both in [1989] 1 Lloyd's Law Rep 548), and by the Italian *Corte di Cassazione*, 25.1.1991 (Foro Italiano, (1991), I, c. 1439). Since then the Court of Appeal referred a question of interpretation to the European Court of Justice, and the Italian *Corte di Cassazione* confirmed the competence of the Court of Genoa to render a negative declaratory judgment. In both countries the final decision has still to be handed down.

of section 10(3) of the 1950 Arbitration Act. The seller objected, invoking the absence of jurisdiction of the English courts on two grounds. First of all, under R.S.C. Order 73, r. 7(1) the intervention of the English courts in terms of the Arbitration Act is conditional on the arbitration being governed by English law or being or about to be held within the jurisdiction. In this case there was not even a valid arbitration agreement. Second, this case clearly fell within the ambit of the Brussels Jurisdiction Convention. According to Article 2 of that Convention competence would lie with the Italian courts as the courts of the country in which the defendants were domiciled. The court of first instance rejected both of these objections.

With reference to the preliminary question of the applicability of the Brussels Convention, Mr Justice Hirst recalled that arbitration is among the matters that according to Article 1 of the Convention are outside its scope.[23] As to the argument based on domestic law, he conceded that the jurisdiction of the English courts in arbitration matters presupposes that the action raised concerns an arbitration regulated by English law or to be held within English jurisdiction, while in the case in hand the very existence of the arbitration agreement was in question. This did not mean, however, that the condition required for the intervention of the English courts had not been satisfied. Indeed, the principle laid down in *The Parouth*,[24] according to which the conclusion of a contract is governed by the law which would have been the proper law had the contract been validly concluded, applied *a fortiori* when it was only the existence of a single clause that was in dispute. Consequently, an express reference to English law in such a single clause was sufficient to hold this same law applicable in order to determine the validity of the clause itself. Nor was there any point in recalling that in cases under R.S.C. Order 73, r. 7(1) the exercise of jurisdiction by the English court was merely discretional, i.e. would have to be excluded if in the instant case England could not be shown to be the most appropriate forum. It may have been true, as the defendants did not fail to point out, that almost everything in this case,

---

[23] The Italian company objected that this exclusion refers only to the so-called auxiliary arbitration procedures, such as the nomination or challenge of the arbitrators, the adoption of interim measures, and the setting aside or the enforcement of the award, but not to disputes as to the existence or validity of an arbitration clause. To answer this argument the judge referred to, *inter alia*, statements contained in the reports by Jenard and Schlosser both of whom, in his opinion, favoured a wide interpretation of the term 'arbitration' in the context of Art. 1 of the Convention. The relevant passages of the two reports are to be found in Report by Jenard on the Convention, [1979] OJ C59/13, and in the Report by Schlosser on the Accession Convention, ibidem, at 93. Note, however, that in a legal opinion which Professor Schlosser recently presented to the European Court of Justice on this case he vigorously rejects his original interpretation of Art. 1(4), favouring instead the inclusion of the kinds of disputes in question within the scope of the Brussels Convention: see Schlosser, 'The 1968 Brussels Convention and Arbitration', in *Riv dir intern priv proc* (1989), 545 *et seq*.   [24] [1982] 2 Lloyd's Rep 351.

beginning with the fact that all the witnesses except one and the other forms of proof were to be found in Italy, would appear at first sight to point to that country as the *forum conveniens*; however, this fact was 'of somewhat limited value since it is an everyday experience nowadays for witness to travel abroad, particularly in Europe'.[25]

The conclusions reached by the judge of first instance with reference to the question based on domestic law were subsequently upheld by the Court of Appeal.[26] If the Italian defendants' appeal was not completely rejected, this was only because the Court of Appeal was hesitant to follow entirely the reasoning of the judge of first instance with regard to the question of the application of the Brussels Convention to the case in hand. In other words, faced with the various arguments put forward by the parties in favour and against the Convention's application, the court preferred not to accept either position, and to refer the question to the European Court of Justice in accordance with Article 2(2) of the 1971 Protocol on the interpretation of the Convention by the Court in Luxembourg.

On this last issue the European Court has now rendered its decision which goes in substantially the same direction as that rendered by Mr Justice Hirst, i.e. 'Article 1(4) of the [Brussels] Convention must be interpreted as meaning that the exclusion provided for therein extends to litigation pending before a national court concerning the appointment of an arbitrator, even if the existence or validity of the arbitration agreement is a preliminary issue in that litigation'.[27]

The Atlantic Emperor nevertheless remains a case of interest for our purposes. Suppose the existence of the contract as such, and not that of the arbitration agreement alone, was at stake, with the consequence that the case would undoubtedly fall under the Brussels Convention. Even if one were to assume, for the sake of argument, that the case was to be decided in accordance with English law as the putative proper law of the contract,[28] under the Convention the outcome would be the opposite to that effectively reached by the two English courts. Indeed, according to the general rule laid down in Article 2 of the Convention, Italiana Impianti should have been sued in Italy, the state of its domicile, or, alternatively,

---

[25] [1989] 1 Lloyd's Rep 553.

[26] More precisely, it was confirmed that the principle that the existence of a single clause, even in the case of an arbitration clause, is determined like that of the contract as a whole on the basis of the law that would be applicable if the contract had been validly concluded. As the Court also refused to interfere with the weight attached by Mr Justice Hirst to certain factors in order to justify the exercise of jurisdiction in the given case since it held them to be matters entirely within his discretion and thus unable to be challenged by a superior court.

[27] See Judgment of 25 July 1991, in Case C-190/89 (not yet published).

[28] As will be demonstrated later in this paper, the decisions of the court of first instance and of the Court of Appeal on this point as well appear more than questionable, at any rate under the regime established by the 1980 Rome Convention on the Applicable Law.

in accordance with Article 5(1), at the place of performance of its obligation of delivery.[29] To affirm the competence of English courts on the ground
that English law is the proper law of the contract (or simply because there
is 'a good arguable case' to assume that it is so), would in no case be
possible, since under the Convention which law is applicable to the dispute
is totally irrelevant for the exercise of jurisdiction.

The situation is different as far as the Italian courts are concerned. They
were seised of a request by Italiana Impianti for a negative declaratory
judgment against Marc Rich. When asked to rule on the jurisdiction of the
Court of Genoa, where the action was brought, the *Corte di Cassazione*
was in substance right not to decide the matter in accordance with the
Convention, but to apply Italian law, and to affirm Italian jurisdiction on
the basis of article 4(2) of the Code of Civil Procedure. The court was,
however, wrong in assuming that the scope of application of the Convention as such is limited to cases where both parties are domiciled in
contracting States.[30] What is true, is that according to Article 4(1) if the
defendant is not domiciled in a contracting State—and Marc Rich is a
Swiss company domiciled in Switzerland—the jurisdiction shall in principle be determined by the domestic law of the forum.[31]

3   The Impact of the 1980 Rome Convention on Applicable Law on Traditional National Methods for the Determination of the Law Governing Contracts

3.1   *Reconsidering the Parties' Freedom of Choice and the Discretionary Power of Courts*

If the purpose of the Brussels Convention was to provide adequate rules
for the allocation of jurisdiction between the courts of the different member States of the European Communities as well as for the recognition and
enforcement of foreign judgments, the 1980 Rome Convention on the Law
Applicable to Contractual Obligations aims at introducing uniform conflict of laws rules. The link between the two Conventions is evident. Since,
in addition to the general domicile rule, the Brussels Convention provides
for a number of alternative fora, and parties are in principle free to agree

---

[29] However, as regards this latter alternative, it should be borne in mind that under the
Convention it is available only if the place of performance is situated in a contracting State,
a condition which does not seem to be fulfilled in the case at hand, where the Italian seller
had to deliver at an oil terminal in Iran.

[30] Since there are a number of provisions in the Convention, including those relating to the
recognition and enforcement of foreign judgments, which do apply even if the defendant is
not domiciled in a contracting State, the refusal of the court to postpone its decision until
the European Court of Justice would have rendered its ruling on the interpretation of Art.
1(1) no. 4, also seems unjustified.

[31] *Corte di Cassazione*, cit., Foro Italiano, (1991), I, c. 1442.

on the competence of any other court, it is important to avoid, to the greatest extent possible, what is commonly known as 'forum shopping'.[32] In theory, there would have been two alternative ways of achieving this objective: either by unifying the substantive laws of the different countries concerned, or by providing uniform criteria for the determination of the applicable law. Yet, given the necessarily slow and difficult process of the unification and harmonization of the former, in practice the only realistic solution available was that of unifying the latter.

The Rome Convention, the preparation of which was decided by the six original member States of the EEC in 1970, but which was finalized with the active participation of Denmark, Ireland, and the United Kingdom after their accession in 1973, is much more of a compromise between the existing domestic laws of all member States than the Brussels Convention.

This is not the place to examine the content of the Convention in detail. Attention will rather be focused on those specific provisions which are of particular interest in the present context. I refer to Article 3(3) and (4) on the one hand, and to Article 4 on the other: the former, dealing with the parties' freedom of choice of the applicable law, introduces a limit to that freedom and ventures to ensure that in any event the choice is made by both parties in full awareness; the latter, dealing with the case where the applicable law has not been chosen by the parties, provides for a number of presumptions for the determination of the applicable law, thereby considerably reducing the courts' discretionary powers in this respect.

3.1.1 *Article 3(3) or a Limit to the Parties' Freedom of Choice*

Contrary to a number of domestic laws,[33] the Convention does not require any connection between the law chosen by the parties and the transaction concerned.[34] Yet are parties free to designate a foreign law as the law governing their contract even in a purely domestic context, i.e. if the transaction concerned is otherwise entirely connected with one country only?

The problem of whether or not the parties' freedom of choice is limited to 'international' cases, i.e. where for a variety of reasons (different nation-

---

[32] On this point see the pertinent remarks of Fletcher, *Conflict of Laws and European Community Law* (1982), 13–15, 148–9, and of Kohler, 'Fortbildung des Brüsseler Gerichtsstands- und Vollstreckungsübereinkommen durch den Europäischen Gerichtshof: Freizügigkeit oder effektiver Rechtsschutz', in *Europarecht: Internationales Privatrecht— Rechtsvergleichung*, ed. Schwind (1988), 125 *et seq.*, esp. 132–3.

[33] The most striking example is given by the United States Uniform Commercial Code, which limits the parties' right to choose the applicable law to jurisdictions to which the transaction bears a 'reasonable relation' (s. 1–105); see also para. 187(2) of the *Restatement Second on Conflict of Laws*, which requires the law chosen to have a 'substantial relationship' to the parties or the transaction, or another 'reasonable basis' for the parties' choice.

[34] See Art. 3(1), which lays down the principle that '[a] contract shall be governed by the law chosen by the parties' without any further qualification.

ality of the parties, or their being domiciled in different States; goods, services, or payment moving from one country to another, etc.) the contract has at least one foreign or international element, is far from purely academic. There are trade sectors, such as maritime transport, insurance, or financing, where parties, even to a purely domestic contract, might prefer to subject it to, for instance, English law and to accept the jurisdiction of English courts.

The extent to which they are permitted to do so under existing domestic laws varies considerably from country to country, although there is a certain preference for a narrow interpretation of the principle of the parties' freedom of choice.[35]

The Convention would, at first sight at least, appear to adopt a much more liberal approach. Indeed, contrary, for instance, to the 1955 Hague Convention on the Law Applicable to International Sales of Goods which states that it applies to 'international sales of goods' and at the same time specifies 'The mere declaration of the parties, relative to the application of a law or the competence of a judge or arbitrator, shall not be sufficient to confer upon a sale the international character' (Article 1),[36] the Rome Convention is intended to apply generally 'in any situation involving a choice between the laws of different countries' (Article 1).

A closer look, however, reveals that this is not entirely true. Article 1 of the Convention has to be read in conjunction with Article 3(3), which specifies 'The fact that the parties have chosen a foreign law, whether or not accompanied by the choice of a foreign tribunal, shall not, where all the other elements relevant to the situation at the time of the choice are connected with one country only, prejudice the application of rules of the law of that country which cannot be derogated from by contract.' According to the official report of Professors Giuliano and Lagarde, this latter provision

is the result of a compromise between . . . the wish on the one hand of certain experts to limit the parties' freedom of choice . . . by means of a correcting factor specifying that the choice of a foreign law would be insufficient per se to permit the application of that law . . . , and on the other the concern of other experts,

---

[35] For an exhaustive comparative survey on this point, see Giuliano, Lagarde, and Sasse van Ysselt, 'Rapport Concernant l'Avant-projet de Convention sur la Loi Applicable aux Obligations Contractuelles et non Contractuelles' (Doc. XIV/408/72 F, Ras. 1), para. 4; see also Lando, 'International Situations and Situations involving a Choice between the Laws of different Legal Systems', in *Harmonisation of Private International Law by the E.E.C.*, (ed. Lipstein) (1978), 15 *et seq.*, esp. 17–18.

[36] In substance the same approach is followed also by the new 1985 Convention on the Law Applicable to Contracts for the International Sale of Goods, which in defining its scope of application refers to contracts of sale between parties situated in different States or to '. . . all other case involving a choice between the laws of different States, unless such a choice arises solely from a stipulation by the parties as to the applicable law, even if accompanied by a choice of court or arbitration' (Art. 1).

notably the United Kingdom experts, that such a correcting factor would be too great an obstacle to the freedom of the parties in situations in which their choice appeared justified, made in good faith and capable of serving interests worthy of protection . . . .[37]

Indeed, even leaving here open the question of the exact nature of a reference to foreign law in cases under Article 3(3), i.e. as a veritable choice of the applicable law (*kollisionsrechtliche Verweisung*) or as a mere incorporation of the foreign law into the contract (*materiellrechtliche Verweisung*),[38] one thing is certain: under the Convention, parties to a purely domestic contract may not elude the application of the mandatory rules provided by the law which otherwise would be applicable simply by designating a foreign law as the proper law of the contract, and/or by agreeing on the competence of a foreign court.

3.1.2 *Article 3(4) or How to Avoid Unwelcome Surprises*

Article 3(4) states that 'The existence and validity of the consent of the parties as to the choice of the applicable law shall be determined in accordance with the provisions of articles 8, 9, and 11'. Of the three provisions, it is Article 8 which is of particular interest in the present context.[39]

First, because according to Article 8(1) '[t]he existence and validity of a contract, or of any term of a contract, shall be determined by the law which would govern it under [the] Convention if the contract or term were valid'. The fact that this provision applies also to choice of law clauses means that under the Convention not only the substantive validity, but also the very existence of an agreement between the parties as to the applicable law is governed by that same law and not, as is the case under a number of domestic laws, either by the *lex fori*, or by the law which would be applicable in the absence of a choice of law by the parties.[40]

---

[37] See Report on the Convention on the Law Applicable to Contractual Obligations, by Giuliano and Lagarde, in *Official Journal of the European Communities* of 31 October 1980, No. C282/18.

[38] For the former opinion see, among others, Treves, 'Norme imperative e di applicazione necessaria nella Convenzione di Roma del 19 giugno 1980', in Treves (ed.), *Verso una disciplina comunitaria della legge applicablie ai contratti* (1983), 25 et seq., esp. 30. For the latter view see Reithmann and Martiny, *Internationales Vertragsrecht*, 4th edn. (1988), 85. For a flexible approach, see Philip, 'Mandatory Rules, Public Law (Political Rules) and Choice of Law in the E.E.C. Convention on the Law Applicable to Contractual Obligations', in *Contract Conflicts: The E.E.C. Convention on the Law Applicable to Contractual Obligations: A Comparative Study*, ed. North 81 et seq., esp. 95–7.

[39] Arts. 9 and 11 deal with the formal validity of the contract and possible cases of incapacity of the parties respectively.

[40] For the different national solutions, see Lando, in *International Encyclopedia of Comparative Law* (1986), iii ch. 24, 'Contracts', para. 81–4, and, with particular reference to common-law theories, North, 'Reform, but not Revolution', in his general course on private international law, at the Académie de droit international, Recueil des cours (1990), i: 9 et seq., esp. 168–174.

Yet, what is even more significant is the exception which the same Article introduces to the application of the putative proper law. Indeed, Article 8(2) states that '. . . a party may rely upon the law of the country in which he has his habitual residence to establish that he did not consent if it appears from the circumstances that it would not be reasonable to determine the effect of his conduct in accordance with the law specified in the preceeding paragraph'.

The importance of this provision with respect to the stipulation by the parties of the applicable law is evident. Choice of law clauses are often included in standard forms which one of the parties simply attaches to his offer or acceptance, or to a so-called 'letter of confirmation' which he sends after the conclusion of the contract with the intent of specifying in writing the terms of the contract which were orally agreed upon. Since domestic laws vary considerably as to the interpretation of silence on the part of the addressee,[41] the question arises of which law should govern the issue. So far basically two approaches have been followed: either that of applying the *lex fori*,[42] or that of deciding the issue in accordance with the law of the State in which the silent party is domiciled.[43]

The solution adopted by the Convention has the merit of providing the necessary degree of flexibility:[44] in case of dispute the silent party is in principle permitted to rely on his own law, but only in order to deny that he assented to the choice of law proposed by the other party and on condition that under the circumstances it would not be reasonable to hold him bound under the putative proper law (e.g. because in previous transactions the parties have already stipulated the same choice of law clause, or the contract was concluded in the state in which the proponent party has his place of business and the other party, who regularly conducts business in that country, should know that according to the law of that State his silence amounts to acceptance). In practice the result will be that no one should any longer be taken by surprise by a clever trade partner imposing a particular law upon him as the proper law of the contract, without his being fully aware of it.

---

[41] See Reithmann and Martiny, op. cit., 148–55.

[42] For this so far prevailing approach, see, among others, Dicey and Morris *On The Conflict of Laws*, op cit. ii: 1176–8.

[43] As was the position of German law before the adoption of the new Act on Private International Law in 1986: see Reithmann and Martiny, op. cit., 166 *et seq*.

[44] See the pertinent remarks of Profaner Gaudemet Tallon, 'Le Nouveau Droit International Privé Européen des Contrats Commentaire de la Convention C.E.E. n° 80/934 sur la Loi Applicable aux Obligations Contractuelles, Ouverte à la Signature à Rome le 19 juin 1980', in *Revue trimestrielle de droit européen* (1981), 273.

3.1.3   *Article 4 or the Reduction of the Discretionary Power of Courts*

Article 4(1) provides that in the absence of an express or implied choice of the applicable law by the parties[45] 'the contract shall be governed by the law of the country with which it is most closely connected'. For the determination of that country the Convention lays down a number of presumptions, the most important of which is to be found in Article 4(2) and is in favour of 'the country where the party who is to effect the performance which is characteristic of the contract has, at the time of the conclusion of the contract, his habitual residence, or, in case of a body corporate or unincorporate, its central administration', or, 'if the contract is entered into in the course of the party's trade or profession, . . . the country in which the principal place of business is situated or, where under the terms of the contract the performance is to be effected through a place of business other than the principal place of business, the country in which that other place of business is situated'.[46]

What constitutes the characteristic performance of any given type of contract is not defined by the Convention. While in unilateral contracts its identification should not be difficult, as far as bilateral contracts are concerned the Giuliano–Lagarde Report, in an attempt to provide further guidance, suggests that it is normally the performance for which payment is due, i.e. depending on the type of contract, the provision of the goods or services, transport, insurance, banking operations, security, etc., which may be regarded as the characteristic performance.[47]

In any event, the characteristic performance test does not apply if the characteristic performance cannot be determined or if it appears from the circumstances as a whole that the contract is more closely connected with another country (Article 4(5)).

This is certainly not the place for a detailed examination of the extent to which the system envisaged in the Convention is innovative with respect to the domestic laws of the member States. Suffice it to mention that the national systems which at first sight appear to be those most affected are, on the one side, the Italian, where so far the determination of the applicable

---

[45] Art. 3(1) provides that the parties' choice 'must be express or demonstrated with reasonable certainty by the terms of the contract or the circumstances of the case'. According to the Giuliano–Lagarde Report, 17, for an implied choice to be recognized as such, it is necessary that the parties have made a real choice although this is not expressly stated in the contract. Examples given of such an implied choice include contracts made on the basis of standard forms which are known to be governed by a particular system of law, a previous course of dealing between the parties, an express choice of law in related transactions between the same parties, reference to specific provisions of a particular national legislation, while the mere choice of a particular forum or place of arbitration is as a rule not sufficient to permit an inference that the law of the forum or of that place shall apply.

[46] The other two presumptions are laid down in Art. 4(3) and (4), and concern contracts relating to immoveables and contracts for the carriage of goods respectively.

[47] Cf. 20.

law was made on the basis of rigid rules laid down in statutory provisions,[48] and at the other end of the spectrum, the English and, to a certain extent at least, the French, where courts have been used to determining the 'proper law' of the contract in a much more flexible manner by weighing all relevant factors against each other.[49]

Nor is it the place for commenting on the at times all too heavy criticism which has been levied against it, in particular by English scholars.[50]

What is important for our purposes is to note that to introduce some restraint on the discretionary power of courts in determining the applicable law in the absence of a choice of the parties, is not only unlikely to do much harm, but might well do some good. This in particular if one considers how often the use of flexible or individualistic methods have led courts to favour the application of their own law.

3.2 *Again:* The Atlantic Emperor

The Atlantic Emperor case can also serve as an illustration of the changes that will follow the adoption of the Rome Convention. To begin with, the case as it came before the Italian courts presented two issues of private international law. First, since the Swiss defendant invoked an arbitration agreement, it was necessary to determine the law according to which the existence of such an agreement should be decided. Second, since the Italian plaintiff based the jurisdiction of the Italian courts on the fact that the sales contract had been concluded in Italy, the law governing the formation of the contract

---

[48] According to Art. 25 of the preliminary provisions to the Italian Civil Code, in the absence of a choice by the parties contractual obligations are governed either by the national law of the parties if they are of common nationality, or by the law of the country where the contract was concluded.

[49] For a more detailed comparative analysis, see Lando, 'The Conflict of Laws of Contracts' in his General Principles, at the Académie de droit international, Recueil des cours (1985), i: 225 *et seq.*, esp. 318–94.

[50] The arguments put forward are not always convincing. Thus, to condemn the Convention just because it replaces '. . . one of the great achievements of the English judiciary . . . , an achievement which produced an effective private international law of contracts, was recognised and followed in practically the whole world and has not at any time or anywhere led to dissatisfaction or to a demand for reform' ('Mann, The Proper Law of the Contract: An Obituary', LQR 107 (1991), 353) is more a profession of faith than an objective criticism. Equally, to accuse the Convention of ignoring the results of general experience and to say that the sole objective, and possible merit, of the system of presumptions laid down in Art. 4 is 'to rescue the German courts from their firmly entrenched but plainly inconvenient doctrine of scission . . .' (Lasok and Stone, *Conflict of Laws in the European Community* (1987), 361), is clearly out of place, if one considers that the last time the German Supreme Court applied two legal systems to the same contract was in a decision of 1924 (RG 27.5.1924 referred to by Kreuzer, *Das internationale Privatrecht des Warenkaufs in der deutschen Rechtsprechung* (1964), 175). For a much more balanced analysis, see, among others, North, 'Reform', op. cit., 194 *et seq.*; and, among non-English scholars, Gaudemet and Tallon, op. cit., 246 *et seq.*, Reithmann and Martiny, op. cit., 87 *et seq.*, and Giardina, 'Volontà delle Parti, Prestazione Caratteristica e Collegamento più Significativo', in Treves (ed.), see n. 38, above., 3 *et seq.*

had to be determined. Both questions were decided by the *Corte di Cassazione* in favour of Italian law.[51]

Under the Rome Convention the result would not be any different. What would differ, however, at least with respect to the second of the two questions, is the method followed.[52] Indeed, while the *Corte di Cassazione* applied Italian law as the *lex fori*, under the Convention the same law would be applicable by virtue of the combined application of Article 8(1), which provides that the conclusion of the contract is governed by the putative proper law, and of Article 4(2) according to which in a sales contract the proper law is presumed to be the law of the seller.

The impact of the Convention is much greater if one were to consider the case as being brought before the English courts.

As will be recalled, in order to affirm their jurisdiction under R.S.C. Order 73, r. 7(1), both the court of first instance and the Court of Appeal invoked the principle of private international law according to which the existence not only of a contract as a whole, but also of any of its individual clauses, is determined on the basis of the putative proper law, and concluded that in the case before them this law was English law.

This is not the place to investigate the extent to which this reasoning is convincing under English domestic law.[53] What is important to note is that it clearly can no longer be upheld under the Convention.

Let us again suppose, for the sake of argument, that the existence of the contract as such, and not that of the arbitration agreement alone, is at stake,[54] and that notwithstanding the absence of any other link with Eng-

---

[51] *Corte di Cassazione*, cit., Foro Italiano (1991), I, c. 1442–3.

[52] With respect to the first question, it is sufficient to recall that according to Art. 1(2)(d) arbitration agreements are excluded from the scope of the Convention.

[53] The principle of private international law invoked in the two decisions under consideration, known as the Dicey Rule, was recently affirmed in 'The Parouth' case, [1982] 2 Lloyd's Rep 351 (CA). In both *The Parouth* and *The Atlantic Emperor* the judges quoted Dicey and Morris *On the Conflict of Laws*, op. cit., ii: 1197–9 in support of their arguments. Apparently, however, they overlooked the fact that in Dicey and Morris the pronouncement of the general principle according to which '[t]he formation of a contract is governed by that law which would be the proper law of the contract if the contract was validly concluded' is followed by the proviso that '. . . there are situations . . . in which the application of the putative proper law would lead to grave injustice to one at least of the parties . . . in such cases that party must be able to rely on the law of his place of business or residence'. In the same text they go on to give the example of an Englishman who risks being bound by a contract since, according to the foreign putative proper law, his silence to the offer of the other party amounts to an acceptance thereto. The suggested solution is that, since such a principle is unknown in his country, he should be permitted to rely on the law of the country of his domicile in order to avoid the application on this point of the foreign putative proper law.

[54] Since arbitration agreements are excluded from the scope of the Convention, the issue will continue in the future to be governed by the relevant English domestic law. Surprisingly enough, in *The Atlantic Emperor* neither the court of first instance, nor the Court of Appeal took into consideration the fact that both the 1958 New York Convention on the Recogni-

land, English law is considered to be the putative proper law of the contract because of a choice of law clause to this effect. Under the Convention the question of the existence of a parties' agreement as to the applicable law is, as a rule, governed by that very law.[55] Yet, as mentioned above, there is an exception to the application of the putative proper law, i.e. a party may invoke his own law if it appears from the circumstances that it would not be reasonable to determine the effect of his conduct in accordance with the former law.[56] Leaving aside the question of the extent to which silence on the part of the recipient of a writing containing a choice of law clause may be considered as an exception under English law,[57] there can be no doubt that in a case such as the one under consideration, the Italian defendant would be entitled to avail himself of this exception and to invoke the application of Italian law in order to demonstrate that his conduct could not have constituted an assent.[58]

4 Conclusions

The attitude of States towards international uniform law has always been somewhat ambiguous. On the one hand they engage in strenuous negotiations for the preparation of uniform rules on the most diverse subject-matters, and once the text of the convention or model law concerned is finalized and adopted by the plenipotentiaries of the various countries, the event is enthusiastically greeted as an important contribution to the progressive unification or harmonization of law throughout the world. On the other hand when it comes to incorporating the uniform law into domestic law, much of the original enthusiasm is lost. Not only do Governments suddenly discover that, in terms of political returns, the unification of law

tion and Enforcement of Foreign Arbitral Awards (Art. II(2)), and the Arbitration Acts of 1950/1979 (Art. 32) require arbitration agreements to be in writing. Had they done so, they would have come to the conclusion they actually reached, since, whatever meaning one may attach in general to this special requirement of form, it can in no way be deemed to be satisfied in cases such as the one under consideration where the arbitration clause was inserted for the first time in a writing which one party sent to the other as confirmation of an already concluded contract. (Cf. with respect to the 1958 New York Convention, Gaja, *International Commercial Arbitration* (1980), i: B.3; with respect to Art. 32 of the Arbitration Act, see *Arab African Energy Corp. Ltd.* v. *Olieprodukten Nederland BV* [1983] 2 *Lloyd's Rep* 419; *Excomm Ltd.* v. *Ahmed Abdul-Qawi Bamaodah* [1985] 1 *Lloyd's Rep* 403.)

[55] See Art. 3(4) read together with Art. 8(1).

[56] See Art. 3(4) read together with Art. 8(2).

[57] On the reluctance of English law to admit that mere silence may ever amount to acceptance, see Treitel, *The Law of Contract*, 6th edn., (1984), 26 *et seq.*; Cheshire, Fifoot, and Furmston, *Law of Contract*, 11th edn. (1986), 47 *et seq.*

[58] According to Italian law, silence may amount to acceptance only in exceptional circumstances, such as the existence of a course of dealing between the parties, or where the party concerned is under a special duty to react: see Gorla in *Formation of Contracts*, ed. Schlesinger (1968), ii: 1176 *et seq.*; Galgano, *Il negozio giuridico* (1988), 64 *et seq.*

is far from gratifying, but also that interested business circles oppose the proposed uniform regime, which at best they consider to be a useless complication, with the result that in most cases the convention or model law does not even reach Parliament, and the product of years of intensive efforts remains a dead letter.

The 1968 Brussels Convention on Jurisdiction and the Enforcement of Judgments in Civil and Commercial Matters and the 1980 Rome Convention on the Law Applicable to Contractual Obligations are clear exceptions. Not only were they adopted within a relatively short period of time by the States which had originally elaborated them, but their persuasive value—above all that of the first, but to a certain extent also that of the second—has even extended beyond the boundaries of the European Communities, thus contributing to the creation of what has been called a veritable *espace judiciaire européen*.[59]

Yet, the importance of the two instruments lies also elsewhere. As illustrated in this paper, they are characterized by the fact that their impact on the municipal laws of the contracting states is not limited to the subject-matters specifically dealt with. By providing strict and uniform jurisdictional rules to the exclusion of exorbitant national jurisdiction, and by requalifying the parties' freedom of choice and reducing the discretionary power of courts in the determination of the applicable law, they should succeed in eliminating, or at least considerably reducing, any sort of 'legal imperialism' on the part of some over-ambitious national courts and clever trade partners.

Of course, also in the future there will be national jurisdictions and laws which will prevail, only from now on it should not be possible to impose them arbitrarily, but their affirmation will have to be justified by a clear choice of the parties or on the basis of objective and certain criteria. This was urged, as far as English jurisdiction is concerned, by Lord Diplock in *Amin Rasheed Shipping Corporation* v. *Kuwait Insurance Co.*,[60] when, in replying to Sir John Donaldson who wished to justify the exercise of English jurisdiction by the supposed international vocation of English courts, he stated that submission to their jurisdiction by foreign litigants should be voluntary and should not be forced upon unwilling defendants by English courts in the exercise of an exorbitant jurisdiction which no English court would ever recognize as possessed by foreign courts.

---

[59] Jenard, 'Les Développements Attendus et Inattendus de la Convention de Bruxelles du 27 septembre 1968 Concernant la Compétence Judiciaire et l'Exécution des Décisions en Matière Civile et Commerciale', *Journal des tribunaux* (1989), 173.

[60] [1984] 1 AC, 67–8.

SOME COMPARATIVE REFLECTIONS

THE RT. HON. SIR THOMAS BINGHAM

Conventions are made when States recognize problems which can only, or can best, be addressed by common action along lines internationally agreed. No one can doubt the growing significance of such conventions. Brussels, The Hague, Warsaw, Vienna, Rome: the list steadily lengthens, and with it the central role of such conventions in the international legal order. The topic addressed by these two complementary papers is accordingly of cardinal importance, particularly to those within the European Community but also to those outside it.

Professor Tallon illuminates the place of international conventions in French law. At first blush the contrast with the English position could scarcely be more striking. Upon ratification by the President (albeit with parliamentary authorization) the convention not only becomes part of the law of France, but also takes precedence over rules of purely domestic origin, an echo perhaps of principles older than the nation-state. In England, as recent decisions of high authority make clear, a convention not expressly enacted into English law is of no more than marginal significance at best.[1]

It does not, however, seem that the high ideals embodied in the French approach have been accepted without demur. Enforcement of a convention obligation may be refused if the other party or parties have not fulfilled their obligations, and it seems to be doubtful whether the courts or the executive are to judge whether they have or not. There appears to have been doubt, now perhaps resolved, whether a convention takes precedence over a later and inconsistent statute. And there has been some uncertainty about the role of the courts in interpreting international conventions, particularly in relation to questions touching on international public order. This uncertainty also is, perhaps, in course of resolution. Overall, the French courts appear to be taking a more assertive position and to be adopting a refreshingly internationalist approach.

The approach of the English judge called upon to interpret an international convention incorporated into English law is probably no different from that of his French counterpart. The so-called literal rule of interpretation does, of course, mean that he will begin by seeking to ascertain the meaning of the provision he is required to interpret from the words used, but the French judge could scarcely fail to do the same. The English judge is permitted, subject to certain safeguards, to have regard to *travaux*

---

[1] *J. H. Rayner (Mincing Lane) Ltd.* v. *Department of Trade and Industry* [1990] 2 AC 418; *R.* v. *Secretary of State for the Home Department* ex parte *Brind* [1991] 1 AC 696.

préparatoires, and regularly does so.[2] He will certainly expect to be referred, and will pay due regard, to the decisions of foreign judges on the same point. He will do his best to appreciate the mischief which the convention was designed to remedy, and the scheme underlying it, seeking to ensure that his resolution of any ambiguity and any interpolation he makes are consistent with that scheme and not inimical to it. But he must also understand that most conventions represent not the conception of a single mind but the outcome of a complex bargaining process in which the interests of different parties have been reconciled by compromise. In the field of interpretation, it is reasonable to hope that the judges—be they French, English, or other—are all internationalists now.

Professor Bonell devotes his paper to consideration of two conventions, the 1968 Brussels Civil Jurisdiction and Judgments Convention and the 1980 Rome Convention on Applicable Law. These Conventions, dealing with different but closely related subject matters, have a common objective: to curb the tendency of national courts to assume jurisdiction over cases which more properly belong elsewhere and to subject to their own law disputes more appropriately governed by another law. The aim is to replace what may become an unseemly tussle by clear and agreed rules applicable to every case.

It is perhaps surprising that courts, many of them over-burdened and over-stretched, should be greedy to assume jurisdiction in contested cases and so add to their workload. Distrust of the unknown, or the little-known, may be one factor: pride in their own law and procedure has almost certainly, at times, been another. A protective attitude towards one's own nationals or residents has probably been another. And it does appear that courts called upon to decide whether a dispute is governed by their own law or that of another State have tended to find in favour of their own. An objective observer would, surely, find it hard to argue that it was not desirable to avoid these expensive and often unseemly disputes by a code of rules agreed among the participating states. It is hard to avoid reference to that most hackneyed of all clichés, the level playing field.

The substance of the rules themselves is, no doubt inevitably, more controversial, although the two basic rules—that a defendant should be sued in the place of his domicile and that a contract should be governed by the law of the country with which it is most closely connected—should not be offensive to English lawyers. It is the provisions governing the parties' freedom to choose their forum or their applicable law, very interestingly analysed by Professor Bonell, which are likely to cause differences of opinion, partly because of the different approach to incorporation of

---

[2] *Fothergill v. Monarch Airlines Ltd.* [1981] AC 251.

contractual terms by reference of continental and common-law countries and partly, perhaps, because old habits die hard. Refreshingly, the Professor does not attempt to disguise his own preference: there is every prospect of an interesting, and important, developing jurisprudence.

5

The European Community and the European Convention on Human Rights: Their Effect on National Law

LEARNING FROM EUROPE— WITH EMPHASIS ON THE EUROPEAN CONVENTION ON HUMAN RIGHTS

HENRY G. SCHERMERS

1 Introduction

The integration of Europe leads to an enormous increase in contacts between the different member States. All European States learn from each other, and this process of learning covers almost all aspects of life and, inevitably, also the law. In this essay I shall focus on a number of particular issues which were raised before the European Commission of Human Rights and which concerned English rules or English practices which, in the opinion of the European Commission and the European Court of Human Rights, could be improved.

2 Applicability of international treaties

One issue where UK law differs considerably from the law of most countries on the Continent is the applicability of treaties. Compared to the United Kingdom, the Netherlands would be placed at the other extreme. What both countries have in common is that they have considerable interests overseas. Whilst the UK could defend its interests with its navy, UK diplomats did not appear to be over-concerned with international law; it was not even a compulsory part of their education. The Netherlands, on the other hand, had no military force to defend its interests and, therefore, always tried to persuade other countries that a careful application of international arrangements was essential in international relations. By making treaties about investment and nationalization the Netherlands tried to protect its interests overseas. This protection fully depended on a scrupulous application of international law. To give an example: Dutch judges have traditionally considered international law as being superior to domestic law and even preceding the Dutch constitution. Now that the force of the British navy is diminishing, it might be wise for the UK to put more emphasis on the direct applicability of international obligations. Both Norway and Denmark, who use the same dualistic system as the UK, intend to abandon it in the near future and give priority to international law over their domestic legislation. A Danish committee recently published a report stating why this should be done. A similar Norwegian report was expected, before the end of 1992. The arguments used in these documents might be of interest to English lawyers.

Application of international law within the domestic legal order can be performed in different ways. In the Netherlands the constitution requires that international treaties take priority over all domestic legislation, including the constitution itself. In several other countries treaties rank immediately after the constitution but take priority over domestic legislation. In Germany and Italy treaties are incorporated into the national legal system at the same level as domestic laws which means that a later law—at least in theory—can overrule a treaty provision. In practice new legislation never expressly sets aside treaty obligations. In all other cases courts tend to interpret new legislation in such a way as not to overrule a treaty obligation and therefore treat it as not being applicable to situations covered by the international obligation. In practice, courts can prevent such conflicts if they are so minded.

In Britain, even though the European Convention on Human Rights is not part of the national legal order, British courts do refer to it and often even take it into account which could be seen as coming close to a direct application. Nonetheless, there are situations where British courts are unable to apply the European Convention on Human Rights. The clearest example where courts have not applied the convention is not from the United Kingdom but from the Republic of Ireland. It concerns homosexual acts between consenting male adults in private. According to the legislation of Northern Ireland of the time, such homosexual acts were a criminal offence. In the *Dudgeon* case the European Court of Human Rights held that the restriction imposed on Mr Dudgeon's private life under Northern Irish law, by reason of its breadth and absolute character, was disproportionate to the aims sought to be achieved and therefore in violation of Article 8 of the European Convention on Human Rights.[1] The Republic of Ireland had exactly the same legislation, stemming from the time prior to its independence. Mr Norris brought a case against the Republic in October 1983 claiming that this legislation equally violated Article 8. The *Dudgeon*

---

[1] *Dudgeon*, judgment of 22 Oct. 1981, Series A, No. 45, 24, 25, 27.

judgment was invoked but the Irish Supreme Court, stating that 'the Convention is an international agreement' which 'does not and cannot form part of [Ireland's] domestic law nor affect in any way questions which arise thereunder'. The Chief Justice in the majority judgment said further: 'this is made quite clear by Article 29 section 6 of the Constitution which declares: "no international agreement shall be part of the domestic law of the State save as may be determined by the Oireachtas".' By a three to two majority decision of 22 April 1983 the Irish Supreme Court refused to follow the European Court's judgment in *Dudgeon* on the ground that the Convention is not part of Irish law. Subsequently Mr Norris brought a complaint under the European Convention of Human Rights which found a breach of Article 8 of the Convention on 26 October 1988.[2] English courts, not bound by a written Constitution, may be more flexible than their Irish counterparts, but the problem remains the same.

It has often been said that a large number of cases are brought against the United Kingdom under the European Convention of Human Rights due to the fact that UK Courts are not permitted to apply the Convention itself. When, in the Netherlands, the Convention has been infringed it will usually be the domestic courts applying the Convention which will redress the situation. In England domestic courts are not allowed to do so. Applying equivalent national rules and using the Convention as background material they may reach the same results. But as they cannot apply the Convention itself, applicants may be encouraged to raise the question in Strasbourg.

The fact that about a fifth of the cases before the Human Rights Court come from the United Kingdom could be seen as a positive factor. Obviously individual applicants are sufficiently informed of their rights and are not prevented from raising their problems in Strasbourg. At the same time however, the large number may be attributed to the inability of the domestic courts to apply fully the convention.

By 1 January 1991 the European Court of Human Rights had decided 177 cases. In 130 of them it found at least one violation. Of the 177 cases 37 (21 per cent) were brought against the United Kingdom. In 27 of the cases brought against the UK at least one violation was found (that is also almost 21 per cent of all violations found). In the cases where the Court found no violation, of the Convention it sometimes did so only after hesitation. In the *Cossey* case, for example, the Court found there was no violation. The case concerned the impossibility of transsexuals obtaining any kind of change to their birth certificates after a change of sex. This can lead to great hardship when official papers are needed. The question came up first in the *Rees* case where the Court, overruling a unanimous

---

[2] *Norris*, judgment of 26 Oct. 1988, Series A, No. 142.

Commission, found no violation by twelve votes to three.[3] The *Cossey* case, decided four years later, concerned virtually the same issue. The Court came to the same decision but the majority had shrunk to ten votes to eight.[4] Furthermore, in both cases the Court reminded the UK Government that since the Convention has to be interpreted in the light of current circumstances, the need for appropriate measures should be kept under review. This corresponds with the opinion of the European Court of Human Rights that the Convention is a living instrument and should therefore be interpreted not in accordance with the meaning it was given when it was drafted, but instead in the light of circumstances existing today. This may well mean that in another five or ten years time English legislation, prohibiting the alteration of a birth certificate, will be held contrary to the Convention.

3   The Convention as a Bill of Rights

The question was discussed whether incorporation of the European Convention on Human Rights into the British legal system would in fact introduce a Bill of Rights superior to any Act of Parliament. Under particular circumstances it would permit, or even charge, the appointed judiciary to overrule the elected parliament. It seems unacceptable that when a democratically elected parliament has adopted a law, probably after duly debating the question of conformity with human rights, an appointed judge may subsequently refuse to apply that law on the ground that, in his opinion, it conflicts with the European Convention on Human Rights. Is this not contrary to the basis of democracy? In England, the doctrine of 'sovereignty of Parliament' might cause additional difficulties.

In practice, this conflict does not frequently occur. When legislating, parliaments do not intentionally overrule the European Convention on Human Rights. When there is doubt whether particular legislation is permissible under the Convention, and when this legislation has been thoroughly discussed in Parliament, the judiciary will take this discussion into account. The only example which I know of from Western Europe, where a constitutional court clearly refused to accept legislation adopted by Parliament, was the case of the German abortion law which in the opinion of the German Constitutional Court was in violation of the fundamental right to life.[5] Even though in practice our judges are careful not to overrule Parliament too quickly, this does not provide a conclusive answer to the problem, a future judiciary might show less respect for Parliament. Lower

---

[3] *Rees* case, judgment of 17 Oct. 1986, Series A, No. 106.

[4] *Cossey* case, judgment of 27 Sept. 1990, Series A, No. 184.

[5] Decision of the Bundesverfassungsgericht of 25 Feb. 1975, EuGRZ (1975), 126; NJW (1975), 573.

courts in the Netherlands have repeatedly refused to apply legislation on the ground that it conflicted with the European Convention on Human Rights or with other treaty obligations. A system which permits the judiciary to overrule the legislature must accept the risk that legislation will be set aside by courts.

However, democracy is a more complicated notion than simply giving priority to the will of Parliament. An elected Parliament is not, necessarily, a guarantee of a fair democratic government. Democracy is, in any case, more than majority voting. The European Court of Human Rights has repeatedly interpreted democracy as including demands of pluralism, tolerance, and broad-mindedness. The German Constitutional Court (*Bundesverfassungsgericht*) enumerated the following fundamental principles for a free democratic system:

- respect for human rights as defined in the Basic Law, in particular the right to life and free development of the personality;
- the sovereignty of the people, the separation of powers, the Government's responsibility to Parliament;
- the principle that administrative acts are governed by the rule of law, the independence of the courts, the plurality of political parties;
- equal opportunity to all political parties;
- the right to found an opposition and to contend with those in power, in accordance with the Constitution.[6]

At least in theory there are also dangers inherent in the doctrine of the sovereignty of Parliament. When there are strong currents in public opinion against foreigners, or against Jews, or against blacks, there may be electoral profit in anti-foreign, anti-Jewish or anti-black legislation. In theory a majority of Parliament can accept legislation which is biased against minorities. Furthermore, modern legislation can be extremely complicated which means that there is a risk that possibly unacceptable consequences of particular legislation may not be identified before they actually arise. Laws which are the result of political compromises are not always the best laws. To protect the population, and especially to protect minorities, judicial control over Parliament may thus be advisable.

Like so often in law, we are confronted with a pair of scales which have to be kept in balance. On the one hand a sovereign Parliament may infringe upon the essential rights of minorities or individuals, on the other hand too powerful a judiciary may be against the democratic system. In practice we try to elect sufficiently responsible people to prevent Parliament from infringing fundamental human rights and at the same time we try to appoint to the judiciary people of sufficient standing and wisdom to

---

[6] Judgments of 23 Oct. 1952 and 17 Aug. 1956, quoted by the European Court of Human Rights in the *Glasenapp* case, Series A, No. 104, 10.

guarantee that the powers of Parliament are suitably respected. In communist countries the Party could instruct judges how to decide their cases. In that kind of society judicial control is unacceptable. In Western Europe, however, we have a strong tradition of an independent judiciary of high standing. Balancing all pros and cons, the advantages of judicial control in our society outweigh the risks and disadvantages. All West European countries, which have judicial control, consider it valuable. But for a very few exceptions, court decisions not to apply legislation because of its conflict with fundamental human rights have been favourably accepted by commentators.

4   Treatment in Prisons

An important yardstick for the protection of fundamental human rights in a particular country is the way it treats its prisoners. It may be that in this respect England can learn from Europe. During the Second World War many leading politicians on the continent of Europe were put in prison by Nazi authorities. Their practical experience of prison sentences has been one of the great forces behind the improvement of prison treatment. The absence of such experience in the United Kingdom may, arguably, be one of the reasons why the treatment of prisoners in the United Kingdom has led to so many cases before the European Commission and Court of Human Rights. The most severe cases concerned prisons in Northern Ireland where people were forced to stand for hours against walls with their hands above their head; were subjected to white noise or deprived of sleep, food, and drink; were forced to do heavy exercises; or were covered by a dark hood over their heads for long periods of time. The European Court of Human Rights considered the treatment not serious enough to be considered torture, but sufficiently serious to constitute inhuman and degrading treatment.[7]

Because of the special situation in Northern Ireland, Northern Irish prisons should not be considered representative of the entire British system. However, in other respects as well British prisons have fallen short of European standards. In three cases the European Court of Human Rights has criticized the United Kingdom for the unjustified limitation of the correspondence of prisoners. Both in 1975 and in 1983 the European Court held that UK rules on prison correspondence were too restrictive.[8] In 1988 and in 1990 new cases concerning the correspondence of prisoners in the UK were brought before the European Court of Human Rights. In these cases the Government acknowledged that correspondence had been

[7] *Ireland* v. *UK*, judgment of 18 Jan. 1978, Series A, No. 25.

[8] *Golder*, judgment of 21 Feb. 1975, Series A, No. 18, 20–22, and *Silver*, judgment of 25 March 1983, Series A, No. 61.

unreasonably restricted.[9] It is not quite clear why the UK courts were unable to settle these issues themselves. Since the Government acknowledged the infringement of the Convention, one would have expected that a presentation of the case before the domestic courts could have solved the dispute. The result may thus be due to an insufficient applicability of the Convention in the domestic legal order, or, perhaps, of an insufficient familiarity with the Convention and its case law in the case in point. It is difficult for an outside observer to do more than speculate.

Another issue where standards in British prisons fell short of the requirements of the European Convention concerned the limitations on the rights of prisoners to consult a solicitor. In 1975 a prisoner, Golder, wished to consult a solicitor with a view to instituting legal proceedings in order to sue a prison officer for libel. The Home Secretary's refusal to grant such permission was considered to be in breach of Article 6(1) of the Convention.[10] The question of the right to seek legal advice was also discussed in the *Silver* case in 1983.[11]

In *Campbell and Fell* the Board of Visitors of one of HM Prisons imposed additional sentences on two prisoners who took part in a prison unrest while denying them legal representation at the hearings. The European Court of Human Rights found a violation of Article 6(3). The Board of Visitors was also not accepted as an independent and impartial court in the sense of Article 6 of the Convention because its judgments had not been passed in public.[12]

There is, in short, a corpus of UK law which may not be entirely satisfactory and which could stand to be improved by greater familiarity with European law and practices.

5 Suspects

According to a number of decisions of the European Court of Human Rights the United Kingdom fell short of the European standards on the protection of persons suspected of criminal activities.

5.1 *The* Malone *Case*

Mr Malone complained about the tapping of his telephone. In an earlier case the European Court of Human Rights had accepted that telephone tapping is covered by Article 8 of the European Convention which guarantees to everyone the right to respect for his private and family life, his

---

[9] *Boyle* and *Rice*, judgment of 27 Apr. 1988, Series A, No. 131, 22 and *McCallum*, judgment of 30 Aug. 1990, Series A, No. 183, 15.

[10] *Golder*, judgment of 21 Feb. 1975, Series A, No. 18.

[11] *Silver*, judgment of 25 Mar. 1983, Series A, No. 61.

[12] *Golder*, judgment of 21 Feb. 1975, Series A, No. 18.

home, and his correspondence.[13] Paragraph 2 of Article 8 permits interference with private and family life, home, and correspondence, if this is necessary in a democratic society in the interest of *inter alia* national security for the prevention of disorder or crime. Such interference must, then, be in accordance with the law. In *The Sunday Times* v. *United Kingdom*[14] the European Court ruled that 'law' does not necessarily mean statutory law. Customary law or case law may also be acceptable provided that it is adequately accessible, formulated with sufficient precision, and compatible with the rule of law (which means that the law must have a certain quality). In the *Malone* case the European Court of Human Rights held that the English law permitting telephone tapping did not fulfil these conditions as it was insufficiently clear. On that ground the Court found Malone's telephone tapping in breach of the Convention.[15]

5.2   *The* Granger *Case*

Mr Granger had been sentenced to five years' imprisonment. When he expressed a wish to appeal against this judgment, legal aid for the appeal was refused. The European Court of Human Rights, considering the length of the sentence and the importance of the appeal to Mr Granger, held that this refusal was an infringement of Article 6(1) and (3)(c).[16]

5.3   *The* Brogan *Case*

To cope with the problems in Northern Ireland special legislation provided that persons could be held in detention for seven days without any judicial control. In the *Brogan* case the Court held that this legislation conflicted with European standards. According to Article 5(3) of the Convention a person arrested or detained, if not released immediately, is entitled to a prompt appearance before a judge or judicial officer. The Court underlined the importance of this provision as a fundamental right protecting the individual against arbitrary interferences by the State with his right to liberty, guaranteed in Article 5 of the Convention. According to the Court, judicial control of interferences by the executive with the individual's right to liberty is essential to minimize the risk of arbitrariness.

The Court was of the opinion that the word 'promptly' in Article 5(3) and even more the French expression '*aussitôt*' is of limited flexibility. Even a period of four days and six hours falls outside the strict constraints as to time permitted by the Article. Too wide an interpretation of the provision would import a serious weakening of a procedural guarantee to the detriment of the individual and would entail consequences impairing the

---

[13] *Klass*, judgment of 6 Sept. 1978, Series A, No. 28.
[14] Judgment of 6 Nov. 1980, Series A, No. 38.
[15] *Malone*, judgment of 2 Aug. 1984, Series A, No. 82, 31–6.
[16] *Granger*, judgment of 28 Mar. 1990, Series A, No. 174, 16–19.

very essence of the right protected by this provision. The Court concluded that there had been a violation of Article 5(3).

In the event, the Government of the United Kingdom was unwilling to adapt its legislation to conform with their ruling. In its opinion it was often, for practical reasons, impossible to give full information about the arrest of a person within a period of time shorter than seven days. It was equally impossible to require a court to make a decision without all information available, or to present information to a court in a confidential way. Any procedure which would allow a court to make a decision on information not presented to the detainee or his legal advisor would represent a radical departure from the principles which govern judicial proceedings in the UK and could seriously affect public trust and confidence in the independence of the judiciary. On these grounds the Government of the United Kingdom invoked Article 15 of the Convention which permits measures derogating from the obligations under the Convention in time of war or other public emergency.

5.4   The Fox, Campbell, *and* Hartley *Case*

Under special legislation a person can be held in detention without judicial control for a long period of time. This, as we have seen, is one of the issues that must be kept under review; but it is not the only one. The basis on which arrests can be made can also be criticized. Under section 11(1) of the Northern Ireland (Emergency Provisions) Act 1978 'any constable may arrest without warrant any person whom he suspects of being a terrorist'. Article 5(1)(c) permits deprivation of liberty only on *reasonable suspicion* of having committed an offence. In the Fox, *Campbell,* and *Hartley* case the Court found that the suspicion which led to their arrest was insufficiently explained as reasonable.[17] In more recent cases arrests have been made on the basis that the Government has a reasonable suspicion on the ground of confidential information obtained from reliable sources that the suspect was involved in particular criminal activity. The Commission referred one of these cases to the Court in order to make sure whether this is sufficient to conclude that there is a reasonable suspicion under Article 5(1)(c).

6   Sentences

In some cases the European Court of Human Rights has had to pronounce upon the discretionary life sentence which has developed in English law as a measure of dealing with mentally unstable and dangerous offenders. Although the dividing line may be difficult to draw in particular cases, it

---

[17] Fox, *Campbell,* and *Hartley,* judgment of 30 Aug. 1990, Series A, No. 182, 15–18.

seems clear that the principles underlying such sentences, unlike mandatory life sentences, have developed in the sense that they are composed partly of a punitive element and partly of a security element designed to confer on the Secretary of State the responsibility of determining when the public interest permits the prisoner's release. With respect to that security element the basis for imprisonment (the existence of mental instability and dangerousness) are susceptible to change over the passage of time. New issues as to the lawfulness of the sentence may thus arise in the course of detention. The European Court of Human Rights has held, therefore, that at various intervals in the execution of their sentences, detained persons are entitled under Article 5(4) of the Convention, to take proceedings to have the lawfulness of their continued detention reviewed by a court. Where such a review was not available in particular instances in the United Kingdom, Article 5(4) was held to have been violated.[18]

In another case a prisoner, freed on parole, was re-called to prison after three years. In this case as well the European Court was of the opinion that the lawfulness of the redetention should be determined by a court. As the re-call was not subject to judicial control the Court found that Article 5(4) of the Convention had been violated.[19]

In another instance a young offender had committed relatively minor crimes and was not considered to be a dangerous person. His life sentence was not considered in violation with Article 5(1); but the European Court of Human Rights held that at some later stage, when the offender could be of the opinion that the situation had changed, he should have a right to take new proceedings before a court. The absence of such a possibility was considered as an infringement of Article 5(4).[20] Likewise in the case of *Thynne, Wilson,* and *Gunnell* the European Court found that there was no review of the case possible and for that reason held that Article 5(4) had been violated.[21]

7   Freedom of the Press

The freedom of the press is guaranteed by Article 10 of the European Convention on Human Rights, which provides:

1 Everyone has the right to freedom of expression. This right shall include freedom to hold opinions and to receive and impart information and ideas without interference by public authority and regardless of frontiers. This Article shall not prevent states from requiring the licensing of broadcasting, television or cinema enterprises.

---

[18] *Thynne, Wilson,* and *Gunnell,* judgment of 25 Oct. 1990, Series A, No. 190, 29, 30, 32.   [19] *X v. UK,* judgment of 5 Nov. 1981, Series A, No. 46.
[20] *Weeks,* judgment of 2 Mar. 1987, Series A, No. 114.
[21] *Thynne, Wilson,* and *Gunnell,* judgment of 25 Oct. 1990, Series A, No. 190, 29, 30, 32.

2 The exercise of these freedoms, since it carries with it duties and responsibilities, may be subject to such formalities, conditions, restrictions or penalties as are prescribed by law and are necessary in a democratic society, in the interests of national security, territorial integrity or public safety, for the prevention of disorder or crime, for the protection of health or morals, for the protection of the reputation or rights of others, for preventing the disclosure of information received in confidence, or for maintaining the authority and impartiality of the judiciary.

The European Court of Human Rights has consistently ruled that the freedom of the press is guaranteed by this Article and that exceptions to it should not be easily allowed, as the freedom of the press is one of the essential elements of modern democratic Government. The European Court of Human Rights has twice found the United Kingdom Government in violation of this provision.

7.1   *The* Sunday Times *Case*

The first case was brought by *The Sunday Times* and concerned a report on Thalidomide. This drug had caused severe deformities in babies born between 1958 and 1961. Between 1962 and 1966 many parents issued writs against The Distillers Company (Biochemicals) Limited, the producer of the drug. The majority of the actions were settled in 1968 following negotiations between the parties' legal advisors. By 1971, 389 claims were still pending. Further negotiations led to proposals for a settlement involving the setting-up of a £3,250,000 trust fund. This proposal was to be submitted in October 1972 to the British court for approval.

On 24 September 1972 *The Sunday Times* carried an article entitled: 'Our Thalidomide Children: A Cause for National Shame'. This examined the settlement proposals then under consideration, describing them as 'grotesquely out of proportion to the injuries suffered'. Compared to the profit of £64.8 million made by selling the drug, it considered a trust fund of £3.25 million to be totally insufficient. A footnote to the article announced that in a future article *The Sunday Times* would trace how the tragedy occurred. On 17 November 1972 the Divisional Court of the Queen's Bench Division granted the Attorney-General's application for an injunction restraining publication of this future article on the ground that it would constitute contempt of court. Accordingly the article was not published before the discharge of the injunction on 23 June 1976. The article appeared in a somewhat amended form in *The Sunday Times* of 27 June 1976.

However, in the autumn of 1972 there was a considerable response from the public, the press, and television. Some radio and television programmes were cancelled after official warnings about contempt of court. On 29 November 1972 the matter was extensively debated in the House of Commons. Shortly before that debate the Distillers Company had increased the value of their proposed trust fund from £3.25 million to £5 million. The parliamentary debate was followed by a further wave of publications, but no further contempt proceedings were instituted.

Following the public criticism the proposed settlement did not materialize. In January 1973 the Distillers Company further increased the value of the trust fund to £20 million. On that basis a settlement was reached in the vast majority of cases. It was approved by a single judge of the Queen's Bench Division on 30 July 1973.

In the meantime, following an appeal by Times Newspapers Limited the Divisional Court's injunction was discharged by the Court of Appeal on 16 February 1973, only to be restored in modified form on 24 August 1973 following the House of Lords' decision of 18 July allowing a further appeal by the Attorney-General. Since not all the parents had accepted the proposed settlement the issue remained *sub judice*.

The dispute before the European Court of Human Rights concerned the question whether the fact that negotiations were being conducted in order to achieve an agreed settlement under the auspices of the court justified this limitation of the freedom of the press. Article 10 of the European Convention permits a limitation of the freedom of the press if this is prescribed by law and necessary in a democratic society *inter alia* for the protection of the reputation or rights of others or for maintaining the authority and impartiality of the judiciary.

With respect to the requirement that the interference must be prescribed by law the European Court of Human Rights held that the word 'law' does not necessarily require a statute. It also covers unwritten law, provided that such unwritten law is adequately accessible to a citizen who wishes to know the legal rules applicable in a given case, and it is sufficiently precise to enable the citizen to regulate his conduct accordingly. In the present case the Court considered that these conditions were fulfilled and held that the interference with the applicant's freedom of expression was thus 'prescribed by law' within the meaning of Article 10(2).

The Court also accepted that the interference with the applicant's freedom of expression was made for the purpose of 'maintaining the authority and impartiality of the judiciary'. It did not consider it necessary to decide whether the interference also fulfilled the purpose of safeguarding the rights of others, as the safeguarding of the rights of litigants was included in the phrase 'maintaining the authority and impartiality of the judiciary'.

The decisive question in the case was whether the interference was 'necessary in a democratic society' for achieving the legitimate aim of maintaining the authority of the judiciary.

According to the Court 'necessary' is not synonymous with 'indispensable' but does not have the flexibility of such expressions as 'admissible', 'ordinary', 'useful', 'reasonable', or 'desirable'. In order to consider a provision necessary the Court held there must be a 'pressing social need' for it. In order to establish the existence of such a pressing social need the Court gives the contracting States a margin of discretion, which, however, is not unlimited. The domestic margin of discretion goes hand in hand with European supervision. This supervision is not limited to ascertaining whether a State exercised its discretion reasonably, carefully, and in good faith. Even when it does so, the exercise of such discretion remains subject to the Court's control as regards the compatibility of its conduct with its commitments under the Convention.

The Court accepted the concern regarding 'trial by newspaper'. If the issues arising in a litigation are aired in such a way as to lead the public to form its own conclusion thereon in advance, the public may lose its respect for, and confidence in, the courts. Nor can it be excluded that if the public were to become accustomed to the regular spectacle of pseudo-trials in the news media, such behaviour might, in the long run, have detrimental effects on the acceptance of the courts as the proper forum for the settlement of disputes. However, this concern could not be decisive in the present case. The proposed article was couched in moderate terms and did not present only one side of the evidence or claim that there was only one possible result at which a court could arrive. It analysed in detail the evidence against Distillers, but also summarized arguments in their favour.

It should also be taken into consideration that the negotiations were very lengthy, continuing for several years, and that at the moment when publication of the article was restrained the case had not reached the stage of a trial. Furthermore, when the injunction was discharged in 1976 there were still a number of parents with outstanding claims. If the injunction was not necessary for the protection of their litigation, it becomes unclear why it had been necessary at all.

Article 10 of the European Convention on Human Rights guarantees not only the freedom of the press to inform the public but also the right of the public to be properly informed. In *The Sunday Times* case the families of numerous victims of the tragedy, who were unaware of the legal difficulties involved, had a vital interest in knowing all the underlying facts and the various possible solutions. To deprive them of this crucial information could only be justified by a very serious threat to the authority of the judiciary.

The Court finally concluded that the interference complained of did not correspond to a social need sufficiently pressing to outweigh the public interest in freedom of expression within the meaning of the Convention. The restraint imposed on the applicants proved not to be proportionate to the legitimate aims of maintaining the authority and impartiality of the judiciary. Therefore, it was not necessary in a democratic society for maintaining the authority of the judiciary. Accordingly, the injunction restraining publication of the article in the *Sunday Times* constituted a violation of Article 10 of the European Convention on Human Rights.

7.2   *The* Spycatcher *Case*

The other infringement of the freedom of the press found by The European Court of Human Rights occured when it took the view that the United Kingdom had violated the Convention in the case concerning Peter Wright's book *Spycatcher*. Two cases were brought before the Court, one by the *Observer* and *Guardian* and the other again by *The Sunday Times*. The Court decided both cases on 26 November 1991.

Mr Peter Wright was employed by the British Government as a senior member of the British Security Service (MI5) from 1955 to 1976 when he resigned. Subsequently, without any authority from his former employers, he wrote his memoirs, entitled *Spycatcher*, and made arrangements for their publication in Australia, where he was then living. The book dealt with the operational organization, methods, and personnel of MI5 and also included an account of alleged illegal activities by the Security Service. Mr Wright had previously sought, unsuccessfully, to persuade the British Government to institute an independent inquiry into these illegal activities. Part of the material in *Spycatcher* had already been published in books by another author and moreover, in July 1984, Mr Wright had given a lengthy interview on television about the work of the Security Service. When he was informed of the intended publication, the Attorney-General of England and Wales instituted proceedings in the Australian courts to restrain publication of *Spycatcher* and of any information contained therein. Whilst the Australian proceedings were still pending the *Observer* and *Guardian* newspapers published, in June 1986, short articles on the forthcoming case in Australia in which they also gave details of some of the contents of the manuscript. The Attorney-General sought permanent injunctions against these defendants.

Where a plaintiff seeks a permanent injunction against a defendant, the English courts have a discretion to grant the plaintiff an interlocutory injunction. Such a temporary restriction pending the determination of the dispute at the substantive trial is designed to protect the plaintiff's position in the interim. In such a case the plaintiff will normally be required to give an undertaking to pay damages to the defendant should the latter succeed in the trial. When it granted such interim injunctions on 27 June 1986 the English court held that the injunctions requested were only temporary and that to refuse them might cause irreparable harm to the Attorney-General's case. Furthermore, the alleged unlawful activities had occurred in the rather distant past so that there could be hardly any compelling interest requiring their publication immediately rather than after the substantive trial.

In the subsequent stages of the interlocutory proceedings both the Court of Appeal and all the members of the Appellate Committee of the House of Lords considered that this initial grant of interim injunctions was justified.

When the Australian courts had rejected the Attorney-General's claim against Peter Wright on 30 March 1987, and when, after that, several English newspapers published certain of the allegations made in *Spycatcher*, the *Observer*, the *Guardian*, and *The Sunday Times* applied for the discharge of the injunctions against them on the ground that there had been significant change of circumstances since they were granted. While this application was still pending, Viking Penguin Incorporated announced its intention to publish the book in the USA on 14 July 1987. On 12 July 1987 *The Sunday Times* printed in its later editions the first instalment of extracts from *Spycatcher*. On 13 July 1987 the Attorney-General commenced proceedings against *The Sunday Times* for contempt of court.

On 14 July 1987 the book was published in the USA. A substantial number of copies were then brought into the United Kingdom. The telephone number and address of US bookshops willing to deliver the book in the United Kingdom were widely advertised in the UK. No steps to prevent imports were taken by the British Government.

When *The Sunday Times* had made it clear that, unless restrained by law, they would publish the second instalment of the serialization of *Spycatcher* on 19 July 1987 the Attorney-General applied for an injunction to restrain them from doing so. On 16 July 1987 the Vice-Chancellor granted this injunction. This new injunction restrained publication by *The Sunday Times* until 21 July, as on 20 July the Vice-Chancellor was to consider the application by the newspapers for discharge of the original injunctions.

Having heard arguments from 20 to 22 July 1987, the Vice-Chancellor delivered a courageous judgment discharging the original injunctions and dismissing the claim for a further injunction against *The Sunday Times*.

The Attorney-General immediately appealed against the Vice-Chancellor's decision. Pending the appeal the original injunctions against the newspapers continued to be in force but no new injunction was issued following *The Sunday Times* announcement that it would publish the second instalment in the serialization of *Spycatcher*.

In a judgment of 24 July 1987 the Court of Appeal held that it was inappropriate to continue the original injunctions in their original form, but that it was appropriate to vary these injunctions to restrain publication of the book in order to restore confidence in the Security Service by showing that memoirs could not be published without authority, to protect the

Attorney-General's rights until the trial, and to fulfil the court's duty of deterring the dissemination of material written in breach of confidence.

On 30 July 1987 the Appellate Committee of the House of Lords gave judgment, holding by a majority of three to two that the original injunctions should continue. In fact they subsequently remained in force until the commencement of the substantive trial in the breach of confidence actions on 23 November 1987.

On 21 December 1987 the High Court (Mr Justice Scott) gave judgment. On the main issue the High Court decided in favour of the newspapers but it continued the interlocutory injunctions pending an appeal to the Court of Appeal.

On 10 February 1988 the Court of Appeal affirmed the decision of the High Court and likewise granted fresh interim injunctions pending an appeal to the House of Lords.

On 13 October 1988 the Appellate Committee of the House of Lords also affirmed the decision of the High Court. It held *inter alia* that since the world-wide publication of *Spycatcher* had destroyed any secrecy as to its contents continuation of the injunctions was not necessary, that the articles of 22 and 23 June 1986 had not contained information damaging to the public interest, and that the information in *Spycatcher* was now in the public domain and no longer confidential.

The Court further held that the *The Sunday Times* was in breach of its duty of confidentiality in publishing its first serialized extract from *Spycatcher* on 12 July 1987, that imminent publication of the book in the USA did not amount to a justification and that accordingly *The Sunday Times* was liable to account for the profits resulting from that breach.

On 8 May 1989 the High Court reached a decision on the Attorney-General's action for contempt of court initiated when *The Sunday Times* had published part of the *Spycatcher* two days before its publication in the USA. The High Court held *The Sunday Times* in contempt of court and imposed a fine of £50,000. On 27 February 1990 the Court of Appeal dismissed the appeal of *The Sunday Times* against the finding that it had been in contempt but concluded that no fines should be imposed. A further appeal by *The Sunday Times* against the finding of contempt was dismissed by the Appellate Committee of the House of Lords on 11 April 1991.

Before the European Court of Human Rights it was not disputed that the injunctions interfered with the applicants' freedom of expression, that they were 'prescribed by law' and that they had legitimate aims, primarily 'maintaining the authority of the judiciary', further 'protecting national security'. The issue before the European Court of Human Rights was whether the interference was necessary in a democratic society.

The European Court first pronounced the following four major principles with respect to its interpretation of Article 10 of the Convention.

(a) Freedom of expression constitutes one of the essential foundations of a demo-cratic society; subject to paragraph 2 of Article 10, it is applicable not only to 'information' or 'ideas' that are favourably received or regarded as inoffen-sive or as a matter of indifference, but also to those that offend, shock or disturb. Freedom of expression, as enshrined in Article 10, is subject to a number of exceptions which, however, must be narrowly interpreted and the necessity for any restrictions must be convincingly established.

(b) These principles are of particular importance as far as the press is concerned. Whilst it must not overstep the bounds set, inter alia, in the 'interests of national security' or for 'maintaining the authority of the judiciary', it is nevertheless incumbent on it to impart information and ideas on matters of public interest. Not only does the press have the task of imparting such infor-mation and ideas: the public also has a right to receive them. Were it otherwise, the press would be unable to play its vital role of 'public watchdog'.

(c) The adjective 'necessary', within the meaning of Article 10(2), implies the existence of a 'pressing social need'. The contracting States have a certain margin of appreciation in assessing whether such a need exists, but it goes hand in hand with a European supervision, embracing both the law and the decisions applying it, even those given by independent courts. The Court is therefore empowered to give the final ruling on whether a 'restriction' is reconcilable with freedom of expression as protected by Article 10.

(d) The Court's task, in exercising its supervisory jurisdiction, is not to take the place of the competent national authorities but rather to review under Article 10 the decisions they delivered pursuant to their power of appreciation. This does not mean that the supervision is limited to ascertaining whether the respondent State exercised its discretion reasonably, carefully and in good faith; what the Court has to do is to look at the interference complained of in the light of the case as a whole and determine whether it was 'proportion-ate to the legitimate aim pursued' and whether the reasons adduced by the national authorities to justify it are 'relevant and sufficient'.

The Court underlined that Article 10 of the Convention does not pro-hibit the imposition of prior restraints on publication but that the dangers inherent in prior restraints are such that they call for the most careful scrutiny on the part of the Court. This is especially so as far as the press is concerned, for news is a perishable commodity and to delay its pub-lication, even for a short period, may well deprive it of all its value and interest. The European Court accepted most of the arguments on which the House of Lords founded its decision of 30 July 1987 to continue the injunctions against the newspapers. Based on the above considerations it found, however, that these arguments were insufficient to fulfil the require-ments of Article 10 of the Convention. In the opinion of the Court, the interest in maintaining the confidentiality of the material contained in *Spycatcher* had, for the purposes of the Convention, ceased to exist by 30 July 1987. The Court concluded that the interference complained of was not 'necessary in a democratic society' and that the United Kingdom had accordingly violated Article 10 of the Convention.

8   Dissenting and Concurring Opinions

In the area of unanimous or dissenting judgments, continental lawyers stand to learn from the English (and, arguably, English lawyers may be interested in continental ideas on the topic). With only a few exceptions (such as the German Constitutional Court) continental courts are bound by the confidentiality of their internal discussions. The judges take a decision by majority vote and that decision is presented to the world as the unanimous decision of the court. Judges are not allowed to disclose how the decision was reached. The underlying idea is that a court decision will be more authoritative where no dissent is revealed. Continental lawyers are far from unanimous in the belief that this is the best situation. But if has been part of continental European legal tradition for a long time and would therefore be difficult to change, even assuming there was wide demand for such a change.

The Court of Justice of the European Communities was established by six continental countries. This may have caused a certain preference against allowing the publication of dissenting and concurring opinions, but there were at least three other, and stronger, arguments against it. In the first place it was considered desirable to appoint the judges for only six years. The founders of the Communities were afraid that dynamism would be lost when judges became too old. As each member State could appoint only one judge there was also a wish to make some sort of rotation possible between judges from different backgrounds. Once it was decided that the judges could sit for only six years, it became essential to their independence that any dissenting opinions should remain secret, otherwise a judge who wished to be re-elected may be tempted to vote in favour of his Government. Even if he would not actually do so, he could be suspected of having done so if he was re-elected.

A second reason for keeping the votes of the judges secret was in order to preserve the confidence of all member States in the Community judical system. It could easily happen that one judge (for whatever reason) would always be out-voted on any particular issue. This might cause people from the judge's member State to mistrust that part of case law ('our own judge always voted against it'). Third, it is important to a European Court that as much unanimity is reached as possible. A compromise solution may be more acceptable than a decision reached by majority vote. Where dissenting opinions are possible, courts are more easily inclined to decide by majority vote, allowing the minority to dissent. Where no dissenting opinions are possible there is a greater pressure to meet the minority by making at least some concessions.

If one accepts the above arguments and concludes that retaining the confidentiality of judicial deliberations is the better system for the Court of Justice of the European Communities, then it may seem inconsistent that the European Court of Human Rights allows the presentation of dissenting and concurring opinions. This Court (of Human Rights) was established with the co-operation of the United Kingdom and Ireland, and that may have been one reason why dissenting and concurring opinions were allowed. But another reason is that the task of this Court differs from that of the Court of Justice of the Communities. Unlike the latter, the Human Rights Court does not have to make decisions affecting national economic interests. Neither does it give preliminary rulings in which the law is interpreted generally. It is unlikely that the Human Rights Court would ever take a series of decisions on a particular issue comparable to the decisions of the Court of Justice of the European Community on issues such as parallel imports, direct effect of directives, or equal pay for men and women. Nor has the Court of Human Rights the power to annul decisions of an international organization. The judgments of the Human Rights Court are entirely limited to legal questions concerning human rights. Furthermore, membership of the Court of Human Rights was not expected to be the principal occupation of the persons concerned.

The advantages and disadvantages of unanimous judgments may thus be open to argument. Perhaps different styles are appropriate to different courts; but the differences are still there and in examining them national lawyers may be given the opportunity to reconsider the strengths and weaknesses of their own approach.

EUROPEAN COMMUNITY LAW AND PUBLIC LAW IN THE UNITED KINGDOM

DERRICK WYATT

This essay addresses the mutual influences which are or might be exerted by national law on European Community law, and by the latter on the law of the member States. This is the 'learning from Europe' which informs the decision making of national judges on the one hand, and the judges in Luxembourg on the other. It is important to emphasize the role of the judges, for they are central to the legal order of Europe, whether they sit in the Court of Justice or Court of First Instance in Luxembourg, or in national courts and tribunals. The national legal systems are clearly open to the influence of EC law because EC law has direct effect in the member States. This brings in its train not only the enforcement of Community rights as part of the law of the member States, but the creation of hybrid remedies, based on national remedies, and adapted to the requirements of Community law.[1] But there is also a more subtle route for the Community system to influence the national systems; namely, the application in a purely national context, by analogy, of principles of Community public law. While the applications of Community law by national authorities and courts in the member States has wrought highly visible changes in the national legal systems, it is those same national systems which provided the starting point for the development of the Community legal system, and it would be wrong to leave out of account, because it is less tangible, the debt owed by Community law to principles of national law and to the procedures of national courts and tribunals.

1 National Influences on European Law

Community law is open to influence from the national systems in a number of ways. In the first place judges appointed to the Court of Justice of the European Communities are not trained exclusively, or even mainly, to practise in the field of Community law, or adjudicate upon Community law issues. They are chosen from those 'whose independence is beyond doubt and who possess the qualifications required for appointment to the highest judicial offices in their respective countries or who are jurisconsults of recognised competence . . .'[2] A judge who is appointed to the European

---

Fellow of St Edmund Hall, Barrister. This article was originally drafted as a lecture. In adapting it for publication, the author has sought to preserve its original character.

[1] Case 199/82 *San Giorgio* [1983] ECR 3595; case C-213/89 *Factortame* [1990] ECR I-2433.   [2] Art. 167 of the EEC Treaty.

Court may have developed his principle expertise in areas of law unrelated to European Community law. Even if Community law is the principal expertise of the new appointee, he will have developed this expertise after education and training in his national legal system, of which European Community comprises a component part.[3] To the extent that Community law is characterized by general principles developed on a case by case basis, the influence of national principles and procedures seems inevitable. That this influence is difficult to attribute to a particular system in a particular case reflects in part the distinct function and purpose of the Community system, which may require the solution of legal problems without a precise analogy in the national law of the member States, and in part the fact that the influence of the national systems is both simultaneous and cumulative. It would indeed be a cause for concern if the legal approach of a particular member State or member States were to dominate or even to seem to dominate in the development of Community law.

Quite apart from any automatic influence of the national legal traditions upon the decision making of the European Courts which might result from the education and training of the judges, Community law invites reception of general principles derived from national law in a number of respects. Two important examples are to be found in Articles 215(2) and 173(1) of the Treaty.

The first makes provision for the liability of the Community in damages in accordance with the general principles common to the laws of the member States. While the Court of Justice has no doubt developed those principles of Community liability which it considers best suited to the requirements of the Community system, taking general account of the principles of State liability in national law, the Court on occasion makes some reference to the processes of comparative analysis which might be involved. With respect to the liability of the Community for invalid legislative acts, the Court stated in *Bayerische HNL Vermehrungsbetriebe GmbH & Co. KG* v. *Council and Commission*:

To determine what conditions must be present in addition to such breach [i.e. breach of a superior rule of law for the protection of the individual] for the Community to incur liability in accordance with the criterion laid down in the case-law of the Court of Justice it is necessary to take into consideration the principles in the legal systems of the Member States governing the liability of public authorities for damages caused to individuals by legislative measures. Although these principles vary considerably from one Member State to another, it is however possible to state that the public authorities can only exceptionally and in special circumstances incur liability for legislative measures which are the result of choice

---

[3] See case 6/64 *Costa* v. *ENEL* [1964] ECR 585 at 593, '. . . the EEC Treaty has created its own legal system which, on the entry into force of the Treaty, became an integral part of the legal systems of the Member States and which their courts are bound to apply.'

of economic policy. This restrictive view is explained by the consideration that the legislative authority, even where the validity of its measures is subject to judicial review, cannot always be hindered in making its decisions by the prospect of applications for damage whenever it has occasion to adopt legislative measures in the public interest which may adversely affect the interests of individuals.[4]

With respect to the application of a time bar which has not been pleaded by the defendant, the Court in *Roquette Freres SA* v. *Commission* stated: 'Actions to establish non-contractual liability are governed, pursuant to the second paragraph of Article 215 of the EEC Treaty, by the general principles common to the laws of the Member States. A comparison of the legal systems of the Member States shows that as a general rule, subject to very few exceptions, a court may not of its own motion raise the issue of time limitation.'[5]

Article 173(1), unlike Article 215(2), makes no express provision for the application of principles of national law. It states that the Court of Justice shall have jurisdiction to review the legality of acts of the institutions on grounds of lack of competence, infringement of an essential procedural requirement, infringement of the Treaty of Rome or of any rule of law relating to its application, or misuse of powers. Yet it would be a mistake to assume that in making such provision the draftsman had done any more than provide the titles for the chapters which were to be written by the Court of Justice in its subsequent case law. The Treaty gives no hint as to the content of the rules of administrative law which the Court is to apply in fulfilling its judicial task. Principles of legal certainty and legitimate expectation, of proportionality and human rights,[6] have been developed in the case law of the Court as a response to the requirements of the Community legal order and against the background of the administrative law traditions in which the judges of the Court were educated and trained, and in which they administered, professed, practised, or adjudicated.

Although it is generally unsafe to attribute a particular legal development in Community law to a particular national legal origin it may be appropriate in this particular context to refer to potential influences of the 'British' approach in Community law. These potential influences are both substantive and procedural.

In terms of substantive influence, the principles of United Kingdom public law (it is misleading to speak simply of English law), along with those of other national systems, have played their part in establishing the principles of natural justice as principles of Community law. Reference in this context[7]

---

[4] Cases 83 and 94/76 etc. [1978] ECR 1209 at para. 5 of judgment.

[5] Case 20/88 [1989] ECR 1553 at para. 12 of judgment.

[6] See Wyatt and Dashwood, *Substantive Law of the EEC* (Sweet & Maxwell, London, 1987), 60 *et seq.*

[7] Brown and Jacobs, *The Court of Justice of the European Communities* (Sweet & Maxwell, London, 1989), 302.

has been made to the *Transocean Marine Paint Association* case, in which Advocate General Warner cited English, Scottish, Belgian, French, and Luxembourg law in support of the principle *audi alterem partem*, and in which the Court adopted the principle as part of Community law.[8] As has been noted, experience of the various national systems is ensured by the multi-national character of the Court of Justice and the Court of First Instance.

What I may be forgiven for describing as 'the common-law approach' is also felt in matters of technique and procedure in the Community legal system. I would refer first to the contribution of United Kingdom lawyers in the use of case law in pleading before the Court of Justice, before which the procedure is principally written. It is not surprising that lawyers from the United Kingdom produce written arguments which made good use of relevant case law. Reference to case law is second nature and they are used to citing cases in written opinions, in skeleton arguments for the Court of Appeal and in written cases for the House of Lords. I would also refer to the good use to which the limited oral procedure is put by British advocates. They need little encouragement to comply with the Court's notes for counsel and refrain from simply reading prepared texts to the Court, since they are accustomed to speaking freely in argument before national courts and tribunals.[9] It is my impression that the judges in Luxembourg engage British advocates more readily in argument than advocates from those member States where debate between bar and bench is less prominent a feature of the judicial process. The reason for this is that British advocates will welcome the opportunity to assist the Court of Justice in this particular way. It is also my impression that it does so assist the Court. It may be that the practices of the Court of Justice are still not ideally suited to getting the most from the admittedly limited oral procedure, and to this I shall return. For the time being, I shall consider possible influences of principles of Community public law on the development of public law in the United Kingdom.

2   Possible European Influences in the Public Law Field

At the beginning of this paper, reference was made to the possibility that Community law might influence the law of the United Kingdom not only by virtue of its direct application in accordance with the Treaty, but also as a result of its general principles being applied by analogy as part of national law. I say at once that I incline to the view that there are certain rules and principles which may well weather at least partial transplantation into the soil of the common law—at any rate in the public law field.

---

[8] Case 17/74 [1974] ECR 1063.
[9] There are, of course, sometimes good reasons why advocates are reluctant to depart from a prepared draft of a speech, e.g. where the advocate is representing a member State.

3   Interpretative Techniques of the European Court

Mention must be made of the interpretative techniques of the European Court, which emphasize the purpose of the provision in issue, whether it be a provision of the Treaty, or of secondary legislation. It is common for the purposive approach to take priority over a literal interpretation of the relevant text. Thus the fact that Article 173 of the EC Treaty does not name the European Parliament as a potential defendant in proceedings for judicial review has not prevented the European Court from entertaining such actions against the Parliament, in cases where acts of the Parliament have had more than merely internal effect.[10] Indeed, the European Court has come close to claiming an inherent jurisdiction, designed to curb abuse of power by the Community institutions, in the name of the rule of law.[11]

But it must be added that the approach of the Court of Justice will vary according to context. For example, the Court will expect to find clear words if it is alleged that the effect of a Community measure is to impose a *charge* on individuals, for a contrary approach would be contrary to the principle of legal certainty.[12]

The European Court then, other than in matters of revenue, tends to be result oriented and pragmatic, and to come close to claiming an inherent jurisdiction to control the abuse of power. Yet it would be wrong to regard these characteristics as distancing the interpretative techniques of the European Court from those employed by the courts of the United Kingdom, providing that like is compared with like. If the interpretative techniques of the European Court are compared with those current in the Chancery Division then the contrast is apparent and substantial. Yet that is not an appropriate comparison to make. A better comparison is between the European Court acting as an arbiter of the legality of Governmental action, both at the national and Community level, and the Divisional Court of the Queen's Bench Division adjudicating upon an application for judicial review. Surely it cannot be said that a purposive approach to the construction of legislation, and the concept of an inherent jurisdiction to curb excess of power, are concepts alien to our domestic system of public law?

4   Common Ground between United Kingdom and European Public Law

The corner-stone of the British system of administrative law is the inherent jurisdiction of the Divisional Court to curb abuse of power on the part of

---

[10] Case 294/83 *Les Verts* v. *Parliament* [1986] ECR 1339.
[11] Case C-2/88 *Zwartveld* [1990] ECR I-3365.
[12] Case 169/80 *Gondrand Frères* [1981] ECR 1931.

Government.[13] Again, in the field of public law, English courts have not been enamoured of a literal approach to the interpretation of statutes. The principles of natural justice are based on implied procedural safeguards interpolated into statutory provisions which on any literal construction would be otherwise construed. More dramatic examples exist. I would refer to *R. v. Registrar General* ex p. *Smith*.[14] In this case a person in a secure mental health unit who had been convicted of murder and manslaughter applied under section 51 of the Adoption Act for details of his birth record. The Registrar General, on medical advice that the person concerned might do harm to his natural mother if he discovered her identity, refused to disclose the relevant details. The person applied for judicial review of this refusal, arguing that he had an absolute statutory right to the information. There were no express exceptions in the Act. Both the Divisional Court and the Court of Appeal refused the application, on the basis that an exception was to be implied on grounds of public policy. Staughton LJ was willing to make such an exception where to do so would prevent serious crime in the future. He stated: 'This is consistent with the growing tendency, perhaps encouraged by Europe, towards a purposive construction of statutes, at all events if they do not deal with penal or revenue matters.'[15]

It has already been noted that in revenue matters, European law equally adopts a more literal approach to interpretation.

Still in the field of public law in the United Kingdom, one of the most recent developments has been recognition of a principle of legitimate expectation. This principle is capable of creating both procedural and substantive expectations in individuals which the courts will safeguard through the procedure for judicial review.[16] This recent creation of the common law may prevent a public authority from changing its position unless required by statute or considerations of the public interest. It would be inaccurate to describe judicial developments in public law of this type as evidencing a literal approach to statutory construction. The literal approach is *one* approach, which is particularly appropriate in certain contexts, but generally inappropriate in the public law field. It is to generate a largely false comparison to describe the judicial tradition of the United Kingdom as being characterized by a literal approach to the construction of legislation, while describing the European approach as being characterized by a teleological approach. Where public law is concerned, it is more accurate to say that the teleological approach has been employed to a greater or lesser extent in the United Kingdom for a number of years,

---

[13] Wade, *Administrative Law*, 6th edn. (Clarendon Press, Oxford), 639.
[14] [1991] 2 All ER 88.   [15] [1991] 2 All ER 88 at 95, d–e.
[16] See e.g. *Attorney-General of Hong Kong* v. *Shiu* [1983] 2 All ER 346; *Khan* [1985] 1 All ER 40; *Ruddock* [1987] 2 All ER 518.

though always subject to the qualification, which is not applicable to the Court of Justice of the European Communities, that general principles of United Kingdom public law are subordinate to statutes and to *intra vires* secondary legislation.

Without overstating the case, it surely must be acknowledged that the approach of the European Court of Justice on the one hand and that of the Divisional Court in the public law field on the other are similar in certain respects. Both approaches are pragmatic and result oriented. Both to a greater or lesser extent go beyond the literal interpretation in order to promote the underlying values of their legal orders.

5   General Principles of European Public Law

The European Court of Justice has developed certain principles which limit the otherwise general discretion of the Council and Commission to take legislative or administrative action under various provisions of the EEC Treaty. These principles include:

1 non discrimination;
2 legitimate expectation; and
3 proportionality.

6   Non-Discrimination

This principle has a basis in Article 40(3) of the Treaty, which provides that common organizations of agricultural markets shall exclude any discrimination between producers or consumers within the Community. Subsequent case law has accorded the principle more general application. In *Ruckdeschel* and *Moulin* the Court stated: 'the prohibition of discrimination laid down in the aforesaid provision [i.e., Art. 40(3)] is merely a specific enunciation of the general principle of equality which is one of the fundamental principles of Community law. This principle requires that similar situations shall not be treated differently unless differentiation is objectively justified.'[17]

7   Legitimate Expectation

The second principle, that of legitimate expectation, has developed independently of any formulation in the text of the Treaty. It has been loosely linked in its origins with principles of German, French, and Belgian administrative law.[18] It has in common with the similarly named principle of United Kingdom administrative law, an attribution of legal consequences

[17] Cases 117/76 and 16/77 [1977] ECR 1753, at 1769, and 1795 at 1811.
[18] Usher, 'Influence of National concepts on Decisions of the European Court' 1 *EL Rev* 1 (1976), 359, 363 *et seq.*

to reliance by private parties upon the conduct or representations of public authorities.[19]

8 Proportionality

The principle of proportionality has some textual basis in the Treaty, in that some Treaty provisions state that the Council may take the measures *required* to achieve a particular end. It has been linked in its origins with the truism that the punishment should fit the crime, and with a principle of German administrative law.[20] However, the principle has developed as a 'common-law' principle from case to case.

The abovementioned principles may be invoked where it is alleged that Community legislative or administrative acts are *ultra vires* the discretionary power vested in the Council or Commission. The Court has taken a further step, and held in a number of cases that the general principles of Community law, which includes those referred to above, condition the legality of *national* measures taken to implement *Community* obligations.[21] Thus a national penal provision implementing a Community regulation or directive could in principle be challenged for being excessive and disproportionate.[22]

9 Should General Principles of Community Law Influence United Kingdom Public Law?

The question arises to what extent the general principles of Community law might influence, or ought to influence the development of purely domestic public law. My own view is that some influence is likely, and desirable, where application by analogy of Community principles constitutes a logical progression of the United Kingdom system of public law. There are certainly practical reasons why the influence of Community will be felt in appropriate cases. Our judges will become familiar with the relevant principles of Community law by applying them in a Community context. If the principles are compatible with the aims of our national system of public law, and assist in the solution of practical problems when they arise, it is likely and appropriate that they will incorporated, *mutatis mutandis*, into our system of public law.

10 Possible Influence of the Principle of Proportionality

Judicial and extra judicial consideration has been given to the principle of proportionality in Community law and United Kingdom law, and I shall

---

[19] Wyatt and Dashwood, op. cit., n. 7, 61 *et seq.*   [20] Usher, op. cit., n. 19, 362, 363.
[21] See e.g. case 5/88 [1989] ECR 2609.   [22] Case C-326/88 *Hansen* [1990] ECR I-2911.

address this principle in more detail. This principle simply stated holds that: 'the individual should not have his freedom of action limited beyond the degree necessary for the public interest.'[23]

The principle of proportionality operates in a number of contexts, and indeed takes colour from its context. It is most rigorous in its application when a member State engages in activity prima facie contrary to a general principle of law, and relies by way of justification upon an exception to that principle, e.g. a member State claims a restriction upon the free movement of goods is justified on grounds of public health.[24] The principle is less rigorous in its application when Community institutions take prima facie lawful action involving a choice of policy. In such a context, the Court of Justice stresses the policy choice available to the institutions, and the political responsibility involved, and will only interfere where the measure is *manifestly inappropriate*, having regard to the objective which the competent institution is seeking to pursue.[25] I think it is important to say that it is proportionality of this latter type which is best fitted for application by analogy in the United Kingdom domestic system of administrative law.

United Kingdom courts have referred to the principle of proportionality in a number of cases. I would refer the reader to:

- *CCSU v. Minister for the Civil Service;*[26]
- *Pegasus Holdings*, per Schiemann J: 'Is there here such [*Wednesbury*] total lack of proportionality or lack of reasonableness';[27]
- *Assegai* per Woolf LJ: 'where the response is out of proportion with the cause to this extent, this provides a very clear indication of unreasonableness in a Wednesbury sense.'[28]
- *Brind v. Home Secretary.*[29]

Three Law Lords in *Brind* accepted the possibility of the future development of the principle of proportionality in United Kingdom administrative law. But Lord Ackner raised the objection that such a development would involve balancing the reasons for and against the decision of the minister in a case such as that before him. It appears from Lord Ackner's treatment of the *Wednesbury* test that he believed that the principle of proportionality would amount to the exercise of an *appellate* rather the *supervisory* jurisdiction.[30]

Yet it seems that in some cases the courts may interfere with discretionary administrative action on the ground that the methods used to achieve

---

[23] Case 11/70 *Internationale Handeslgesellschaft* [1970] ECR 1125 at 1127 *per* Advocate General Dutheillet de Lamothe.   [24] Case 104/75 *De Peijper* [1976] ECR 613.
[25] Case 331/88 *Fedesa*, judgment of 13 Nov. 1990.
[26] [1984] 3 All ER 935 at 950, *per* Lord Diplock.   [27] [1989] 2 All ER 481 at 490.
[28] (1987) *The Times*, 18 June.   [29] [1991] 1 All ER 720.
[30] [1991] 1 All ER 720 at 735.

a lawful purpose so clearly go too far as to be unlawful. I would refer to *Wheeler v. Leicester City Council.*[31] In this case a city council's refusal to allow a rugby club to use a council recreation ground for 12 months was held to be unlawful. Three members of the club had gone on a rugby tour of South Africa. The council demanded that the club condemn the tour in very precise terms dictated by the council. The club condemned the tour, but not in the precise terms dictated by the council. The House of Lords held that the ban on the club's use of the ground must be quashed. The grounds were that the ban was *Wednesbury* unreasonable, procedurally unfair, and amounted to punishment in the absence of wrongdoing. It was accepted by the House of Lords that the overall purpose of the council was lawful—the promotion of good race relations in Leicester. But they had gone the wrong way about it.

Lord Roskill said: 'Persuasion, even forceful persuasion, is always a permissible way of seeking to obtain an objection. But in a field where other views can equally legitimately be held, persuasion, however powerful, must not be allowed to cross that line where it moves into the field of illegitimate pressure coupled with the threat of sanctions.'[32] Later on he said: 'If the club had adopted a different and hostile attitude, different considerations might well have arisen. But the club did not adopt any such attitude.'[33]

The point seems to be this: the city council went too far, in view of the compliant attitude of the club. It might have been different if they had been hostile, but they were not. This reasoning assumes that means must be adjusted to ends according to circumstance. It is the reasoning of proportionality. Lord Templeman said: 'The council could not properly seek to use its statutory powers . . . for the purpose of punishing the club where the club had done no wrong.'[34] This did not mean that the council would have been bound to allow the use of its premises by a racist organization. That was not the case in point. If it *had* been the case in point, no doubt either the club would have been guilty of doing something wrong, in which case it could have been punished, or the ban would have been justified by the concern of the council to maintain good race relations, i.e. the ban would not have been 'punishment'. The council's ban was not bad *per se*, but only to the extent that it was an excessive and disproportionate response to the behaviour of the club. It was only to that extent that it could be considered as 'punishment'.

The embryonic principle of our administrative law that no person may be punished unless he or she has done something wrong is far easier to

---

[31] [1985] 2 All ER 1106, [1985] AC 1054. Possible explanation of *Wheeler* in terms of the principle of proportionality is considered by Jowell and Lester, 'Beyond *Wednesbury*: Substantive Principles of Administrative Law' *PL* (1987) 368 at 376, 377; Craig, *Administrative Law*, 2nd edn. (Sweet & Maxwell, London, 1988), 297.
[32] [1985] 2 All ER 1106 at 1111 e.   [33] Ibid. at 1112 a.   [34] Ibid. at 1113 e.

state as a conclusion on particular facts than to apply consistently in practice. It may in its present state of development be described as a conclusion in need of a conceptual basis. It cannot be said that very adverse exercise of administrative discretionary power infringes the principle. Both the concept of 'punishment' and 'wrong' are largely metaphorical in the context. Where the purpose of the alleged punishment, as in *Wheeler*, is itself lawful, the legality of the means may raise squarely the question of proportionality. To this extent at least questioning the merits of administrative decisions is clearly part of our system of administrative law. As an aspect of *Wednesbury* unreasonableness, and as a criterion for the principle that no one be punished except for some wrongdoing, the principle of proportionality has surely some role to play in the evolution of our system of administrative law.

11   The Oral Procedure in the European Court of Justice

It has already been noted that the traffic in ideas between the European Court and the national courts is a two-way process and it concerns procedural as well as substantive matters. As far as procedural matters are concerned, the United Kingdom system has certain specific contributions to make to the administration of justice by the Court of Justice and the Court of First Instance. First, in the oral presentation of cases, and second, in certain aspects of judicial reasoning.

The short oral procedure in the Court of Justice (addresses average fifteen to twenty minutes) is still in some respects under utilized. Pressure on judicial time is likely to ensure that the oral procedure is not expanded. It may (rightly) be dispensed with in some cases.[35] Yet in Article 177 proceedings the oral procedure may be of considerable importance. It is at the hearing that all interested parties for the first time have an opportunity to comment on each other's arguments. This is because written observations by the various interested parties are submitted simultaneously to the Court. Even if parties in the national court are aware of each other's arguments, other parties may appear when the case is referred to Luxembourg (always the Commission, often other member States, sometimes the Council).[36] In a recent publication the President of the European Court was generous enough to commend the approach of the English or Scottish advocate as a model to be followed in addressing the Court in the oral procedure.[37] It is perhaps permissible to make a suggestion as to how the

[35] Art. 44(a) of the Rules of Procedure of the Court of Justice of the European Communities, [1991] LOJ 176/7 at L176/16.

[36] Art. 20 of the Protocol on the Statute of the Court of Justice of the European Economic Community.

[37] *Butterworth's Guide to European Court Practice* (Butterworths, London, 1991).

Court's conduct of cases at the oral stage might be improved. The most successful oral procedures are those in which the Court indicates in advance, perhaps by a request in writing addressed to one or other of the parties, which matters it considers to be significant.[38] In any case, it is of enormous help to an advocate to have an indication from the Judge Rapporteur of issues regarded by the judge as significant. One would expect it equally to be of assistance to the Court of Justice. It seems that, despite the predominance of written arguments, the oral procedure exerts an influence in at least some cases. This emerges from references, in Advocate General's Opinions and in judgments of the Court, to arguments which were only raised at the oral stage. A modest suggestion to the Court of Justice is that it circulate with the report for the hearing a note of those issues on which the Judge Rapporteur would wish to have clarification, subject always to the practical constraints imposed upon the Court by its large case load, and without prejudice to the freedom of the parties to conduct their cases as they wish.

12 Judicial Reasoning in the European Court

As the jurisprudence of the Court of Justice develops, inconsistencies inevitably emerge in the case law of the Court of Justice. It would be strange if it were otherwise. Again, the Court of Justice, while in general adhering to a consistent case law where it already exists, may depart from its previous case law.[39] Where this happens in the United Kingdom, the court in question would explain the relationship between the decision made, and previous inconsistent decisions, and explain the reasons for the discrepancy.[40] The European Court does not always do this.[41] To an extent it is possible to attribute this to its character as a tribunal embracing traditions other than that of the common law. But since the purpose of endowing the Court of Justice with such an extensive jurisdiction is to ensure the uniform interpretation of Community law in the member States, it is this purpose, rather than the traditions of the judges, which ought to exert the more powerful influence on the evolution of the jurisprudence of the Court. Furthermore, Advocates General in both common-law and civil-law traditions may deliver opinions containing a comprehensive critical analysis of the Court's case law to date.[42] The collegiate character of the Court's

---

[38] A notable example is case C-112/89 *Upjohn* v. *Farzoo*, judgment of 16 Apr. 1991.
[39] See e.g., case C-10/89 *SA CNL-SUCAL NV* v. *HAG GF AG* [1990] ECR I-3711.
[40] See e.g., *Murphy* v. *Brentwood DC* [1990] 2 All ER 908 HL.
[41] See case C-302/87 *Parliament* v. *Council* [1988] ECR 5615; cf. case C-70/88 *Parliament* v. *Council* [1990] ECR I-2041.
[42] For examples see the Opinion of Advocate General Jacobs in case C-10/89, n. 40, at 3725 *et seq.*; Opinion of Advocate General Van Gerven in case C-145/88 *Torfaen BC* v. *B & Q PLC* [1989] ECR 3851 at 3865 *et seq.*

judgments need not rule out a similar analysis in those cases in which it becomes important to clarify the state of the law (as the experience of the Privy Council demonstrates). Uncertainty may result in needless references to the Court of Justice, with attendant delays and costs. In this context the mode of judicial reasoning employed by the English and Scottish courts is conducive to maximizing the useful effect of the European Court's decisions, while, for example, the model of the *Conseil d'État* would be less appropriate to that end. The present practice of the European Court is somewhere in between, and would benefit in certain case from further common-law influence.

13 Influence of European Court Procedure on Procedure of United Kingdom Courts

European Court procedure is principally a written procedure. The procedure of courts in the United Kingdom is principally oral. There is probably room for more use of written procedure in the United Kingdom. The procedure for judicial review of administrative action in the United Kingdom includes the possibility for an application for leave for judicial review to be made in writing.[43] The grounds for relief in Form 86a often contain, in difficult cases, substantial legal argument. This no doubt proves of assistance to a judge considering a written application for leave to apply, and may well prove of assistance to judge or judges hearing the application, since the written argument in the grounds for relief sets the scene for the hearing and may serve to expedite the proceeding and save costs.[44] In addition to an affidavit in reply, it might be appropriate for a respondent to be entitled, or required, where the judge so directs, to file a short statement of legal argument in response to the application. Such a direction would perhaps be expected in legally difficult cases, and indeed applications made with a view to a reference to the Court of Justice under Article 177 of the Treaty would often fall into this category. The legal statement might be described as grounds for refusal of relief, being a counterpart to the grounds for relief section of Form 86a. As pressures on the Crown Office list increase, any possible saving of judicial time from such an innovation would surely be welcome. That said, I have no doubt that the procedure before English courts should remain an oral procedure with written elements, while the procedure in Luxembourg will in an increasing number of cases be a written procedure in which even the short oral procedure is waived.

A characteristic of the organization of the Court of Justice and of the Court of First Instance is the assistance provided to judges by the rather

---

[43] RSC Ord. 53 r. 3(3).   [44] RSC Ord. 53 r. 6(4).

inappropriately titled Legal Secretaries. These legal attachés assist the judges at all stages of the judicial process, including the drafting stage, but are not present at judicial deliberations. Without these excellent lawyers supporting the judges, it would be impossible for the Court of Justice to cope with its heavy case-load. It is tempting to consider the possibility that senior judges in the United Kingdom might be assisted at appropriate stages of the judicial process by qualified 'clerks' or legal attachés. A step may have been taken in this general direction by the appointment of a number of 'in-house lawyers' to the Court of Appeal. The Court of Appeal's (Civil Division) *Review of the Legal Year* 1989–90 states:

In future every application and appeal will be allocated to one or other of the lawyers, according to subject matter, and they will be personally responsible for monitoring and expediting its progress. What was missing in the original system was not administrative, but legal expertise . . . Of all the changes and improvements in the organisation and procedures of the Civil Division of the Court of Appeal over the last 8 years, I have no doubt that the arrival of the in-house lawyers is the most important and has the greatest potential for improving the service which we offer to the public. That said, it has to be recognised that we are breaking new ground. The Criminal Division has had a large number of in-house lawyers for several years, but the problems which confront that Division are somewhat different. We shall have to learn by experience how their expertise can best be used, but improvements in the light of experience will simply be a bonus. The essential steps of bringing legal professional knowledge to bear on case management and the administrative process has already been taken.

It is important to note that the above development is confined to the use of in-house lawyers in case management and the administrative process. It would be a further and different step to involve in-house lawyers in the decision making and drafting process.

The problems of the Court of Justice and the Court of First Instance on the one hand, and the courts of the member States on the other, are not identical, and even if they were, different solutions might be thought appropriate by those concerned. Yet it is often possible to be enlightened by the experience of others, and United Kingdom lawyers who practise regularly before the Courts in Luxembourg more often than not find at least some element in European practice and procedure which they believe might justify adoption *mutatis mutandis* in the United Kingdom.

The Impact of European Law on English Human Rights and Public Law

The law of the EC and the principles of the European Convention on Human Rights ('the Convention') already pervade large areas of English law. Their impact, of course, differs. EC law is directly applicable as part of the domestic law of England. In the event of conflict, EC law prevails. English statutes have to be construed, if possible, so as to give effect to EC directives. In contrast, the Convention is not part of our domestic law: even so, the courts of this country now frequently refer to the Convention in human rights cases; where an English statute is ambiguous the courts construe the statute in accordance with the principles of the Convention, applying the presumption that Parliament, in enacting the statute, must have intended to comply with the treaty obligations of this country. There is now high judicial authority for the view that, even in the absence of a statutory ambiguity, the court should give effect to the Convention whenever possible: see Lord Goff in *Attorney-General* v. *Guardian Newspapers (No. 2)* ([1990] 1 AC 109, at page 203).

This process may well accelerate in the near future. As to EC law, the decision of the European Court of Justice in the *Marleasing* case ([1992] 1 CMLR 305) requires English statutes to be construed 'so far as possible' so as to give effect to a European directive in all cases and not only in cases where the directive preceded the passing of the statute. EC law has been, and will continue to be, of fundamental importance in the development of English sex discrimination law. Finally, and potentially of most importance, the European Court of Justice has incorporated into EC law the human rights norms stated in the Convention. As a result, in the ever-widening areas of English law subject to EC law, the Convention (although not directly incorporated into English law) has been indirectly incorporated via the EC.

As a result of this increasing impact of EC and Convention law, many English judges are being brought into contact with these non-common-law principles and are having to grapple with the conflict between two quite different legal cultures. To take an example from public law, proportionality is a concept adopted both by the European Court of Justice and the European Court of Human Rights. Although not yet finally accepted as part of English public law, it can only be a matter of time before it is.

In a case involving EC law the English court in judging the legality of administrative action taken under an English statute passed to give effect to a directive would, in my view, have to consider whether the act complained of was proportional to the objective sought to be obtained by the directive. If the decision in *Marleasing* remains good law, the English court will have to construe an English statute (regardless of when passed) so as to conform to EC law: this will indirectly lead to the conclusion that the English statute only authorizes acts which are proportional. Once this stage is reached, it is only a short step to the view that in all cases Parliament in legislating only intends to authorize administrative action which satisfies the test of proportionality. Similarly, in relation to human rights under the Convention, despite the decision in *Brind* ([1991] AC 696) it seems to me possible that the courts will sooner or later reach the conclusion that Parliament in enacting legislation in general terms did not intend to authorize actions which contravene the Convention, it being a treaty to which this country is a party. As a result, the human rights jurisprudence of Strasbourg will enter English law generally.

For myself, I welcome this tendency. The full development of the English law of judicial review is to an extent hampered by its historical development. In English law the legality of an executive act ultimately depends on whether it was *intra vires* the statutory power under which it was done, which in turn requires the court to attribute to the legislature certain implied intentions as to the manner in which the powers it confers are to be exercised, e.g. that the rules of natural justice will be complied with and that all, and only, relevant matters will be taken into account. European administrative law is not so confined: both EC and Convention law are founded on written constitutions which have been held to impose certain requirements on administrative action. These principles regulate all administrative action as general principles of law: issues of *vires* become largely irrelevant. It may well be that under this influence English law can move in the same direction.

Finally, European law may influence the intense pragmatism of the English judicial method at least in the field of human rights. I believe that the common-law method of building the law incrementally on a case by case basis is valuable and I hope we never depart from it completely. But in the field of human rights it has dangers. The common-law method is inclined to concentrate on 'the merits' of the parties in the particular case before the court and to shape the law in such a case so that the meritorious win and the undeserving lose. In cases involving, say, freedom of the press or the rights of a prisoner, this leads English courts to concentrate unduly on the often disreputable behaviour of those who are asserting their human rights to the detriment of the underlying principles. It is my hope that the less pragmatic and more principled approach inherent in the Convention and the Strasbourg jurisprudence will lead English courts to give greater emphasis to the importance of protecting the basic human rights regardless of the merits of the person who is seeking to rely on them. It is easy to afford a saint his human rights: but a sinner has the same rights.

6

Developments in Environmental Law

FROM SOVEREIGNTY TO COMMON GOVERNANCE: THE EC ENVIRONMENTAL POLICY

FRANCESCO FRANCIONI

1 Introduction

The purpose of this paper is not to provide an exhaustive analysis of the legal and political issues arising from the implementation of the European Community's regulations in the field of environmental protection. Its aim is more modest: i.e. to respond to the challenge posed by the theme this series of essays—learning from Europe—and to try to explore what lesson lawyers and judges in the United Kingdom may draw from the growing role of the Community's regulatory policies in the area of environmental protection. Such growing role is met by the member States with mixed reactions. On the one hand, there is a sense of great expectation regarding the capacity of the Community to bridge competing national interests and develop a true common policy based on the assessment and implementation of the 'general' Community interest in protecting the environment over the whole of Europe. On the other hand, there is the awareness that the expansion of Community regulatory powers, especially after the adoption of the Single European Act (SEA)[1] and the (possible adoption of the) Maastricht Treaty on European Union,[2] necessarily occurs at the expense

---

[1] The Single European Act was signed in Luxembourg on 17 Feb. 1986 by the Foreign Ministers of the 12 member States, and entered into force in July 1988. OJ: [1987] OJ. L169/1. The title of this agreement is due to the merging into a single text of the provisions modifying the treaties establishing the European Communities (EC) and the provisions on the European political co-operation in the field of foreign policy. On the environmental provisions of the SEA, see Kramer 'The Single European Act and Environmental Protection: Reflections on Several New Provisions in Community Law', *Common Market Law Rev*, 659–88; Koppen, *The Community Environmental Policy: From the Summit in Paris, 1972, to the Single European Act, 1987*, Working Paper 88/328 (European University Institute, Florence, 1988); Zacker, 'Environmental Law of the European Economic Community: New Powers under the Single European Act', *Boston College Int Comp Law Rev* (1991), 249 ff. On the specific effects of the European environmental policy in Britain, see Haigh, *EEC Environmental Policy and Britain*, 2nd edn. (1987).

[2] Maastricht, 7 Feb. 1992. Reprinted in *ILM*, 31 247 ff. Although this Treaty is not yet in force, it is worth mentioning for two significant modifications it introduces in the present

of the national powers and sovereign rights of member States. This gives reasons for concern especially to those member States that have already developed their own tradition of environmental protection and, not without reason, are proud of their independent approach. This seems to be the case with the United Kingdom, at least if one is to judge from recent official and public opinion reactions to Community initiatives involving encroachment upon the national process of environmental regulation and control.[3]

One must note also that the distrust of the European institutions tends to be greater in this field than in others— such as agriculture, competition, transport, trade policy, etc.—because of the relatively recent emergence of the EC environmental competence. As a latecomer in a world of competing environmental actors the EC and its environmental policy present a Janus-like face. On the one hand, such policy partakes of the qualities of regulatory federalism, based on the delegation of powers from member States to federal agencies in view of subjecting to the latter's control those activities that are considered of social significance and which otherwise would fall entirely within the competence of member States. On the other hand, it presents itself as a carefully balanced system of international obligations whose implementation remains in the hands of national authorities with a minimum measure of delegation of administrative functions to the institutions of the Community.

In assessing the problems and opportunities that are offered by the newly-established EC environmental policy, the following discussion will address three main themes. The first concerns the general imprint that contemporary international law makes on the EC environmental policy as a consequence of the world-wide patterns of legal co-operation followed

regime of environmental protection by the Community. The first one concerns the decision-making process. Environmental measures would be adopted by majority decision as a rule, rather than by way of an exception (new Art. 130s(1)) and new powers would be given to the European Parliament under the so-called 'co-operation procedure' (Art. 189 (c)). The second modification consists of the transfer from Title VIII ('Environment') to Part One ('Principles') of the first clause of Art. 130r(4) providing that the 'Community shall take action relating to the environment to the extent to which the objectives referred to in para. 1 can be attained better at Community level than at the level of individual member States'. In the new Treaty of European Union this clause would become part of the general principle of 'subsidiarity' applicable across the board to every type of action the Community wants to undertake in areas in which it does not have exclusive competence.

[3] See, particularly, the recent controversy aroused by the Commission's complaint to the United Kingdom Government alleging non-compliance with directive 85/337 EC on environmental impact assessment. Although the terms of the Commission's complaint are not public, it is reported to relate to several major projects including: (1) the construction of the M3 link (Twyford Down case); (2) the East London River Crossing; (3) the Channel Tunnel rail link and passenger terminal; and (4) the road link between Hackney Wick and the M11. The Commission's complaint is reported to have included a request that projects be halted, something that has been generally perceived in the United Kingdom as a policy of intervention in what is believed to be an essentially domestic matter.

in combating environmental degradation. This co-operation finds expression in an abundance of new treaties, international declarations, and emerging customs that have the effect of gradually eroding traditional concepts of unfettered State sovereignty and domestic jurisdiction in the governance of transnational environmental problems. The second theme concerns the identification of the scope of EC powers in the field of environmental protection and the analysis of the effects that the variable treaty basis of such powers will ultimately have on the forms and modes of regulatory action at Community level. The third theme concerns the extent to which, in the light of this EC quasi-federal competence, member States—and, for the purpose of this essay, the United Kingdom—may retain, or regain national competence to develop and implement an independent regulatory policy of environmental protection. This problem appears to be of special significance if viewed within the perspective of the single European market whose functioning postulates the disappearance of intra-community barriers to trade, including technical barriers due to measure of environmental protection.

2   The Making of a Modern International Environmental Order

The rise of modern international environmental law is a fairly recent phenomenon. It can be traced to a threefold movement within three different stages of legal development.

The first stage was characterized by purely 'incidental' and 'ancillary' protection of the environment by the operation of rules of international law—customary or treaty law—which were primarily intended to protect interests and values different from environmental integrity. Examples of these rules can be found in early treaties concluded at the beginning of this century such as those for the protection of birds useful to agriculture and of seals valuable, for their fur.[4] Here, the subservient role of nature conservation *vis-à-vis* the primary economic concern of resource management and exploitation is clearly expressed in the title of the treaties. Similarly, the most important arbitral award, while often quoted as the matrix of modern international law on responsibility for environmental harm, the *Trial Smelter Arbitration (US v. Canada,* 1941),[5] was a case arising out of the context of bilateral relations involving claims for economic damage in the context of classical good-neighbourliness rules. The environmental protection obtained in this arbitral award by the United States against the noxious transborder emissions caused by a Canadian foundry was only incidental or consequential to the protection of the American farmers'

---

[4] Paris Convention on the Protection of Birds Useful to Agriculture, 19 Mar. 1902: Treaty of Washington on the Protection of Seals, 7 Feb. 1911.
[5] *UN Rep Intl Arb Awards,* (1949), iii: 1907 ff.

economic interests and to the implementation of classic private law principles of nuisance.

The first step in the process of gradual development of the modern body of international environmental law was marked by the elevation of the environment to the dignity of a value worthy of international protection *per se* and independent of other considerations, such as economic damage or good-neighbourliness. This concept was formally inaugurated by the 1972 Stockholm Declaration on the Human Environment which, for the first time, set forth the duty to prevent damage to the environment of other States in autonomous terms, independent of economic injury or geographic proximity. Following the Stockholm Declaration, important conventions were adopted, including the Geneva Convention on Long Range Transboundary Air Pollution with subsequent Protocols,[6] and the 1986 Vienna Conventions on Early Notification and Assistance with Regard to Radiological Contamination, which were adopted in the wake of the Chernobyl disaster and in the realization that nuclear contamination could extend well beyond neighbouring States.[7]

The second stage in the development of international environmental law coincided with the overcoming of the bilateral-transboundary pollution approach and the recognition of the general obligation of every State to prevent also the environmental deterioration of spaces and natural components beyond national jurisdiction such as the high seas, Antarctica, and the ozone layer. Manifestations of this new concern can be found in the provisions of the 1982 Law of the Sea Convention,[8] the 1985 Vienna Convention on the Ozone Layer, with the Montreal Protocol of 1987,[9] and the 1991 Protocol on the Protection of the Antarctic Environment.[10] More recently, there has been increasing emphasis on the preservation of global ecological conditions such as climate.[11]

---

[6] See text in Burhenne (ed.), *Beitraege zur Umweltgestaltung, Internationales Umweltrecht Multilaterale Vertrage* (Berlin) 979:84, hereafter cited as Burhenne. For the text of subsequent protocols, ibid. 979:84/A, B, and C.

[7] Convention on Early Notification of a Nuclear Accident, Vienna, 26 Sept. 1986, Burhenne, 986:71; Convention on Assistance in the Case of a Nuclear Accident or Radiological Emergency, Vienna, 26 Sept. 1986, ibid. 986:72. For a comment, see Sand, *Chernobyl: Law and Communication* (1988), 40 ff.

[8] See esp. Art. 194. The text of the UN Law of the Sea Convention is reproduced in *ILM* 21 (1982), 126.   [9] Burhenne, 985:22 and 985:22/A.

[10] The Consultative Parties to the Antarctic Treaty (Washington 1959) have adopted an additional Protocol on environmental protection at the end of a special consultative meeting concluded in Madrid on 4 Oct. 1991. For a comment see, Francioni, 'Il Protocollo di Madrid sulla Protezione dell'Ambiente Antartico', *Rivista di diritto internazionale* (1991), n. 4.

[11] On the question of the greenhouse effect there is no binding instrument in force yet. However, a number of proposals and declarations exist addressing the problem and indicating possible measures to prevent or mitigate the adverse effects of climate change. See particularly, EC Council Resolution on the Greenhouse effect and the Community, [1989] OJ C183/4; UNEP, Governing Council Decision on Global Climate Change of 25 May 1989, in

The third aspect of the progressive development of international environmental law can be traced to the process of gradual erosion of sovereign rights in the management of natural resources which, although they remain located within the territory of a single State, without an outward element of transborder effects, are perceived to be worthy of international protection by the international community as a whole. This is the case with the protection of endangered species, such as elephants,[12] preservation of biodiversity, and conservation of rain forests.

This threefold expansion of the contemporary practice in the field of environmental protection does not only reflect different degrees of environmental awareness on the part of the international community. It represents also *different stages of elaboration of new legal principles and techniques* required by the specificity and gravity of the problem of environmental deterioration. For instance, the passage from the first stage to the second stage of development as described above was greatly facilitated by the fashioning of the *erga omnes* obligations. i.e. obligations owed by every State to the international community as a whole and whose breach causes an injury to all States and not only to the one(s) directly and tangibly affected by their breach.[13] This concept has its origin and most immediate application in the field of the general environment.[14] The binding restraints accepted by treaty or unilateral declarations in the field of renunciation of nuclear testing in water and atmosphere and of the protection of the ozone layer[15] attest to the increasing acceptance of this type of obligation in the field of environmental protection.

Other legal doctrines have accompanied the introduction of *erga omnes* obligation and helped clarify the conceptual framework in which

28 *ILM* 25 (1989) 1330; Bergen Ministerial Declaration on Sustainable Development in the ECE Region, 16 May 1990.

[12] Convention on International Trade in Endangered Species of Wild Fauna and Flora, Washington, 3 Mar. 1973, in Burhenne, 973:18. On the specific question of preserving the elephants, see M. Glennon, 'Has International Law Failed the Elephants?' *AJIL* 84 (1990), 1 ff.

[13] In the well-known passage of the *Barcelona Traction* case, the international Court of Justice recognized the existence of 'obligations of a State toward the international community as a whole' and added that they '. . . are the concern of all States . . . all States can be held to have a legal interest in their protection; they are obligations *erga omnes*', *ICJ Reports* (1970), 3, 32.

[14] Such extension results from the Restatement of the US Foreign Relations Law, st. 601 and 902 comment, and is widely recognized in legal doctrine. See G. Handl, Territorial Sovereignty and the Problem of Transnational Pollution *AJIL*, (1975), 50, 58 ff.; Kiss, 'Survey of Current Developments in International Environmental Law', in *IUCN Environmental Policy and Law Paper* (1976), 48 ff.; Springer, *The International Law of Pollution*, (1983), 158 ff.; Smith, *State Responsibility and the Marine Environment: The Rules of Decision* (1988), 94 ff.

[15] Treaty Banning Nuclear Weapons Tests in the Atmosphere, in Outer space and Under Water, made at Moscow on 5 Aug. 1963 and entered into force on 10 Oct. 1963, 480 *UNTS* 43.

international environmental law is evolving today. One can mention the principle of the common heritage of mankind, which postulates that humanity as a whole, and not States individually considered, has a legal title to the use of spaces and resources beyond national jurisdiction, such as the international sea-bed area and outer space. Under this principle States or groups of States may act only as trustees of humanity when carrying out activities in such international areas and may not, therefore, invoke their pioneering role as a basis for asserting sovereign rights along the pattern of old colonial days. The inescapable implication of this legal formulation is that States are bound to protect the environment of international spaces as an integral part of the general interest.

In a similar vein the International Law Commission's (ILC) draft articles on State responsibility (Article 19) have introduced the notion of international crimes which includes crimes against the environment. Although this notion remains to be fully developed, it is clear that it involves a different regime of State responsibility—permitting, *inter alia*, the subjection of the transgressor to punitive measures by *any* member of the international community, in addition to the obligation to make reparation to the direct victim.[16] Article 19 of the ILC's draft expressly mentions massive pollution of the oceans or of the atmosphere as a possible hypothesis of an international crime. The strong reactions in the international community to the devastating environmental consequences of the Iraqi war, and the express mention of them in SC resolution No. 687 of 3 April 1991 as a ground for war reparation, signal that the time is ripe for the codification of this new category of international crimes besides those already regulated in the four Geneva Conventions of 1949.[17]

The final point I wish to stress is that the emergence of modern international law of the environment entails a corresponding erosion of the concept of domestic jurisdiction, and thus of sovereign rights. This occurs not only with regard to the growing body of treaties regulating the various aspects of transborder pollution, but also with regard to regulatory policies issued for the conservation of elements of the environment which are entirely localized within the territory of the target State and which, under traditional concepts of territorial sovereignty, would not be the proper subject of international regulation. Protection of tropical forests and of species of fauna and flora are prominent examples of this new pervasive reach of international environmental law in the sphere of domestic sovereignty. The

[16] For a thorough discussion of the rationale and implications of the category of international crimes, see Weiler, Cassese, and Spinedi, *International Crimes of State* (1989).

[17] Resolution No. 687 reaffirms that Iraq '. . . is liable under international law for any direct loss, damage, *including environmental damage and the depletion of natural resources . . . as a result of Iraq's unlawful invasion and occupation of Kuwait*' (emphasis added). S/RES/ 687 (1991) 8 Apr. 1991.

UN Conference on Environment and Development held in Rio de Janeiro in June 1992, has highlighted this issue (especially with regard to biodiversity) in an attempt to reconcile global environmental concerns with national interests in resource exploitation and economic development. It is undeniable that this diplomatic agenda sets us a world apart from the epoch in which Justice Holmes of the US Supreme Court held (*Missouri* v. *Holland* (1990))[18] that the proper exercise of foreign relations powers in the federal context was to be tested on the basis of the criteria whether the object of the regulation was 'stationary' or moving across State frontiers!

The evolving structure and scope of international environmental law, as outlined above, has not yet led to the generalized setting up of international institutions endowed with supranational regulatory and enforcement powers binding on States and private actors alike. Some limited institutional machinery has been developed in certain areas such as marine pollution, trade in endangered species, and protection of the ozone.[19] However, they remain the exception in a world where, as a rule, States retain their sovereign right to decide whether to become bound by treaties establishing institutional arrangements, such as intergovernmental commissions or consultative meetings of State parties, aimed at setting legal standards, co-ordinating policies, and implementing environmental standards through supervision and consultation. In contrast, the European Community represents the most advanced and sophisticated model of institutional law-making and enforcement of environmental regulatory powers. In the following section it is examined both for its intrinsic interest as a form of proto-federal regulation, and for its possible role as a model for the transition from a regime of national regulation based on sovereignty to a regime of supranational governance of shared environmental problems at a regional or global level.

3   The Legal Foundation and Scope of the EC Environmental Policy

As is known, Community action in the environmental field did not rest on an express grant of competence until the adoption in 1986 of the SEA. The Treaty of Rome did not contain any express reference to the environment nor did it require that the Community should protect it in one way or another. This notwithstanding, EC initiatives in environmental matters had reached a considerable intensity and scope even before 1986. This was facilitated by the European Court's expansive reading of the Treaty objectives (Article 2) and by the general provision of Article 235 on implied

[18] 252 US 420 (1920).

[19] For a detailed examination of the institutional models emerging from the current treaty practice in the field of the protection of the environment, see Boyle, 'Saving the World? Implementation and Enforcement of International Environmental Law through International Institutions', *Journal of Env Law*, (1991) iii: 229 ff.

powers. However, such tenuous legal basis did not fail to attract criticism and the occasional challenge of the Community's competence to act in this field. Italy, for instance, in an attempt to counter the Commission's infringement action under Article 169 for failure to implement environmental directives on detergents and on the sulphur content of fuels, questioned their direct applicability and contended that they had to be treated as international agreements. The Court rejected this argument basing the EC competence on Article 100 (approximation of laws) and on the previous adoption of the Community's Action Programme on the Environment, as well as on the General Programme for the elimination of technical barriers to trade.[20] Similarly, in the United Kingdom, the House of Lords Committee on the European Communities expressed doubts as to EC competence in environmental protection in the absence of an express grant of powers limiting the original sovereignty of national parliaments in the area.[21]

In spite of these familiar instances of member States dragging their feet the Community's competence to deal with environmental problems was established by the European Court of Justice in the *cause célèbre* concerning the disposal of waste oils within the Community territory. In the case *Procureur de la Républic* v. *Association de Défence des Brûleuers d'huiles usagées*[22] the Court affirmed the validity of a directive establishing a mandatory system of waste oils disposal by stating that:[23]

The principle of freedom of trade is not to be viewed in absolute terms but is subject to certain limits justified by the objectives of general interest favoured by the community provided that the rights in question are not substantially impaired. There is no reason to conclude that the directive has exceeded those limits. The directive must be seen in the perspective of environmental protection, which is one of the Community's essential objectives.

Following this decision one could safely say (1) that even before the SEA the EC had incorporated environmental protection within the range of objectives indicated in Article 2 of the Treaty of Rome; (2) that for the attainment of such objectives, the Community could rely on Article 100 (approximation of laws) and on Article 235 (implied powers) to the extent that specific limiting measures were deemed necessary; (3) that, at least in the Court's jurisprudence, Community regulatory action in this field could be buttressed by the Community's environmental programmes originally meant to be mere policy statements.

With the adoption of the SEA a firm foundation was established for EC environmental policy. Title VII of the SEA provides an independent legal

---

[20] *Commission* v. *Italy* cases 91/79 and 92/79 [1980] ECR 1099, 1115.

[21] House of Lords Select Committee on the EC Communities, *Approximation of Laws under Art. 100 of the Treaty of Rome* (London, 1978); ibid. *Environmental Problems and the Treaty of Rome* (London, 1979).

[22] ECR 1985, 531 ff.   [23] Ibid. 548 ff.

basis for Community regulation with respect to a wide range of objectives including: (1) the preservation, protection, and improvement of the environment; (2) protection of human health; and (3) the prudent and rational utilization of national resources (Article 130r). This legal basis is concurrent with other treaty provisions also suitable for providing legal justification for Community regulation. The relevant treaty provisions, however, are not interchangeable; their application entails different decision-making processes, i.e. unanimity or majority voting, as we shall see later in this section. Furthermore, the great number and the variety of environmental regulatory measures—which are attested by the more than 170 binding texts adopted as of 1990—underscore the practical importance of defining the basis and scope of Community powers in this field.

At the risk of excessive schematization, the following scheme can be utilized to identify the legal basis for Community regulatory action regarding the environment:

1 Articles 130r–130t of the SEA, apply to regulation intended primarily to protect the environment and unrelated or only indirectly related to the elimination of barriers to the functioning of the single markets.
2 Articles 100 and 100A provide the legal basis for the adoption of Community directives for the approximation of member States' legislation in view of establishing the internal market; here the Community's regulation of environmental problems is only a consequence or secondary effect of the primary goal of removing environmental barriers to trade as they may arise from different technical and environmental requirements in member States.
3 Finally, a narrower basis for environmental action can be found in treaty provisions granting the Community specific authority over a field of the Common Market where regulation necessitates an environmental component or pursues *also* an environmental objective. Examples of this further basis can be found in regulations, directives, or decisions adopted in the field of agriculture under Article 43. In this field, the overlapping of environmental concerns and economic integration may actually be systemic rather than occasional. How are we to decide whether measures intended to regulate pesticides, fertilizers, drainage, land consolidations, technology in animal reproduction, or plant genetics are to be considered part of agricultural policy or of environmental regulation?

Other provisions capable of providing a concurrent basis for environmental regulation are those on the common commercial policy. The Community's competence in this field under Article 113 can be exercised in areas that significantly affect the environment. Given the increasing connection between trade and environmental protection, the symbiotic relationship between competences under Articles 130r and 113 can become quite problematic. At present, concurrence of competences occurs in the areas of restrictions of trade on endangered species under the CITES Convention;[24] regulation of transboundary movement of waste;[25] and restrictions on substances that deplete the ozone under the Vienna Convention and the Montreal Protocol on the Elimination of Chlorofluorocarbons.[26]

This multiple-choice system of Community competence is not governed by a set of precise rules applicable to the selection of the appropriate legal basis for the different types of environmental regulations. This may be surprising in light of the practical consequences deriving from the choice of one treaty provision rather than another; measures under Article 130r, as already mentioned, are to be adopted by unanimous consent, while measures under Article 100a, as well as those under Articles 43 and 113, are to be adopted by qualified majority. Besides, Article 100a requires active involvement of the European Parliament in the preparation of the Commission's proposal while Article 130r requires only consultation. Further, the original choice of the treaty basis for the proposed measure will ultimately determine to what extent member States are allowed to be exonerated from its application on grounds of special national interests.[27]

The lack of precise rules applicable to the choice of the proper legal basis for any given measure may certainly be explained—although not entirely justified—by the increasing complexity of the tasks required from the EC as a consequence of the SEA. This complexity and the overriding objective of completing the internal market by the end of 1992 was leading some authors to suggest a criterion of subsidiarity of environmental policy with respect to market integration. This means that whenever a certain Community policy can be based on specific treaty provisions, such as agriculture under Article 43, harmonization of market conditions under Articles 100 and 100a, or commercial policy under Article 113, these specific treaty provisions should be dominant.[28] As a consequence, the general environmental provisions of Articles 130s f. would have the

---

[24] Note 12, above.

[25] *Convention on the Control of Transboundary Movements of Hazardous Wastes and their Disposal, Basel, 22 March 1989, ILM 28 (1989) 652 ff.*   [26] N. 6, above.

[27] Harmonization measures adopted by the Council acting by a qualified majority under Art. 100a are subject to national derogation on grounds of 'major needs' including the protection of the environment, provided the Commission finds that they are not discriminatory or a disguised restriction of trade between member States. On the other hand, Art. 130r admits national independent measures whenever the environmental objectives set out in its first paragraph may be better attained by individual State action rather than by common action. Further, Art. 130t allows member States to maintain or introduce more stringent protective measures than those adopted in common pursuant to Art. 130r. On these provisions, see section 5, below.

[28] Pernice, 'Kompetenzordnung und Handlungsbefugnisse der Europäischen Gemeinschaft auf dem Gebiet des Umwelt-und Technikrechts', *Die Verwaltung* (1989), 34 ff.

residuary role of 'subsidiary' provisions which would come in to play only when no other treaty provisions were applicable to the relevant measures.

At first sight, support for this opinion could be found in a recent decision of the European Court on the reduction of pollution by waste from the titanium dioxide industry.[29] This case concerned an intra-institutional dispute between the Commission, supported by the Parliament, and the Council. The Commission had originally presented a proposal for a directive on the harmonization of the plans to reduce industrial pollution resulting from titanium dioxide and had used Article 100a as its legal basis. The Council, instead, adopted the directive on the basis of Article 130s thus leaving the Parliament with a mere consultation role rather than a role of active co-operation and initiative as contemplated by Article 100a (1). The Court, in its decision of 11 June 1991 favoured the adoption of Article 100a on the basis of the argument that whenever a measure pursues the double objective of protecting the environment and of securing the internal market, the latter should prevail and the procedure of Article 100a must be followed.

The decision of the court is correct in as much as the primary purpose of the relevant titanium dioxide directive[30] was to harmonize conditions of competition in the relevant industrial sector. But it cannot be taken as an endorsement across the board of the criterion of subsidiarity of Articles 130r f.

In our view the problem of the choice of the appropriate treaty basis for the adoption of measures that aim at the same time at market unification and environmental protection cannot be solved on the basis of the rigid criterion of subsidiarity of Article 130r. This criterion is unacceptable because it is not based on any textual element of the Treaty and because it would unduly reduce the scope of Articles 130r f. in a way as to detract from the spirit of the SEA which aims at elevating environmental protection to the dignity of an independent Community objective. Besides, there is no merit in the argument that Articles 130r and 130s would concern only decisions on 'what action is to be taken by the Community' rather than decisions on specific binding measures. This argument proves 'too much' in so far as it would relegate Article 130r to the domain of policy determinations. It is clear instead, from the language of Article 130t, that Title VIII permits the adoption of specific binding measures. The correct approach to this problem, thus, requires that, rather than adopting a mechanical criterion of subsidiarity of Articles 130r and 130s, the choice of the legal basis of a given measure be dictated by a process of balancing of the two competing finalities: environmental protection and market

---

[29] Case C-300/89 decided on 11 June 1991. The only text available at the date of 15 November 1991 is the original French.   [30] Dir. 89/428, [1989] OJ L201/56.

integration. Whenever the preponderant object and purpose of the measure is environmental protection Article 130r should be preferred even if the measure aims at, or has the effect of, ironing out differences in the relevant market sector that may lead to distortion of trade and competition. Similarly, if the primary objective of the measure is to harmonize conditions of competition or trade in a certain industrial, service, or agricultural sector, the environmental component or effects of the measure should not prevent the application of Article 100a or of a more specific provision such as Article 43 or 113.

The soundness of this more flexible approach is confirmed by the practice of the Community's institutions. For example, the Commission based a proposal for a directive on the prevention of water contamination by nitrates resulting from agricultural activities on Articles 130r f., rather than on the more specific Article 43, when it recognized that the predominant interest pursued by that directive was not agricultural policy but rather environmental protection against excess concentration of livestock in environmentally sensitive areas.[31] By the same token, the European Court has correctly indicated that the proper basis of Community measures is Article 43 whenever the measure has a predominant effect on the marketing of agricultural products. The precedent of *United Kingdom* v. *Council*[32] concerning the use of hormones in animal feeds was decided on the basis of the exclusive relevance of Article 43 to the United Kingdom's objections, and mainly because of the overriding objective of the measure to guarantee uniformity of production and marketing conditions in the context of the common agricultural policy.

Certainly, in this process of balancing the competing interests and goals connected to a proposed regulatory measure, Community institutions will perform a discretionary function in which political expediency and jurisdictional considerations will combine in view of the final determination of the controlling treaty basis. This discretionary function will most likely require the adoption of political, rather than jurisdictional, criteria, in the Community's decision as to whether market integration or environmental protection should provide the rationale and legal justification of a given regulatory measure. In this political context the EC environmental policy differs from the corresponding experiences of federal regulatory intervention—e.g. the United States' experience with the Environmental Protection Agency (EPA)—where the legal basis, the scope, and the patterns of intervention, are cast *a priori* in the relevant federal statutes. These statutes are implemented through independent agencies and on the basis of federal funding whose concession or withdrawal constitutes the system of incen-

---

[31] See the Commission's proposal in [1989] OJ C54/4.
[32] Case 68/86 [1988] ECR 855.

tives and sanctions to induce compliance with the relevant environmental programmes. All of this, of course, occurs within the general framework of the national constitution. In the EC, the present system is still quite far from this federal model. Not only does it lack an independent enforcement system, but even at the legislative process it still requires international bargaining and negotiation for every measure, so as to ensure proper accommodation of various competing interests, which include the member States' interest in safeguarding their original sovereign rights to regulate the environment; the general interest of the Community to pursue market integration; and finally the independent interest of the Community to set its own environmental agenda. The way in which accommodation of these different interests is achieved, especially through majority decision making and active involvement of the Parliament in the co-operation procedure may gradually help the transition toward a 'federal' model of institutional environmental policy management. This transition can certainly be facilitated by the institutional reform achieved by the SEA and foreseen by the Maastricht Treaty, as well as through the jurisprudence of the Court. This expectation, however, does not authorize us to conclude that member States have already given up their sovereign right to contract the obligations concerning the protection of the environment on a case by case basis along the 'international law' model based on the process of consensus building within the relevant Community organs.

4 Community Action, Member States' action, or both?

The above considerations concerning the ambivalence of the criteria to determine the legal basis for Community regulatory action on the environment are applicable *mutatis mutandis* also to the question of when such Community action—as opposed to individual States' regulation—is required to achieve the objectives of environmental protection set out in the SEA. As is known, the criterion adopted by Article 130r is that of 'subsidiarity' of common action. Article 130r(4) requires the Community to take such action only to the extent to which the environmental objectives set forth in the SEA, i.e. '(i) to preserve, protect and improve the environment; (ii) to contribute towards protecting human health; (iii) to ensure a prudent and rational utilization of natural resources' . . . can be attained '*better*' at a Community level than at the level of the individual member States.' In the Maastricht Treaty the 'better' clause of para. 4 has been taken away from the specific context of Article 130r and elevated to the dignity of a general principle of the Treaty under Article 3b. There is no doubt that such provisions are based on a sound principle of environmental political economy. No one could argue that Community regulations are needed for every national, regional, or local problem concerning, for example, the protection of local lakes, domestic habitats, or specific local problems relating to land management or waste disposal. On the other hand, however, one cannot automatically infer, *a contrario*, that action by the Community is better in every case of transboundary pollution or of protection of the international environment or common global areas. Recent practice shows that with regard to the latter, the EC has in some cases taken common action—e.g. the participation in and implementation of the Vienna Convention and Montreal Protocol on the Ozone Layer[33]—whereas in other cases, it has taken no role, leaving to the States the primary, or rather, the *exclusive* responsibility of environmental regulation. A recent example of 'exclusive' State action is provided by the protection of the Antarctic environment. The special national interest of the United Kingdom and of other claimant countries—and the necessity of preserving the security arrangement reached with the Treaty of Washington of 1959—posed a formidable political obstacle to the Community's common action in the negotiation and elaboration of the Madrid Protocol on Environmental Protection Supplementing the Antarctic Treaty (October 4 1991).[34]

Given this uncertain Community practice and the inherent relativity of the criteria applicable to establishing whether and under which circumstances common action is better than national regulation, the issue arises as to whether the 'better' clause of Article 130r (which, if and when Maastricht comes into force will have to be read in conjunction with Article 3b of that Treaty) has any normative value or is rather a mere political guideline which theoretically could leave member States free to decide that national regulation is always better than common action. Some commentators have favoured the latter opinion (Kramer, above, note 1) relying on the general language of Article 130r (4), on the apparent absence of binding criteria for the allocation of responsibilities between Community and member States, and on the necessity of judging each case on its substantive merits. These are certainly respectable arguments. At a policy level they may offer the advantage of freeing Community action of the constraints of a strict application of the subsidiarity principle so as not to paralyse such action until crushing evidence is provided that individual State regulation would not offer a viable alternative.

However, I believe that these arguments may not be pushed to the extreme of making the 'better' clause of Article 130r(4) (now included in Article 3b of the Maastricht Treaty) devoid of any legal significance. First of all, it would be contradictory for the SEA to lay down a set of elements indicating what is the notion of the general Community interest in the protection of the environment and at the same time deny any normative

---

[33] See Council regulation 594/91 of 4 Mar. 1991.
[34] For the negotiating history of this instrument see Francioni, n. 9, above.

value to the criteria upon which the Community organs are to decide how and by whom such general interest is to be pursued. Second, although at the present formative stage of a European environmental policy the parameters under which such decision is to be made are likely to be more political than legal, one should not foreclose the possibility that at a more advanced stage a clearer contour of the common EC environmental interests will emerge. In this perspective, we do not see any reason why the practice of the Commission and the jurisprudence of the Court should not lead to the fleshing out of the principle of subsidiarity as has occurred in other areas in which expansion and strengthening of Community competence has had a corresponding erosion of member States' sovereign rights.

If this is correct, the recognition of a legal value of the 'better' clause of Article 130r must be deemed to be more consistent with the purpose and object of Community law than the opinion attributing to this clause only a political content. At the practical level, a consequence of this recognition is the possibility of judicial review by the European Court of the way in which the clause is implemented. Such possibility ought to be left open at least in the most clear cases of abuse of power, manifest error, or misuse of power. Besides, even in areas which do not fall within the Community's exclusive competence, exercise of judicial review over this clause could indirectly extend to the actual merits of a case when by reason of the nature, scale or effects of the proposed action the environmental objectives may not be adequately achieved by independent member States' regulation. The circumstances—sufficient to justify such a review on the merits may be exemplified as follows:

1 When past experience has unambiguously shown that the solution of member States' action is ineffective or even detrimental with regard to the objectives of environmental protection indicated in Article 130r.
2 When the decision not to adopt a common action was taken on the basis of scientific and technical assessment that later proved to be erroneous.
3 When scientific and technical developments have rendered obsolete or inadequate previous decisions leaving a particular environmental problem within the competence of member States. This case is exemplified by global warming, acid rain, and deforestation where the increased scientific knowledge of the phenomena erodes the rationale for individual States regulation and highlights the linkages between the various national sources of pollution.
4 Finally, when previous Community decisions in the same area have unambiguously shown that the better approach is the common one, because of proven detrimental effects of the isolated action. This proof can be derived from Community decisions to take common action with third countries or international organisations in the same area of environmental problems.

It is still too early to assess the role of the European Court with regard to member States' or the Commission's attempt to bring the 'better' clause contained in Article 130r(4) and in Article 3b of the Treaty of Union within the scope of its judicial review. If the approach suggested above will be followed, the Court will have the opportunity of contributing to the gradual shaping of formal criteria capable of allocating competence between member States and the Community. This allocation, obviously, will not occur in a vacuum: it will be made possible by the substantive body of decisions, regulations, directives, declarations, and programmes which will make up the map to guide the Community in deciding which tasks belong to it and which must be left to member States on account of the 'better clause'. In this way, the political decision as to *how* the environmental objectives must be achieved will be matched by the legal decision as to *who* is the proper actor to carry out the action necessary to achieve those objectives.

5   The Risk of Renationalization of Environmental Policies

The problem discussed above indicates that unclear allocation of competence between the Community and member States may result in the renationalization of environmental policies. This risk, however, derives more explicitly from two other provisions of the SEA: Articles 130t and 100a(4), which allow national departure from the common environmental regulation on account, respectively, of a higher level of environmental protection and of 'major needs' relating, *inter alia,* to the protection of the environment.

Article 130t provides that: 'The protective measures adopted in common pursuant to Article 130s shall not prevent any member State from maintaining or introducing more stringent protective measures compatible with this Treaty'. This provision is premised on the notion that in the field of environmental protection, Community powers and the relative enactment of regulatory measures do not have pre-emptive effect on national powers. The former are intended to guarantee that minimum environmental standards are met Community-wide. The latter may still be used even in a field occupied by Community regulations in order to safeguard the right of individual countries to try harder than the rest in their endeavour to protect the environment. This concept is rather unique in the Treaty: the only similar provision is Article 118a(a) of the SEA concerning social policy. Its implication is that action by the Community in the environmental field— unlike other fields of EC policy such as agriculture, transport, and competition etc.—does not terminate the member States' power to legislate.

This situation of potential or actual concurrence between Community measures and member States' legislation has clear advantages from the point of view of the national interest to preserve the capacity to carry out an independent environmental policy. It may also counterbalance the excesses of a centralized approach—which are feared particularly in the United Kingdom—especially in view of averting the risk of scarce sensitivity to the variety of environmental problems and priorities in the different regions of the Community. Besides, faced with the endemic problem of enforcement of the Community's environmental measures, the recognition of a concurrent regulatory power of member States may lead to more effective implementation of environmental standards that have been tailored to suit specific ecological situations.

At the same time, the solution adopted in Article 130t presents certain inconveniences. The most obvious one is the risk that under the guise of more stringent environmental standards member States may introduce new barriers to trade. This risk is already apparent from a number of recent controversies ranging from the compulsory system of glass bottles return in Denmark and Germany,[35] restrictions on the use of plastic bags in Italy,[36] and the banning of diesel cars in Greece.[37] All these controversies hinge on the fundamental questions whether the more stringent measures adopted by individual States are compatible with the Treaty despite their unquestionable restrictive effects on the free movement of goods. The EC Court has contributed to the solution of this question by developing a permissibility test in the recent dispute of *Commission* v *Denmark*.[38] In this case the Commission challenged a Danish scheme devised to regulate the beverage market and presenting the following features: (1) the introduction of a compulsory system of re-usable containers for beer and soft drinks; (2) the exclusion of all metal containers and (3) the allowance of a limited quota for non-approved containers, which nonetheless remained subject to a deposit and return system. Undoubtedly, this system was intended to protect the environment from one of the most widespread sources of waste—empty cans and bottles—and to conserve the energy needed to produce new containers. The Commission, however, based its action on the alleged creation of quantative restrictions to the free move-

---

[35] On 1 Dec. 1988, Germany adopted a regulation imposing a mandatory deposit system for plastic bottles used as beverage containers. The objective of this measure was to limit further increase of the use of plastic, a legitimate environmental goal, but its effects on trade became a concern for the Commission—which has brought infringement proceedings against Germany (case 1104/88)—because of the higher cost of transport of glass bottles—heavier than plastic—to German importers of beverages from other member States.

[36] See Law 397 of 9 Sept. 1988, on industrial waste, and Law 475 of 9 Nov. 1988, respectively in G.U. . . . .

[37] Greek legislation does not permit the use of private diesel motor vehicles on the grounds of pollution control. The Community has found this legislation disproportionate in so far as the problem of air pollution that such legislation intends to address exists only in the urban areas of Athens and Tessaloniki. This does not justify a total ban.

[38] Case 302/86, of Sept. 20 1988.

ment of goods, contrary to Article 30 of the Treaty. In its decision of 20 September 1988, the European Court approached the permissibility issue on the basis of a threefold test: first, the restrictive measure must be proportional to the objective of environmental protection; second, the measure must avoid any discrimination against foreign products; and finally it must be necessitated by the unavailability of other means which would be capable of reaching the same objectives without introducing restrictions on trade. On the basis of this test the Court held the Danish scheme permissible.[39]

The three-pronged test formulated by the European Court is very important for the future because it is premised on the recognition that environmental protection is a fundamental objective of the Community to be considered on an equal footing with free circulation of goods and therefore capable of limiting the application of Article 30 of the Treaty.

The limit of the aforementioned criteria, however, is that they are primarily intended to provide a framework of reference for dispute settlement. Yet, in the field of environmental protection, it is difficult to deny that prevention of disputes is better than reliable methods of adjudication. If this is true, the focus must be on what is the best approach to avoid this type of dispute between member States and the Community. The answer to this question is the development of an EC policy based on a high standard of environmental protection in every regulatory initiative concerned with market integration. This goal can be pursued through the avenue clearly indicated by the SEA, and precisely by Article 100a(3) which requires that 'the Commission, in its proposals . . . concerning . . . environmental protection . . . will take as a base a high level of protection'. Although cast in general language, this provision contains the unambiguous mandate for the Community to strive towards achieving a high level of environmental protection so as to reduce the justification for member States enacting more stringent national standards. Obviously, the lower the level of environmental protection adopted by the Community and the less complete the web of common regulatory standards, the more justifiable becomes the member States' claim to 'be cleaner than the rest'.[40] To be fruitfully pursued, the strategy indicated in Article 100a(3) requires abandoning or attenuating member States' distrust of a strong Community policy for the environment. Countries such as the United Kingdom who have a tradition of resistance to the expansion of Community regulatory powers at the expense of member States' sovereignty, may need to reassess their position with regard to environmental policy. The lesson to be learned in this field may be that there

---

[39] Ibid. considerations 9, 10, and 21 of the judgment.

[40] This expression is used by Koppen 'The Role of the European Court of Justice in the Development of E.C. Environmental Policy', unpublished paper (European University Institute, 1991).

is much to lose in obstructing a generalized use of community powers for the achievement of a common high level of environmental protection. At the same time, there may be a lot to be gained in raising the common level of environmental protection, not only in terms of 'harmonious development' and general well-being, but also in view of foreclosing national regulatory initiatives which, however well intended they may be, unavoidably will be the source of conflict with the overriding goal of free movement of goods within the single market.

The other provision leaving the door open to the renationalization of environmental policy within the Community is Article 100a(4). This provision, as is known, permits a member State to contract out of harmonization measures adopted by majority vote for the establishment and functioning of the internal market. The grounds for contracting out are the 'major' needs referred to in Article 36 and the protection of the environment or the working environment. This provision raises several issues. The first is who can contract out? The State or States opposing the measure, or any member irrespective of the position taken at the time of the negotiation and adoption of the harmonization measure? In our opinion nothing in the language of Article 100a indicates or implies a restriction of the opting-out clause to the dissenting States. From a policy point of view such a restriction would become a powerful incentive to raising objections against harmonization measures in order not to foreclose the future possibility of opting out on grounds of major needs. Further, the more liberal interpretation of this clause is required by the dynamic nature of the relationship between the Community and member States in the management of environmental policies. Major national needs requiring the application of national law may be identified only after some time has elapsed since the adoption of the harmonization measures; thus the notification of the exemption procedure under Article 100a(4) ought to also be deemed permissible for States which did not originally oppose the measure.

Another issue connected to the interpretation of Article 100a(4) is whether this clause permits only the application of more stringent national standards or also derogations in favour of looser national regulation. The answer to this question can be found in the language and the rationale of Article 100a(4). The language is clear: 'major needs must be related to . . . the protection of the environment'; thus national measures can only be permitted if they tend to raise the level of protection and not to lower it. As to the *ratio legis*, one must observe that Article 100a requires that the Community will take 'as a base a high level of protection'. This provision would be incompatible with member States being allowed to create further regulatory gaps by lowering the standards of environmental protection.

Finally, the issue arises as to whether States availing themselves of the opting-out procedure under Article 100a(4) are allowed to apply only existing law at variance with Community regulation or whether they may also enact new measures. A restrictive interpretation appears to be more consistent with the language of Article 100a, which uses the phrase 'apply national provisions'; its plain meaning is 'to maintain in force', and not 'to introduce or enact' new provisions. Besides, it would be rather bizarre for such a provision to contemplate the introduction of new national regimes whose fate would ultimately be that of disrupting the single market.[41]

5   Concluding Remarks

With the single market programme moving swiftly forward towards the magic year of 1993, it becomes ever more apparent that there is a close connection between the functioning of the unified market and the European policy of environmental protection. A point that this paper has tried to stress is that it will be increasingly difficult for member States to avail themselves of the benefits and opportunities of the former without accepting the loss in terms of sovereignty and independent regulatory capacity with respect to the latter.

A second point that needs to be stressed in our conclusions is that with the completion of the single market agenda, by way of harmonization of laws and removal of barriers to trade, a new emphasis is now placed on 'negative integration'. This concept indicates the achievement of a unified internal market by way of 'mutual recognition' of national norms and regulations, even if they have not been harmonized in accordance with Article 100a to the extent that their application has a bearing on the functioning of the internal market. The technique of mutual recognition entails that when a product is made in a given EC country in conformity with its laws and administrative rules, such product shall be freely allowed to circulate in the Community even if it does not entirely conform to technical rules in force in the importing country. This principle was first applied by the European Court of Justice in the well-known *Cassis de Dijon* case and it has since been fostered in many other market areas including beer, pasta, vinegar, and yoghurt.[42]

There is hardly any doubt that the principle of mutual recognition may work as a powerful factor of integration and of development of a quasi-federal structure. Its role may become very similar to the one performed by the 'commerce clause' in the federal system of the United States of

---

[41] This view is supported and further elaborated by Kramer 'The Single European Act and Environmental Protection: Reflections on Several New Provisions in Community Law', *Common Market Law Rev* 24, 659, at 680 ff.

[42] *Rewe-Zentral AG* v. *Bundesmonopolverwaltung fur Branntewein* ('Cassis de Dijon'), case 120/78, [1979] ECR 649. For the German beer case, see *Commission* v. *Germany*, case 178/84 [1988] 1 CMLR 780.

America, with the attendant spill-over effects not only in areas of economic integration but also of social organization. It may also prove to be more agreeable to member States than the process of positive integration through directives intended to harmonize national laws. Such process, as is well known, is resented by member States as an imposition of a political agenda on national parliaments, and is not the least important cause of the widespread difficulties encountered by member States in ensuring timely compliance with the EC directives. However, in the specific field of environmental protection, negative integration by way of mutual recognition presents also some disadvantages. The most evident one is the possibility of export of environmental hazards related to products and to industrial and management processes, as well as of the relocation of production plants in the least environmentally demanding regions. In a single market where the four freedoms of movement of goods, capital, persons, and services are guaranteed, a 'full faith and credit' clause of legal environmental requirements is likely to encourage firms to shop for the more permissive systems so as to cut costs and obtain a competitive advantage. Ultimately, this might cause a 'downward' competition among member States' environmental legislation, an outcome that is hardly consistent with the objectives and spirit of the new environmental powers under the SEA.

It is perhaps too early to assess whether this process is actually taking place. To avert its occurrence, however, it will be necessary for the EC to continue the process of regulatory intervention in order to guarantee a uniform and satisfactory level of environmental protection. This should aim at filling the regulatory gaps in European legislation, with a view to eliminating a source of incentives (attraction or retention of economic investments) to member States to soften their respective environmental legislation. Ultimately, the lesson to be learned from Europe in the field of environmental protection is that the market and competition alone will not guarantee a uniform satisfactory level of environmental protection throughout the Community. To achieve such common level, 'rules' are needed and the institutional reform undertaken by the SEA, especially by the introduction of the majority decision principle, makes regulatory action by the Community more realistic and effective. Obviously, the legal-institutional machinery is only a tool: to make it effective, national attitudes of distrust toward the European institutions must yield to a new fiduciary relationship and to a sense of shared responsibility for the promotion of a common interest. If these conditions are met, the market and competition may even work the miracle of stimulating an 'upward' race by member States towards a level of environmental protection higher than the uniform one applicable Community-wide.

DEVELOPMENTS WITH RESPECT TO COMPENSATION FOR DAMAGE CAUSED BY POLLUTION

H. BOCKEN

1 Introduction

In this essay I propose to highlight a number of possible solutions to some of the problems related to compensation for damage caused by pollution. More particularly I shall focus on the way this issue is dealt with by the European Community and the Council of Europe.

The European Community has recently entered the area of tort law. The directive of 25 June 1985 on liability for defective products was the first EC legislative document on the subject. More recently, the concern for consumer interests has given rise to a draft directive on liability for defective services.[1]

In the area of environmental protection, article 11(3) of directive 84/631 on the transborder movement of toxic waste[2] called on the Commission to establish special rules on liability and insurance with respect to damages caused by transborder movements of toxic waste. The Fourth Environmental Action Programme[3] instructed the Commission also 'to consider the scope for the better definition of responsibility in the environmental field'.

The first comprehensive legislative document on environmental liability to be issued by the Community is the proposal of 1 September 1989 for a Council directive on civil liability for damage caused by waste[4] (hereafter proposed waste liability directive). After extensive discussion in the European Parliament, the Commission submitted an amended proposal on 28 June 1991.[5] This proposal has opened the debate at Community level with respect to a number of difficult legal and policy questions relating to liability for environmental damage. However, whether it will ultimately be adopted or not remains uncertain. On several points it is, in fact, in conflict

---

[1] [1991] OJ C12/8.   [2] [1984] OJ L326 31.
[3] [1986] OJ C328 6, (s. 2.5.5).   [4] [1989] OJ C251 3.
[5] [1991] OJ C192 6. See P. Renaudière, 'Proposition de Directive concernant la Responsabilité Civile pour les Dommages Causés par les Déchets', unpub. paper presented in Nov. 1989 for the Belgian Association of Environmental Law; C. H. C. V. De Villeneuve, 'Les Développements au Niveau des CE en Matière de la Responsabilité et de l'Assurance pour Dommages Causés à l'Environnement', in *Verzekering Van Milieuschade: Assurance des Dommages Causés par la Pollution, Insurance of Environmental Damage'*, ed. H. Bocken and D. Ryckbost (Story-Scientia, Brussels 1991) (hereafter *Insurance of Environmental Damages*), 249–234; C. H. W. M. Sterk, 'De Aansprakelijkheid voor Gevaarlijke Afvalstoffen', *WPNR* (1991), 73–80 and 89–94; P. Luiki and D. Stephenson, 'European Community Waste Policy: at the Brink of a New Era', *International Environment Reporter*, 17 July (1991), 403–11; Sturms, W., 'Internationale Ontwikkelingen m.b.t. Aansprakelijkheid voor Milieuschade', in W. Braams, A. van Oevelen, en W. Sturms, *Risico-Aansprakelijkheid voor Milieuschade* (WEJ Tjeenk Willink, Zwolle, 1992), 115.

with the Council of Europe draft convention on civil liability for damage resulting from activities dangerous to the environment[6] (hereafter COE draft convention). The (unofficial) January 1992 version of this draft indicates that the EC is intending to become a party to the convention. This, however, does not solve the problem of precedence between the two instruments. According to Art. 27, 'in their mutual relations, Parties which are members of the European Economic Community shall apply Community rules and shall therefore not apply the rules arising from this Convention except insofar as there is no Community rule governing the particular subject concerned...'

The problems raised by the confrontation of tort law and pollution damage require a fundamental reflection. The EC Commission has for some time now been promising the publication of a general policy paper on liability for environmental damage which will take the form of a 'Communication from the Commission to the Council and Parliament'. The repeated postponement of the publication of the paper indicates the difficulty that the EC is experiencing in determining its own position on a number of issues. In the meantime, the Commission is also including provisions on liability and financial guarantees in the proposal for a directive on landfills[7] and in an amended draft directive on the elimination of PCBs.[8]

Special attention must also be paid to the Geneva Convention on civil liability for damage caused during carriage of dangerous goods by road, rail, and inland navigation vessels (hereafter CRTD), adopted on the initiative of the Economic Commission for Europe of the United Nations on 10 October 1990.[9] A comparative analysis of the subject is further stimulated by a profusion of legislative initiatives at national level on the European Continent.[10] In this respect the German Environmental Liability

---

[6] Council of Europe, Dir/Jur (91)3, Strasbourg, 22 July 1991. See among others S. Ercmann, 'Problems of Waste Management and Disposal: National and International', paper presented at the Conference on Law and Economics of Environmental Policy (Paris, 4–5 Apr. 1991), 17; Sturms, op. cit. (n. 5), 132–42.

[7] 23 Apr. 1991 (art. 14, 17, and 18), [1991] OJ C190 1.

[8] 22 Oct. 1991 (art. 6), [1991] OJ, C299 9.

[9] A Convention on Liability and Compensation for Damage in Connection with the Carriage of Dangerous Goods by Sea (HNS Convention) is being prepared by the International Maritime Organization.

[10] Special liability rules with respect to the compensation of pollution damages have been enacted in among others Sweden (Environmental Damage Act of 1986, English translation in *Ministry of the Environment; Swedish Environmental Legislation* (Stockholm, 1990), 61); Norway (Pollution Control Act of 1981, as amended in 1989, ss. 53–64); Germany, see following note; Belgium (among others art. 7 of the toxic waste act of 22 July 1974); Portugal (Basic Environmental Law No. 11 of 7 Apr. 1987, French translation in *RJE* (1988), 189); and in Italy (Act No. 349 of 8 July 1986 (art. 18)). Of interest is also a Dutch bill on pollution liability (Voorstel van wet tot aanvulling van de Boeken 3, 6 en 8 Nieuw BW. met regels betreffende de aansprakelijkheid voor gevaarlijke stoffen en verontreiniging van lucht, water of bodem, Tweede Kamer, 1988–9, No. 21.202., zoals gewijzigd bij de nota van

Act of 10 December 1990[11] is of particular interest. Moreover, these new developments have to be seen in the perspective of the general law of torts and of better known specific compensation mechanisms as elaborated in the US legislation[12] and in treaties on nuclear damages[13] and on the pollution of the sea by oil.[14]

2   The Specificity of Damage Caused by Pollution

An adequate system of liability for pollution damages can only be based on a correct analysis of the specificity of environmental pollution and of the damage caused by it. A brief sketch of some of the mechanics of pollution and pollution damage may thus be desirable.

In general, one can say that pollution is the result of the release in the air, water, or soil of substances which negatively affect the quality of the environmental medium into which they have been released. This in turn, causes damage to man and nature. Hereafter, some of the main elements of the process are further developed.

2.1   *The Release of Polluting Substances into the Environment*

Pollution of the environment is the result of the release[15] of substances, energy, or—more exceptionally—organisms into the air, water, or soil.

wijziging 21202, No. 7. See W. T. Braams. *Aansprakelijkheid voor gevaarlijke stoffen en milieuverontreiniging* (Deventer, 1989); n. 5, above, 25ff.

[11] 'Gestetz über die Umwelthaftung' *BGBl* (1990) i: 2634. English translation by W. Pfennigstorf, published in *Pollution Insurance Bulletin* (July 1991), 8. See R. Ganten, 'Deliberations on a New Law on Liability for Environmental Damage in the Federal Republic of Germany: A Model for Europe?', Paper given on the occasion of the Elizabeth Haub Prize Award Ceremony (Brussels, 29 Feb. 1988); W. Pfennigstorf, 'Developments in the Federal Republic of Germany in Liability and Insurance for Environmental Damage', in *Insurance of Environmental Damage*, op.cit., 183–209; G. Aager, 'Das neue Umwelthaftungsgesetz', *NJW* (1991), 134–43; H. Scherer, 'Strict Liability for Environmental Damage in Germany', *International Business Lawyer* (1991), 309–10. See also the Genentechnikgesetz of 1990.

[12] See especially the Comprehensive Environmental Response, Compensation, and Liability Act of 1980 (PL, 96–510) as amended by the Superfund Amendments and Reauthorization Act of 1986 (PL, 99–499). (W. Mc Clain, *US Environmental Laws, 1991* (Bureau of National Affairs, Washington DC, 1991).

[13] Paris Convention on Third-Party Liability in the Field of Nuclear Energy of 29 July 1960 and additional Protocol of 28 Jan. 1964; Brussels Convention of 31 Jan. 1963 on Third-Party Liability in the Field of Nuclear Energy of 1963 and additional Protocols of 16 Nov. 1982.

[14] International Convention on Civil Liability for Oil Pollution Damages of 29 Nov. 1969 (hereafter Oil Pollution Convention) and the Convention for the Establishment of an International Fund for Compensation of Oil Pollution Damages of 1971 (hereafter Fund Convention).

[15] One of the earliest explicit legal definitions is to be found in s. 107(22) of the US Comprehensive Environmental Response, Compensation, and Liability Act of 1980 (hereafter,

That this may be an obvious fact is explicitly recognized in more recent environmental legislation. According to the UK Environmental Protection Act,[16] section 1(3), pollution results from 'the release in any environmental medium, . . . of substances which are capable of causing harm to man or other living organisms supported by the environment'.[17] The German Environmental Liability Act imposes strict liability for damage which results from any change caused to the environment. According to article 3, the latter is the case if the damage is caused by substances, vibrations, noise, pressure, rays, gases, vapours, temperature, or other phenomena that have spread in the ground, air, or water. The foregoing definitions of pollution imply that the 'environment' is considered to consist of air, water, and soil.[18] Man and nature are thus not considered to be part of the environment but are 'living organisms supported by' it.[19] In this conceptual framework, a special liability rule which is to cover most pollution damages cannot, in its application, be limited to the 'environment' alone. The CERCLA[20] solves the problem by considering land, air, and water, taken together with fish, wildlife, and biota, to constitute 'natural resources' which are protected by a special liability rule.

Not all recent proposals proceed from the same analysis. The COE draft convention does not attach particular importance to the release or dispersal of pollutants but proceeds from a definition of the values to be protected by the special liability rule it establishes. Thus it defines 'environment' as including air, water, soil, nature, the cultural heritage, and landscapes[21] and attaches liability to activities dangerous to the environment (the handling, storage, production, or discharge of substances or organisms, activities involving radiation, and installations or sites for the treatment or disposal of waste).

CERCLA). It illustrates the various ways in which the release can take place: '"release" means any spilling, leaking, pumping, pouring, emitting, emptying, discharging, injecting, escaping, leaching, dumping or disposing into the environment (including the abandonment or discarding of barrels, containers, and other closed receptacles containing any hazardous substance or pollutant or contaminant)'.

[16] Environmental Protection Act 1990, with annotations by S. Tromans.

[17] Release is further defined in s. 1(10).

[18] This is explicitly stated in the UK Environmental Protection Act, s. 1(2): 'The environment consists of all, or any of the following media, namely, the air, water and land and the medium air includes the air within buildings and the air within other natural or man-made structures above or below ground'. See in the same sense, CERCLA, s. 101(8).

[19] UK Environmental Protection Act, s. 1(3). [20] Note 3, 2.

[21] Art. 2(11): 'Environment includes natural resources both abiotic and biotic such as air, water, soil, fauna and flora and the interaction between the same factors, property which forms part of the cultural heritage and the characteristic aspects of the landscape. The proposed waste liability directive limits itself to define 'impairment of the environment' as 'a significant physical, chemical or biological deterioration of the environment'.

2.2 *Sources of pollution*

The release at the origin of the pollution may be sudden or gradual, intentional or accidental, legal or illegal. It generally occurs in one of the following manners:

1 Residual pollution is the result of the way in which we dispose of the residues of our activities. A very well-established system for doing so is to release them directly in the environment (e.g. gas exhausts from a chimney, liquid discharges in a river, abandonment of solid waste on land). In recent times we have become aware that the potential of the environment to absorb residues is limited. We therefore collect solid waste and waste water and treat them e.g. in incinerators or water treatment plants. The result, however, is again a release in the environment, be it reduced in volume and made less dangerous. As their adequate treatment is often costly, solid and other wastes are often intentionally discharged in the environment, in violation of environmental law.
2 Of a totally different nature is accidental pollution. Most of the spectacular pollution incidents of the last decades have been of this type (*Torrey Canyon, Amoco Cadiz, Exxon Valdez,* Seveso, Bhopal, Sandoz, Chernobyl . . .).[22] Unlike residual pollution, accidental emissions are the result of unintended, unforeseen, and unwanted incidents occurring as a result of carrying out dangerous activities.
3 A third category of releases results from the normal use of a variety of chemicals. As chemicals are often volatile or difficult to apply with precision, their use entails in many cases a spill and, as an unintended side-effect, an emission in the environment (e.g. CFCs in spray cans, pesticides, and fertilizers).

The diversity of pollution sources has its impact on public environmental law as well as on the resolution of damage cases.

In order to prevent pollution, environmental law has recourse to a multitude of policy instruments. Emission limitations; product, process and construction standards; and economic instruments such as taxes and subsidies, may all be used to limit residual emissions. Safety measures of various types will be necessary to prevent accidental pollution. The administrative structure must be in place in order to take remedial action after its occurrence. Finally, product standards will be essential to control pollution in the third category.

As far as compensation for damage is concerned, a variety of more or less well-established liability rules, governing nuisance and industrial

---

[22] Accidental pollutions seem to be the only category, the size of which has been effectively studied. See especially the studies of H. Smets, e.g. 'Le Coût de l'Indemnistaion des Tiers Victimes de la Pollution Accidentelle en France' in *Insurance of Environmental Damage*, (n. 5), 97 and references.

accidents as well as the use of products may come into play, together with the more recent strict liability rules elaborated specifically for the compensation of pollution damages.

2.3 *The Dispersal of Pollutants*

Once released, the pollutants can generally no longer be controlled. They are often transported over a large distance, depending on the nature of the pollutant and the medium in which they are released. They mix with other pollutants and synergetic effects may occur (e.g. acid rain). In any event, since the pollutants are dispersed[23] in either air, water, or soil the 'normal' quality of air, soil, and water is thereby affected.

The dispersal of the pollutants is an aspect of the pollution process which is most relevant for the tort law. It lies at the basis of many difficulties that face victims in their attempts to establish the causal relationship between pollution damage and a specific source of pollution.

2.4 *The Deterioration of the Quality of Air, Water, and Soil*

The dispersal of pollutants in turn changes the composition of the environmental medium in which they are spread. The presence of foreign substances becomes 'pollution' as soon as they cause or can cause harm.[24] From an ecological point of view, there is harm if there is a negative effect on the health of living organisms or if their physical support or ecosystem is threatened. For man harm will, in addition, result from damage to his personal, moral, or material interests.[25]

The objective of pollution control legislation will thus ultimately be to guarantee that the environment maintains the quality necessary to continue to sustain man and other living organisms in a satisfactory way. An essential part in modern environmental policy-making has thus become the establishment of quality objectives. This concept, which appears to have originated in the US Clean Air Act of 1970, has also been adopted by the European Community in various directives which have been instrumental in its adoption in national legislation of the member States.[26]

Quality objectives reflect the level at which the environment is considered to have potential negative effects. They are not directly binding on the citizen but constitute an injunction to the public authorities who are to take it into account in setting emission standards, delivering permits, and planning environmental controls. Quality objectives may, however, also

---

[23] The dispersal of the pollutants is an element of the definition of 'effect on the environment' in art. 3(1) of the German Environmental Liability Act: '. . . phenomena that have spread in the ground, air or water'.

[24] UK Environmental Protection Act, s. 1(3).

[25] UK Environmental Protection Act, s. 1(4).

[26] See e.g. UK Environmental Protection Act, s. 3(4).

have an effect on tort law as they indicate the level of pollution which should not be tolerated.

2.5 *Pollution Damage*

Pollution has various negative effects. To a large extent, they result in compensatable damages of a traditional type. However important they are in fact, physical injury and death, property damage, loss of amenities, economic damages, moral damages, pain, and suffering can also result from other sources than pollution. As such, they do not raise unusual problems under liability law.

By contrast, other negative effects of pollution raise substantial problems. To a large extent pollution affects 'collective' rather than individual interests. Traditional liability rules, however, are normally only concerned with individual interests.

The category of negative effects of the pollution which is most challenging to traditional legal concepts is that of ecological damages. In essence it consists of damage to the ecosystem itself (e.g. the endangerment of the ozone layer) or to parts of nature which have not been individually appropriated by man (e.g. extinction of wild species or death of marine animals as a result of oil pollution).[27]

Also important in pollution cases is the expenditure made by public authorities pursuant to pollution incidents,[28] either to prevent or limit the emission of pollutants or their dispersal, to avoid exposure to pollutants of protected interests (e.g. evacuation), or to clean up the polluted soil or water. The amounts of money involved in fighting marine oil pollution and cleaning up polluted soils are staggering.

2.6 *Major Issues*

A comparative and systematic, be it summary, description of the issues raised by the compensation of damages caused by pollution, falls outside the scope of this paper. So in this presentation I shall first describe the development of strict liability for pollution damages (section 3), in section

---

[27] To a certain extent, ecological damages may overlap with damages of a more traditional type. Economic losses resulting from the reduced use of the physical environment (losses suffered by a fisherman as a result of the pollution of the sea e.g.), is a well-known category. The same goes for damages to certain individually held goods which have an ecological dimension of a different nature than their monetary value. A landmark tree, e.g. is something other than firewood. Damage to these goods raises difficulties at the level of the valuation of the damage. Problems of this type may be difficult; they are not new. Countries which recognize the concept of moral damage already have experience with translating into money values for which no market exists.

[28] Expenditure made apart from a specific pollution incident, with a goal of providing the authorities with the necessary personnel and equipment to fight pollution naturally cannot be compensated on the basis of liability law, among other reasons, because there is no causal relationship between this expenditure and a specific source of pollution.

4 a number of issues relating to the concept of damage will be examined, and finally in section 5 I shall look at possible solutions to the difficulties of establishing causation, including the creation of environmental compensation funds.

3 The Development of Strict Liability for Pollution Damage

In most countries, victims of pollution can attempt to rely on a variety of legal theories in order to claim compensation.[29] Over the years, however, it has become apparent that traditional tort rules do not provide an adequate mechanism for the compensation of damages resulting from the application of dangerous modern technologies.[30] Nuisance rules are mainly relevant to neighbourhood problems. Where negligence is a condition for liability, the victim may be left uncompensated either because there was no negligence on the part of the polluter or because it cannot be proved. In a growing number of countries, the courts and the legislators have thus been developing for some time now strict liability rules under which the victim no longer has to establish negligence or any other tortious behaviour on the part of the defendant. In recent years, strict liability appears to have become the rule with respect to pollution damages.

Generally, strict liability proceeds from the conviction that he who for his own benefit exposes others to exceptional risks, should also bear the losses if the risks materialize.

3.1 *Area of Application*

The recent development of strict liability in the area of pollution damages is not without precedent.[31] In France, for example, the courts have, on the basis of article 1384 CC,[32] developed a rule according to which the custodian of a thing is, irrespective of fault, liable for damage caused by the thing.

---

[29] For a comparative general survey, see H. Bocken, 'Sanctions de Droit Civil Contre la pollution', *TAR* (1975), 67 and *Preventie, toerekening en schade door herstel van schade door milieuverontreiniging*, Preadvies voor de Nederlandse Vereniging voor Rechtsvergelijking, (Kluwer, Deventer, 1983) (hereafter 'Preventie'), 45–86; P. Wetterstein, *Damage from International Disasters in the Light of Tort and Insurance Law: General Report for the 8th World Congress of AIDA* (Copenhagen, 1990), 2–180. See also J. M. Van Dunné, *Aansprakelijkheid voor Milieuschade bij door Lozingen Vervuild Havenslib* (Instituut voor Milieuschade, Rotterdam, 1991), 49–55 and references.

[30] See generally, F. H. Lawson and B. S. Markesinis, *Tortious Liability for Unintentional Harm in the Common Law and the Civil Law* (CUP, 1982), 142; H. Kötz, 'Gefährdungshaftung', in *Gutachten und Vorschläge zur Uberarbeitung des Schuldrechts* (Bundesanzeiger Verlagsges, Köln, 1981), ii: 1783.

[31] See generally, H. Bocken, *Preventie*, 49.

[32] See generally, G. Viney, *Les Obligations, La Responsabilité: Conditions* (LGDJ, 1982), 751 ff; B. Starck, *Droit Civil: Obligations; Responsabilité Délictuelle*, 3rd edn. by H. Roland; and L. Boyer, *Litec* (Paris, 1988), 209.

In Belgium, the rule is restricted to damage caused by a defect of the thing.[33] According to case law, the defect is an 'abnormal characteristic'. However, it does not follow that the thing is defective merely because it is dangerous. This interpretation of article 1384 by the Belgian courts is important, especially with respect to accidental pollution due to defective installations.[34]

In the common-law countries, one finds the rule of *Rylands* v. *Fletcher*:[35] whoever makes a non-natural use of his land by bringing on to it objects which are likely to cause a mischief if they escape, is liable for the harm thus caused. The rule may apply to a variety of pollution cases. The *Cambridge Water Company* case, however, demonstrated that the rule has been substantially weakened by a tolerance for industrial activities.[36]

In recent times, the legislators of many countries have, by special legislation, introduced strict liability for a variety of potentially dangerous technologies and installations. Many of these rules are directed towards pollution damages. A few examples illustrate their scope.

An area of great concern has been pollution resulting from transportation. In the wake of the *Torrey Canyon* accident, a number of countries adopted in 1969 the International Convention on Civil Liability for Oil Pollution Damage according to which the owner of an oil tanker is strictly liable for the damage resulting from the pollution of the sea by oil. On 10 October 1989, the CRTD Convention was adopted. It imposes strict liability on the carrier for damage caused during carriage of dangerous goods by road, rail, or inland navigation vessels. In the framework of the IMO, a convention is being prepared with respect to liability and compensation for damage in connection with the carriage of dangerous goods by sea.

A well-known strict liability rule, established by the treaties of Paris and Brussels,[37] governs nuclear plants and the transportation of nuclear material.

In the US, the most important strict liability rule relating to pollution damages is that imposed by section 107 of the CERCLA, which imposes strict liability for clean up costs and damages to natural resources caused by the release of hazardous substances.[38]

---

[33] See generally, L. Cornelis, *Beginselen van het Belgische Buitencontractuele Aansprakelijkheidsrecht* (Brussels, 1989), i: 456; for a general survey of strict liability in Belgian law, see H. Bocken, 'Van Fout Naar Risico', *TPR* (1984), 329–415 and 'La responsabilité sans Faute en Droit Belge', in *Memoriam Jean Limpens*, (Kluwer Rechtswetenschappen, Antwerp 1987), 85–111.

[34] H. Bocken, *Het Aansprakelijkheidsrecht als Sanctie tegen de Verstoring van het leefmilieu* (Brussels, 1979), 262.

[35] (1868) 1 Exch 265; (1868) 3 App Cas 330 (HL). See generally R. W. M. Dias and B. S. Markesinis, *Tort Law* (Clarendon Press, Oxford, 1989), 343.

[36] *Cambridge Water Company* v. *Eastern Counties Leather* PLC and *Same* v. *Hutchings and Harding, The Times*, 23 Oct. 1991. See on the subject, S. Tromans, 'Environmental Liability', *Env Pol & L* (1992), 43; N. Atkinson, *Journal of Environmental Law* (1992), 105.

[37] See n. 13.   [38] See n. 14.

Paragraph 22 of the German Waserhaushaltgesetz of 1957 and article 36 of the Swiss Gewassershutzgesetz impose strict liability for water pollution.

The Belgian Act of 22 July 1974 imposes strict liability on the producer of toxic waste for all accidents caused by the waste, even if it is during their final elimination in a waste treatment installation operated by a third party. This law has inspired the proposed EC waste liability directive which holds the producer of the waste liable, irrespective of fault (article 3). If, however, the waste has been lawfully transferred to an authorized disposal installation, liability is, correspondingly, transferred to the disposing concern. Other draft directives impose strict liability on the operator of a landfill and on those who eliminate PCBs.[39]

Recently, strict liability rules with a more comprehensive area of application have been developed or in the process of being adopted. The COE draft convention concerns broadly defined 'activities dangerous to the environment including the handling, storage, production, and discharge of dangerous substances or organisms, activities producing radiation, and the operation of installations for the treatment or permanent disposal of waste' (article 2, 1–5). The Swedish Act of 30 April 1986 concerning damage to the environment, provides compensation, irrespective of negligence, for damage caused by pollution resulting from operations performed on real property. The Norwegian Pollution Control Act (section 55), as amended, also imposes liability on the owner of real property or of any object which causes pollution damage. The German Environmental Liability Act (section 1) imposes strict liability for pollution damages resulting from industrial installations. The Dutch Bill of 28 June 1989 concerns liability for dangerous substances and pollution of the air, water, or soil.

Although there is a clear tendency to broaden the scope of strict liability rules with respect to pollution, a number of substantial limitations are to be taken into account in order to make the liability manageable and ensure the liability insurance or other risk spreading mechanisms remain available.

Most often, the strict liability applies only to prospective pollution.[40] The CERCLA is an exception insofar as it has a retroactive application to 'historic' pollution.

Finally, one also finds in these enactments the traditional nuisance test of looking for what is tolerable in a particular locality. Local conditions may, therefore, be of paramount importance.[41] A more modern approach of the problem would be to refer to pollution which does not exceed the environmental quality objectives.

[39] See n. 7 and 8.

[40] COE draft convention, Art. 5; proposed waste liability directive, art. 13; German Environmental Liability Act, art. 23.

[41] COE draft convention, s. 5; Swedish Environmental Damage Act, s. 1, German Environmental Liability Act, s. 5.

3.2 Defences

As indicated, in most if not all of the above cases, the victim no longer has to establish negligence on the part of the defendant. The latter, however, generally has the possibility of escaping liability by establishing that the damage was caused by varying external factors such as an Act of God, exceptional natural phenomena, *force majeure*, or fault of the victim or of a third party. Strict liability rules are not consistent in this respect. To the same extent it is difficult to generalize with respect to their more or less strict or absolute character.

In this respect, the proposed waste liability directive seems to be very lenient since it exempts the producer from liability whenever the damage or the impairment results from *force majeure* as defined in Community law. The latter concept is very broad. According to the European Court of Justice, *force majeure* refers to an abnormal and unforeseeable event taking place outside the will of the defendant and which he could not prevent even if he took due care.[42] The wide exemption seems to correspond to the notion of *force majeure* in French and Belgian law.

The COE draft convention (Article 8) adopts a more limited list of causes of exemption. Liability is more particularly excluded if the damage was caused (1) by an act of war, hostilities, civil war, insurrection, or a natural phenomenon of an exceptional, inevitable, and irresistible character; or (2) by an act of a third party committed (appropriate safety measures notwithstanding) with the intent to cause damage. Comparable provisions are found in the CRTD (article 5, sections 4a and 5) and the Oil Pollution Convention of 1969 (Article III, 2(a)). The German Environmental Liability Act excludes liability in the event that the damage was caused by an Act of God. The COE draft convention furthermore excludes liability if the damage was caused as a result of the compliance with an order or compulsory measure of a public authority or by a dangerous action lawfully taken in the interest of the victim.[43] The draft directives on landfills and on the elimination of PCBs do not address the question of exemptions.

3.3 Canalization of Liability

Yet another important feature of strict liability rules which benefits victims is the fact that liability is no longer determined on the basis of actual causation between the damage and the activities of the defendant. This is explicitly recognized in the COE draft which refers to 'the causal link between the incident and the damage' (Article 10). Liability is by law

---

[42] Case 145/85, *Denkavit* v. *Belgium* [1987] ECR 565.

[43] The draft convention also excludes liability if the damage was caused by pollution at tolerable levels to be anticipated under local relevant circumstances. See n. 15.

allocated (canalized) to a determined category of persons who have a certain control over the installation or activity involved in the incident which is the cause of the damage.[44] A multitude of policy considerations, both with respect to the allocation of the losses and the preventive effect of the liability rule appear to have directed various solutions all of which benefit the victim in that he no longer has to identify the one person among the many connected with the installation or activity whose acts actually brought about the damages.

Sometimes liability is channelled to a single class of person. Often this is the person who has the actual or legal control over the means of transportation or over the installation from which the pollution originates. Thus the International Oil Pollution Convention allocates the damage to the owner of the oil tanker (Article 3); the CRTD, holds liable the carrier (Article 5(1)); the Paris Convention on Nuclear Damages, the operator of a nuclear plant; the COE draft convention channels the liability to the operator of the dangerous activity. In the draft directive on landfills (article 17) and the amended directive on the elimination of PCBs (article 6(b)), the operators of the landfill and of the installation are respectively held liable. In a number of cases, the producer of the polluting product is to bear the losses. Thus, the Belgian Act on toxic waste of 22 July 1974 (article 7) holds liable the producer of toxic waste. The producer is also the first party to be liable according to the product liability directive of 25 July 1985 and the proposed waste liability directive (articles 2 and 3).

In some cases the position of the victim is improved by the fact that there is a cascade of potentially liable parties on whom liability is imposed in the event that there is no liable party of a higher category. The proposed waste liability directive is a good example. If the waste has been imported, the importer is liable. If the producer or the importer cannot be identified, or the waste is in transit, the person who has actual control over the waste is liable. Finally, if the waste is legally transferred to a licensed waste treatment installation, liability is transferred to the operator thereof.

Thus strict liability is the broadest type of liability as several categories of potentially liable parties can jointly and severally be held liable. A striking example is section 107 of the CERCLA which in fact imposes liability on almost anybody who produced, stored, transported, or attempted to eliminate the dangerous substances which were released.[45]

3.4 *Limitation of Liability*

To some extent, strict liability may also be intended to protect the operators of certain installations against the consequences of full liability for pollution damages.

---

[44] Bocken, 'Van Fout Naar Risico', *TPR* (1984), 373.   [45] See further, n. 31.

In a number of cases, the strict liability is financially limited, generally to a certain amount per incident.[46] This is the case in the Oil Pollution Convention (Article V, 1984 Protocols, Article 6), the CRTD (Article 9), and the Paris Nuclear Convention (Article 7(b)). Article 15 of the German Environmental Liability Act provides for a limitation of 160 million DM per incident, for both personal and property damage. The COE draft convention leaves the matter to national law (Article 12). No limitation is provided for in the proposed waste liability directive and in the draft directives on landfills and the elimination of PCBs.

Under certain circumstances, the limitation of liability, however, cannot be invoked. In the COE draft convention, this is the case if the damage is the result of an act committed with the intent of causing damage or recklessly and with knowledge that such damage would probably result (Article 12(2)). The CRTD (Article 10) and the Oil Pollution Convention (Article V, 2, 1984 Protocols, Article 6(2)) contain a comparable clause.

The potentially liable party will be additionally protected if the rights of the victim are limited to a claim under the strict liability provision and if recourse to common law remedies is excluded. Thus, the victim cannot circumvent the limitation of liability provided for. A solution of this type has been adopted in the Paris Convention on Nuclear Damages (Article 6), the Oil Pollution Convention (Article III, 4),[47] and the CRTD (Article 5(6)). Most statutory instruments, however, only create a new cause of action, without excluding recourse to common law. Often it is explicitly stated that the rights of the victims under other provisions are not affected. The COE draft convention (Article 27) is an example; and so is the German Environmental Liability Act (section 18). The proposed waste liability directive does not directly address the issue. As the proposal is based on Article 100A, that Article will also determine to what extent member States can depart from the directive. It is interesting to note that Article 27(2) of the COE draft convention states that Community rules shall prevail over the Convention with respect to the mutual relations of the member States.

4   The Nature and Dimensions of Pollution Damages

4.1   *Response Costs*

Expenditure made by public authorities in order to limit an emission or the spreading of the pollutants or to clean up the pollution, may be extremely important. In most countries the authorities can be compensated under

---

[46] This limitation of liability is said among others, to improve the possibility of obtaining adequate liability insurance.

[47] This is the reason why the *Amoco Cadiz* victims sued in the USA which has not ratified the Oil Pollution Conventions.

general liability law. There are, however, exceptions. Belgian courts, for example, have for a time adopted a different solution[48] following the argument that the legal obligation (on the basis of which the public authorities act) interrupts the causal relationship between the 'response cost' and the third party's negligence. The present case law, however, is less restrictive and it allows recovery if the public authority has only a secondary duty to clean up the pollution, the party being primarily liable to do so, having neglected its obligation.[49] Also statutory provisions explicitly allow the recovery of response costs.[50]

To avoid difficulties of this type many legislators have taken measures to ensure, by introducing strict liability, a more easy recovery of expenditure made by public authorities. No doubt the most striking example in this respect is to CERCLA, section 107, which imposes on a wide range of potential defendants strict liability for response costs incurred pursuant to a release of a hazardous substance. Another typical example is article 85 of the Belgian Act of 24 December 1976 which imposes on the authorities the obligation to recover the cost of remedial action undertaken by the civil protection administration or the local fire brigades from the owner of polluting substances.

The 1984 Protocols to the Oil Pollution Convention (Article 1(7)), the CRTD. (Article 1(11)), and the COE draft convention (Article 2(10)) equally institute a strict liability for preventive measures, defined as 'any reasonable measures taken by any person after an incident has occurred to prevent or minimize damages'. The proposed waste liability directive (art. 4(1)(b)(iii) provides for the possibility of obtaining an injunction ordering the reimbursement of costs lawfully incurred in taking preventive measures (including the cost of any damage caused by the preventive measures).

A specific problem arises when preventive measures or remedial action are taken not by public authorities but by private parties. This problem is easy to solve if the person having a property interest exposed to pollution personally takes measures to prevent or limit the damage. Normally these expenses will be recoverable under general tort law.

More difficult is the case where a public interest group incurs expenses to prevent ecological damage. In this instance, the objection will be raised in many countries that under general tort law the public interest group is not pursuing a private interest and that it has not suffered personal damage.[51] The recent decision of the court in Rotterdam in the *Borcea* case[52]

---

[48] Cass. 28 Apr. 1978, RW (1978–9) 1695; 7 Apr. 1979, RW (1978–9), 2664.

[49] Cass., 13 May 1988, RW (1988–9), 1126; Cass., 15 Nov. 1990, JLMB (1991), 867.

[50] See more extensively, H. Bocken, 'Milieuwetgeving en Onroerende Goederen. Aansprakelijkheid voor de Kosten van Bodemsanering, *TPR* (1992), 32; 'La Réparation des Dommages Causés par la Pollution: La Situation en 1992', RCDC (1992) No. 16 ff 296.

[51] See further, note 68.

[52] District Court of Rotterdam, 15 Mar. 1991, *TMA* (1991) 1, note by Van Maanen.

indicates an alternative solution. Thus in this case the court allowed a society for the protection of marine birds to recover the expenditure made in cleaning birds after a marine oil spill caused by the defendant on the basis that the general interest in the protection of birds must also be seen as the plaintiffs' own interest. Some national legislation, and most recent international (draft) treaties, go in the same direction. Thus the CERCLA (section 107(4)(B)) allows recovery of any necessary response costs incurred by any other person consistent with the national contingency plan. The proposed waste liability directive (art. 4(3)) explicitly recognizes the right of public interest groups to obtain reimbursement of the cost of preventive measures. As indicated above, the Oil Pollution Convention, the CRTD, and the COE draft convention all define preventive measures as any reasonable measures taken by any person after an incident has occurred in order to prevent or minimize loss or damage (Art. 2(10)).

4.2 Ecological Damage

4.2.1 The Concept of Ecological Damage

The traditional liability case involves two individual parties, the tortfeasor and the victim. As indicated above, pollution damages often do not fit into this scheme insofar as they affect collective rather than individual interests.

Traditional liability law requires the claimant to show that his personal rights or legally protected interests have been infringed. Damages affecting collective interests only, or interests of a third party, do not generally give legal rights. In any event, they do not meet the substantive requirements of tort law.

More and more, however, 'ecological damage', is being recognized as a separate category of actionable harm.[53] The US legislature was one of the first to do so. Section 107(f) of the CERCLA, establishes liability 'in the case of an injury to, destruction of, or loss of natural resources.'[54] 'Natural resources' means 'land, fish, wildlife, biota, air, water, ground water, drinking water supplies, and any other such resources belonging to, . . . held in trust by . . . the United States . . .' (section 101(16)). Later, the Italian Act No. 349 of 8 July 1986 (art. 18) recognized the concept of *damno ecologico*. The Norwegian legislation[55] provides liability for interference with common rights. At international level we find the 1984 Protocol to

---

[53] See generally, the not yet published proceedings of the colloquia 'Le Dommage Écologique en Droit Interne, Communautaire et Comparé; Congrès de la Société Française pour le Droit de l'Environnement' (Nice, 21–2 Mar. 1991) and 'Verantwortlichkeit für Ökologischen Schäden' (Bonn, Jan. 1992), organized by Prof. Will of the Universität des Saarlandes. On the latter colloquium, see H. U. Marticke, 'Liability for Ecological Damage', *Env Pol & L* (1992), 28.

[54] See R. Stewart, 'Recent Developments in the Field of Liability for Hazardous Waste under CERCLA and Natural Resource Damages in the US', *TMA* (1991), 89–97.

[55] Pollution Control Act of 13 Mar. 1981, as amended in 1989 (art. 57).

the Oil Pollution Convention which refers to 'compensation for impairment of the environment'. The CRTD contains a similar provision (Article 1(10)(c)). Most interesting is also the proposed waste liability directive. It defines 'impairment of the environment' as 'any significant physical, chemical or biological deterioration of the environment' which does not constitute personal or property damage. According to the COE draft, 'damage' includes 'loss or damage by impairment of the environment' insofar as it does not constitute personal injury or property damage (Article 8(c)).

Other legislators, however, have not (yet) followed suit. For example, the Swedish Environmental Damage Act of 1986 (section 1), the German Environmental Liability Act, and the Dutch Bill do not recognize ecological damage as a separate category. The German Environmental Liability Act only provides for a special rule for the measurement of damages in the event where damage to property constitutes at the same time an impairment of nature or scenery. According to section 16 of the Act, expenses incurred in the restoration of polluted property are not to be considered unreasonable for the sole reason that they exceed the value of the property. Ecological damage which does not constitute damage to property is not covered by the Dutch Bill.

The compensation of damages to the ecosystem or to natural resources which are not subject to individual property rights, raises two distinct questions. The first is how damages of this nature can be compensated; the second, who can act as a plaintiff.

4.2.2 *How to Compensate for Ecological Damage*

The monetary evaluation of pure ecological losses is particularly difficult as there is no market for most of the values involved. The problem, however, is not an entirely new one. In a variety of cases, judges have had to adopt more or less arbitrary solutions when compensating victims who have suffered emotional or aesthetic losses.

A similar problem arises with respect to property damage with an ecological dimension. The solution is reasonably easy if it is possible to replace the object; in that case the replacement cost determines the amount of the compensation. If replacement is not feasible, as in the case, for example, of the destruction of a landmark tree, things are more difficult. If one takes only into account the normal market value of the property, its ecological dimension will be ignored. The value of the tree is not expressed by the price of the firewood or of the veneer it could provide. Generally, a more or less arbitrary evaluation is made on a case by case basis. In certain countries, however, attempts have been made to develop more sophisticated methods to quantify in a more systematic way the value of property with an ecological dimension. Belgian courts, for example, tend to determine the value of a tree by making use of a formula in which various elements such as the species, the age, and the location are all taken into account.[56]

The difficulty is even greater when pure ecological damages are concerned. How should one, for example, evaluate the ecological damages resulting from the loss of marine life caused by oil polluting a swamp? In the interesting case of the *Zoe Colocotroni*[57] a tanker polluted the coast of Puerto Rico. The lower court determined the value of the marine organisms destroyed by the oil pollution by establishing the theoretical population of the area before the pollution and by multiplying the number of each species by the price for which the animals could be bought from specialized traders.

A method by which one tries to determine the nominal value of parts of the environment which have not been individually appropriated is, in my opinion, rather arbitrary. Nevertheless, some countries are not unwilling to require this monetary evaluation. For example, according to the CERCLA section 107(f), 'the measure of damages . . . shall not be limited by the sums which can be used to restore or replace such resources'. Pursuant to section 301(c)(1), regulations for natural resource damage assessment were promulgated in 1986 by the Department of the Interior.[58] Even more explicit is the US Oil Pollution Act of 1990, section 1006(d) of which determines that natural resources damages will be measured not only by the cost of restoration but also by the 'b) diminution in value of those natural resources pending restoration plus c) the reasonable cost of assessing those damages'. The Italian Act No. 349 of 8 July 1986 (article 18) instructs the judge to determine equitably the amount of the compensation due in the event of damage to the environment in equity, taking into account the degree of fault of the defendant and the advantages he obtained from the pollution. There is a growing body of legal writing which supports a monetary evaluation of ecological damages.[59]

From an ecological point of view, restoration of the environment is preferable to monetary compensation. This consideration, together with the difficulties involved in measuring the value of natural resources, has lead a number of legislators to limit recovery for ecological damages to the restoration costs. Typical in this respect is the 1984 Protocol to the Oil Pollution Convention (Article 2(3)) which provides that 'compensation

---

[56] For further references, see H. Bocken, *RGDC* (1992), No. 13, 293; H. Bocken, I Traest, L. De Jager, *Bomen; Eeen Overzicht van het Recht in het Vlaamse Gewest van Toepassing op Bomen* (Story-Scientia, Brussels, 1992), 145ff, 219ff.

[57] *Commonwealth of Puerto Rico v. Zoe Colocotroni*, 628 F 2d 652. See H. Bocken, *Preventie*, 35.   [58] CFR pt. 11 (1990).

[59] For further references, see the reports to the colloquia mentioned in n. 51 and M. Rémond-Gouilloud, 'From Economics to Law: Improving Compensation for Damages from Accidental Pollution', OECD doc. ENV/EC/ECO/ 91(13).

for impairment of the environment other than loss of profit from such impairment shall be limited to costs of reasonable measures of reinstatement actually undertaken or to be undertaken'. The CRTD (Article 1(9)(c)) contains an identical provision. The proposed waste liability directive explicitly requires national law to open the possibility for a claim for 'an injunction ordering the reinstatement of the environment and/or ordering the execution of preventive measures and the reimbursement of costs lawfully incurred in reinstating the environment and in taking preventive measures (including costs of damage caused by preventive measures' (Article 4(1)(b)(iii)). The Norwegian Pollution Control Act, as amended (article 58), limits the claim in the event of damage to common rights on the environment to the reasonable restoration expenses. The COE draft convention (Article 2(7)(c)) limits the compensation for damages caused by impairment of the environment (other than for loss of profit from such impairment), to the cost of measures of reinstatement actually undertaken or to be undertaken (Article 1(8)(c)). The draft is interesting insofar as it explicitly refers to the possibility to 'compensate' the loss of ecological value by the introduction in the environment of equivalent components to the one destroyed. The US Oil Pollution Act of 1990 equally opens the possibility of 'acquiring the equivalent of the damaged natural resources' (section 1006(d)).

Restoration of the polluted environment, however, is an objective which is not always easy to achieve. Environmentalists and polluters may take a different view on the extent of the measures that need to be taken. Scientists will disagree on the chances of success of certain measures. Thus the legislator has, occasionally, with great difficulty tried to formulate policy guidelines for the judge. Most legislation, however, resorts to a more general restriction. The 1984 Protocols to the Oil Pollution Convention (Article 2(3)), the CRTD (Article 1(11)) and the COE draft convention (Art. 2(9)) require the restoration measures to be reasonable. The proposed waste liability directive contains a more elaborated but equally unclear limitation. One can not claim restoration measures if their cost substantially exceeds the benefit arising for the environment from such restoration and other measures may be undertaken at a substantially lower cost (Article 4(2)). Probably the approach taken by the CERCLA is the more sensible one, even though it is very complicated. It requires a case by case analysis and subjects restoration efforts to careful but time-consuming and costly preliminary studies. The restoration efforts should also be consistent with the National Contingency Plan.[60]

---

[60] CERCLA, s. 104.

4.2.3   *Who Can Act as a Plaintiff?*

The common goods of nature are not the object of individual property rights. In civil law countries they have the status of *res nullius* or *res communes*. Thus the individual citizen is not normally entitled to act as a plaintiff to recover ecological damages.[61] Generally the solution is to allow public authorities to act as plaintiffs. In the US, the legislature has, in a large number of statutes, confirmed the 'public trust doctrine' on the basis of which the Government not only has the duty to protect the environment, but is also entitled to claim compensation in the event of damage to the environment which it controls[62] (see e.g. the CERCLA section 107(f)). On the basis of the theory that natural resources are State property, the law of certain former Soviet republics gives the State the right to claim compensation for environmental damages.[63] Similar solutions have been adopted in a number of countries, among which are Italy[64] and Norway[65] (Pollution Damage Act, article 58). Except insofar as public interest groups are concerned,[66] neither the proposed waste liability directive nor the COE draft convention determines who can act as a plaintiff in the event of ecological damage but leaves the matter to the national legislator.

Much attention has also been paid to the possibility of environmental associations acting as plaintiffs in order to obtain monetary compensation in natural resource damages cases.[67] In France, some associations have the right to claim compensation in the event of criminal offences involving the violation of certain environmental statutes. In this case they are not required to show that they have suffered personal damage.[68] No other country seems to have adopted this approach insofar as a damages award is concerned.

---

[61] This does not preclude an action to obtain damages for the losses resulting from his reduced use of the environment (see e.g. COE draft convention which provides for the compensation of loss of profit resulting from impairment of the environment (art. 2(8)c). The US Oil Pollution Act of 1990, s. 1002(b)(2)A and C, does not limit compensation to the loss of economic use of natural resources. It recognizes as compensative both the 'loss of use of natural resource' and the 'loss of subsistence use of natural resources'.

[62] See e.g. CERCLA, s. 107(f); Oil Pollution Act of 1990, s. 1006(b).

[63] Z. Brodecki, *Ecological Damages in International Law* (Polish Institute of International Affairs, Warsaw, 1990), 133.   [64] Act No. 349 of 8 July, 1986 (art. 18).

[65] Pollution Control Act of 13 Mar. 1981, as amended, art. 58.

[66] See No. 28, below.

[67] More readily accepted is the possibility for associations to sue for an injunction. In the US, many environmental statutes provide for a citizens suit which enables any person to ask for an injunction against activities violating certain environmental statutes. Other countries grant similar rights to associations. In Belgium and The Netherlands bills are pending to the same effect. Reports on the subject in Belgian, French, German, Dutch, and US law are contained in *Vorderingsbevoegdheid voor Milieuschade: Le Droit, pour les Associations de Défense de l' Environnement, d' Ester en Justice*, ed. H. Bocken (Story-Scientia, Brussels, 1988).

[68] See M. Prieur, 'Le Droit des Associations de Protection de l' Environnement d' Ester en Justice' in *Vorderingsbevoegdheid voor Milieuverenigingen: Le Droit, pour les Associations de Défense de l' Environnement, d' Ester en Justice* (previous note), 58.

The legislature, however, seems less reluctant to allow associations to act as plaintiffs if only restoration measures can be claimed in the event of ecological damages. For example, both the proposed waste liability directive (art. 4(3)) and the COE draft convention (Article 20) explicitly grant associations the right to ask for an injunction ordering preventive measures or measures of reinstatement.

4.3 *The Size of the Damages*

A common characteristic of all types of compensation actions for pollution damage is their potentially very large dimension. One sees this clearly in the major accidental pollution cases of recent years which have assumed on catastrophic dimensions.[69] The compensation to be paid may in a number of cases exceed the financial resources of the liable party. The need for insurance against the possibility of such awards is thus obvious.

The most common technique of insuring financial responsibility,[70] is liability insurance. It not only protects the victim against insolvency of the liable party; it also realizes a spreading of the losses, to the benefit of the potential polluter. Liability insurance, however, is only effective if it covers at least a very substantial part of the liability of the operator. One is only too well aware of the problems that exist, both in the US and Europe, with respect to the availability of comprehensive liability insurance.[71] The situation is basically the same with respect to variations of insurance such as captive insurances, insurance pools, co-operative arrangements and other risk retention groups by which insurers and potentially liable parties try to overcome the problem.

In a limited number of cases, compulsory liability insurance is required as a guarantee from a potential polluter. In Belgium, for example, where strict liability is frequently imposed in other areas, operators of certain treatment facilities for toxic waste and persons engaged in trading in or importing of toxic waste are under the statutory obligation to have liability insurance. A comparable obligation rests on collectors of used oil.[72] The amended draft directive on the disposal of PCBs also imposes compulsory insurance on the eliminator (art. 6(b)).

Most national or international provisions which require financial guarantees, however, also accept solutions other than liability insurance, such

---

[69] After the oil spill off the coast of Alaska, Exxon agreed to pay 1125 billion US dollars in damages and spent 2.5 billion in clean up costs (*International Environment Reporter*, (9 Oct. 1991), 542).

[70] For a general survey, see H. Bocken, 'Alternative Compensation Systems for Pollution Damages', OECD, ENV/ECO, 89.8 (hereafter 'Alternative Compensation Systems'), 12–22.

[71] See the reports in *Insurance of Environmental Damages* (n. 5); 'OECD, Pollution Insurance', *Environment Monographs* 42 (Paris, 1992).

[72] Royal decree of 9 Feb. 1976, art. 6 (4) (2) and art. 12; Flemisch region, executive decree, 25 July 1985, art. 7(3).

as bank guarantees or guarantees from parent corporations. A similar solution has, for a long time now, been adopted by the Paris Convention on Nuclear Damages (Article 10) and in the Oil Pollution Convention (Article 7) and is also provided for in the CRTD (Article 13). The proposed waste liability directive states in article 11 that the liability of the producer and of the eliminator shall be covered by insurance or any other financial security. The draft landfill directive also provides the obligation to give financial guarantees to cover the cost of the closure procedures and aftercare operations at the landfill site (article 17). The COE draft convention (Article 13) leaves it to the national legislature to ensure that 'where appropriate, taking due account of the risks of the activity and of the financial capacity of the operator, operators carrying out dangerous activities ... be required to have and maintain insurance or other financial security up to a certain limit and of such type and terms as specified by national law ...' The German Environmental Liability Act (article 19) provides that the operator of certain listed installations, may use liability insurance or financial guarantees offered by public authorities or financial institutions. Article 53 of the French Act No. 87-565 of 22 July 1987 makes the delivery of permits for the exploitation of certain dangerous installations subject to the constitution of financial guarantees.

In a limited number of cases, victims of pollution damage find protection against the insolvency of the operator in environmental funds financed by taxes levied on potential polluters. Typical guarantee funds, however, are rare in the area of pollution damages. They protect the victim against insolvency of the potential polluter. They generally do not constitute risk-spreading mechanisms to the benefit of the potential polluter. An example of a fund of this type is the Toxic Waste Guarantee Fund, established by article 10 of the Belgian Act on Toxic Waste of 22 July 1974. This fund, financed by levies on the producers of toxic waste, was to assume, in case of default, the obligations of the producer of the toxic waste (who is strictly liable for all damages caused by the waste). The fund, however, has not yet been actually set up. The draft EC landfill directive sets up a 'Landfill Aftercare Fund' to be financed by contributions from landfill operators (article 18). The fund is to cover the costs of aftercare and remedial measures at closed landfills insofar as they cannot be directly charged to the landfill operator.

5   Individual Liability or Compensation Funds

Even the introduction of strict liability and liability insurance does not fully protect the victim of pollution damages.[73] Liability is based on evidence of

---

[73] H. Bocken, 'Deficiencies of the System of Liability and Liability Insurance as a Mechanism for the Indemnification of Environmental Damage Suffered by Individual Victims' in *Insurance of Environmental Damage* (note 5), 133.

causality. The victim of pollution thus has to identify both the nature of the pollutant and the source of the emissions, which may be very difficult, or may require lengthy and expensive investigations. In case of multiple polluters, or of a synergy of pollutants, the task becomes almost impossible. If the factual causation cannot be established, the victim of pollution will remain uncompensated.

Even where the nature and the source of pollution is identified, the victim may not be able to satisfy the substantial requirements of tort law. He may not be able to show negligence, or the case may fall out of the reach of a narrowly defined strict liability rule. Moreover, the defendant may be able to establish *force majeure* or other valid defences. Especially where strict liability applies, there may also be a monetary limit for liability. Finally, whatever the basis for liability, the relevant statute of limitations may bar claims relating to historic pollution.

In some countries, courts and legislatures have reacted in several ways in order to improve the position of victims with respect to the burden of proof of causation.

A first solution is to depart from the rules of evidence and to reduce the burden of proof for the victim. According to articles 4 and 6 of the original proposed waste liability directive, the plaintiff shall be required only to show the overwhelming probability of the causal relationship between the waste and the damage. This provision, however, attracted much criticism and was abandoned in the amended proposal. The latter refers the matter of burden of proof to national law; the burden of proof may, however, not be higher than the standard burden of proof in civil law. The preliminaries of the COE draft convention also claims that the convention is intended to alleviate the burden of proof for victims of activities dangerous to the environment. Article 10 of the draft, however, states (only) that the court, 'when considering evidence of the causal link . . . shall take due account of the increased danger of causing such damage inherent in the dangerous activity'. The German Environmental Liability Act is more specific and provides for a rebuttable presumption of causation to the disadvantage of installations which are likely to cause the emission (articles 6 and 7).[74] Quite explicit is also section 3 of the Swedish Environmental Damage Act of 1986: 'Damages shall be considered to have been caused as a disturbance as referred to in paragraph one above if, in view of the nature of the disturbance and the damage, of other possible

---

[74] If there are facts supporting the assumption that an installation has caused the damage, the occupier of the installation and public authorities are to provide the victim, at its request, with extensive information on the subject of the operation of the installation (arts. 6 and 7). On causation and pollution liability in German law, see generally J. Köndgen in, *Multiple Causation and Joint Tortfeasors in Pollution Cases According to German Law in Transboundary Pollution and Liability*, ed. Van Dunné (Lelystad, 1991), 99.

causes of the damage, and of other circumstances, there is a substantial probability of a causal connection'.[75]

Another possible approach is to modify the substantive rules on causation. A number of authors have in this context advocated 'market share' liability as a model for 'pollution share liability'.[76]

An example of a third type of solution is to be found in the CERCLA, section 107, which designates as potentially liable parties a large group of persons who possibly may have had only a very remote connection with the actual release of pollutants. Under the CERCLA, liability can rest upon generators of hazardous waste, transporters, operators of waste sites, past and current property owners, and possibly also on parent companies and financial institutions.[77] Under a strict liability rule of this type, liability indeed is no longer based on actual causation between the damage and the activities of the defendant but is, through an unrebuttable presumption of causation, canalized to the group of potentially liable parties designated by the legislature.

In other countries, one has rightly—in my opinion—more readily accepted the fact that a number of pollution damages fall outside the reach of any system of individual liability. If one wishes to help the victims of pollution from non-identified sources or pollutions which do not give rise to liability, the only effective solution is to have recourse to mechanisms of collective compensation.[78]

Financing the compensation of pollution from general tax revenues is contrary to the 'polluter pays' principle and should be rejected save in some exceptional situations. First-party insurance taken out by the potential victim of pollution is a theoretical possibility but should, even if it were sufficiently available, be rejected for the same policy reasons. One can, however, conceive that (compulsory) pollution insurance should be taken out by the polluter for the benefit of those he exposes to pollution. An original compensation system of this type has been adopted in Sweden with the Swedish Pollution Victims Insurance Scheme.[79] It consists of

---

[75] English translation in *Ministry of the Environment; Swedish Environmental Legislation* (Stockholm, 1990), 60.

[76] E. Snijder, 'Van Market Share Liability naar Pollution Share Liability', *TMA* (1990), 141–50; J. Van Dunné, op. cit. n. 29, 43–7.

[77] For a survey of the liability of each category of potentially responsible parties, see *Environmental Dispute Handbook: Liability and Claims*, ed. D. Carpenter, R. Cushman, and B. Roznowski (Wiley Law Publications, New York, 1991), chs. 6 to 13.

[78] For further references, see Bocken, *Preventie*, 101 and 'Alternative Compensation Systems' (n. 7), 22–3.

[79] Ordinance on Environmental Damage Insurance of 25 May 1989. An English translation is to be found in annex to C. Olderz, 'Swedish Environmental Damage Insurance: A New Concept of Insuring Personal Injuries or Property Damages, Caused by Environmental Disturbances', in *Insurance of environmental damage* (n. 5), 376; H. Bocken, 'Alternative Compensation Systems' (n. 7), 25–8.

compulsory insurance to be taken out for the benefit of the victims of pollution damages, by the enterprises carrying out certain environmentally dangerous activities. The Swedish Pollution Victims Insurance is most interesting. It protects the victim against the polluter's insolvency, avoids the difficulties of establishing causation, and it also provides compensation if a tort claim fails as a result of the application of the statute of limitations.

From a comparative point of view it would appear that damage which cannot be compensated under tort law (either because no liability arises or because the polluter has not been identified), is increasingly indemnified through compensation funds financed mainly by contributions from potential polluters. Thus, the financial burden of the loss is not borne by one individual polluter but is spread over a group of operators creating a similar risk.

The first pollution compensation funds originated as a response to the pollution of the sea resulting from the transportation of crude oil, CRISTAL and the International Oil Pollution Compensation Fund. They mainly come into play when the damage exceeds the ceiling of liability, or when the defendant can invoke a valid defence.[80]

In the last decade the number of funds has substantially increased. Most of them, however, concentrate on clean-up costs; the US Superfund set up by the CERCLA is a typical example.

Only exceptionally do environmental compensation funds cover personal or property damage suffered by private parties. One of the more important funds covering private damages is the Dutch Air Pollution Fund[81] which provides compensation for damages resulting from air pollution occurring above Dutch territory which are not covered by insurance. This occurs only when the victim cannot obtain compensation, as the source of pollution remains unidentified, or where it is impossible to furnish the evidence required for a successful tort claim. The Dutch Air Pollution Fund certainly does not cover the majority of the uncompensated damages caused by air pollution; nevertheless it plays a substantial role in the indemnification of damages, especially in the agricultural sector.

Another interesting compensation fund is the California Hazardous Substance Account[82] which is meant to compensate for damage suffered by private parties as a result of releases of hazardous substances. It is intended to fill the major gaps of the liability system. The nature of the damages which can be compensated, however, is severely limited so that the California scheme has not had in practice a major success.

[80] H. Bocken, 'Alternatives to Liability and Liability Insurance for the Compensation of Pollution Damages', *TMA* (1987), 84 and references.
[81] M. Bakker, 'Het Fonds Luchtverontreiniging' in *Insurance of environmental damage*, 345; H. Bocken, 'Alternative Compensation Systems' (n. 70), 32–5.
[82] H. Bocken, 'Alternative Compensation Systems' (n. 70), 30.

The EC is aware of this problem but has not yet developed a clear policy on the subject. Further study of the matter is considered necessary. According to article 11(2) of the proposed waste liability directive, as amended, the Council shall by the end of 1992, draft rules that will govern the case of the unidentified and insolvable polluter. 'In this regard the Commission shall study the feasibility of the establishment of a European fund for compensation for damage and impairment of the environment caused by waste'.

Under certain conditions, compensation funds not only benefit the victims of pollution damages but can also allow the operators of polluting installations to spread the losses from liability for pollution damages.

This objective can, for example, be achieved if a limitation of liability is adopted, the fund providing compensation for damage in excess of the ceiling. This—probably—would also make obtaining liability insurance more easy. To a large extent, the International Oil Pollution Compensation Fund created by the Brussels Convention of 18 December 1971[83] operates to this effect.

Subject to the economic and political difficulties of providing sufficient resources, a comprehensive environmental compensation fund may have substantial advantages[84] in that it theoretically allows the elaboration of an adequate compensation system without a fundamental departure from traditional liability rules or the introduction of compulsory liability insurance. From the point of view of the victim, unlimited strict liability is no longer necessary if a fund provides compensation in cases where the polluter is insolvent or unidentified, or where no liability arises. A system could thus be conceived in which the first layer of the losses is compensated by the polluter on the basis of strict liability. A compensation fund would (up to a second ceiling which should be sufficiently high) compensate damages exceeding the limit of personal liability as well as those caused by non-identified and, in certain cases, non-liable, polluters. The system would thus be comparable to that operating in Belgium in the area of automobile accidents where the gaps in the liability system are fairly adequately filled by the Automobile Guarantee Fund.[85]

6 Conclusion

Technology has to be adapted to the requirements of the protection of the environment. Until the development of a technology which is safe for man

---

[83] International Convention on the Establishment of an International Fund for Compensation for Oil Pollution Damage. See also the additional Protocol of 1984.

[84] See H. Smets, 'Pour une Indemnisation Garantie des Victimes de Pollution Accidentelle' and H. Bocken, 'Complementary Compensation Mechanisms: A general Environmental Damage Fund?' in *Insurance of environmental damage*, n. 5, 397 and 425.

[85] H. Bocken, 'Alternative compensation systems', 35–9.

and the environment, damage caused by pollution will have to be compensated in one way or another.

The introduction or generalization of strict liability for pollution damage is reasonable. It is more equitable that environmental damage be borne by the person who benefits from the polluting activities than by the unfortunate victim. It is equally undesirable that pollution damages are borne by society as a whole.

Strict liability further implements the 'polluter pays' principle and promotes the internalization of the financial burden of the pollution damage in the cost of the products the production of which gave rise to the pollution. This internalization in turn may contribute to the development of environmentally-sound technology.

In fact many countries already apply a variety of strict liability rules applicable to specific forms of pollution damage. The consolidation of these rules into a comprehensive, and at the same time manageable and transparent, set of rules applicable to all or a majority of pollution damages would, in my opinion, constitute a considerable progress.

In establishing a compensation system for pollution damage, one should, however, sufficiently take into account the interests of the potentially liable party. Where possible the latter should be able to quantify in advance his potential liabilities and to spread them, e.g. through liability insurance. As far as possible, the ability to insure against claims resulting from environmental damage should be increased, be it through imposing compulsory liability insurance or otherwise. Under certain conditions, a financial limitation on the strict liability may also be desirable. This, however, would require the establishment of compensation funds which can be used when damage exceeds the ceiling of liability. If this fund can, at the same time compensate the victim whenever the defendant is insolvent or unidentified, full protection will be achieved.

SOME COMPARATIVE REFLECTIONS

STEPHEN TROMANS

1 Common Issues

The essays by Professors Bocken and Francioni provide much useful food for thought for an English environmental lawyer. Most UK practitioners, I suspect, first encountered environmental law in the lecture room in the context of the common law rules of nuisance and *Rylands* v. *Fletcher*. Many others will have learned their law before the full significance of the EC environmental dimension was appreciated, and when 'Common Market law' was seen as a subject of peripheral interest regulating matters such as the dimensions of beetroots.

Times have changed, and fast. In the US, and throughout Europe, the common law relating to environmental damage has been supplemented, and in some cases superseded, by statutory duties and powers. The environment has achieved a dominant position in EC policy, with the potential to become an all-pervasive factor in shaping policy and making law.[1] Environmental law is, perhaps *par excellence,* an area where national law makers can learn from each other's mistakes and successes. Not all environmental damage is the result of pollution, but certainly pollution is a universal problem—and always has been, as the existence of early laws on nuisances attests. Professor Bocken points out, correctly, that pollution can stem from any of three basic activities: the disposal of residues; accidental escapes; and releases occurring in the normal use of products or substances. Such activities are universal, though their exact nature and intensity are, of course, variable.

It could be thought, then, that the national laws which govern pollution and its consequences might share some common features. However, that is not so. The reason is that laws are made within a particular legal and political tradition, and the issue of the law's response to pollution is essentially a political, rather than a technical one. The questions posed by pollution of the environment are, however, the same, ever if the national answers may be different. These are:

1 How should damage to, or impairment of, the natural environment (as opposed to persons or property) be treated?

MA, Solicitor, Partner and Head of Environmental Law Department, Simmons & Simmons.
[1] In particular following the Maastricht Treaty on European Union of 7 Feb. 1992, and in the light of the proposed Fifth Community Action Programme on policy and action in relation to the environment and sustainable development, COM (92) 23 Final, vols. i and ii, 27 Mar. 1992. See also David Wilkinson, *Maastricht and the Environment* (IEEP, Apr. 1992) and *EC Environmental Policy in the Melting Pot* ENDS Report 209 (June 1992), 14.

2 How should the law recognize the fact that pollution will often involve the violation of common interests?

3 By what mechanism should the law seek to ensure that ecological damage is prevented, or where damage has occurred that it is remedied?

4 If damage cannot be remedied or the environment cannot be fully restored (or will take time to recover) should that damage be compensated, to what level, and who should receive compensation?

Many of these questions will ultimately resolve themselves, for those practically involved in the process, into the issue of: who should pay for prevention, restoration, and compensation, and how much?

This in turn raises the question of what should be the objectives of good environmental protection law. Clearly it should aim to prevent pollution, but few would argue that the law should seek to avoid all harm (even were that possible) irrespective of cost. But beyond that, if environmental damage occurs, the law may seek to do certain things:

• At the bare minimum it should seek to compensate those who have suffered personal injury or damage to their property.

• More controversially, it may compensate those whose economic interests have been affected by the damage (the fisherman whose catches are affected; the hoteliers whose trade is disrupted).

• Going further, it may 'compensate' those whose personal or group interest in and appreciation of the natural environment has been affected— this may include people who have never visited the affected area, but who are affronted by its violation.

• The law may seek to indicate society's disapproval by punishing those responsible for, or implicated in, the pollution incident: fault *may* be relevant here.

• The law may, at the same time, be concerned with ensuring the environment is restored, at the cost of those responsible or implicated. Again, fault *may* be relevant, though if the concern is simply to achieve restoration, the policy may be that the 'polluter' should pay irrespective of fault. In reality, application of the 'polluter pays' principle is rarely concerned with the totally dispassionate exercise of restoration, and punitive elements will often be present.

• The law may seek, by means of a particular regime of liability, to influence future conduct—for example, strict laws relating to liability for waste may have, amongst their objectives, the encouragement of waste minimization.[2] Similarly, strict rules of liability relating to a particular method of waste management, such as landfill, may indirectly seek to

---

[2] For example, the proposal for a Council directive on Civil Liability for Damage Caused by Waste [1991] OJ C192/6.

encourage the use of other methods of waste management which are currently perceived as more environmentally benign.[3]

Two final points may be made in concluding these initial comments: they are not entirely unconnected. First, modern science makes it possible in theory to detect contaminants at minute concentrations, and indeed possible in practice if the necessary resources for monitoring, analysis, and interpretation are made available. Political considerations, or the precautionary principle, may lead to the setting of maximum admissible concentrations for certain substances at levels which in reality represent a 'surrogate zero'.[4] In other words, presence of a substance is equated to contamination, and may result in a breach of the relevant legal standards. However, many commentators would draw a fundamental distinction between presence or contamination on the one hand, and pollution on the other.[5] The distinguishing characteristic is harm, or the capacity to cause harm: it is that which marks the borderline at which contamination becomes pollution. Certainly, that is the test provided for in the most recent UK legislation.[6] 'Pollution of the environment' means pollution of the environment due to the release (into any environmental medium) . . . of substances which are capable of causing harm to man or any other living organisms supported by the environment.'

This is also recognized by Professor Bocken in his essay where he says: 'The presence of foreign substances becomes "pollution" as soon as they cause or can cause harm', paraphrasing the UK's legislative definition.

However, harm or potential harm may be irrelevant so far as EC law is concerned, which may in turn have consequences in terms of liability, or in determining who bears the cost of complying with the necessary standards. Literally millions of pounds are currently being spent by UK water supply undertakers in fulfilling undertakings as to the removal of pesticides from drinking water.[7] The requirement for this expenditure stems from the relevant EC directive on drinking water, and is not based on toxicological criteria. Certainly in the UK there is currently no legal mechanism for shifting the cost of compliance from the water companies, their customers and shareholders, through to any other party who might be regarded as responsible for the presence of pesticides in the environment, namely agricultural and industrial users, and producers.[8]

---

[3] Proposal for a Council directive on the landfill of waste COM (91) 102 Final-SYN 335.

[4] For example, some of the parameters in Annex 1 of directive 80/778/EEC on the quality of water intended for human consumption [1980] OJ L229.

[5] M. W. Holdgate, A *Perspective on Environmental Pollution* (Cambridge, 1979); Royal Commission on Environmental Pollution Tenth Report, *Tackling Pollution: Experience and Prospects* (Cmd. 9149, paras. 1.9–1.13).

[6] Environmental Protection Act 1990, s. 1(3); see also s. 29(3).

[7] See Water Industry Act 1991, ss. 18, 19.

[8] The problem of nitrate pollution from diffuse sources is addressed by the power to designate 'nitrate sensitive areas' under s. 94 and Sch. 12 of the Water Resources Act 1991; see also directive 91/676/EEC [1991] OJ L375.

A more specific example of the same problem is provided by the case of *Cambridge Water Company Ltd.* v. *Eastern Counties Leather PLC and Hutchings and Hardings Ltd.*[9] Activities at two industrial tannery sites had led to the presence of organochlorine solvents in groundwater abstracted by the water company. There was no evidence that the concentration of organochlorines was injurious to health, and the judge had little doubt that there was 'an immense margin of safety' in the prescribed figures. For all that, the water was legally unfit for supply for human consumption, and it was to the judge unimportant that such standards 'might be thought to be arbitrarily set, or to be variable'.

The second point relates to fairness. As Professor Bocken so rightly points out, in establishing a system for compensation of pollution damages one should sufficiently take into account the interests of the potentially liable party. It is all too easy for vigorous application of the polluter pays principle to overlook that point, particularly where liability regimes are seen as a means of expressing disapproval of conduct, influencing future behaviour, or simply making a political point. It is sometimes also convenient to forget that principles such as joint and several liability may, in pollution cases, operate very harshly against some potentially responsible parties, as may extreme standards for clean-up.[10]

2 The Common Law: Potent Tool or Spent Force?

For many years after the Industrial Revolution, the common law of nuisance represented the main legal means of environmental protection in Britain.[11] The worst excesses of air pollution from the nascent chemical industry were not the subject of even limited legislation until 1863.[12] Today, the common law relating to pollution in England and Wales, whilst undoubtedly effective on occasions, at other times seems woefully inadequate. There are many problems, procedural and substantive, but the main problems are, first, the emphasis on concepts of fault, reasonableness, and foreseeability, rather than strict liability and, secondly, the limited notion of what constitutes actionable damage.[13]

The first problem is best illustrated by reference to the recent *Cambridge Water Company* case. As mentioned above, it was found on the balance

[9] Queens Bench Division, 31 July 1991 (Mr Justice Ian Kennedy).

[10] The prime example being the US 'Superfund' legislation, though the Dutch concept of 'multifunctionality' as a standard for the clean up of contaminated land is also relevant.

[11] See for example, C. Gearty, *The Place of Private Nuisance in a Modern Law of Torts CLJ* (1989), 214 and articles cited there.

[12] See E. Ashby and M. Anderson, *The Politics of Clear Air* (Oxford, 1981).

[13] On the damage point, for a striking recent example see *Merlin* v. *British Nuclear Fuels PLC, JEL* 3 (1991), 122 (no remedy for contamination of residential property by radioactivity from nuclear reprocessing plant, resulting in substantial depreciation in value). For a general survey of the problems, see S. Tromans, *Environmental Liability Environmental Policy and Law*, 22 (1992), 43.

of probabilities that the two tannery companies had each contributed
to the relevant groundwater pollution. In the case of *Eastern Counties
Leather PLC*, the judge found there had been frequently recurring spillages
of a few gallons or litres of solvent caused by handling the drums in which
the material was stored: these spillages had occurred over a period up to
1976, when bulk storage commenced. There was also a second plume of
pollution from ECL's works resulting from the dumping of solid waste on
land or in settlement tanks. In the case of the second tannery, HHL, the
evidence was less clear, though the judge found there were circumstances
which could have led to the escape of animal oil contaminated by solvent
('sod oil'), such pollution being very much less significant than that from
ECL's site.

Cambridge Water Company were less successful in their submissions on
the law. Their claim was based on the strict liability principles of the rule
in *Rylands* v. *Fletcher*, negligence and nuisance. The problem with the
Rylands v. *Fletcher*[14] principle, as the judge pointed out, is that it has been
qualified and confined over the years by reference to the contrast of natural
and non-natural user, in particular with respect to industrial uses of land,
for example:

I should hesitate to hold in these days and in an industrial community it was a non-
natural use of land to build a factory on it and conduct there the manufacture of
explosives.[15]

The manufacturing of electrical and electronic components in 1964, which is the
material date, cannot be adjudged to be a special use nor can the bringing and
storing on the premises of metal foil be a special use in itself . . . The metal foil was
there for use in the manufacture of goods of a common type which, at all material
times were needed for the general benefit of the community.[16]

So in the Cambridge Water Company case it is perhaps not surprising that
the judge found the storage of the relevant industrial solvents not to be a
non-natural use. In so holding he took into account the degree of 'special
risks' created by the activity, the magnitude and location of the storage
and the benefits of creating employment. Essentially the decision was one
of policy as to the allocation of risk:

In reaching this decision I reflect on the innumerable small works that one sees up
and down the country with drums stored in their yards. I cannot imagine that all
those drums contain milk and water, or some like innocuous substance. Inevitably
that storage presents some hazard, but in a manufacturing and outside a primitive
and pastoral society such hazards are part of the life of every citizen.

---

[14] (1868) 1 Exch 265; (1868) 3 App Cas 330 (HL)
[15] *Read* v. *J. Lyons & Co. Ltd.* [1947] AC 156, 174 (Lord Macmillan).
[16] *British Celanese Ltd.* v. *A. H. Hunt (Capacitors) Ltd.* [1969] 1 WLR 959, 963 (Lawton J).

In other words: we all live in a chemical society.[17] Those storing chemicals must exercise the degree of care demanded by the law and will be liable if they do not. But if an escape and consequent harm occurs despite the exercise of proper care, society at large rather than the polluter must bear the cost.

Cambridge Water Company were similarly unsuccessful in basing their claim on negligence and nuisance. Here the problem was that the judge found that 'the reasonable supervisor' overseeing the operation of the plant would not have foreseen any environmental hazard from small re-peated spillages:

> ...he would, I believe, have supposed that the majority would have evaporated harmlessly either directly or by drying out of the ground, and as to that proportion that would remain I entirely doubt whether, even if he has reflected upon the way in which an aquifer is re-stocked that he would have concluded that detectable quantities of solvent would be found down-catchment.

Nor in relation to HHL's premises, the judge held, would the reasonable supervisor have concluded that occasional dribbling or overflowing of waste sod oil from drums would have affected the aquifer.

What the reasonable supervisor would or should anticipate today, in the light of current knowledge about groundwater contamination is, of course, another matter; but as a question of policy, the judge was certainly wary of penalizing the polluter on the basis of hindsight:

> There must be many areas within England and Wales where activities long-ceased still have their impact on the environment, and where the perception of such impact depends on knowledge and standards which have been gained or imposed in more recent times. If it is right as a matter of public policy that those who were responsible for those activities, or their successors, should now be under a duty to undo that impact (or pay damages if a cure is impractical), that must be a matter for Parliament. The common law will not undertake such a retrospective enquiry.

The decision thus gives little hope for development of a coherent system of risk allocation by the common law, or for the use of negligence or foresight-based concepts in a rapidly evolving area of science and technology. Can legislation do any better?

3 Legislative Solutions

The first point to make, which is obvious to anyone familiar with UK legislation, is that its approach is piecemeal. Legislation can perhaps be

---

[17] See H. D. Crone, *Chemicals and Society: A Guide to the New Chemical Age* (Cambridge, 1986) and J. V. Rodricks, *Calculated Risks: The Toxicity and Human Health Risks of Chemicals in our Environment* (Cambridge, 1992).

likened to a weapon in the hands of the regulators. If so, then different countries favour different forms of armament. US legislation, such as CERCLA and SARA,[18] may perhaps be likened in its technical complexity, range, and effect on target to a Cruise missile. The Dutch legislation on contaminated land has the simplicity and scope of a blunderbuss:[19] 'In a case of soil contamination . . . Our Minister may order the person with rights to the property on which the source of contamination is situated to take appropriate measures to eliminate that source or to restrict the contamination or its effects as far as possible.' UK legislation by contrast can be likened to a number of different armaments, from the peashooter to the bazooka, but all aimed at different targets and with triggers of varying sensitivities.

Some are activated by a criminal conviction;[20] others require no crime to have been committed but may lead to an offence if an order for remedial steps is not complied with.[21] Some have the capability to create strict and retrospective liability.[22] Some bite on the polluter,[23] others on a subsequent innocent landowner.[24] Separate rules apply to different environmental media or different pollutants.[25]

It may be argued that the UK legislative approach has always been piecemeal and pragmatic and that what matters is that the law works effectively and equitably in its relevant context, rather than it being totally consistent. But if the Government, as it does, endorses the principle that the polluter should pay,[26] surely it should be possible to devise a conceptually coherent framework of liability?

Perhaps the problem is that civil liability issues are too much bound up with issues of regulation, licensing, and criminal liability, and indeed, are usually something of an afterthought. Quite correctly, Parliament regulates different processes and different substances in different ways and by different statutory provisions. However, that is no reason why the provisions on civil liability and clean-up powers (such as they are) should be different. It would be quite possible to have a separate and general legislative regime dealing with environmental damage and its consequences, leaving the

---

[18] The Comprehensive Environmental Response, Compensation, and Liability Act 1980 and the Superfund Amendments and Reauthorization Act 1986.

[19] The Soil Clean-up (Interim) Act, s. 12(1), which came into force on 15 Jan. 1983.

[20] Environmental Protection Act 1990, ss. 26, 27.

[21] Environmental Protection Act 1990, s. 80.

[22] Environmental Protection Act 1990, s. 61.

[23] Environmental Protection Act 1990, s. 59, Water Resources Act 1991, s. 161.

[24] Environmental Protection Act 1990, s. 61.

[25] For example, Part I of the Environmental Protection Act on prescribed processes; Part II on waste; Part III on statutory nuisances; Part VI on generally modified organisms; The Water Resources Act 1991 on pollution of controlled waters.

[26] Cm 1200, *This Common Inheritance: Britain's Environmental Strategy* (Sept. 1990), para. 1.25.

administrative provisions on licensing and other forms of control to the individual Acts on waste, water, pesticides, air pollution, etc. It is a question of policy whether compliance with the terms of any administrative licence should provide a defence against civil liability for resulting damage, though logically there is a very strong argument that the two issues are distinct.

Until there is such a system, the position seems likely to remain confused and arbitrary, perhaps increasingly with attempts to bring the facts of a case within a statutory regime to which they do not wholly correspond.[27]

Any such regime could proceed on a variety of policy goals or assumptions, as referred to in the first section of this paper, and there may undoubtedly be conflicts between those goals and there will inevitably be many different questions to be grappled with. These issues were discussed at length in the report of the House of Lords European Communities' Committee Sub-Committee F (Environment) in its report *Paying for Pollution*.[28] They include:

- strict liability versus fault
- injury to the environment and the concept of damage
- on whom should the liability rest?
- joint and several liability
- retrospection
- limitation periods
- burden of proof
- relationship to insurance

Another important objective is the minimization of transaction costs in allocating liability, though to push this objective too far may unacceptably infringe principles of equity: the adoption of 'market share' liability rules may be a case in point.

For many industrialized countries (the UK being no exception) one of the most difficult policy issues is dealing with the legacy of past pollution, especially soil and ground water contamination. Here the conflict of fairness as against effective response to environmental problems arises most starkly. The original polluters are rarely to be found—it is current landowners, occupiers, and their mortgagees who represent the main, or only, obvious targets. Moreover, there is the issue, which arose in the *Cambridge Water Company* case of applying today's standards to yesterday's actions in terms of allocating liability. Should strict liability be confined to current or prospective, as opposed to historic pollution? In a recent paper on

---

[27] See, for example, R. Kidner, 'Toxic Waste and Strict Liability for Products' *NLJ* (1988), 379. And in a different context, see Dr H. U. Paeffgen, 'Overlapping Tensions between Criminal and Administrative Law: The Experience of West German Environmental Law', JEL 3 (1991) 247.   [28] Session 1989–90, 25th Report, HL Paper 84.

Contaminated Land[29] Mr John Hobson of the Department of Environment's Directorate of Pollution Control and Wastes concluded:

it is clear that there are still issues to resolve to take all the effects of the legacy of contaminated land. It can be seen that our objective for determining who should pay for clean up must be to ensure equity and efficiency both now and in the long term . . . By developing a strategic balanced approach with clear priorities and targets we can optimise the use of all our resources.

Undoubtedly, there is much that the UK can learn from Europe. But also there is much which can potentially be learnt from the US federal and state provisions, and from Canada and Australia. Left to itself, the UK might well choose to follow paths other than those of its close European neighbours. However, the UK is a member of the European Community, in which the pressure for common principles of environmental liability is on the increase. Part of this pressure comes from the adoption of the various non-EC measures referred to in Professor Bocken's essay. But, those pressures aside, is there genuine justification for the Community attempting to impose common rules on environmental liability? Professor Francioni's essay presents a compelling justification in general terms for such harmonization. Yet such intervention may be more difficult to justify in specific terms. Of course, pollution *can* raise transboundary issues, and there may well be a need for common rules in that context: however, the great majority of environmental liability issues probably arise wholly or mainly within the national jurisdiction. Similarly, environmental measures can be justified on the basis of approximating legislation to avoid barriers to trade. But exactly what barriers to trade *are* posed by differing regimes of environmental liability and why are they any worse in consequences than, say, differing rules on liability for road accidents? In truth, the justification for the immense effort involved in achieving common rules on environmental liability is whether they succeed in achieving a high level of environmental protection.

The main thrust of the Community's activities so far have lain in the field of waste, in particular the amended proposal for a Council directive on civil liability for damage caused by waste.[30] The preamble to this proposal bases it both on the internal market and on the environmental protection justification in reaching the conclusion that it should not be limited to damage and impairment of the environment occurring during transfrontier movements of waste. And yet the amended proposal issued in July 1991 leaves considerably more discretion to national laws of member States than did the original version. Areas where national laws may be determinative include:

---

[29] Conference paper, given early in 1991.   [30] [1991] OJ C192/6.

- identity of the plaintiff
- remedies
- burden of proof
- whether and to what extent loss of profit and economic loss are recoverable
- conditions of standing for common interest groups or associations
- rules on non-material damage

Maybe taken as a whole those areas where the proposed directive is definitive outweigh such matters, but the scope for national variation remains formidable, as perhaps, realistically it must.

4   Conclusions

Neither Professor Francioni nor Professor Bocken have attempted to be specific about the ways in which the UK may learn from Europe, or vice versa: nor will I. However, it is clear that there is much learning to be done before even a conceptual scheme of liability for ecological damage can be formulated, let alone translated into a workable legal framework. Nor should that learning necessarily be restricted to the EC—environmental problems tend to manifest themselves in much the same way the world over, and the EC may do well to learn from the successes (and equally important, the failures) of the USA.

That said, English lawyers with their common-law traditions will probably require some reorientation if the EC presses forward with any proposals for a common environmental liability regime. However, that change of mind-set may not in fact be so fundamental as some commentators would suggest: British lawyers seem to have assimilated without too much difficulty the EC-led rules on product liability.

What is clear is that, the world over, common-law or judge-made solutions are being seen as inadequate to protect the environment. A statutory framework is essential and a coherent and fair system which protects the environment seems unlikely to be achieved by the current piecemeal and pragmatic UK legislative approach. It is also salutory to remember that more law does not necessarily mean a better environment—perhaps that is the first and fundamental lesson yet to be learnt.

7

The Scottish Reaction —
An Epilogue

DAVID EDWARD

Most Scots are aware of the fact, and proud of it, that their law is different from other peoples' and, in particular, different from that of the English. Asked to say what the differences are, they might point to the third ('not proven') verdict; to the jury of fifteen deciding guilt by simple majority vote; to the system of prosecution by a public prosecutor independent of (but with power to direct) the police; or perhaps to the almost universal jurisdiction in civil and criminal matters of the local judge, the sheriff. In fact, none of these characteristics of the Scottish legal system owes anything to European influence, or only very remotely.

As proof of the European credentials of Scots law, it is frequently said that it is based on Roman law. But this is true, and always has been true, only in limited (albeit important) areas of private law. In those fields where Scots law is most civilian, the greater flexibility of English law has often been seen as something to be followed rather than avoided—see, for example, Professor George Joseph Bell's Preface to his *Commentaries on the Law of Scotland and the Principles of Mercantile Jurisprudence* published in 1804, and the current Lord Advocate's Maccabaean Lecture on the *Codification of Commercial Law in Victorian Britain.*[1]

Admittedly, Scots law has not had to go through the contortions of English law in order to recognise the *jus quaesitum tertio.* But the late Professor J. D. B. Mitchell used to maintain that Lord President Cooper's forthright rejection in 1951 of the floating charge, as being conceptually incompatible with Scots law,[2] set back the post-war recovery of the Scottish economy by a vital ten years. So the civilian inheritance of Scots law may have been, at best, a mixed blessing.

Again, it is often said that Scots law is based more on principle than precedent. But the average observer of proceedings in a Scottish appeal court would need a big pinch of salt with which to swallow that assertion. It was, after all, the two Scots judges in the House of Lords who dissented in *Woolwich Equitable Building Society* v. *Inland Revenue Commissioners,*[3] where the English majority overturned more than a century of precedent

---

[1] [1992] 108 LQR 570.   [2] *Carse* v. *Coppen,* 1951 S.C. 233.
[3] [1992] 3 WLR 366.

on the basis of reasoning from principle proposed by the Regius Professor of Civil Law at Oxford. The reality is that, for most practical purposes, the Scottish legal system belongs firmly within the common-law family, and its most notable peculiarities are home-grown rather than European. Indeed, its most unusual feature might even be shocking to the continental observer. Scots criminal law remains substantially 'common law', only the more contemporary types of criminal offence being defined in legislative texts. Does this offend against the principle *nulla poena sine lege?*

The foregoing paragraphs may seem an odd way to begin the Scottish postscript to a book of essays whose Introduction portrays the Scots as being more European, and more internationally-minded, than the English. But we should not lose sight of Gibbon's maxim that 'The laws of a nation form the most instructive portion of its history.'[4]

Scots law, with all its eclectic borrowings and homegrown idiosyncrasies, is a reflection of Scotland's history. If Scots lawyers are more internationally-minded than the English, it is not because Scots law, as such, is more international—indeed the contrary is certainly true—but because the Scottish system is not, and has never claimed to be, self-sufficient. In this respect Scots law is no different from the law of other small jurisdictions throughout the European continent. They have inherited or borrowed much from Roman law, from canon law or from one of the great modern codifications. But, to a greater or lesser extent, they have retained some of their customary law or adapted other peoples' law to the needs and preferences of their own people. So their lawyers are necessarily, to some extent, comparative lawyers. This creates a habit of mind which may, for want of a better word, be called 'international'. It is this unaccustomed habit of mind which the process of European integration is now forcing upon lawyers who have been trained, and who have taught or practised, exclusively in one of the larger, self-sufficient systems. In former days it was possible for English, French, and German lawyers to view the legal map of Europe as divided between large monolithic structures—between common law and civil law, or between the Anglo-Saxon, Napoleonic and Germanic systems—to one of which they (and everyone else) belonged. They must now come to terms with the fact that Europe's legal map is more of a patchwork, the variety of whose individual patches has to be taken into account both in the human rights and law reform activities of the Council of Europe and in the more pervasive demands of the European Community.

The early experiences of English lawyers in the Community were often such as to cause exasperation, both to themselves when faced with ready-made solutions devised by continental lawyers, and to those same continental lawyers who tended to see the common law as a cuckoo in the

---

[4] *Decline and Fall of the Roman Empire*, ch. 44.

Community nest. Now, partly as a result of English influence, it is recognized that schemes for legal harmonization or reform are more likely to be adopted and implemented if they take account of what exists on the ground.

The search is for solutions that offer compatibility rather than uniformity of laws. This search for common ground between diverse legal systems is unlikely, on the whole, to home in on the distinctive doctrinal solution of one of the major systems. The chosen solution is more likely to be eclectic or 'homegrown European'.

The result is that lawyers from the big, previously self-sufficient, systems now find themselves in the same position as Scots lawyers and lawyers from other small jurisdictions. By force of circumstances they have to become comparative lawyers. As the new Master of the Rolls showed in his 1991 F. A. Mann Lecture,[5] and as the contributions to this book have shown again, this is both an informative and an enriching experience.

In his essay 'What is Comparative Law?',[6] Professor J. F. Garner observes that a study of the diversities between legal systems 'can be justified not only as a fascinating intellectual exercise, but also by reason of the wider knowledge they may bring to the basic principles of any one particular native system of law. They are also, of course, an essential tool in the preparation of law reforms in any one jurisdiction.' One does not have to search very far in recent writings on law reform to find it said by lawyers and laymen that England should abandon the adversarial system of criminal trial and plump for the *juge d'instruction*. But, as Professor Delmas-Marty observes in her contribution to this book, 'To the French lawyer, however patriotic he may be, this sudden admiration in England for the *juge d'instruction* looks distinctly odd'. The *juge d'instruction* is not, as is often asserted, an institution common to the 'civil-law systems' in general. Many never had such an institution in the first place, and others that did have abandoned it.

On the other hand, overall judicial control of the criminal process (of which the institution of *juge d'instruction* is only a part) *is* characteristic of most other systems. The Scottish system of public prosecution reflects this approach, although its historical origins are feudal rather than Napoleonic.[7] Perhaps it is because the Scottish system is not fully understood as a compromise between adversarial justice and judicial control that, until the Runciman Commission began to make detailed enquiries, English law reformers have taken very little interest in it. The crucial point, made by Mr Spencer in his paper here, is that a number of important tasks should

---

[5] T. H. Bingham: '*There is a World Elsewhere?: The Changing Perspectives of English Law*'; [1992] 41 ICLQ 513.

[6] In *Droit Sans Frontières: Essays in Honour of L. Neville Brown*, (Hand and McBride, eds.) (Holdsworth Club, Birmingham 1991) 14.

[7] See *Stair Memorial Encyclopaedia of the Laws of Scotland*, Vol. 17, para. 530.

be done by someone in the interval between police investigation and trial which, in English criminal procedure, are usually done by nobody at all. In Scotland they are done by the Lord Advocate or his deputies, by the local Procurator Fiscal or, in some instances, by the local Sheriff.

In another respect, however, England may unconsciously be moving in the same direction since the Chief Inspector of Prisons is now a judge. Both England and Scotland should perhaps spend more time studying the French institution of *juge de l'application des peines* than that of *juge d'instruction*. The lesson to be learned from the discussion of the *juge d'instruction* surely is that useful borrowing from other systems depends on a proper understanding of what is being borrowed in its native context. The intellectual effort required is illustrated by the contributions of Professor Lorenz on the contractual *jus tertii* and Professor von Bar on liability for economic loss. It might be added that incautious assimilation of English and Scots law in both these fields has caused some confusion on both sides of the border.

The European Community does not, as such, contribute to the process of law reform outside the areas in which harmonization of laws is necessary to achieve Community objectives. But the fact of being in the Community and being forced to 'do' comparative law in a practical context contributes enormously to the capacity of lawyers from all the Community countries to make the good comparisons that lie at the root of using other peoples' law in the process of law reform.

The need to learn is not confined to lawyers teaching and practising within their own national systems. No-one stands in more need of the insights that good comparison can give than those in the European Courts who have to find solutions compatible with, and so far as possible acceptable in, a wide variety of national jurisdictions. In this connection it is worth adding something to what has been said by Professor Henry Schermers and Dr Derrick Wyatt about the dissenting judgment and the oral hearing. Common-law observers of the EC Court of Justice generally find the absence of dissenting opinions a marked defect, and some of the arguments put forward against dissenting opinions are not very convincing given that they are allowed both in The Hague and in Strasbourg. But there is another consideration: the principle of collegiality.

Collegiality in the process of judgment means more than a willingness to sign a text that reflects the majority view and to keep silent about one's private dissent. It is true that the result has to be decided by majority vote if there is a difference of opinion. But that is often only the first stage in the process of deliberation and discussion of a draft judgment. The minority are entitled to, and do, contribute actively to the debate after the decision of principle has been taken. They will help to point out flaws and obscurities in the draft and, by the end of several sessions, it may be very difficult to remember who was in the majority and who in the minority on the first vote. Sometimes the process of discussing a draft will show that the minority was right in the first place and drafting must begin again. So collegiality becomes an attitude of mind. One of the current members of the EC Court of Justice has commented that 'deliberation is the heart of our activity'. Even more than in those national systems where it is indigenous, the process of judicial debate behind closed doors is one of the most important ways in which Community judges adapt their own habit of mind to a developing legal system in which the doctrinal position is seldom clear and even more rarely settled. This in turn affects the attitude of the Court to oral procedure.

Oral procedure in which the pleader simply repeats what has already been said in writing is not a profitable use of judicial time. It may be helpful that the pleader should summarize his arguments and draw attention to the salient points, but even here some of the effect will be lost in simultaneous interpretation. Dr Wyatt is right in saying that oral procedure at Luxembourg is usually best when the Court has indicated in advance the points on which it wishes to hear further argument. There is still a psychological problem.

Those who are familiar with court practice in the common-law world know that oral pleading there is not simply a matter of presenting arguments in a more or less lucid oral form. The debate between counsel and judge, sometimes sharp and not always kind, plays an essential part in defining the issues in the case, weeding out useless arguments and refining the good ones. The judge, who is himself an advocate by training and often still an advocate by instinct, may well ask questions or suggest propositions that will find no place in the judgment and may even reflect a position quite inconsistent with the eventual result.

It is more difficult for the judge bred in the collegial system to play this role. A question asked by a judge in anything but the most hypothetical way may give the impression of *parti pris*. It may be embarrassing to his colleagues and even shocking to an advocate bred in the same system who expects his judge to display total impartiality until the last stage of judgment. The cut and thrust of debate about facts and law that is so characteristic of common-law court procedure finds no place in most other systems, and the difficulties of introducing it to Luxembourg are only compounded by the problem of language. Similarly, it is not altogether straightforward to introduce more written procedure into British courts. The Master of the Rolls has observed[8] that, 'it could be said that England has captured the worst of both worlds, by accepting written submissions without very significantly shortening oral arguments'.

---

[8] F. A. Mann Lecture, 1991, see n. 5, above, at 526.

Professor Markesinis remarks in his Introduction that the aim in the series of seminars which gave rise to the present book was 'to discuss developments that were actually taking place whether we (or the majority of our compatriots) liked them or not'. A legal world without dissenting judgments and with only a skeletal form of oral procedure is not one in which common lawyers find themselves readily at home. But the European system is not monolithic. It is susceptible to change and will change in response to informed challenge. So, it is hoped, is the common-law system to which Scotland, very substantially, belongs.

Those who are engaged in learning from Europe can help in this process as teachers. A better understanding of other systems brings with it a clearer knowledge of one's own. Of all exercises in legal exposition, the most difficult is to explain what one has hitherto taken for granted. What lawyer can say with a clear conscience that he has never, when called upon for an explanation, replied 'It is so because it is so'? What lawyer would not be happy to be able to do better?

Index